T0311873

Historicizing Self-Interest in the Modern Atlantic World

This volume historicizes the use of the notion of self-interest that at least since Bernard de Mandeville and Adam Smith's theories is considered a central component of economic theory.

Having in the twentieth century become one of the key-features of rational choice models, and thus is seen as an idealized trait of human behavior, self-interest has, despite Albert O. Hirschman's pivotal analysis of self-interest, only marginally been historicized. Historicizations of self-interest, however, offers new insights into the concept by asking why, when, for what reason and in which contexts the notion was discussed or referred to, how it was employed by contemporaries, and how the different usages developed and changed over time. This helps us to appreciate the various transformations in the perception of the notion, and also to explore how and in what ways different people at different times and in different regions reflected on or realized the act of considering what was in their best interest. The volume focuses on those different usages, knowledges, and practices concerned with self-interest in the modern Atlantic World from the seventeenth to twentieth centuries, by using different approaches, including political and economic theory, actuarial science, anthropology, or the history of emotions.

Offering a new perspective on a key component of Western capitalism, this is the ideal resource for researches and scholars of intellectual, political and economic history in the modern Atlantic World.

Christine Zabel is Head of the Early Modern Department at the German Historical Institute in Paris, France. She is currently completing a book on the economic and financial history of speculation, especially in early modern France. She is particularly interested in the history of political economy, financial mathematics, the history of knowledge and early modern republicanism(s). She is the author of the book *Polis und Politesse. Der Diskurs über das antike Athen in England und Frankreich, 1630–1760* (2016).

Political Economies of Capitalism, 1600-1850
Series editors: Carl Wennerlind, *Barnhart College, US,*
John Shovlin, *New York University, US,* and
Philip J. Stern, *Duke University, US*

This series seeks manuscripts exploring the many dimensions of early modern political economy, and especially the ways in which this period established both foundations for and alternatives to modern capitalist thought and practice. We welcome submissions that examine this history from a variety of perspectives—political, intellectual, cultural, economic, scientific, social, spatial, or others—and in contexts ranging from the local to the global. Potential themes include efforts to understand how natural philosophy and political economy were intertwined and how they shaped prevailing worldviews of both individual actors and states; the uneasy coexistence of liberty and coercion in labor, commodity, and financial markets; the tension between commercial activities, social virtues, and political stability; the interplay between commercial, military, and political power at home and overseas; the incongruity between ideal categories, such as free trade, and real world practices. While we will consider traditional monographs, our primary focus is on the publication of shorter interpretive and conceptual books (50-70,000 words). We believe that this format is ideal for the development of broad arguments and perspectives, providing authors with the opportunity to develop their ideas in a flexible and accessible format. We are also open to proposals for other forms of scholarship, both innovative and traditional, such as collaborative works, edited collections, and critical textual editions.

Authors interested in submitting a proposal, please feel free to contact any of the series editors.

Commercial Cosmopolitanism?
Cross-Cultural Objects, Spaces, and Institutions in the Early Modern World
Edited by Felicia Gottmann

Historicizing Self-Interest in the Modern Atlantic World
A Plea for Ego?
Edited by Christine Zabel

For more information about this series, please visit: https://www.routledge.com/Political-Economies-of-Capitalism-1600-1850/book-series/CARL

Historicizing Self-Interest in the Modern Atlantic World

A Plea for Ego?

Edited by Christine Zabel

Routledge
Taylor & Francis Group

LONDON AND NEW YORK

First published 2021
by Routledge
2 Park Square, Milton Park, Abingdon, Oxon OX14 4RN

and by Routledge
52 Vanderbilt Avenue, New York, NY 10017

Routledge is an imprint of the Taylor & Francis Group, an informa business

© 2021 selection and editorial matter, Christine Zabel; individual chapters, the contributors

The right of Christine Zabel to be identified as the author of the editorial material, and of the authors for their individual chapters, has been asserted by her in accordance with sections 77 and 78 of the Copyright, Designs and Patents Act 1988.

All rights reserved. No part of this book may be reprinted or reproduced or utilised in any form or by any electronic, mechanical, or other means, now known or hereafter invented, including photocopying and recording, or in any information storage or retrieval system, without permission in writing from the publishers.

Trademark notice: Product or corporate names may be trademarks or registered trademarks, and are used only for identification and explanation without intent to infringe.

British Library Cataloguing-in-Publication Data
A catalogue record for this book is available from the British Library

Library of Congress Cataloging-in-Publication Data
A catalog record has been requested for this book

ISBN: 978-0-367-90122-6 (hbk)
ISBN: 978-1-003-02274-9 (ebk)

Typeset in Times New Roman
by KnowledgeWorks Global Ltd.

Contents

Figures and table

Figures

Table

Contributors

Rafe Blaufarb is a Professor of French history at Florida State University, where he directs the Institute on Napoleon and the French Revolution. His most recent monograph was *The Great Demarcation: The French Revolution and the Invention of Modern Property* (2016). He is currently conducting research for a new book on privilege in Old Regime and Revolutionary France.

Simone De Angelis is Professor of History of Science and Director of the Centre for the History of Science at the University of Graz, Austria. His main research areas are the history of science and medicine, the history of human sciences, life sciences and anthropology, Renaissance and Enlightenment Studies, integrated history, and philosophy of science. He is the author of *Anthropologien. Genese und Konfiguration einer ›Wissenschaft vom Menschen‹ in der Frühen Neuzeit* (2010).

Christof Dejung is Professor of Modern History at the University of Bern, Switzerland. He is the author of *Commodity Trading, Globalization and the Colonial World: Spinning the Web of the Global Market* (2018) and a co-editor of *Foundations of World-Wide Economic Integration: Power, Institutions and Global Markets, 1850–1930* (2013), *Auf der Suche nach der Ökonomie: Historische Annäherungen* (2014) and *The Global Bourgeoisie: The Rise of the Middle Classes in the Age of Empire* (2019).

Inger Leemans is Professor of Cultural History at Vrije Universiteit Amsterdam and PI of *NL-Lab*, at the Humanities Cluster of KNAW (Royal Netherlands Academy of Arts and Sciences). Her main research areas are: cultural economy, emotion/sensory studies, and digital humanities. Inger Leemans is also Director of ACCESS, the Amsterdam Center for Emotion and Sensory Studies, and one of the hosts of the History of Finance platform (https://history-of-finance.org). She was principal investigator of the working group "Affective Economies—Knowledge and the Market" in the international research project "Creating a Knowledge Society in a Globalizing World, 1450–1800." Currently, she is working on the project "Affective Economies: A Cultural History of Stock Trading."

Ted McCormick is Associate Professor of History at Concordia University in Montreal. He is the author of *William Petty and the Ambitions of Political Arithmetic* (2009), which won the 2010 Jon Ben Snow Prize from the North American Conference on British Studies. He is currently completing a study of demographic thinking in England and the British Atlantic, c. 1500–1800.

Daniel Menning is Associate Professor at the Institute of Modern History, University of Tübingen, Germany. His current research projects explore the history of stock market bubbles and speculation in history. His publications focus on projecting in 1720 and on discourses about and techniques for speculation around 1900.

Ulrich Pfister has been full Professor of Economic and Social History at the University of Münster since 1996 and obtained his PhD in 1984 from the University of Zürich. He has published on regional export industries, family and historical demography, the history of international financial relations, church history, and religious practice in rural areas. Recent publications focus on agrarian history and the aggregate development of the German economy, c. 1500–1880.

Gisèle Sapiro is Professor of Sociology at the Ecole des Hautes Etudes en Sciences Sociales Paris and Research Director at the CNRS (CESSP). She is the author of *La Guerre des écrivains, 1940–1953* (1999; Transl. *French Writers' War*, 2014), *La Responsabilité de l'écrivain* (2011), *La Sociologie de la littérature* (2014), *Los Intelectuales* (2017), *Les Ecrivains et la politique en France* (2018), and has (co)edited eight collections.

Friederike Scholten-Buschhoff is currently finishing her PhD at the University of Münster, Germany. She studies the history of rural areas, particularly in Westphalia, focusing on the economics of noble estates; 2010 Bachelor of Arts (History, English); 2014 Master of Arts (History); 2014–2018 Project member: "Rural estates in Westphalia and Rhineland," 1650–1850, University of Münster; since 2018: Analyst and Key Account Manager Kleffmann Group Lüdinghausen.

Koen Stapelbroek is Associate Professor at Erasmus University Rotterdam and Director of the Helsinki Centre for Intellectual History. He published *Love, Self-Deceit and Money: Commerce and Morality in the Early Neapolitan Enlightenment* (2008) and a range of articles and edited volumes on European eighteenth-century political thought and the history of commercial institutions.

Cornelius Torp is Professor of Modern History at the University of Bremen. Recently, he served as the DAAD Hannah Arendt Visiting Chair for German and European Studies at the University of Toronto and was a Research Fellow at the Freiburg Institute for Advanced Studies (FRIAS) and a Marie Curie Fellow at the European University Institute in

Florence. Among his recent books are *Gerechtigkeit im Wohlfahrtsstaat. Alter und Alterssicherung in Deutschland und Großbritannien von 1945 bis heute* (2015) and *The Challenges of Globalization. Economy and Politics in Germany 1860–1914* (2014). He is also the author of numerous articles in journals ranging from *Central European History* to *Germany History* and the editor of *Economic Crises and Global Politics in the 20th Century* (2014, ed. with A. Nützenadel), as well as of *Challenges of Aging: Pensions, Retirement and Social Justice* (2015).

Christine Zabel is Head of the Early Modern Department at the German Historical Institute in Paris. She is currently completing a book on the economic and financial history of speculation, especially in early modern France. She is particularly interested in the history of political economy, financial mathematics and the history of science/history of knowledge. She is also the author of the book *Polis und Politesse. Der Diskurs über das antike Athen in England und Frankreich, 1630–1760* (2016).

Acknowledgements

Most of the contributions to this volume originate from a conference on the "Knowledge(s) of Self-interest" that was held at the Kulturwissenschaftliches Institut (KWI) Essen in February 2019. The conference and this publication were funded by the Fritz Thyssen Foundation. I am very grateful to the KWI and the Fritz Thyssen Foundation for their very generous support.

I also want to thank Stefan Brakensiek, who supported the endeavor with practical help, good advice and insightful comments. I am also grateful to Angelika Köffer, who made the administrative side of the project a pleasant and easy experience for everyone, especially for me. I am indebted to Carolyn Jones, who proofread all contributions with an eagle eye, and to Julia Theresa Krusen, who tirelessly double-checked all the contributions' notes, even in late night shifts. I'd also like to thank Jiayun Hu, who helped with the final steps of the production.

I would like to thank all those who participated in the conference, those who contributed with a paper or a presentation as well as those who commented on them. And of course, special thanks go to all the contributors to this volume. I am very glad that you embarked with me on this journey of inquiry about the different histories of self-interest.

Düsseldorf, July 2020

Introduction

The search for self-interest and the problems with its historicization

Christine Zabel

In a lecture series on political economy, initiated by his friend Pierre Bourdieu and given at the Parisian Collège de France in the early 1980s,[1] the economist Albert Hirschman explained that interest was "one of the most central and controversial concepts in economics and, more generally, in social science and history." He went on to lay out how, despite the changes that the concept had undergone since the sixteenth century, it "has stood for the fundamental forces, based on the drive for self-preservation and self-aggrandizement, that motivate or should motivate the actions of the prince or the state, of the individual, and, later, of groups of people occupying a similar social or economic position (classes, interest groups)." Although Hirschman presented a narrative that explained how self-interest went from being a concept that described political conduct to one that referred to human behavior more broadly, then to one that portrayed economic behavior, self-interest "can cover—to the point of tautology—all of human action."[2]

Similarly, examples of references to "self-interest" or "self-interested behavior" are numerous and disparate in our present-day world. Politicians' or political parties' motives are questioned by evoking their self-interest (their wish to gain votes); in this case, the allusion to self-interest is an external attribution and an interpretation of an individual's or a group's behavior from outside. But we also often appeal directly to our own or to somebody else's self-interest when we emphasize that it will be good for us if we work out, or follow a healthy diet; or, when we argue for the political organization and representation of minority groups. Self-interest is commonly defined as "the act of considering the advantage to yourself when making decisions, and deciding to do what is best for you."[3] In this sense, self-interest seems to be an intellectual disposition shared by human beings that helps to transfer and break down goals into concrete options, between which we can choose. In other words, it is self-interest that helps us to contemplate the consequences of our decisions and actions and choose the option that promises the best outcome for us. Self-interest, thus, can appear as egoistic, egocentric, selfish, self-centered, and inconsiderate; or alternatively it can spur self-awareness, realize an act of self-defense, or be empowering. In the light of the concept's ubiquity, we might wonder, however, what can actually be explained by allusions to self-interest?

Despite the broader meaning of self-interest, in many instances the notion also bears a decisively economic, and mostly pejorative, component. In this case, self-interest is placed in relation to, or is equated with, profit-seeking: for example, when we speak of the "greenwashing" of certain products; or when we point to management policies and (bad) working conditions for employees that companies' proprietors and managers perpetuate in order to maximize profits. A reference to self-interest, then, gives us an explanation for the exploitation of resources or of people, or serves to question the purity of motives behind actions, even if those actions have a positive outcome on the public good. It is used to voice suspicion and mistrust of decision-makers, leaders, or more generally "other people," acting in a deeply capitalist and profit-seeking world. And in such a world, where the pursuit of profit seems to be the first rule, everybody appears to be, and to act in ways that are, self-interested. The pursuit of self-interest, then, figures as the natural state of existence in a commercial, and indeed, capitalist society—as many economic thinkers, since Bernard de Mandeville's *Fable of the Bees* (1714) and Adam Smith's *The Wealth of Nations* (1776), have pointed out. This tradition of thinking about self-interest as a characteristic feature of economic action led the Irish political economist Francis Edgeworth, who famously applied mathematical calculus to economics, to explain in his *Mathematical Psychics* of 1881 that "The first principle of Economics is that every agent is actuated only by self-interest."[4]

With the emphasis on the economic bearings of the term, it is hardly surprising that self-interest became a key component of the *homo oeconomicus* model as it emerged as the foundation of economic theory in the nineteenth and twentieth centuries, rapidly becoming the "prevalent model of human behavior in mainstream economics."[5] Although Adam Smith and John Stuart Mill are often considered the first inventors of the model, the (anglicized) notion of "economic man" was, according to Joseph Persky, first introduced by the end of the nineteenth century (around the same time that Edgeworth confirmed self-interest's function as the main mover for economic action) by another Irish economist and mathematician, John Kells Ingram, in *A History of Political Economy* (1888). Similarly, the latinized version *homo oeconomicus* was first used by Maffeo Pantaelleoni in his *Principii di economia pura* (1889).[6]

Homo oeconomicus, as modeled in the social sciences, has since been characterized by rationality and a capacity for logical thought and calculation, along with behavior based on the selfish pursuit of an individual's own benefit and profit.[7] The *homo oeconomicus* model (or the Restricted Resourceful Expecting Evaluating Maximizing Man model, short RREEMM) thus endorses and comprises a triadic complex including self-interest, rationality, and mathematical computation; and within this triad, self-interest functions as the main impulse. It is self-interest that sets goals, and that uses rational capacities and mathematical computation in order to pursue those aims that promise the best outcome. In other words, self-interest is the foundation on which rationality and mathematical computation operate.

In the social sciences, critics have developed numerous other models. They have referred to the ancient Greek *zoon politicon* in order to designate *homo politicus* (who is defined by his or her interest in the public good). Other modifications include: *homo sociologicus* (this model was developed by Ralf Dahrendorf and understands humans as social beings who are deeply shaped and defined by society, thus deferring to society's expectations and values); *homo hierarchicus* (this model goes back to Louis Dumont's *Homo hierarchicus: Le système des castes* from 1966, in which he studied the Indian caste system); *homo sustinens* (this model was developed by Bernd Siebenhüner and emphasizes sustainability as a guiding principle of national and international politics); *homo cooperativus/homo heterogenus* (the model on which the concept of sustainable economy is founded, which goes back to Holger Rogall's *Neue Umweltökonomie* from 2002); we also have models of *homo aciotus, homo moralis, homo ethicus, homo kantiensis*— the list could go on.[8]

The criticisms voiced against the *homo oeconomicus* model have in common that they oppose assumptions made about human self-interest. Many critics including Jon Elster have pointed out that humans do not always or exclusively pursue selfish goals, but also aspire to higher moral values; and that they are thus capable of deeply empathic behavior. According to this view, humans are not always motivated by self(ish) interests alone, and they are able to incorporate the consideration of others' needs into their own interest.[9] Such critics admonish that, even though the simplicity of models might be preferable, models must still reflect complex reality. And even one of the first apologists of the *homo oeconomicus* model, Francis Edgeworth, admitted that:

> The moral constitution of the concrete agent would be neither Pure Utilitarian nor Pure Egoistic [...] between the two extremes Pure Egoistic and Pure Universalistic there may be an indefinite number of impure methods; wherein the happiness of others as compared by the agent (in a calm moment) with his own, neither counts for nothing, nor yet "counts for one," but *counts for a fraction*.[10]

Accordingly, Jon Elster, who developed a theory of limited rationality, opposes the model's one-dimensional design with other "plausible stories," e.g. with the observation that humans do not always act selfishly:[11]

> Suppose that someone asserts that self-sacrificing or helping behavior is conclusive proof that not all action is self-interested or that emotional behavior is conclusive proof that not all action is rational. One might conclude that there are three irreducibly different forms of behavior:

rational and selfish, rational and non-selfish, and irrational. The drive for parsimony that characterizes good science should lead us to question this view. Could it not be in one's self-interest to help others? Could it not be rational to be swayed by one's emotions? The first step toward finding a positive answer is telling a plausible story to show how these possibilities could be realized. [...] By telling a story one can transform an issue from a metaphysical one into one that is amenable to empirical research. The question now is whether the premises of the story are true, not whether it is possible or impossible to explain one range of phenomena in terms of other, less complex phenomena.[12]

Not only has it been pointed out that self-interest cannot be equated with egotism, but also, the model's rational component has been criticized. Against the (neo-classical) model of *homo oeconomicus* and its mathematical rationality, behavioral economics (which gained much public attention, not least through the Nobel Memorial Prizes in Economic Sciences awarded to behavioral economists) seeks to incorporate psychological and neuroscientific observations into economic theory. Behavioral economists have developed various theories that point in one way or another to the limitations of human rationality: the "theory of bounded rationality" emphasizes that decision-makers' rationality is limited by their cognitive disposition, their capacities to influence a decision, and by the time within which they have to make a decision; the "prospect theory" goes back to Daniel Kahneman's and Amos Tversky's experimental work, which studied decision-making in situations of risk and uncertainty. Kahneman and Tversky generated empirical data to support doubts about the utility-maximization concept and showed that people choose lower utility and higher certainty when facing risky choices that promise gains (risk aversion); but that people seek risk when they fear loss, which leads to decisions that promise less utility, but manage to avoid loss.[13]

The behavioral economist Richard Thaler, therefore, assesses that economics has relied for too long on mono-theoretical assumptions derived from universal axioms, and he makes the fictional figure of the *homo oeconomicus* accountable for the discipline's misinterpretations of economic developments and its deficient predictive ability:

The problem is with the model being used by economists that replaces homo sapiens with a fictional creature called homo oeconomicus (Econs) [...] Compared to this fictional world of Econs, Humans do a lot of misbehaving, and that means that economic models make a lot of bad predictions [...] Virtually no economists saw the financial crisis of 2007–8 coming, and worse, many thought both the crash and its aftermath were things that simply could not happen.[14]

Such a critique indicates that self-interest is not necessarily, or always, accompanied by rational calculation, nor does it necessarily, or always, spur rational behavior. Instead, according to Thaler (or many empirical studies), people misbehave in many ways: They cannot optimize as well as the model suggests; to the actor confronted by many options, it is not always clear which one really is the best, or best represents his or her self-interest. Economic actors rarely have all necessary information available at the decision-making moment, nor are they necessarily able to calculate and weigh the information at hand rapidly enough for their decision-making-process.[15] In addition, people often appear to do things that would be irrelevant in a world of Econs (Thaler mentions the examples of buying or expecting a present for a wedding anniversary). In light of these misbehaviors, Thaler argues for a more realistic and "enriched" approach to economics.

The philosopher Laurie Paul has similarly pointed to the problem of making rationally informed decisions, especially in situations of big, transformative life choices. In *Transformative Experience,* she describes situations that are epistemically challenging, because the decision-makers cannot compare the present lived experience with the alternative lived experience—for example, when confronted with the decision whether or not to have children. In these situations, the decision-makers cannot *rationally* know what they want. In other words, they cannot know through an assessment based on experience what their preferences are, until or unless they have had the experience themselves; the testimony of others, or studies, might offer some guidance but, according to Paul's argument, these cannot substitute for the lived experience. Paul thus emphasizes that in transformative life choices, the self lacks experience to decide *rationally* what is in its own best interest.[16]

If options are not easily prioritized or rationally assessed, as Richard Thaler, Daniel Kahneman, Laurie Paul, and many others have pointed out, then the following questions arise: when and how can we consider our self-interest, and how much time do we need to become aware of or to consider it? How do self-interest and rationality relate to each other? And does self-interest have similar effects in different realms of society? The latter question has led Dan Usher, the author of *The Economics of Voting: Studies of Self-Interest, Bargaining, Duty and Rights* to inquire about self-interest's impact on voting strategies:

> The central proposition in economics is that the world's work gets done satisfactorily when each person does what is best for himself alone. [...] the great lesson of economics is that, [...] the outcome is order rather than chaos and that the resulting order is in some sense desirable. Self-interest generates a satisfactory outcome in markets for ordinary goods and services within an appropriate framework that only government can provide, including the protection of life and property, resolution of disputes, provision of roads, bridges and schools, dealings with other countries and the mitigation of inequality of income when deemed in the interest of the community as a whole. The economics of voting is the study of whether—subject to what qualifications and to what extent—an equally

satisfactory outcome is attained in government, too, when laws and leaders are chosen by majority rule voting and when each person votes for whatever seems best for himself alone. The economics of voting is about when self-interest may be relied upon in voting as well as in markets, and, if not, what other considerations must be introduced.[17]

Similarly, political scientists such as Peter Egge Langsæther and Goeffrey Evans have undertaken to question ideas about self-interest, for example, the correlation between class affiliation and political preferences, and tested such assumptions for eighteen Western European countries.[18]

Though self-interest is often treated as an evident category, the critiques of the *homo oeconomicus* model, as formulated predominantly in the social sciences, demonstrate the challenges of arriving at a formal definition. Self-interest does not necessarily equal egoistic or selfish behavior; nor is there a clear-cut line that helps us to decide whether it pertains to the rational or the passionate realm (or how perceived self-interest defines our conception of rationality altogether), nor whether it is a virtue or a vice. When considering different choices, it is, furthermore, not necessarily clear to actors—nor to their observers, for that matter—which options will really lead to their best interest. It is not always obvious, either, which outcome might actually constitute one's best interest. A possible definition of self-interest is also complicated on an epistemological level: if self-interest does not consist (or at least does not consist exclusively) of (mathematized) calculations or prioritizations based on perfect information, it is difficult to pinpoint where self-interest translates into intellectual processes. It is hard to tell, then, whether we can train, teach or inspire "the act of considering the advantage to yourself when making decisions," or, on a praxeological level, what qualifies as a self-interested action, behavior, practice, or routine. Similarly, we might wonder whether harnessing or taming self-interest is an ethical, moral, or intellectual endeavor, or one that can only be materialized in actions. In short, it is not entirely clear whether self-interest encompasses self-interested behavior, or self-interested intention, or whether it is an intellectual undertaking (the process of prioritizing, or weighing, and calculating options), or whether it is, like wind, detectable only by its effects. Again: What, then, is self-interest?

One way to address this question was offered by the above-mentioned development economist Albert O. Hirschman, who, with his study of self-interest, wanted to challenge his fellow economists to think about the "political consequences of economic growth."[19] It was his frustration with contemporary social sciences and grand theories (especially with development theories—instead, he argued for case-by-case studies of developing countries) that led Hirschman to embark on a *historical* survey of the concept. Deeply critical of the neo-conservative version of capitalism, and the political repercussions of capitalist structures, Hirschman wondered how capitalism could have become so discouraging and disappointing. He thus agreed with other economists that self-interest was a main ingredient of capitalist culture and, therefore, of economic behavior. Unlike them, however, he did not engage in a discussion of self-interest as a universal, or inborn, human characteristic. Reacting to "right-wingers" who were using references to self-interest "to make a case for unfettering individuals from intrusive states,"[20] Hirschman's goal was not to refute the model of *homo oeconomicus* by providing yet another model. Rather, the historical inquiry into the different definitions and euphemistic turns of self-interest was, for him, a window that allowed him to see and understand the implicit and explicit repercussions of capitalism in order to change them for the better. Hirschman's historical survey thus went hand-in-hand with his refusal to follow the ideologies and big theories that shaped the social science of the 1960s and 1970s, and, instead, he sought to encourage the intellectual pursuit of alternatives. Accordingly, his ideal (not model) figure, "the possibilist," took the freedom to imagine and envision what was possible, instead of merely concentrating on the probable, thus enacting his or her "right to a non-projected future." It was Hirschman's profound belief that human actions were infused by our understanding of the world, and that in order to change our actions, we would have to change our ideas about it. And this was made possible not by turning to abstract theory, but by concentrating on the foundations and underlying currents that shape our world.[21]

Not least for this reason, Hirschman was fascinated by those early modern authors who directly addressed the political repercussions of an interest-based social order. He did not share their optimism about an economic growth ideology from which, as history had revealed, only some individuals or regions benefited. Yet, Hirschman was optimistic enough about humankind to suggest that there must once have been good reasons to endorse this economic value that underpinned a capitalist world order. Indeed, it was the very hope of finding those good reasons that led him to embark on his historical survey of the notion. Accordingly, Hirschman attempted "to figure out how capitalism was initially understood *before* its triumph in order to present alternative perspectives *after* its triumph."[22]

He began his seminal work *The Passions and the Interests* in 1972, during his year at the newly founded Institute for Advanced Studies at Princeton University. Hirschman was still a Harvard Professor at the time; however, he became a permanent member of the Institute in 1974, and remained one until his death in 2012. In that volume, the economist unfolded how great hopes were once placed in self-interest and an interest-based social order. Many commentators and thinkers of the eighteenth century believed that commerce had polishing effects on the manners of a people, and that it could operate as a bastion against despotic aspirations and was, therefore, an effective tool in domestic politics. There was also a widespread belief that commerce would, on an international level, create and maintain peace between states (the doux-commerce thesis). Furthermore, as Hirschman showed, the free pursuit of self-interest was thought to bring stability and predictability: if everyone could freely follow their own interest and seek their own profit, individual actions became, in this view, more predictable. This, in turn, made the world more governable, as James Madison and Alexander Hamilton believed. The latter declared: "The safest reliance of every government is on man's interest. This is a principle of human nature, on which all political speculation, to be just, must be founded."[23]

In *The Passions and the Interests*, Hirschman also explained our various and ambiguous uses of the concept of self-interest by showing how "interest" became a key concept, and an "infatuation" in the seventeenth and eighteenth centuries,[24] gradually replacing the pursuit of older passions such as the striving for glory or honor. In his analysis (which he condensed for his Paris lectures), he unraveled the three main ways in which self-interest began to be used euphemistically. As early as the late Middle Ages, the term "interest" was coined in order to make the practice of requiring borrowers to pay interest on loans (condemned as usury in Canonic law) sound respectable.[25] Far from being outdated, this euphemism was, according to Hirschman, still viable in the economics of his days: it assumed that individual, self-centered, and rational calculation of their own expected costs or gains helped individuals to choose their best options, disregarding the costs to other people.

In the sixteenth and seventeenth centuries, rational calculation was also central to the second euphemism that emerged when interest inflicted itself on political language infused by Machiavelli's ideas (Machiavelli's *The Prince* was a point of departure for Hirschman's analysis). This was what subsequently came to be called the "reason of state doctrine": hiding a ruler's private or personal interest behind the assumption that his or her interests as a ruler were identical with those of the state, here "interest" referred to a prince's or sovereign's rational calculation of the necessities of state.

[I]n the early modern age, "interest" was not only a label under which a ruler was given new latitude or was absolved from feeling guilty about following a practice he had previously been taught to consider as immoral: the term also served to impose new restraints, as it enjoined the prince to pursue his interests with a rational, calculating spirit that would often imply prudence, and moderation.[26]

In the early seventeenth century, the prince's interests were set in opposition to untamed and vicious passions (such as the pursuit of glory and honor) that in the Middle Ages and the Renaissance had been endorsed as heroic virtues. This was the doctrine promulgated by another author who was key to Hirschman's analysis, the duc de Rohan, in his *De l'intérêt des princes et États de la chrétienté* (*On the Interest of Princes and States of Christendom*) published in 1638.[27] According to Hirschman, "the interest doctrine" freed the ruler from "certain traditional restraints (or guilt feelings) only to subject him to new ones that were felt to be far more efficacious than the well-worn appeals to religion, morals, or abstract reason." Such new restrictions upon a ruler's power sparked hopes that "statecraft would be able to produce a more stable political order and a more peaceful world."[28]

This interest doctrine, which, in the sixteenth and seventeenth centuries, was powerful mainly in the context of statecraft, assumed an opposition between interest and passion (an opposition that Rohan was the first to introduce). In the decades to come, this dichotomy was used to help interpret the conduct not only of rulers, but also of everyone else: "Most of human action was suddenly explained by self-interest," to the point that a new paradigm was born.[29] Despite the "infatuation," or maybe because of it, self-interest remained, as Hirschman pointed out, remarkably undefined; nor was it ever really clear how self-interest related to the passions or to reason. However, according to Hirschman, it was exactly this dichotomy between passion and reason that gave rise to the concept of interest:

> Once passion was deemed destructive and reason ineffectual, the view that human action could be exhaustively described by attribution to either one or the other meant an exceedingly somber outlook for humanity. A message of hope was therefore conveyed by the wedging of interest in between the two traditional categories of human motivation. Interest was seen to partake in effect of the better nature of each, as the passion of self-love upgraded and contained by reason, and as reason given direction and force by that passion. The resulting hybrid form of human action was considered exempt from both the destructiveness of passion and the ineffectuality of reason. No wonder that the doctrine of interest was received at the time as a veritable message of salvation![30]

From this broad focus on human interest, it was a rather small step to narrow the concept again: this time, however, to its economic component, which is still visible to us today. We know, from Hirschman's analysis, that the role played by Machiavelli, in the emergence of the interest doctrine against the backdrop of the reasons of state theory, was then re-enacted by Mandeville, in the emergence of the economic reading of the doctrine. Mandeville described the positive effects that such private passions as the striving for material gain could have on public welfare. Now "interest" became a euphemism (a third time) for more pejorative terms such as "avarice."[31] In these early stages of the interest doctrine, interest-based behavior—whether attributed to a ruler or to any individual—meant that actions were based on rational calculation, and to contemporaries of the seventeenth and early eighteenth century rational calculation seemed more desirable than a world deeply shaped and ruled by passions.[32] The eventual rehabilitation of the passions in the course of the eighteenth century then provoked a new evaluation of self-interest, and many thinkers, such as the Third Earl of Shaftesbury, Samuel Butler, or David Hume, became highly critical of self-interest and thought the passions might bring welcome change to a world ruled by self-interest.[33]

While Hirschman's narrative proved powerful—his influence on other scholars of self-interest is testimony to that—it remains somewhat fluid when it comes to explaining the shift of the concept from one realm to another, especially from the political to the economic sphere. Hirschman himself alluded to the speculative nature of his answers. In *The Passions and the Interests,* he conjectured that it might have been the "old association of interest and money-lending," or, with regard to seventeenth-century France, it might also be that "with power so concentrated and seemingly so stable at the time, economic interests constituted the only portion of an ordinary person's total aspirations in which important ups and downs could be visualized." Hirschman shared yet another idea: the advantages offered by the intellectual asset of predictability might have brought about the economic reading of self-interest, because the reduction of human interest to material interest seemed to make actions more predictable.[34] Further, in his Paris lecture, he stated:

> The interests of the vast majority of people, that is, of those outside of the highest reaches of power, came to be more narrowly defined as economic, material, or "moneyed" interests, probably because the non-elite was deemed to busy itself primarily with scrounging a living with no time left to worry about honor, glory, and the like.[35]

Pierre Force, the author of *Self-interest before Adam Smith,* accordingly wondered "how one goes from the interest doctrine (selfish motives are behind all human actions) to economic science (self-interest explains *economic* behavior, but not all types of human behavior)."[36] Furthermore, reading Hirschman's account, one is also left to ponder the question of what happened to self-interest in the political realm after the concept received its economic meaning, a question that Rafe Blaufarb raises in his contribution to this volume. Without doubt, this volume is, like many other studies of self-interest, deeply indebted to Hirschman, but its goal is not to verify Hirschman's grand narrative step by step. Rather, inspired by Hirschman's wish to historicize the notion of self-interest, it engages with his account, yet also seeks to take the attempt further and find other ways to do so.

In light of the difficulties in discussing the nature of self-interest—clearly, the meaning of the term is not self-evident—historicization(s) of self-interest can offer new insights into the concept by asking why, when, for what reason and in which contexts the notion was discussed or referred to, how it was employed by contemporaries, and how the different usages developed and changed over time. This might help us to appreciate the subtle, or not so subtle, transformations in the perception of the notion, and also to explore how and in what ways different people at different times and in different regions reflected on or realized the act of considering what was in their best interest. A historicization of self-interest, then, acknowledges that the question of what it means to be self-interested depends on context rather than on a natural state of things. In other words, it will lead us to explore the various and particular moments in which self-interest was discussed or practiced; a historicization of self-interest is, therefore, necessarily an ongoing, and challenging, process.

Historians rely for their analyses on sources rather than on models, and are thus dependent on what has been handed down. Thus, a particular challenge for them is the study of the *self* in self-interest. While desires and interests can be pursued by individuals, corporations, groups, or societies, and can be described and narrated from within and from without, the self, thought of as an entity of its own (though existing in relation to others), can only be tracked down in the tension (or overlap) between the self's own desires and others' expectations.[37] The self acts, then narrates, and explains those actions, desires, or interests vis-à-vis a present or imagined audience, and thus follows *self*-interest in the light of others' expectations and observations, imagined or real. In other words, as Martin Buber puts it, the self needs the other (*Du*) in order to create a self-identity.[38]

This means that, for a historical study of self-interest, it would be desirable to juxtapose both views of the self; however, in many cases, we lack one side of the story (most often the view from within), or we have only retrospective accounts that try to make sense of past actions. In many instances, we do not have (timely) ego-documents that describe self-interest in relation to others' ideas about the self. Furthermore, it is not entirely clear how much (self-)awareness and (self-)reflexivity we can or should expect from our sources; often we are left to read between the lines in order to reconstruct the self's interests. We are at times able to trace self-perceptions,[39] but often enough we can only approximate the self's desires and interests according to our knowledge of an individual's class, gender, race, religion, language, or education. Or, we may choose to analyze how others viewed the decision-making of a particular person. In other words, in both those cases, we study attributed selves.

Given this fact, historians may tend to opt, not unlike Hirschman, for an approach that focuses on the histories of ideas or on the intellectual histories of self-interest, or that analyzes the languages and discourses concerned with the concept by exploring how contemporaries perceived, thought and talked about, or used references to self-interest. Such language-based approaches also allow us to reflect on the different vernacular traditions and translations of self-interest in the context of its semantic field. A language-based historical inquiry thus explores how different notions of the semantic field relate one to another, and how the various notions can be translated into other languages. In addition to the latinized *egoism* or *egocentrism* (and their vernacular equivalents), we find *self-interest, selfishness,* or *self-love* in English; in French, we refer to *intérêt personnel* or *amour propre*; in Italian, we speak of *interesse personale* or *autostima*; in German, we find *Eigennutz* or *Eigeninteresse*; in Dutch, there is no term that literally translates as self-interest, but a set of words that are related to the notion, such as *hebzucht, winzucht, eigenbaat*, and *eigenbelang*. In this volume, Inger Leemans explores the use of these terms and concepts through the Dutch seventeenth and eighteenth centuries.

Historians of self-interest face yet other challenges if they wish to take approaches that do not rely exclusively on the analysis of ideas or languages, but attempt to relate a person's choice, the outcome of a decision, and a person's or group's intentions or preferences that led to a decision. To uncover the latter, historians might follow, more or less intuitively, an approach based on what the economist Paul Samuelson in 1938 called the "theory of revealed preferences": if a person chooses x instead of y, although both x and y are available, we can conclude that the person prefers x over y. In other words, such an approach assumes that decision-makers reveal their preferences in their choices. As observers, we thus deduce from choice to preferences, while "from the point of introspection of the person in question, the process runs from preference to his choice."[40] While a choice might reveal, or at least help us to detect, a person's preferences, historians might go beyond such deductions to wonder about the factors that influenced, or maybe even coerced, those preferences. Preferences in this sense, then, do not necessarily equate to self-interest.

The search for self-interest is complicated by another reflection. Despite the fact that the passage of time discloses information about the effect of decisions made, and one might think that this would make the study of self-interest easier, we cannot assume that a decision was always and mainly motivated by self-interest because its results eventually turned out to be beneficial to the decision-maker. To take the outcome of a decision that we, as historians, know, and use it as a retrospective criterion for a study of self-interest would overlook those cases of self-interest that did not lead to positive outcomes for the decision-makers, even though they were inspired or provoked by the same motive. It would also disregard the fact that effects can be serendipitous, and that a decision may lead to an outcome that no one could have foreseen, but that happens to align perfectly with the decision-maker's interests. Also, goals might be adapted during the process of decision-making, or of the action, and might change according to circumstances and thus cease to correspond with the original intention. To equate the outcome of a person's decision with the decision-maker's interest is, thus, an undesirable shortcut. Historians cannot, therefore, easily adopt an economic approach (defined by Gary Becker as the "combined assumptions of maximizing behavior, market equilibrium, and stable preferences, used relentlessly and unflinchingly"[41]), at least not without reflecting on his or her own observations; nor can they straightforwardly assume stable preferences, or the validity of the utility-concept. Rather, historians might want to study whether such modeled assumptions hold true when looking at different historical situations and contexts of individual or collective actions.

If serendipitous, unforeseen effects cannot necessarily relate to a decision-maker's interest or intentions, then self-interest must adhere to either an ad-hoc or a long(er)-planned private prognosis of a decision's outcome. In order for self-interest to guide actions, or for an intellectual reflection to be translated into action, the desired outcome must be considered at least possible, if not probable. For their prognosis, decision-makers might need empirical data or information; more sophisticated decision-makers might have developed observational skills, and the capacity to balance different variables, for such a prognosis must be based on more than mere imagination. A decision-maker's interests, however, might not always be unbiased or considered rational or utility-maximizing; choices can also be infused by strong, deeply ingrained emotional connotations and feelings, as the histories of stock market and their crashes, for example, have shown.[42]

A historicization of self-interest could, then, focus on three main topics. The first is the prognostic and temporal character of self-interest and self-interested action: was self-interest translated into strategic thinking or agency? Did it consist of an ad-hoc assessment, or was it a part of a broader, planned, and projected future? How did such assessments change in the course of the process and through interactions with others? The second topic is the knowledge and intellectual skills involved in, or needed for, a reflection of self-interested goals or self-interested behavior (including knowledge about concrete circumstances, or mathematical and computational skills). Third, there is the relationship between self-interest and emotions or psychological dispositions: which feelings and emotions could have influenced the self's interests? How could one feel self-interest—how could it be embodied?

There is certainly an abundance of (historical) analyses that are in one way or another implicitly concerned with self-interest. The notion is prevalent in many different areas of study: for example, in classical economic philosophy or the history of economic thought;[43] in the analyses of (financial) capitalism and the various attempts to tame it;[44] in the history of commercial and financial trust;[45] or, probably most prominently, in the various analyses of the so-called "projecting age" or the "age of improvement."[46] But self-interest also plays an important role in studies of the (self-)perceptions of "early capitalists,"[47] and is similarly significant for the analysis of knowledge markets.[48] Yet, despite Hirschman's indisputable influence on the analysis of the subject, very few studies have followed his endeavor and explicitly focused on the historicization of the concept.

It was only the crisis of Western capitalism around the turn of the millennium that provoked new studies of self-interest: in 2003, Pierre Force enriched the discussion with his book *Self-interest before Adam Smith*.[49] He took Hirschman's survey as a point of departure for his own analysis, but concentrated more on the distinction between *self-interest* and *self-love*. Force's work is also devoted to the discussion of axiomatical principles; however, he opens out Hirschman's perspective by showing how Jean-Jacques Rousseau's psychological assumptions about human passions influenced Adam Smith's economic theory. He then deviated decisively from Hirschman by unraveling how *The Wealth of Nations* reconciled a republican perspective on human passion with the economic (and more liberal) doctrine of commerce (as Montesquieu and James Steuart had done).

The economist Steven G. Medema then published in 2011 his *The Hesitant Hand: Taming Self-Interest in the History of Economic Ideas*,[50] in which he explicitly demonstrated the fact that the economic crises of the early 2000s and the social discussions they provoked made a historical analysis of self-interest more urgent than ever before. Medema then shed light on the history of economic thought and the ways in which the taming of self-interest was envisioned. As Medema made clear, ever since Adam Smith's market analysis, economic theories have predominantly deliberated upon the competences and responsibilities of market control. Medema then unraveled a connection between earlier dealings with self-interested behavior and our own dealings with economic crises (which are based on either condemnations or a defense of self-interested behavior).

In their edited volume, published in 2016, the Germanist Sandra Richter and the historian Guillaume Garner shed light on the economization (*Ökonomisierung*) of the seventeenth century. In the volume, the editors distanced themselves from any kind of neo-classical premise of the economy and from the rationality verdict of a *homo oeconomicus* model. Instead, the editors employed a broader notion of the economy that also includes ethical questions, or questions concerning "efficiency." Furthermore, their definition of the economy also includes actions and institutions which are targeted at the production, circulation, and distribution of material or immaterial resources. Richter and Garner's volume thus included "the economy of knowledge" and "knowledge of the economy." However, in that publication, knowledge predominantly refers to political economy and arithmetic and so remains in the world of the seventeenth-century *republic of letters*.

Many of the existing histories of self-interest have in common that they explicitly or implicitly consider Adam Smith's market analysis a milestone in modern economic thought (and thus analyze the economy before or after Adam Smith). There is also a tendency to assume that it is the history of classical economic thought that is concerned with the subject of self-interest. What is lacking is an approach to the topic that focuses on the different knowledge(s) and practices applied to the creation, calculation, education, embodiment, or limitations of self-interest. Such an approach can incorporate a larger group of recipients of knowledge or practices and can, furthermore, include not only explicit, but also implicit or tacit knowledge about self-interest that can manifest itself in practices, in representations, or in materials.

Furthermore, the temporality of self-interest has not yet been sufficiently studied in the humanities:[51] self-interest figures in agency-theories predominantly as a forward-looking objective, which offers guidance for decisions in the present that should maximize profit in the future. Self-interest, however, also includes different forms of knowledge, most notably empirical or experiential (thus backward-looking knowledge); moreover, it incorporates present observations as well as projections for the future. A historicization of our comprehension of rationality thus has to reflect on this threefold temporal aggregation of knowledge concerned with self-interest. Exploring the different temporalities of self-interest will also allow us to inquire about the prognostic character of self-interested reflections and actions as well as about the relationship between self-interest and our notion of rationality.

Furthermore, in the available literature, we find a strong bias toward studies focused on the early modern period and the Enlightenment. This is hardly surprising when we consider how Hirschman's influential analysis unfolded an ideological transformation, in which violent passions such as the striving for glory, honor, and ambition were increasingly replaced as social values by commercial virtues such as the rational pursuit of one's own self-interest—a process that, according to Hirschman, occurred in the seventeenth and eighteenth centuries. There is also a tendency to study the British histories of profit-seeking. Such an interest is easily explained by Britain's commercial power in the eighteenth century, but also by its rise as the first industrialized power, which has inspired a considerable tradition of exploring British (globalized) capitalism, consumerism, or its "projecting age." This is not to say that we lack Dutch or French studies that are (at least implicitly) concerned with the emergence of a new age of profit-making.[52] Arnaud Orain's recent monograph *La politique du merveilleux*[53] is a good example of such an analysis that focuses on the rise of a new, powerful "Leviathan," known as John Law's System, that inspired and liberated the individual wish for profit.

This volume, however, sets out to widen not only the temporal scope, from roughly the seventeenth to the twentieth century, but also the regional focus, integrating French, English, Dutch, German, and North American histories of various dealings with self-interest. The volume aims to inquire about the knowledge(s) involved when enacting or speaking about self-interest at specific places or moments in time. It also inquires about the embodiments of self-interest, and about the calculations included in self-interest; it asks whether self-interest can be learned or inspired, and whether there were models of emulation for self-interest (or for harnessing self-interest); it focuses on different vernacular traditions, readings, or translations of self-interest. Very different approaches to the topic are assembled here, including classical political and economic theories. In addition, the volume broadens its scope to the history of actuarial science and mathematics, the history of emotions, and anthropology. The following chapters also look at a broader group of recipients or actors concerned with self-interest, by focusing on knowledge-regimes and their various practices.

The first part of the book considers the creation and calculation of self-interest against the backdrop of the interest of a nation. Ted McCormick's chapter combines a focus on projecting and self-interest and inquires into "projecting" as a source of ideas about self-interest. By focusing on the Hartlib Circle during the 1640s and 1650s, he illustrates how the proposals for projects of improvement that came from this circle, and its engagement with the figure of the "projector," constructed self-interest as a good compatible with the interest of a nation. Christine Zabel's chapter, by contrast, focuses on the difficulties encountered when trying to honor both individual interest and the interest of a nation, by examining the calculations and techniques of discounting the Old Regime's annuity schemes at the French revolutionary Comité des Finances. The chapter studies not only how these calculations evolved, but also in what ways changing political positions or ideas influenced the calculations (and vice versa).

The second part studies contemporary attempts to understand and to learn about the operations of self-interest. Koen Stapelbroek sheds light on commercial sociability and the management of self-interest in Isaac de Pinto's writings, who defended the practice of credit and state debts as a way of reining in the "Jealousy of Trade" and as a means to international peace, defended self-interest as a tool that helped individuals to be successful in the marketplace. Simone De Angelis reconstructs a line of self-interest-related argumentation which proceeds from the antagonism between Cumberland and Hobbes and leads on to the relationship between Smith and Rousseau. In particular, the chapter focuses on the post-1750 debate on moral philosophy. Christof Dejung, in turn, examines the genealogy of the concept of "embeddedness" as it was established by social anthropologists in the first half of the twentieth century, to distinguish colonial societies from Western capitalism characterized by self-interest. By examining the transfer of the concept to Western societies and the continuing disputes in economic anthropology about its exact meaning, the chapter aims to provincialize (in Dipesh Chakrabarty's term) the notion of the economy and to point out how difficult it is to establish what we actually mean when we talk about "the economy."

The third section of the volume focuses on feelings involved in the pursuit of self-interest, and the embodiments and practices of self-interest. Inger Leemans offers an introduction to the Dutch terminology, and the transitions these terms underwent in the seventeenth and eighteenth centuries, in order to explore the cultural discourses on (self-)interest in the Dutch Republic. She shows that from a very early stage the commercially oriented Dutch Republic embraced commercial drives as a central force in human behavior and viewed them as embodied passions. Yet the "self" of self-interest was never dominant in Dutch discourse, as interest was described as a social drive, a force essential to the fabric of society. Ulrich Pfister and Friederike Scholten-Buschhoff then explore practical knowledge concerned with self-interest in German rural areas against the backdrop of the "Industrious Revolution" in household management, and changes in the management of rural estates during the "Great Transformation." They investigate the relationship between self-interest and practical knowledge of estate management, and whether practical knowledge informing self-interested behavior was anchored in propositional knowledge of self-interest. Daniel Menning then studies the pursuit of self-interest in emotional communities, by focusing on popular discussions of stock market investors in the United States around 1900. He analyzes a paradox in contemporary stock market dealings: investors were pursuing their self-interest, yet their very immersion in a society of speculators tended to cause them to lose the ability to speculate successfully. The chapter traces the explanations for such phenomena given by socio-psychological theorists and authors of advice manuals on stock market speculation, who explained this negative aspect of self-interest in terms of mass psychology; yet, the chapter also follows individuals who attempted to circumvent those threats to their ability to speculate self-interestedly.

The fourth and final section focuses on the different ways to tame self-interest, or to conceptualize it as a limitation. Rafe Blaufarb's chapter starts where Hirschman's analysis of self-interest in the political realm ended. Although Hirschman had shown that the early modern interest discourse originated in the theory of reasons of state, he did not follow the notion in the political sphere after its shift to the economic realm. Blaufarb proposes to explore interest as an enduring political problem for the early modern French monarchy by shedding light on the French jurists' construction of an elaborate royal-domanial regime to constrain and channel the monarch's property rights. Cornelius Torp, by contrast, studies the interconnection of the political and economic interest story by exploring the conceptualizations of legitimate material self-interest and its interactions with the anti-gambling movement in nineteenth-century America. Focusing on these interconnections allows him to conclude that the prohibition of legal gambling opportunities culminated at a moment in which the profit motive became central to the Western world. The anti-gambling discourse served as a foil to distinguish socially acceptable economic operations and legitimate self-interest from illegitimate forms of economic activity. Gisèle Sapiro then uses the concept of disinterestedness as an axiological operator and analyzes the various definitions and uses of the concept and its construction of oppositions with interest and self-interest in the writings of eighteenth-century French, English, and German thinkers, tracing the intertextuality and debates among these thinkers in a transnational perspective.

The volume offers some different, out of many possible, attempts to look at the histories of self-interest. However, the historical inquiry into the concept of self-interest and its impact on our world should not end here. Self-interest's impression on gender, sexuality, race, or the treatment of minorities should be further examined. The relationship of self-interest and the creations of various markets, including human trafficking (in its historical and modern meanings) should be studied, and inquiries made about education in self-interest or the religious repercussions of an interest-based social order. Far from being exhaustive itself, this volume is presented with the wish to inspire more, different, and new approaches to the study of self-interest that go beyond the regional focus on the Atlantic world; that reflect some of the above-mentioned possible subject areas, or perhaps come up with yet other topics.

Notes

1 Jeremy Adelman in his short Introduction to Albert O. Hirschman's "The Concept of Interest: From Euphemism to Tautology," in *The Essential Hirschman,* ed. Jeremy Adelman, 2nd ed. (Princeton: Princeton University Press, 2015), 195–213, 195.
2 Hirschman, "The Concept of Interest," 195–96.
3 *Cambridge Dictionary* (Cambridge, UK: Cambridge University Press, 2014), https://dictionary.cambridge.org/de/worterbuch/englisch/self-interest.
4 Francis Y. Edgeworth, *Mathematical Psychics. An Essay on the Application of Mathematics to the Moral Sciences* (London: C. Kegan Paul & Co: 1881), 16–17. See also Pierre Force, *Self-interest before Adam Smith: A Genealogy of Economic Science* (Cambridge: Cambridge University Press, 2003), 7.
5 Aneta Kargol-Wasiluk, Anna Wildowicz-Giegiel and Marian Zalesko, "The Evolution of the Economic Man: From Homo Oeconomicus to Homo Moralis," *Gospodarka Narodowa* 29, no. 1 (February/March 2018): 33–57, 34.
6 John J. Persky, "The Ethology of Homo Oeoconomicus," *Journal of Economic Perspectives* 9, no. 2 (1995): 221–31. The edition here used: John K. Ingram, *A History of Political Economy* (New York: The Macmillan Company, 1902). The edition here used: Maffeo Pantaelleoni, *Principii di Economia Pura,* 2nd ed. (Firenze: G. Barbèra, 1894). See also Kargol-Wasiluk, Wildowicz-Giegiel and Zalesko, "The Evolution of the Economic Man," 34.
7 Kargol-Wasiluk, Wildowicz-Giegiel and Zalesko, "The Evolution of the Economic Man," 34 and 36.
8 See Kargol-Wasiluk, Wildowicz-Giegiel and Zalesko, "The Evolution of the Economic Man," 34–35; Ralf Dahrendorf, *Homo Sociologicus. Ein Versuch zur Geschichte, Bedeutung und Kritik der sozialen Rolle,* 17th ed. (Wiesbaden: VS Verlag für Sozialwissenschaften, 2010); Louis Dumont, *Homo hierarchicus. Le système des castes et ses implications* (Paris: Gallimard, 1979); Bernd Siebenhüner, *Homo Sustinens. Auf dem Weg zu einem Menschenbild der Nachhaltigkeit* (Marburg: Metropolis, 2001); Holger Rogall, *Neue Umweltökonomie – Ökologische Ökonomie: Ökonomische und ethische Grundlagen der Nachhaltigkeit, Instrumente zu ihrer Durchsetzung* (Opladen: Leske + Budrich, 2002); Holger Rogall and Katharina Gapp, "Homo heterogenus – das neue Menschenbild in den Wirtschaftswissenschaften," in *Wirtschaftsanthropologie,* ed. Claus Dierksmeier, Ulrich Hemel, and Jürgen Manemann, (Baden-Baden: Nomos, 2015), 99–115.
9 See for this section Force, *Self-Interest,* 10, Jon Elster, "Social Norms and Economic Theory," *Journal of Economic Perspectives* 3, no. 4 (1989): 99–117; Robert H. Frank, *Passions Within Reason: The Strategic Role of Emotions* (New York: W. W. Norton, 1988).
10 Francis Y. Edgeworth, *Mathematical Psychics. An Essay on the Application of Mathematics to the Moral Sciences* (London: C. Kegan Paul & Co, 1881), 16; and Amartya K. Sen, "Rational Fool: A Critique of the Behavioral Foundations of Economic Theory," *Philosophy and Public Affairs* 6 (1977): 317–44, 317; see also Force, *Self-Interest,* 10.
11 Jon Elster, *Nuts and Bolts for the Social Sciences* (Cambridge, UK: Cambridge University Press, 1989), 52–60 and Force, *Self-Interest,* 10.
12 Elster, *Nuts and Bolts,* 7–8.
13 Friedrich August von Hayek, *Individualism and Economic Order* (Chicago: Chicago University Press, 1996); Jon Elster, *Sour Grapes: Studies in the Subversion of Rationality* (Cambridge, UK: Cambridge University Press, 1983); Daniel Kahneman, "Maps of Bounded Rationality: Psychology for Behavioral Economics," *The American Economic Review* 93, no. 5 (Dec 2003): 1449–495;

Daniel Kahneman and Amos Tversky, "Prospect Theory: An Analysis of Decisions Under Risk," *Econometria* 47, no. 2 (March 1979): 264–91; Daniel Kahneman and Amos Tversky, *Choices, Values, and Frames* (Cambridge, UK: Cambridge University Press, 2000); Herbert Simon, "Bounded Rationality and Organizational Learning," *Organization Science* 2, no. 1 (1991): DOI: https://doi.org/10.1287/orsc.2.1.125; Richard H. Thaler and Cass R. Sunstein, *Nudge: Improving Decisions About Health, Wealth and Happiness* (New Haven, CT: Yale University Press, 2008). See also Kargol-Wasiluk, Wildowicz-Giegiel and Zalesko, "The Evolution of the Economic Man," 34 and 36.

14 Richard H. Thaler, *Misbehaving. The Making of Behavioral Economics* (New York/London: W. W. Norton & Company, 2015), 4–5.

15 Thaler, *Misbehaving*, 5–11; see also Kargol-Wasiluk, Wildowicz-Giegiel and Zalesko, "The Evolution of the Economic Man," 34.

16 Laurie A. Paul, *Transformative Experience* (Oxford: Oxford University Press, 2014), especially pp. 5–19.

17 Dan Usher, *The Economics of Voting: Studies of Self-Interest* (Oxford/New York: Routledge, 2015), 1.

18 Peter E. Langsæther and Geoffrey Evans, "More than Self-Interest: Why Different Classes Have Different Attitudes to Income Inequality," *The British Journal of Sociology* (February 2020). DOI:10.1111/1468-4446.12747.

19 Albert O. Hirschman, *The Passions and the Interests. Political Arguments for Capitalism Before Its Triumph*, 3rd ed. (Princeton: Princeton University Press, 2013), 3.

20 Jeremy Adelman in his short introduction to Hirschman's Paris lectures. See Adelman, *The Essential Hirschman*, 195.

21 See Albert O. Hirschman, "Political Economics and Possibilism," in *The Essential Hirschman*, 1–34; Jeremy Adelman, "Introduction," in *The Essential Hirschman*, vii–xvii, xii and xvii, as well as his biography of Albert O. Hirschman: Jeremy Adelman, *A Worldly Philosopher: The Odyssey of Albert O. Hirschman* (Princeton: Princeton University Press, 2013), especially chapter 3, 115.

22 Jeremy Adelman, "Afterword," in *The Passions and the Interests*, 137–43, 140.

23 Cited after Hirschman, "The Concept of Interest," 202.

24 Hirschman, "The Concept of Interest," 204.

25 See Hirschman, "The Concept of Interest," 196.

26 See Hirschman, "The Concept of Interest," 198.

27 See Hirschman, "The Concept of Interest," 197–98.

28 See Hirschman, "The Concept of Interest," 198.

29 Hirschman, *The Passions and the Interests*, 42.

30 Hirschman, *The Passions and the Interests*, 42–44; and Force, *Self-Interest*, 7.

31 See Hirschman, "The Concept of Interest," 199.

32 See Hirschman, "The Concept of Interest," 200.

33 Hirschman, *The Passions and the Interests*, 47.

34 Hirschman, *The Passions and the Interests*, 39–40, also 54.

35 Hirschman, "The Concept of Interest," 200.

36 Force, *Self-Interest*, 4.

37 A good, and for this chapter inspiring, example that explains this tension between the view from within and the view from without is Kate Kirkpatrick's new biography of Simone de Beauvoir. See Kate Kirkpatrick, *Becoming Beauvoir: A Life* (London/New York: Bloomsbury Academic, 2019).

38 Martin Buber, *Ich und Du* (Stuttgart: Reclam, 1995).

39 See, for example, Margaret C. Jacob and Catherine Secretan, eds., *The Self-Perception of Early Modern Capitalists* (New York, NY: Macmillan, 2008)

40 See Paul A. Samuelson, "A Note on the Pure Theory of Consumer's Behavior," *Economia* 5/17 (1938): 61–71; but also Amartya Sen, "Behavior and the Concept of Preferences, in Rational Choice: Readings in Social and Political Theory," ed. Jon Elster (Oxford: Blackwell, 1986), 60–81.

41 Gary S. Becker, "The Economic Approach to Human Behavior," in *Rational Choice*, ed. Jon Elster, 108–22, 110.

42 See, for example, Daniel Menning, *Politik, Ökonomie, Aktienspekulation: 'South Sea Bubble und Co.' 1720* (Berlin/Boston: DeGruyter, 2020).

43 See, for example, Susan James, *Passion and Action: The Emotions in Seventeenth-Century Philosophy* (Oxford: Clarendon Press, 1997); Emma Rothschild, *Economic Sentiments: Adam Smith, Condorcet and the Enlightenment* (Cambridge, MA: Harvard University Press, 2002).

44 See David Henderson, *Misguided Virtue: False Notions of Corporate Social Responsibility* (London: The Institute of Economic Affairs, 2001); Perry Gauci, ed., *Regulating the British Economy, 1660–1850* (Farnham: Ashgate, 2011); Jürgen Kocka and Marcel van der Linden, eds., *Capitalism: The Reemergence of a Historical Concept* (London: Bloomsbury, 2016); Simon Middleton and James E. Shaw, eds., *Market Ethics and Practices, 1300–1850* (Oxford/New York, NY: Routledge, 2017); Anne Murphy, *The Origins of English Financial Markets: Investment and Speculation before the South Sea Bubble* (Cambridge: Cambridge University Press, 2009); Larry Neal, *The Rise of Financial Capitalism: International Capital Markets in the Age of Reason* (Cambridge: Cambridge University Press, 1990); James Taylor, *Creating Capitalism: Joint-Stock Enterprise in British Politics and Culture, 1800–1870* (Woodbridge: Boydell, 2006).

45 See, for example, Fontaine Laurence, *L'Économie morale: Pauvreté, credit et confiance dans l'Europe préindustrielle* (Paris: Gallimard, 2008); Christine McLeod, *Heroes of Invention: Technology, Liberalism and British Industry, 1740–1914* (Cambridge: Cambridge University Press, 2007).

46 See Eric Ash, *The Draining of the Fence: Projectors, Popular Politics, and State Building in Early Modern England* (Baltimore, MD: John Hopkins University Press, 2017); David Alff, *The Wreckage of Intentions: Projects in British Culture, 1660–1730* (Philadelphia, PA: University of Pennsylvania Press, 2017); Toby Barnard, *Improving Ireland? Projectors, Prophets and Profiteers, 1641–1786* (Dublin: Four Courts Press, 2008); Richard Drayton, *Nature's Government: Science, Imperial Britain, and the 'Improvement' of the World* (New Haven, CT: Yale University Press, 2000); Frédéric Graber and Martin Giraudeau, eds., *Les projets: Une histoire politique (XVIᵉ–XXIᵉ siècles)* (Paris: Presse des Mines, 2018); Richard Hoyle, ed., *Custom, Improvement and the Landscape in Early Modern Britain* (Farnham: Ashgate, 2011); Ted McCormick, *William Petty and the Ambitions of Political Arithmetic* (Oxford: Oxford University Press, 2009); Joel Mokyr, *A Culture of Growth: The Origins of the Modern Economy* (Princeton: Princeton University Press, 2017); Maximillian E. Novak, ed., *The Age of Projects* (Toronto: University of Toronto Press, 2008); Paul Slack, *The Invention of Improvement: Information and Material Progress in Seventeenth Century England* (Oxford: Oxford University Press, 2015); Sarah Tarlow, *The Archeology of Improvement in Britain, 1750–1850* (Cambridge: Cambridge University Press, 2007); Koji Yamamoto, *Taming Capitalism Before its Triumph. Public Service, Distrust & 'Projecting' in Early Modern England* (Oxford: Oxford University Press, 2018).

47 See, for example, Jacob and Secretan, eds, The Self-Perception; Thomas Leng, *Benjamin Worsley (1618–1677): Trade, Interest and the Spirit in Revolutionary England* (Woodbridge: Boydell, 2008); Alexandra Shepard, *Accounting for Oneself: Worth, Status, and the Social Order in Early Modern*

England (Oxford: Oxford University Press, 2015); Larry Stewart, *The Rise of Public Science: Rhetoric, Technology, and Natural Philosophy in Newtonian Britain, 1660–1750* (Cambridge: Cambridge University Press, 1992).

48 See, for example, Margaret C. Jacob, *The First Knowledge Economy: Human Capital and the European Economy, 1750–1850* (Cambridge: Cambridge University Press, 2014); Vera Keller, *Knowledge and the Public Interest, 1575–1725* (Cambridge: Cambridge University Press, 2015).

49 Force, *Self-Interest.*

50 Steven G. Medema, *The Hesitant Hand. Taming Self-Interest in the History of Economic Ideas* (Princeton: Princeton University Press, 2009).

51 "Intertemporal choice-theory" problematizes the time gap between decisions made and the outcome of decisions in the social sciences.

52 See, for Dutch histories of profit and for Dutch economic history more broadly, for example: Joel Mokyr, *Industrialization in the Low Countries, 1795–1850* (New Haven, CT: Yale University Press, 1976); Steven Schama, *The Embarrassment of Riches: An Interpretation of Dutch Culture in the Golden Age* (Berkeley/Los Angeles, CA: University of California Press, 1988), Jan de Vires and Ad van der Woulde, *The First Modern Economy: Success, Failure, and Perseverance of the Dutch Economy, 1500–1815* (Cambridge, UK/New York, NY: Cambridge University Press, 1997).

53 Arnaud Orain, *La politique du merveilleux. Une autre histoire du Système de Law (1695–1795)* (Paris: Fayard, 2018).

Part I
Creating, inspiring, and calculating self-interest

1 Improvement, projecting, and self-interest in the Hartlib Circle, c. 1640–1660

Ted McCormick

The unnatural origins of self-interest

Perhaps no concept in economics is as apparently natural as self-interest.[1] It is the engine that drives the individual economic actor; at the same time, it supplies an analytical criterion by which the rationality of past actions is assessed and the likelihood of future ones predicted. It has always been with us, and is universal. Certainly, individuals may have a better or worse understanding of their interests, and they determine these with reference to different timeframes and kinds of good. Historically, too, self-interested behavior has faced complex and varied constraints. Indeed, if the key economic fact of the modern era—for some historians, at least—is the rise of free enterprise, then the central insight of modern economic thought is the corresponding realization that the untrammeled pursuit of individual self-interest leads, as if guided by an invisible hand, to the good of society as a whole. Beginning in the eighteenth century, this interest had only to be liberated by the progress of Enlightenment ideas to transform the world for the better.[2]

One of the enduring virtues of Albert O. Hirschman's *The Passions and the Interests* is that it complicated the intellectual side of this story. Writing his manuscript in the early 1970s, Hirschman was frustrated by what he called "the incapacity of contemporary social science to shed light on the political consequences of economic growth," a problem he blamed on a failure to grasp the ideological roots of economics.[3] His book sought the origins of "interest" in changing philosophical ideas about passions. Long denigrated as a source of disorder and sin, the passions came by the seventeenth century to be seen as drivers of human action, and ultimately as susceptible if not to being subdued then at least to being differentiated and balanced against each other, the merely selfish restraining the politically destructive. During the eighteenth century, greed in particular—so Hirschman argued—came to be described less as a passion and more as an interest, indeed *the* interest. Because it was natural, its operations were predictable; analytically speaking, it made popular behavior legible. In practical terms, it kept the peace.

The Passions and the Interests underlined the ideological origins and purposes of arguments for self-interest—that is, in Hirschman's terms, capitalism. Selfish behavior may have been part of human nature, by this account, but conceptualizing self-interest as the fundamental and legitimate spring of action became acceptable, and then imperative, because it solved a political problem. Generations of political-economic writing that took this solution for granted naturalized the concept and put it beyond critical scrutiny. Yet, Hirschman's account also imposed a chronology that makes apparent anticipations of self-interest in earlier, non-canonical sources harder to interpret. Focusing as it did on canonical works of moral and political philosophy, his book had little to say about the ephemeral pamphlets and proposals that made up the bulk of "economic writing" in the seventeenth century, at least in England—a kind of writing in which concrete economic interests were often directly and explicitly at stake.[4] Still less did this intellectual history accommodate the kinds of profitable, material, technological "improvements," innovations, and schemes that many figures retrospectively classified as "economic writers" pursued in the workshops, on the estates, and in the colonies of the seventeenth-century British world.[5] Inasmuch as ideas of interest, and of self-interest, animated "projects" for improvement and clung to the figure of the "projector" as the architect and purveyor of these profitable designs, this was a significant oversight.

Taking up Hirschman's fundamental insight into the ideological origins of the concept of self-interest while building on more recent work in the histories of improvement and projecting, this chapter aims to bring seventeenth-century projects and projecting into a discussion of interest and its ideological origins. It focuses in particular on projects emerging from the network of philosophers, inventors, Protestant ecumenists, and social reformers centered on the London-based, German-born intelligencer Samuel Hartlib (c. 1600–1662) and known as the "Hartlib Circle."[6] Reaching the peak of its activity in the 1640s and 1650s, in a time of civil conflict and political experimentation, the Hartlib Circle was the matrix for a multitude of projects whose authors invoked and negotiated a plethora of interests even as they proposed to improve, reform, or transform the nation and the world around them. Because of this, because several of Hartlib's associates enjoyed some prominence either as scientific figures or as economic writers after the Restoration, and because Hartlib's voluminous papers have been preserved, it is extraordinarily rich ground for tracing ideas about self-interest in shifting practical as well as intellectual contexts.[7]

The picture that emerges is far messier than the elegant portrait Hirschman sketched. It reveals the practical combination of ideas his account separated. As this chapter will argue, the Hartlibian record indicates a deeper ambiguity in attitudes toward self-interest or self-seeking (as embodied in the figure of the projector), a greater complexity in the language of "interest" (as borne out in Hartlib's archive), and an earlier appreciation of the benefits, if not the necessity, of self-interest for the common good (in projects predicated on enclosure, in particular), than Hirschman's argument allows. At the same time, however, this examination highlights some of the ideological functions of self-interest that Hirschman grasped and further illuminates some of the problems that self-interest seemed to solve. Indeed, reading seventeenth-century projects through the lens of *The Passions and the Interests* lets us see not only the role of self-interest in projecting, but also the extent to which the conceptualization and promotion of self-interest was itself a kind of project.

Projecting and self-interest

What did a projector look like? In March 1661, William Petty—soon to be knighted by the restored king, Charles II—sent "certain proposals for the improvement of Ireland" to the Duke of Ormond, Charles's new Lord-Lieutenant of Ireland. Petty introduced his proposals, which included a land registry, with a disavowal: "I do not appear a projector to shark for my necessities." Well might he protest. His service to the recently overthrown Cromwellian regime had made him one of the greatest non-noble landowners in Ireland; a registry would protect his holdings against the claims of dispossessed royalists and Irish Catholics. That alone might raise questions about Petty's motives, but that was not all. As he bragged, he had "scaped pretty well in several new proposals already," and was willing to be "laughed at once more," if need be.[8] In fact, Petty had acquired his estates thanks to his own "Down Survey" of Ireland, undertaken from 1653 to 1657.[9] As master of the survey, he had been responsible for assessing the quality and extent of confiscated Irish Catholic lands—lands from which Cromwell's soldiers, London investors, and Petty himself were all to be paid. Neither his skill at framing his ideas (in part by casting rivals, including the Surveyor-General, Benjamin Worsley, as devious, incompetent, and self-interested projectors) nor the profit they brought him went unremarked.[10] Ormond would live to complain of both. Facing the end of his career under James II, the duke wrote in 1686 that "Sir William Pet[t]y"—already pitching schemes to James's new favorites—"thinks it prudence to secure himself by applications to men in power & if hee can not save all will try to save one."[11]

To his critics, Petty's career was one long, twisted thread of self-seeking behavior. As they watched his lucrative service to the Protectorate morph into a frenetic scramble for royal patronage, they saw the prudence of the political survivor intertwined with the ambition of the parvenu, the pursuit of privilege and office fueled by hunger for wealth and fame. Yet, the moral cast of these motives depended on perspective. What was avarice to the Baptist soldier or usurping pride to the dispossessed royalist might seem to others no more than the reasonable enjoyment of just reward for ingenious labor in the public interest. This was all the more true because, in science, politics, and economy alike, projecting—the framing of schemes for improvement of all kinds—was the medium of Petty's machinations.[12]

As his disavowal of the name suggests, projects, projecting, and above all the figure of the projector had a strongly negative rhetorical charge. Petty had been stung by it before, and would be again. A 1662 broadside attacking the new Hearth Tax singled out the "pur-blind" Petty's role in this "Painted Project":

> But was this done, my Gracious Liege, for You?
> No, though at first it might make a shew,
> As Painted Projects use, t'inhance Your Rents,
> Their Subtle Sconces moulded worse intents
> Than pur-blin'd Eyes discover'd; for they sought
> Either by Farming what their Brokage wrought,
> Or by their Agents to ingratiate
> Your Smile for whom they did negotiate.[13]

A year later, another ballad mocked Petty's plan for a double-hulled ship in the same terms. Noting that Petty "had many Acres got,/By measuring of Land a Spot," it suggested that, "gaping for [further] promotion," he "Doth now project upon the Water."[14] As balladeers would have it, obsequious projectors hid private interest behind a veil of service, whether to king and country or to the advancement of knowledge. Yet even sympathetic observers, who dwelt on the public benefits of these same projects, did not deny their private profitability nor their authors' desire of name or place. As Daniel Defoe would come to describe it in his *Essay upon Projects*, projecting in itself was neither good, bad, nor indeed neutral, but a morally complex endeavor that aligned—or bound together—a tangle of private motivations and public interests.[15]

It is, therefore, surprising that the historiographies of self-interest, projecting, and the public good have, until recently, rarely intersected.[16] Through the seventeenth and into the eighteenth century, in Britain and Ireland, promoters of various improvements, inventions, and innovations strove to avoid the label of projector because of the self-interest it connoted and the tensions between self- and public interest it implied.[17] To be a projector was to promote the common good while seeking private advantage, to tie the "luciferous" augmentation of knowledge or skill to the "lucriferous" pursuit of material gain.[18] Inasmuch as self-seeking reflected human vices such as avarice or pride, projecting was morally fraught. The moral difficulties with projecting were not simply reflections of inherent vice, however; they were also economic. Aligning the projector's just reward with the good of the commonwealth might require the recruitment of patrons, publics, or the state, and often necessitated the calculated dissimulation or concealment not only of personal motives but also of useful knowledge itself. Of course, the projector might simply lie for profit. But even where projectors were not charlatans or fools, they were understood to be holding something back. Like alchemists—with whom they shared a great deal, in practice and in persona—they promised to effect grand transformations by mysterious means; their very reticence put their knowledge as well as their intentions in doubt.[19] It was not only, as writers such as Defoe and later Samuel Johnson emphasized, that their ideas were untried, but also that they remained secret even as their power was advertised. Behind the projector's promises lay the possibility that private interest—however defensible in itself—might compromise or indefinitely postpone public benefit.

The historian of science, Charles Webster, showed long ago that tensions between self-interest and the common weal surfaced repeatedly in the Hartlib Circle's promotion and criticism of projects during the 1640s and 1650s—the context for Petty's earliest essays in improvement, as well as for his first moves toward economic thought. As Webster argued, Samuel Hartlib's project for an "Office of Address"—an institution for the systematic collection and communication of scientific and other information, modeled on Théophraste Renaudot's *Bureau d'addresse* in Paris and influencing many other proposals, including Petty's—was an attempt to resolve the conflicting concerns of individual projectors, overcome their self-interest in the name of Christian charity, and make their efforts serve the greater good.[20] Other Hartlibians, as Webster also showed, sought to involve either Parliament or, later, the Cromwellian Protectorate in the active promotion of reforms making for the public interest. The means of intervention varied. Some projectors sought privilege or offices; others envisioned improvement as the central task of the state. In the agricultural and mineralogical writer Gabriel Plattes's utopian version of England, *A Description of the Famous Kingdome of Macaria* (1641), unimproved land might be seized from its owners and reassigned to those who would improve it as directed.[21] To adopt the terminology of Hirschman's account, private passions had to be harnessed or restrained more or less forcefully from above, and *made* to serve the interest of the state—or the commonwealth.[22] As Hartlib wrote in an undated "Memorandum on the Office of Address": "Much wrong may bee done by these Men [i.e., those running the Office] to the Subjects of this Commonwealth, if their Proceedings be not Regulated by Authority;" "Much wrong may bee done to *the* Publick Interest of the State itselfe, if *the* Worke bee not committed to trustie hands."[23]

The era of unfettered self-interest anchoring a predictable society and stable polity was still waiting, it would seem, for Bernard Mandeville and his successors.[24] Yet, recent scholarship raises historical and methodological questions about this view. Paul Slack's recent study of improvement, for instance, locates positive reassessments of self-interest and the satiation of individual appetites with late-seventeenth-century economic writers such as John Houghton and Nicholas Barbon. As Slack's account indicates, however, these arguments drew on a legacy of commercial and technical improvement projects that went back much further; in Houghton's case, at least, they echoed Hartlibian ideas.[25] Even if we see Interregnum-era projects as merely influencing, rather than producing or embodying, new ideas about self-interest, then, it makes sense to re-examine their influence. As both the most significant and the best-documented locus of projecting in the period, and as a crucial incubator for several later economic writers and advocates of improvement, the Hartlib Circle is an obvious place to start.

Methodologically speaking, meanwhile, both recent and some not-so-recent work on projects suggest that exploring changes in economic and social thought requires looking beyond the canon of moral and political philosophy—from Machiavelli to Montesquieu—on which Hirschman and other intellectual historians have largely focused. Nearly thirty years ago, Kevin Dunn examined Scottish reformer John Dury's view of the public good as the sum of private goods and pamphleteer William Potter's linkage of individual spending to economic prosperity, notwithstanding Hartlib's ambivalence toward the market.[26] Thomas Leng's 2008 study counterposed Benjamin Worsley's "vision of an amoral world governed by international competition and the force of self-interest" with other Hartlibians' more altruistic, pan-Protestant utopianism.[27] Vera Keller, still more recently, has contrasted the Hartlib Circle's "Christianized" rendering of the public interest with the Royal Society's "discourse of advancement [of epistemic empire, which] claimed to displace mercenary motivations"—the self-interest of mechanics and projectors—"with the incentive of fame."[28] Koji Yamamoto, meanwhile, has surveyed a range of Hartlibian responses to the problem of "distrust of the projector," a problem centered on the legitimacy of self-interest.[29]

This historiography indicates that there is a more complex history of self-interest in the projects of the Hartlib Circle, and in the pursuit of scientific improvements generally, than historians of economic or moral thought have tended to acknowledge. While it is true that private interests were easiest to conceptualize in opposition to each other and therefore in tension with the public good, the nature of this tension and the mechanisms for relieving it were by no means agreed. Indeed, recent work has undermined the coherence of "the Hartlib Circle" as an intellectual unit. Hartlibians differed, and they differed in particular over self-interest. For one thing, while anxiety over the character and aims of the projector often served to crystallize negative assessments of self-seeking behavior, they did not invariably do so; facilitating the projector's pursuit of profit or name could, at least sometimes, be seen as essential to getting work done. More interestingly, from a theoretical perspective, projectors and their patrons among Hartlib's contacts, at least sometimes, invoked the self-interest of those they projected their work *upon*: the farmers who would profit from new agricultural techniques, for example, or the Fen-men whose health would be improved by drainage, or the Irish Catholics who would come to see that English houses, gardens, and markets served them better than wretched cabins and insalubrious bogs. Seen through the lens of the projector, self-interest was not always a destructive passion, or an anti-social force to be suppressed or constrained by authority; it might be mobilized to support improvement. It might even be essential to progress.

The meanings of "interest"

In this as in other questions, however, projecting presents special challenges to the intellectual historian. Projectors were, almost by definition, concerned with advancing specific projects rather than with elaborating or defending the principles or theories that substantiated their plans; they were often located, too, on the margins rather than at the center or in the upper echelons of established disciplines and settled institutions.[30] All this often gives a pragmatic, ephemeral, fragmentary, and inconsistent feel to their written legacy, even in the cases where there is a substantial written legacy with which to work.[31] Of many, perhaps most, projectors, including some who were quite widely known in their time, scant traces remain—in the form of pamphlets, correspondence, manuscript proposals, wish-lists, or mere mentions in second-hand commentary. (Hartlib's journals, the "Ephemerides", are full of such fleeting references.) At the same time, projects often ranged over areas only later divided between disciplines. So, for instance, a technical improvement in agriculture, a modification of the landscape, or an organizational reform of trade might be justified in terms of a combination of scientific, social, and religious ideas and envisioned as having a combination of intellectual, material, and political outcomes.[32] There is little question of reconstructing explicit or fully fledged theories of self-interest as a spring of human action from such sources; theorizing the springs of human action was not their purpose.

On the other hand, the archive preserves a shared vocabulary and set of reference points by means of which ideas about self-interest could be articulated. Setting aside its specific financial meaning, which was well established by the seventeenth century, the word "interest" often denoted a share in the use or ownership of land. The agricultural and religious reformer John Beale, for example, referred to his "having an interest in sandy land" as disposing him to prefer asses to horses as draft animals.[33] Perhaps by extension, it could also mean either a financial stake or a legal right or privilege in a particular trade. Thus in 1648, John Dury suggested that the Huguenot projectors Hugh L'Amy and Peter Le Pruvost, then advancing a new fisheries scheme, might "deale [...] with all those that pretend to an interest or a right to any trade" affected.[34] Its connection to exclusive privileges might tie this idea of interest to monopolies, a negative association for many in Hartlib's network.[35] Yet, Hartlib's friends also applied the term in the same basic sense to their own projects. When the mechanical inventor Cressy Dymock began finding out "engagers" for his seed drill in 1649, for example, he expressed his hope "that my best friends [...] should haue the greatest interest in this much [more?] certain and advantagious busines".[36] "Interest" here suggested not only or primarily intellectual or spiritual concern (though both may have been assumed), but a material stake in the technology and a corresponding claim on the benefits it promised. Even in the context of projects geared toward the security of global Protestantism or the moral reformation of society, the pursuit and reward of individual interests need be no bad thing.

In the crucial context of the search for patronage, "interest" could also mean a stake *in* powerful individuals: a share of their time, goodwill, or attention. Here, interest expressed the value of interpersonal networks. Thus, an unknown correspondent described *Ireland's Naturall History* (written by the Dutch émigrés Gerard and Arnold Boate, and printed under Hartlib's direction in 1652) as "a means of giving [Hartlib] interest" with influential men.[37] Seeking Oliver Cromwell's support for fruit-tree cultivation, Ralph Austen told Hartlib in 1655 of one "worthie Col: Kelsey" who "hath a great interest in his Highnesse;" embodied in "frequent access" to the Lord Protector, this interest "will be very instrumental [...] to affect our desires."[38] Interest in this sense could be exploited to advance interest in other senses, for the good of yet other kinds of interest. A letter from Dymock, written when his "engine for setting corn" was garnering attention in Sweden, neatly illustrates this confounding plethora of interlocking kinds and levels of interest. One of Hartlib's Swedish contacts, Dymock wrote, proposed "to make use of his interest there, for the procuring a pattent, in which [...] hee offers to ioyne mÿ name and interest mutuallÿ with his owne." Yet "though I reiect not to haue an interest bÿ name in the pattent," Dymock continued, he feared lest "mÿ owne condition [be] made worse" if "after I haue sent the tooles and Instructions [...] itt should please the Queene [...] to refuse to grant a pattent." If promises were to fall through, "I [will] haue parted with soe much of mÿ Interest without the Least hope or reason, much lesse returne."[39] Dymock wanted assurances that his partner's interest in decision-makers at court would secure their common interest in a patent before he would give up his present interest in the invention. Advance payment would help.

These interrelated uses of interest frequently centered on the individual, but it required no great leap to imagine "particular" interests adhering to groups with shared concerns distinct from the general, public, or civil interest to which they were often contrasted. Reference to "particulars" in this collective sense often evoked the pursuit of narrow "advantage," as when Dury complained to Culpeper about "particular men" engrossing imported or scarce "comodities" for "privat advantage."[40] This was a familiar example of selfish and decidedly immoral mercantile behavior. On the other hand, much as with "interest," the "private advantage" or "private benefitts" of a group could be consistent with "publique advantage" and instrumental to driving improvement forward; as we shall see below, Dymock's promotion of his engines for Barbados, which would most directly benefit a specific class of private planters, furnishes an example.[41] At the same time, the contrast between the particularity of some interests and the generality of others was not always clear-cut. At a time of confessional conflict both at home and across Europe, there was frequent reference, for instance, to the "Protestant Interest." This usage made interest synonymous with a distinct spiritual and political "cause." In some contexts, this cause was closely connected or even equivalent to the national or "English interest," if not to something still more "common;" but in others, to the contrary, it might be identified with a particular confessional "party."[42]

Interest, in short, might be individual, collective, or general. It might inhere in money, in land, in goods, in ideas, or in persons. Private and public interests—whether single or collective—in any of these things might conflict or coincide. There seems to have been little or no idea, in practice, of extinguishing or wholly suppressing any of these interests, those of individual agents perhaps least of all. If self-interest was not avowedly described as a natural, predictable spring of action, the motive power of particular interests was nevertheless an ineradicable aspect of social and political (and, by extension, scientific and technological) activity. Curiously, the voluble John Beale came very close to articulating an idea of individual self-interest when he spoke of "proper interest." This referred not to human motivations, however, but to the chemical operations of spirits in food, drink, and digestion. Discussing his "philosophy" of liquors in a long letter to Hartlib, Beale argued that the "fiery" properties of various substances were held in place by colder matter. He wrote that:

> The fiery spirits, if they bee restrained to drive their operations towards & about the center, & not <sufferd> to expire & to desert their proper interest; & to breake the Covenant of Vnion, Then they will feede on the cruder parts, & consume them, or convert them into the like noble substance; or quench some of their owne fury in reduceing their adversary into a better accord.[43]

Thus, salt gradually "consumes the rheumatique grossenes of beefe, & bacon [...] into a seasonable relish" or, "(with the helpe of runnet) will, in two or three yeares, make cold cheese-curd."[44] Here, it was the "proper interest" of a spiritual agent to be contained within a larger "Covenant of Vnion," within which it could both feed itself and improve its surroundings by following its natural bent. Implicit in this was an idea of "proper interest" not only as a matter of physical and chemical nature but also as a criterion for assessing the interactions of different individual agents as components of a complex, dynamic system. Beale did not draw the analogy between the "proper interests" of his fiery spirits in a chemical union and those of the people around him in a political or social one. Given that he wrote within a decade of the English Civil War, in the midst of chronic political breakdown, and at a moment of especial concern about the power of "covenants" to bind individuals to polities or factions, however, the parallels may have been obvious.[45]

Aligning interests

The tangle of interests navigated by projectors stands in sharp contrast to the discrete philosophical positions of Hirschman's intellectual history. The latter located the origins of self-interest in a contest, played out in works of moral and political philosophy over the seventeenth and eighteenth centuries, between three "ways of shaping the pattern of human actions."[46] The first, "coercion and suppression" of the passions, originated with Augustine and received a substantial fillip in the sixteenth century from Calvin and his followers in Europe and America, for whom a repressive moral program became a key function and justification of civil government.[47] The second solution, ostensibly better grounded in psychological reality, was "harnessing the passions." Here, too, the state was imagined to play a central role, but now less as a repressive force than as "a civilizing medium" or an agent of a kind of "alchemical transmutation"—a task that came, in the early Enlightenment, to seem unscientific.[48] Finally, there emerged a third idea. This was "to utilize one set of comparatively innocuous passions to countervail another more dangerous and destructive set or [...] to weaken and tame the passions by such internecine fights in *divide et impera* fashion."[49] Rooted in the work of Francis Bacon and Baruch de Spinoza, this belief in the tendency of autonomous passions toward mutual constraint was applied to politics by Thomas Hobbes, who based his vision of an original social contract—or "covenant"—upon it. His critics, however, distinguished among the passions, elevating some to the level of rational "interests" and setting them against the rest in a continual, permanent system of countervailance.[50]

Given their long-standing historiographical association with Puritanism, one might expect at least the more avowedly Calvinist Hartlibians to have favored the first solution. Certainly, the Commonwealth and the Protectorate, most notably during the rule of Cromwell's Major-Generals, saw new exertions of state power against the passions.[51] Whatever they may have felt about the passions, however, some Hartlibian figures evidently did not see the selfish pursuit of particular "interests" and "advantage" in these terms.[52] In their schemes, the state was as often as not employed to assure, not to restrain, private concerns. To this extent, the notion of "harnessing" interests—using the civilizing power of the state to bring them together, the better to serve the common good—seems much closer to the mark. It captures, for example, Gabriel Plattes's suggestion in *Macaria* that the state enjoin and monitor the improvement of private estates. The landowner who failed to adopt improved methods of husbandry was to be "admonished" both of "the great hinderance which [he] doth to the Common-Wealth" *and* of "the prejudice to himself," but coercive expropriation was a matter of last resort.[53] Perhaps paradoxically, it may also make sense of the fact that many projects—Petty's Down Survey is one example—were also, in effect, applications for office.[54] In circumstances where private advantage and public good might otherwise conflict, eventuating in corruption or the loss of useful knowledge, the state was invited to take up the projector's interest and make it a public concern.

One of the most fully articulated examples of a project employing the state to harness disparate and corruptible private interests occurs in John Dury's advice to L'Amy and Le Pruvost, who were promoting a series of interlinked schemes for the employment of the poor, the improvement of the fishery, and the development of new trades across the English Atlantic. Writing to Sir Cheney Culpeper in the later 1640s, Dury dismissed Culpeper's suggestion that Le Pruvost ("a man truely of a public spirit & a good Christian") seek a fourteen-year patent for the plan. In the first place, this was "because I could not imagine it profitable either to him or to his worke." But a deeper reason was that "if hee should seeke a Patent [...] then his worke would seeme a proiect indeed and a kind of monopoly in Trade." This would be all the more troublesome, Dury observed, because "hee is a stranger." For Le Pruvost "to come amoungst the Natives to drive a trade by vertue off a patent which others understand not to bee beneficiall to the public" would generate "soe much opposition of envie & jeallousie against him" that the intended improvement would never take place. The nature of the work, moreover, was such that it "can not bee done but by a State, whose interest must bee engaged in it to cary it on," whose protection alone would attract "Complices" to it, and whose ownership of the "designe" was only logical as "itselfe is principally concerned."[55] Le Pruvost's patent:

> Must bee an Ordinance which the State should make for the Regulating of its owne Profit, to arise from his undertakings wherin the common Idle poore people of all sorts will bee set a worke by Land and Sea which will be infinitly beneficiall to particulars, when all the Idle hands shall bee set a work not only to maintaine themselves but uphold the Public and bring a benefit to it [...] Soe that not only in the way of Policy but in respect of Christianitie his worke will bee usefull to the State, For multitudes of people that are without Rule, in a manner desperate and wilde under noe goverment shall bee reduced to certain employments and brought under [Inspectors?], who may bee directed how to teach them and order in their callinges to the attainment of knowledge and the exercise of Temperance of Rightousnes and Godlinesse.[56]

The civilizing power of government would be in full effect, channeling the pursuit of particular advantage in socially and spiritually, as well as economically, profitable directions. Dury described the resulting state as a kind of godly trading company:

> [I]f the State will Regulat the way of it [...] they shall not only open a way for their owne subjects to improove their estates, and employ their stockes to better advantage for themselves and the public, then hitherto theie have don (by which meanes the [subiects?] become as it were their Factores, & the State by a Prudentiall Addverse is the Principall Trader and doth mannage all their meanes with equalitie for their good) but the Stockes and estates of forrainers will bee drawn in, to increasse the trade and make it beneficiall to the publique.[57]

State regulation would ensure the advance of the common good without prejudice to particulars. Public morals, private benefits.

Yet the idea of harnessing passions from above fails to accommodate other projectors' expedients for recruiting private support for their publicly beneficial work. When Cressy Dymock sought support for his perpetual motion machine—which he explicitly treated as a matter of both particular and general advantage—it was chiefly by selling "interests" in it to private investors with the promise of future profit; a 1650 agreement, for instance, describes his sale of "one eleaventh share part or interest in and vnto all profits, vses, advantages or contracts, which shall hereafter arise or bee in or concerning the said Invention."[58] Put to use, as Dymock elsewhere envisioned, on Barbadian plantations, his engine would reduce agricultural production costs, allowing for a shift from animal to enslaved labor, and thereby permit more land to be used for raising cash crops rather than fodder.[59] Here, the interests of the projector, the investors who backed him, the planters who adopted his improvement, and the colonial power in the material benefits to be enjoyed would align themselves without any specific political intervention, and certainly without recourse to any top-down "civilizing" program. (The enslaved, indeed, were evidently not seen as having any interest worth mentioning.) From the projector's perspective, there was indeed a lot of harnessing of interests to be done. But doing so might be more a matter of accessing, conveying, and controlling information—Hartlib's role as an "intelligencer," and the possibility of the Office of Address as a node of intelligence loomed large here—than of transforming the pattern of human actions.[60] The pursuit of individual profit and the improvement of the commonweal did not conflict.

Nevertheless, Hartlib and his correspondents spent considerable time and effort negotiating the relations between the profits of particulars and the task of wider reformation. Breakdowns were frequent and could be acrimonious. Cheney Culpeper's transformation from an enthusiastic supporter of improvement projects to an embittered skeptic is illustrative. In a dozen letters to Hartlib written between July and November 1648, Culpeper moved from fervent questions about Petty's project for a seed drill, through promises to support both the "corn engine" and its inventor, to recriminations when Petty ultimately declined to reveal his machine except on terms (unspecified in the surviving letters) that left Culpeper feeling cheated—not for the first time.[61] "[A]ll that I can say," Culpeper concluded, "is that I haue soe little good fortune in the company of these ingenuous men that I shall not ouer fondly, shut vp with any more."[62] Not only "Mr Petty his late carriage" but also the earlier case of William Wheeler, a pretended inventor whose very name became synonymous with empty promises, and others "hathe bred in me a resolution, not to trowble my thowghts any farther with these kinde of people."[63] Koji Yamamoto has examined the problem of trust that this and similar exchanges reveal; these were the unhappy flip-side of the mutual benefit that the alignment of interests Hartlib sought promised.[64]

As Culpeper remarked, "I am sorry mr Petty fayles soe muche towards me, & am confidente he will little aduance his owne endes by these wayes."[65] The projector's own interest, if only he would see and act on it, was also the public's. If he did not, the "weakenes & jealousie that dwell in him" would ensure that "excellente thinges [...] will finally be loste" to the projector and the world alike.[66] Neglecting self-interest might harm the public good.

Projecting self-interest

Besides harnessing, aligning, or otherwise managing existing interests, Hartlibian projectors sometimes sought to create them—not least when such interests were required for projects to succeed. Paradoxically, it is in the notion of individual interests as *outcomes* rather than merely factors or conditions of projecting that their comments seem closest to an idea of self-interest as a natural and desirable spring of action. In at least one context, the creation of individual interests was a concrete matter: land. As agricultural historians and others have shown, improvement was related to the enclosure of land—including the conversion of commons into freehold—in complex and changing ways.[67] Broadly speaking, however, Hartlibian writers championed enclosure and the creation of private holdings as a key preliminary stage of agricultural improvement and indeed of universal reformation.[68] Dymock, with his faith in the power of human art aided by divine inspiration to transform the earth's productivity, harped on the advantages of a "single" as opposed to a "mixt interest" in land as the starting point for material and moral change.[69] In a 1649 "Memorandum on the Advantages of Enclosure," he offered a series of calculations showing "how farre & mutch more excellent inclosure & single interest is before, beyond the common feild &, mixt Interest."[70] Under enclosure, he wrote:

> One neygbour cannot thus trespas on other vnlesse willfully & manifestly[.] Each man shall bee blest according to his good endeavour[.] Many comodityes found to bee vendible, not formerly knowne or vsed for sutch, And those that are aboundantly increased both in quantitye & quallitye, & soe made more staple, Thus this kingdome might within one age iustly merritt the title of the garden of the world [...] Nor could there bee any other pore but Indigents, & they would easily & plentifully bee supplyed[.] The wealth of each perticuler thus encreased would soe vastly advance the publique revennue[.][71]

A change in land tenure would mean a change not just in incentives to improvement but also in the people themselves: their behavior would become more moderate, more orderly, and—much as for Hirschman's Enlightenment thinkers—more predictable: "men's minds would bee soe mutch more settled & fitt to serue god & thinke of goodnes by how mutch more their affaires would bee contracted into order & more Moderate

& inobled labour."[72] Other Hartlibian writers similarly touted enclosure's complex import; Ralph Austen and John Beale—two champions of orchard-keeping and cider-making—argued for the spiritual as well as material "profits" of enclosure, and likened the enclosed garden to paradise.[73] In the Restoration, Petty would trumpet the material benefits of his Irish projects, which included the creation of houses with gardens for Irish peasants to exploit commercially (rather than subsisting on potatoes), in similar terms.[74]

Yet, paradise was still a long way off. The introduction of lucriferous inventions might awaken a sense of self-interest in individual members of the public. Dymock, like Petty, expressed confidence that once his perpetual motion was put to work in Barbados, "by the strong arguments of gaine and ease shall many thousands bee invited perswaded to plant there that now (lyke meer droanes) liue here vpon the spoyle of their owne or other men's estates."[75] The prospect of private gain that technology held out would drive individuals to make choices for their own good that unintentionally benefited the commonwealth. But both these men and others saw that mere arguments of gain alone might not suffice. Ranged against many projects, of course, were pre-existing interests—trading concerns, monopolies, and privileges which might need to be coordinated, bought off, or regulated out of existence with Parliament's help. A more fundamental obstacle to invention and improvement, however, was an ignorance of true self-interest on the part of those who, in the projector's judgment, stood to gain. As Le Pruvost noted, after complaining about the obstructions thrown up by monopolies, "Mais ny l'Interest des pauures, ny leur propre Interest proposé, n'a peu leur ouurir les aureilles a escouter a ce bien public et particulier."[76] Such refusal to listen to the voice of self-interest might proceed from understandable distrust of dubious novelties; hence the importance of disavowing that projects were "projects" and their authors "projectors." But it might also proceed from a more positive attachment to older and less profitable ways of doing things.

In "custom," some projectors and improvers discerned a deep-rooted barrier not only to specific changes but, beyond these, to something like the unfettered operation of rational self-interest.[77] Custom was a complex and ambiguous idea; it embraced a variety of established structures, institutions, practices, ideas, and habits. It might include, for example, the persistence of "mixt" rather than "single" interests in land noted above—a matter of long-standing legal and property-holding arrangements. It also had more intangible cultural, ideological, and even psychological dimensions, however. In an early letter to Hartlib discussing the prospects for the Office of Address, Cheney Culpeper observed that men "wowlde not [...] open themselues thowgh to theire owne advantage":

> I cannot but adde to this the Irishe humor, of keepinge theire olde barbarous custome of plowinge by horses tayles, & (for a visible & wofull example in this Kingdome), all the Royalistes are alltogether fownded

on that <Roman> Catholik principle of doinge as theire Fathers did, euen to a continuance in grosse degree of slauery; all this notwith-standinge, my opinion is that those, whose spirits God hathe raysed out of this mudde of Custome, muste indeauor (at the leaste) to improue theire talents towards others[.][78]

In this light, part of the point of scientific and economic projects was pre-cisely to raise people out of "this mudde of Custome," whether that meant the "barbarous" humors of the Irish, the "slauery" of Catholic superstition, or the sheer pigheadedness of simple farmers. Custom in this construc-tion was not merely old but backward, not merely wrong but irrational. Describing his travails in getting farmers to test new methods of plowing, Dymock lamented: "Soe wonderfully are the bores [i.e., boors] of England wedded to their owne olde customes without reason nay oft against itt. And if reall experience soe mutch exceed olde custome in a trifle," he continued, "what may itt bee supposed to doe in matters of greater Consequence[?]"[79] Counterpoised to custom, in this line of thinking, was an idea of self-in-terested behavior that associated the calculated pursuit of private gain with the fruits of experience and reason and, by the same token, with the advancement of the common good.

It will not do to present this as a definitively Hartlibian theory of self-interest, or for that matter as a worked-out theory of self-interest at all. Elements of the three non-religious "solutions" to shaping human action that Albert Hirschman outlined in *The Passions and the Interests* are visible in different parts of the Hartlib papers, and seemingly incompatible views are sometimes present in the works of a single author. The Hartlib Circle is neither a missing chapter of, nor a simple preface to, Hirschman's account. Still, Hartlibian projectors such as Dymock and proponents of improve-ment such as Culpeper effectively described the rational and free pursuit of private gain as a spring of action favorable to the advancement of the com-mon good and far preferable to the irrational, barbarous, and slavish adher-ence to custom they saw as the alternative. Restoration projectors, including veterans of Hartlib's network, adopted similar views in promoting their own schemes. If some of these men are best known today as economic thinkers, their Hartlibian pedigree and still more their eagerness to dissociate them-selves from the antisocial connotations of "projecting," while preserving space for private gain in the pursuit of public interest, indicates that much of what we sometimes see as precocious social theorizing can better be read as the legacy of forgotten projects. By the same token, the failures as well as the successes of such projects may tell us more than the canons of political and economic thought about the origins of the concept of self-interest.[80] If Interregnum projectors' fragmentary musings on problems of interest did not amount to formal contributions to the history of economic or social thought, they nevertheless provided new and vital fuel for "political argu-ments for capitalism before its triumph."

Notes

1 See Andrew M. Kamarck, *Economics as a Social Science: An Approach to Nonautistic Theory* (Ann Arbor: University of Michigan Press, 2002), 22.
2 See Joel Mokyr, *The Enlightened Economy: An Economic History of Britain 1700–1850* (New Haven: Yale University Press, 2009).
3 Albert O. Hirschman, *The Passions and the Interests: Political Arguments for Capitalism before Its Triumph* (Princeton: Princeton University Press, 1977), 3.
4 See Julian Hoppit, "The Contexts and Contours of British Economic Literature, 1660–1760," *Historical Journal* 49, no. 1 (March 2006): 79–110.
5 See, for example, Koji Yamamoto, *Taming Capitalism before Its Triumph: Public Service, Distrust & 'Projecting' in Early Modern England* (Oxford: Oxford University Press, 2018); Vera Keller, *Knowledge and the Public Interest, 1575–1725* (Cambridge: Cambridge University Press, 2015); Paul Slack, *The Invention of Improvement: Information and Material Progress in Seventeenth-Century England* (Oxford: Oxford University Press, 2015).
6 On the Hartlib Circle, see Charles Webster, *The Great Instauration: Science, Medicine and Reform, 1626–1660* (London: Duckworth, 1975).
7 Mark Greengrass, Michael Leslie, and Michael Hannon, eds., *The Hartlib Papers* (Sheffield: Digital Humanities Institute, University of Sheffield) [available at https://www.dhi.ac.uk/hartlib] [hereafter HP].
8 William Petty to James Butler, Duke of Ormond, March 1, 1660/1, in *Calendar of the Manuscripts of the Marquis of Ormonde, K.P. Preserved at Kilkenny Castle*, n.s., vol. 3 (London: Historical Manuscripts Commission, 1904), 11.
9 On the Down Survey, see William J. Smyth, *Map-Making, Landscapes and Memory: A Geography of Colonial and Early Modern Ireland c. 1530–1750* (Cork: Cork University Press, 2006), 166–97; Aaron J. Henry, "William Petty, the Down Survey, Population and Territory in the Seventeenth Century," *Territory, Politics, Governance* 2, no. 2 (2014): 1–20.
10 Petty described Worsley as "having been often frustrated as to his many severall great designes and undertakings in England" and hoping "to improve and repaire himselfe upon a… more credulouse people"; William Petty, *History of the Cromwellian Survey of Ireland, A.D. 1655–6, Commonly Called "the Down Survey,"* ed. Thomas A. Larcom (Dublin: Irish Archaeological Society, 1851). See also William Petty, *Reflections on Some Persons and Things in Ireland, by Letters to and from Dr. Petty* (London: Printed for John Martin, James Allestrey, and Thomas Dicas, 1660). On Worsley, see Thomas Leng, *Benjamin Worsley (1618–1677): Trade, Interest and the Spirit in Revolutionary England* (Woodbridge: Royal Historical Society/Boydell Press, 2008).
11 James Butler, Duke of Ormond, to Sir Robert Southwell, October 27, 1686, British Library Additional MS 21484, f.64.
12 On improvement, see Slack, *Invention of Improvement*. Vera Keller and I have elsewhere distinguished the radical promises of "projects" from the gradual "improvements" Slack emphasizes; Hartlibians pursued both, however, and it is not clear that their engagements with self-interest differed. See Vera Keller and Ted McCormick, "Towards a History of Projects," *Early Science and Medicine* 21, no. 5 (2016): 423–44, at 427–28.
13 Richard Braithwaite, *The Chimneys Scuffle* (London: s.n., 1662), 8.
14 "In Laudem Navis Geminae E Portu Dublinij ad Regem Carolum IIdum Missae" ["In praise of the twin-hulled boat sent from the port of Dublin to King Charles II"] (1663), in Andrew Carpenter, ed., *Verse in English from Tudor and Stuart Ireland* (Cork: Cork University Press, 2003), 390–401, at 391–92 (lines 23–24 and 54) and 401 (line 356).

15 Daniel Defoe, *An Essay upon Projects* (London: R. R. for Tho. Cockerill, 1697), 10–18.
16 But see Keller, *Knowledge and the Public Interest.*
17 See Koji Yamamoto, "Reformation and the Distrust of the Projector in the Hartlib Circle," *The Historical Journal* 55, no. 2 (2012): 375–97.
18 See Kevin Dunn, "Milton among the Monopolists: Areopagitica, Intellectual Property and the Hartlib Circle," in *Samuel Hartlib and the Universal Reformation: Studies in Intellectual Communication*, ed. Mark Greengrass, Michael Leslie, and Timothy Raylor (Cambridge: Cambridge University Press, 1994), 177–92.
19 See William R. Eamon, "From the Secrets of Nature to Public Knowledge: The Origins of the Concept of Openness in Science," *Minerva* 23, no. 3 (September 1985): 321–47, at 325–26.
20 Webster, *Great Instauration*, 369. More recently, see Dunn, "Milton among the Monopolists," 177–78, which describes the office as "an ambiguous mediator between the market (private interests) and the public good." See also Keller, *Knowledge and the Public Interest*, 193–94. On Renaudot, see Kathleen Wellman, *Making Science Social: The Conferences of Théophraste Renaudot, 1633–1642* (Norman: University of Oklahoma Press, 2003).
21 [Gabriel Plattes], *A Description of the Famous Kingdome of Macaria; Shewing Its Excellent Government: Wherein the Inhabitants Live in Great Prosperity, Health, and Happinesse; the King Obeyed, the Nobles Honoured; and All Good Men Respected, Vice Punished, and Vertue Rewarded* (London: Printed for Francis Constable, 1641), 4.
22 Hirschman, *The Passions.*
23 Samuel Hartlib, "Memorandum on the Office of Address" (undated), in HP 63/7/4A-5B.
24 See Edward J. Hundert, *The Enlightenment's Fable: Bernard Mandeville and the Discovery of Society* (Cambridge: Cambridge University Press, 1994), 221.
25 Slack, *Invention of Improvement*, 129. Houghton took up some of Hartlib's and Petty's ideas about the utility of gathering and publishing scientific, economic, and political information in *A Proposal for Improvement of Husbandry and Trade* (London: s.n., 1691).
26 Dunn, "Milton among the Monopolists," 181–86.
27 Thomas Leng, *Benjamin Worsley (1618–1677): Trade, Interest and the Spirit in Revolutionary England* (Woodbridge: Royal Historical Society/Boydell Press, 2008), 37.
28 Keller, *Knowledge and the Public Interest*, 199, 245.
29 Yamamoto, *Reformation and the Distrust of the Projector*; Yamamoto, *Taming Capitalism before Its Triumph*; see also David Alff, *The Wreckage of Intentions: Projects in British Culture, 1660–1730* (Philadelphia: University of Pennsylvania Press, 2017).
30 Keller and McCormick, "Towards a History of Projects".
31 On the fragmentary character of seventeenth-century scientific archives, see Elizabeth Yale, "With Slips and Scraps: How Early Modern Naturalists Invented the Archive," *Book History* 12 (2009): 1–36; Yale, *Sociable Knowledge: Natural History and the Nation in Early Modern Britain* (Philadelphia: University of Pennsylvania Press, 2015).
32 See, for example, Eric Ash, *The Draining of the Fens: Projectors, Popular Politics, and State Building in Early Modern England* (Baltimore: Johns Hopkins University Press, 2017); Chandra Mukerji, *Impossible Engineering: Technology and Territoriality on the Canal du Midi* (Princeton: Princeton University Press, 2015).

33 Letter, John Beale to Hartlib, March 2, 1657, HP 31/1/64a–65b, at 64a.
34 Copy Letters in Hand B, John Dury to Cheney Culpeper, September 25, 1648, HP 12/23a–26b, at 23b.
35 See Dunn, "Milton among the Monopolists". On the wider context, see William R. Eamon, "From the Secrets of Nature," 336–37.
36 Copy Letter in Hartlib's Hand, Cressy Dymock to?, May 25, 1649, HP 62/50/3a–4b, at 3b–4a.
37 Letter, [M. M.?] to Hartlib, October 17/27, 1652, HP 8/7/3a–4b, at 3b.
38 Letter, Ralph Austen to Hartlib, 1655, HP 41/1/82a–83b, at 82a.
39 Copy letter in Scribal Hand G, Cressy Dymock to Hartlib, February 26, 1653, HP 62/28/1a–4b, at 1a and 2a.
40 Letter, John Dury to Cheney Culpeper, September 25, 1648, HP 12/23a–23b, at 23a.
41 Cressy Dymock, "Memorandum about Engines", undated, HP 62/8a–8b, at 8a.
42 See, for example, Letter, John Dury to Hartlib, October 24, 1654, HP 4/3/50a–51b, at 50b–51a.
43 Letter, John Beale to Hartlib, May 8, 1658, HP 52/26a–43b, at 39b.
44 Ibid.
45 On the idea of a "National Covenant" in Interregnum Britain and Ireland, see Allan I. Macinnes, "Covenanting Ideology in Seventeenth-Century Scotland," in *Political Thought in Seventeenth-Century Ireland: Kingdom or Colony*, ed. Jane H. Ohlmeyer (Cambridge: Cambridge University Press, 2000), 191–200. On covenants as the basis of union in early modern English political and social thinking more generally, see Phil Withington, *The Politics of Commonwealth: Citizens and Freemen in Early Modern England* (Cambridge: Cambridge University Press, 2005), 51–84.
46 Hirschman, *The Passions*, 15.
47 Ibid.
48 Ibid., 16.
49 Ibid., 20.
50 Ibid., 31–32.
51 See most recently Bernard Capp, *England's Culture Wars: Puritan Reformation and Its Enemies in the Interregnum, 1649–1660* (Oxford: Oxford University Press, 2012).
52 On the ambivalent implications of Calvinism for judging self-interested behavior, see Yamamoto, "Reformation and the Distrust of the Projector," 390.
53 Plattes, *Macaria*, 4.
54 There is a detailed account in Petty, *History of... "the Down Survey"*; see especially 7–8.
55 Copy Letter in Hand B, John Dury to Cheney Culpeper, undated, HP 12/72a–75b, at 72b–73a.
56 Ibid., HP 12/73a.
57 Ibid., HP 12/73b.
58 Copy Agreement re Invention in Hartlib's Hand, Cressy Dymock, November 6, 1650, HP 58/10a–11b, at 10b.
59 Cressy Dymock, "Memorandum about Engines", undated, HP 62/8a–8b, at 8a.
60 A recent examination of "intelligencers" is Vera Keller, "Mining Tacitus: Secrets of Empire, Nature and Art in the Reason of State," *British Journal for the History of Science* 45, no. 2 (2012): 189–212.
61 See several letters from Culpeper to Hartlib in HP 13/225a–234b and 237a–243b.
62 Letter, Sir Cheney Culpeper to Hartlib, October 11, 1648, HP 13/244a–245b, at 244a.

63 Letter, Sir Cheney Culpeper to Hartlib, November 1, 1648, HP 13/246a–247b, at 247a.
64 Yamamoto, "Reformation and the Distrust of the Projector", especially (concerning Wheeler) 386–89.
65 Letter, Sir Cheney Culpeper to Hartlib, October 4, 1648, HP 13/243a–243b, at 243a.
66 Letter, Sir Cheney Culpeper to Hartlib, August 14, 1649, HP 13/260a–261b, at 261a. (Culpeper here speaks in particular of William Wheeler.)
67 See Joan Thirsk, "Agricultural Change: Policy and Practice, 1500–1750," in Chapters from the Agrarian History of England and Wales, 1500–1750, vol. 4, ed. John Chartres (Cambridge: Cambridge University Press, 1990), 54–109; Andrew McRae, *God Speed the Plough: The Representation of Agrarian England, 1500–1660* (Cambridge: Cambridge University Press, 1996), 135–68; Julian Hoppit, *Britain's Political Economies: Parliament and Economic Life, 1660–1800* (Cambridge: Cambridge University Press, 2017), 66–101.
68 See Simon Schaffer, "The Earth's Fertility as a Social Fact in Early Modern Britain," in *Nature and Society in Historical Context*, ed. Mikuláš Teich, Roy Porter, and Bo Gustafsson (Cambridge: Cambridge University Press, 1997), 124–47; Katherine Bootle Attié, "Enclosure Polemics and the Garden in the 1650s," *Studies in English Literature, 1500–1900* 51, no. 1 (2011): 135–57; Sarah Hogan, *Other Englands: Utopia, Capital, and Empire in an Age of Transition* (Stanford: Stanford University Press, 2018), 156–70.
69 See, for example, Letter, Cressy Dymock to Hartlib?, with plans of farm, undated, HP 62/29/1a–4b, a version of which was printed in Samuel Hartlib, *A Discoverie for Division or Setting Out of Land, as to the Best Form* (London: Printed for Richard Wodenothe, 1653).
70 Cressy Dymock, "Memorandum On The Advantages Of Enclosure," 1649, HP 64/18/1a–2b, at 1b.
71 Ibid., HP/64/18/2a.
72 Ibid., HP 64/18/2b.
73 See Katherine Bootle Attié, "Enclosure Polemics and the Garden in the 1650s", 135–57.
74 William Petty, *The Political Anatomy of Ireland* (London: Printed by D. Brown and W. Rogers, 1691), 98–101.
75 Cressy Dymock, "Memorandum about Engines," HP 62/8a–8b, at 8a.
76 "But neither the interest of the poor, nor their own proposed interest, could open their ears to hear this public and private good." Letter, Peter Le Pruvost to John Dury and Hartlib, September 10, 1649, HP 12/28a–29b, at 28b.
77 On the relationship between custom and improvement, see Paul Warde, "The Idea of Improvement, c. 1520–1700," in *Custom, Improvement, and the Landscape in Early Modern Britain*, ed. Richard W. Hoyle (New York: Routledge, 2011), 127–48.
78 Letter, Sir Cheney Culpeper to Hartlib, [1646?], HP 13/284a–285b.
79 Letter, Cressy Dymock to Hartlib, undated, HP 62/9/2a–2b, at 2a.
80 See Keller, *Knowledge and the Public Interest*, 11–12.

2   Reckoning self-interest at the French revolutionary Comité des Finances

Christine Zabel

French revolutionary fiscal policy could not escape its indebtedness to the past: by taking on the old regime's debts as a sacred obligation,[1] the members of the National Assembly not only promised to protect individual interests (individual property), but also acknowledged at the same time the need to translate the fiscal past into a new present.[2] This bound the new regime to the old in a particular way. Most old regime credit was provided by private investors, who purchased life annuities from the French crown.[3] In such a scheme, the creditor sold the promise of future annual income (*rentes*) in exchange for a lump-sum payment to the debtor (the French state). These contracts were complicated by the fact that in such a life annuity contract, the *nominee(s)* (which could be an individual or a group, on whose life the contract was contingent), the *subscriber* (purchaser), and the *shareholder* or *beneficiary* (the party who received the annual income; this right could even be passed on in a *rente perpétuelle*) did not have to be, and mostly were not, one and the same person. The duration of the payments, as well as interest rates, thus varied greatly according to the longevity of the nominee(s) and also according to the number of nominees, etc. In other words, the debtor (the government) could only lose over time; this was one significant reason why, during the old regime, the French government was more than once not able to amortize its debts. In such a case, the French monarchy had the legal option to declare bankruptcy, which it did ten times before the Revolution (in 1559, 1598, 1634, 1648, 1661, 1716, 1722, 1759, 1770–71, and 1788). The declaration of bankruptcy enabled the monarchy to default on parts of its obligations.[4] This was made easier by the fact that an annuity was *de iure* not a loan. Creditors invested "à fonds perdu"; in other words, the sale of the annuity was based on the simple assumption that the king could never be obliged by human law to pay back a loan, but would do so only out of goodwill.[5] Moreover, in the view of various commentators and *parlements*, the crown's declaration of bankruptcy was—and this might seem counterintuitive to modern readers—morally defensible, because it protected French citizens from excessive tax increases. According to this view, such a default policy would be detrimental only to financiers, who "were 'monsters' preying on French subjects."[6] Such an interpretation reflected (unsurprisingly) a deeply moral understanding of finance: because those financiers had acted out of self-interest alone, they had forfeited their right of protection by their monarch. By declaring bankruptcy, so the argument went, the crown protected its (good) citizens' interests. With those arguments at hand, the monarchy was, as some economists argue, "a persistent default risk because of institutional obstacles to raising taxes."[7] In July 1789, the National Assembly's oath never to pronounce the infamous word "bankruptcy" took away any legal possibility of falling back on a default policy that could put an abrupt end to repayments. The revolutionaries were thus more accountable to the French crown's creditors than the French king had ever been. This put the following question at the very center of all revolutionary endeavor: how could one reconcile individual interest and the interest of the nation? In other words, how could one begin a new regime while being bound by old debts? And more concretely: what should one do with these old debts? How could one come up with a morally, politically, and fiscally sound plan to amortize them?

More than a year into the Revolution, it was still not clear what to do with these debts, as demonstrated by Pierre-Hubert Anson (1744–1810), a Parisian deputy of the third estate, member and *rapporteur* of the Comité des Finances. As the deputy made clear, the well-being of the nation now depended upon devising a plan for how to deal with these specific credits.[8] The choice of liquidation scheme depended not least on detailed computations of the debts and of how they would evolve. However, these calculations were very difficult to undertake. In 1790, it was extremely hard to work out how much the French state would, in future, have to pay those creditors. This dearth of information was partly due to an absence of good data,[9] but, more importantly, to a lack of mathematical expertise capable of reckoning annuities with several contingent variables such as "longevity of multiple nominees," "variable interest rates," etc. These computational challenges, though, had to be resolved swiftly, if the Assembly were to reconcile the different interests at play before they put the entire revolutionary project at risk. Anson thus reminded the Assembly of the urgency of the issue:

> You have decreed thus, that all the different projects concerning the mode of liquidation of the public debt that one might present to you, will be discussed with the circumspection, the duration & the slowness that is advisable for a deliberation of that importance. [...] However, don't forget, Messieurs, that the diverse interests, which fight each other, can (also) fight against the truth; it is the Legislator who ought to determine once and for all the uncertain opinion (even) of the best citizens, & that it is not possible to delay the judgment of this grand question which is subject to your decision any longer.[10]

To Anson, it seemed clear that there could be only *one* solution that represented the "interest of all," and which ought to be communicated with complete clarity to all participants.[11] Thus, according to the deputy, mutually antagonistic interests did not balance each other out, as Mandeville and other mid-century economists had believed,[12] but had to be brought into alignment by the general will. Hence, the Assembly was challenged to identify the single best solution. Yet, how could he achieve this?

The political decision as to whether particular sets of interests were legitimate or illegitimate depended not only on political values and discussions, but also, in no small part, upon sophisticated calculations. The interest of the French nation—to become free of debt—was clear, but it was far from obvious how this goal was to be achieved. What Albert O. Hirschman unraveled in his *The Passions and the Interests* as crucial to incipient capitalist culture (which is the seemingly simple belief that the man who "pursues his interest, he himself will do well since, by definition, 'interest will not lie to him or deceive him,'")[13] thus seems to have a much more complicated story. What if the pursuance of self-interest was not as self-evident as Hirschman (or Rohan, to whom he was referring) imagined? Similarly, to many critics of the *homo oeconomicus* model in the social sciences, who have pointed to the problem of limited information or limited capacities to oversee all information available to decision-makers,[14] Anson referred to a crucial problem of decision-making processes: on the one hand, the deputies should reflect carefully, without haste, and with all information at their disposal. On the other, such reflections were also subject to urgent political exigencies; in short, a decision had to be made swiftly. The question which arises, therefore, is one that Hirschman did not pose in his account of self-interest: What kind of knowledge or information is needed to pursue self-interest appropriately? And how could one balance the need to gather information and cautiously reflect on it with the pressure to act in a timely manner?

Furthermore, if we agree with Keith Baker that "'Interest' is a symbolic and political construction, not simply a pre-existing social reality," and that the interests and claims of social groups "are continually being defined (and redefined),"[15] we need to inquire about how these articulations of various social interests could be condensed into the *one* (national) interest to which Anson was referring and which the Assembly had to communicate to all—at the time preferably referred to by semantics of "public interest." To address these questions might give us another piece of the puzzle of why the "positive appraisal of self-interest during much of the eighteenth century did not," as Hirschman pointed out, "survive the age of the French Revolution and the Napoleonic Wars."[16]

One way to answer these questions would be to read Anson's statement about contesting interests which had to be unified through one general will with an exclusively revisionist interpretation of the French Revolution (à la Furet) in mind.[17] While a Marxist-inspired reading had emphasized the class struggle between nobility and bourgeoisie that led to 1789, and also to the later radicalization of the Revolution, revisionists refuted such assumptions, for they thought these arguments about class antagonism lacked empirical evidence.[18] Rather, some prominent revisionists, such as François Furet and Norman Hampson, explained the Revolution (as well as its later radicalization) with ideological arguments. According to their analysis, extreme ideas that would eventually lead to the so-called *terreur* were already built into radical Enlightenment philosophy. According to these revisionists, the National Assembly was increasingly controlled by Jacobin radicalism that disseminated a naïve version of Rousseau's *volonté générale* and discarded a plurality of opinions and interests. It defended a Rousseau-ian unitary will that allowed for only one rational truth. Accordingly, every opposition to such a unitary truth was interpreted as selfish and counter-revolutionary.[19]

As we can see from this, the question of revolutionary dealings with different individual and collective interest(s) (be it the antagonism of class struggle or of ideas) lies at the very heart of many of our readings of the Revolution. Such readings, however, do not necessarily address whether these dealings with and struggles between different interests changed in the course of the Revolution, or which factors influenced the definition of republican truths. Timothy Tackett has prominently and successfully proposed an approach to the Revolution that shifts away from such a broad inquiry about its genesis and instead argues for an examination of revolutionary experiences and of the changing values of the revolutionaries.[20] The present contribution is inspired by Tackett's suggestion, as it seeks not to think about the Revolution from its later developments (which means from its well-known condemnation of self-interest), but rather to look at the development of revolutionary dealings with self-interest. The chapter seeks to shed light on two very specific moments of revolutionary experience: the autumn of 1789 and the late summer of 1793. More specifically, this contribution will inquire about the kind of knowledge that was generated and used in order to calculate and articulate interests, and proposes to examine the calculations and techniques of discounting the old regime's annuity schemes at the Comité des Finances. It inquires not only how these calculations evolved, but also in which ways changing political positions or ideas might have influenced the calculations, or—and this is especially important—vice versa. As we will see, fiscal and actuarial expert knowledge provided the template on which supposedly ideological political and moral ideas about the national interest could be articulated. The national interest and the question of valency of self-interest were expressed in very specific ways, which took, at this stage of the Revolution, the form of calculations, and of data and numbers.[21] For its analysis, the chapter will use the minutes of the Comité des Finances as well as those of the National Assembly, and the accounts given by members of the Comité. Furthermore, it will look at papers and essays written by individuals such as Anson or his co-members, as well as by mathematicians and statisticians, who worked toward a solution to the fiscal challenge.

Screening, sorting, and organizing data: The first months of the Comité des Finances

In order to get a full picture of the national debts, the National Assembly voted, on July 11, 1789, for the creation of a Comité des Finances. This was by far the largest and most diverse of the revolutionary committees, with sixty-four assigned members, of whom thirty-four represented the *généralités* and thirty the *bureaux* (however, the number of members varied).[22] The Comité was given various assignments, all of which were concerned with the budgetary crisis. It was required to: come up with a plan for the rapid reimbursement of debts; review the tax system; and make inquiries about how the state departments could save money, etc. Because of its wide range of responsibilities, the Comité decided on August 11, 1789 to subdivide into nine different Cabinets, one of which was the Cabinet des Finances. To the latter was assigned the study of the "life annuities and perpetual annuities," the "interests in bills of exchange," and the "pledges representing the interest of finance."[23] Seven members were chosen for this Cabinet: two members of the nobility (M. le duc d'Aiguillon and M. le duc de Biron) and two members of the clergy (M. l'archevêque d'Aix and M. l'abbé de la Salcette) as well as three representatives of the third estate (M. Périer, M. Couderc, and M. Anson).[24]

After the first weeks of the Comité's existence, the different Cabinets, who had met separately, reported back on the data they had managed to assemble. At their 10th session on August 28, 1789, M. Anson, member of the Cabinet of Finances and deputy of the third estate, reported on the current work at his Cabinet. While most of the other Cabinets were able to share their initial results, Anson had to communicate the difficulties facing his own: it was lacking the necessary data for a first assessment. The report ended with the agreement that "This department is very busy, and the final account can only be given in a few days."[25] On September 2, the duc de Liancourt inquired about the Cabinet's work once again and the Comité assigned the "day after tomorrow" for its report.[26] However, we find no evidence in the minutes of the Comité that such a report took place on September 4.[27]

The Comité's work as a whole consisted of discussing data (which, during the old regime, had been gathered by the *fermes générales*, and was now assembled by the Cabinets), of sorting letters, queries, and complaints, and also of deliberating on proposals and essays they had received. After reviewing the content of and motivation behind those complaints or proposals, they had to decide which ones were of interest to the nation and should thus be forwarded to the National Assembly. One essay that proposed a reform of the fiscal regime was presented to the Comité on November 5, 1789. The baron d'Harambure spoke in the name of a certain baron de Cormeré, a former employee of the Controller General and specialist on the tax system. It was resolved in this 29th session that his plan should be reviewed and that the author should be queried about "the basis of his calculations, and who would guarantee for their exactitude," before further decisions could be made.[28] The minutes of the Comité do not mention the report further, but we know that on November 21, 1789 the baron de Cormeré spoke at the National Assembly and asked permission to present his reform plans. However, the comte de Castellan argued against such an exposition, because he thought the Assembly's time too valuable. He instead recommended that Cormeré's plan be sent back to the Comité des Finances, where it should be reviewed in detail. The Assembly consented to the plan, deciding, however, that Cormeré's plan would be annexed to that day's proceedings,[29] where we find it attached as *Mémoire sur les finances et sur le crédit*.[30]

In his *Mémoire*, Cormeré reckoned the debts caused by *rentes perpétuelles* to amount to about 62,500,000 livres (later on he gave the number of 62,677,245 livres),[31] and the debts caused by *rentes viagères* (life annuities) to 105 million. He claimed to know how to reduce the latter debts to a sum of 55,000,000 in total.[32] With his *Mémoire sur les finances* was also bundled another *Mémoire général sur le crédit et sur les finances*,[33] in which Cormeré made clear that his main reform endeavors focused on renewing the French tax system. However, he also aimed at liquidating the debts caused by annuities:

> There are no more expensive loans than those taken out in annuities. […]
> These baits have not escaped the speculators: their eagerness to invest in annuity loans is an irrefutable proof: these loans have multiplied excessively over the last 12 years; their interest is an excessive surcharge on the people, and their extinction […] presents only a means of liberation that is too slow, and greatly inferior to the interest of the capital […].[34]

In his opinion, the National Assembly should decree the immediate reimbursement of annuities held by foreigners, as, according to Cormoré's calculations, one-third to one-half of the annuities' debts were owed to foreigners.[35] The author thus elegantly avoided the question of what constituted a citizen's legitimate self-interest, by contrasting illegitimate, foreign self-interest with that of the French nation. This juxtaposition helped his argument for a one-time repayment of the debts, because, as he made clear, the new French state needed to pursue its own interest in the face of foreign interests.[36]

Cormoré then strengthened his argument with his calculations of the projected duration of payments: out of the 105,000,000 livres of debts due to *rentes viagères*, more than three-quarters dated back to annuities sold since 1777, in other words to annuities that had already been in the process of repayment for twelve years; the other quarter derived from annuities sold between 1766 and 1777, except for a remainder of annuities worth 9,000,000 livres that originated even earlier.[37] Cormeré concluded from this (and probably from his knowledge of average life expectancies) that the annuity payments would go on for at least another thirty to forty years, if the Assembly did not decide to reimburse these annuities. Following the state's interest on this matter and satisfying foreign annuity-holders with a one-time payment was thus an act of self-defense:

> It follows from this statement, that the interest of the State does not solicit less powerfully than that of the balance of trade, a Decree which

grants to the administrators of the National Fund (Caisse Nationale) the faculty to reimburse life annuities [...] The debt is recognized, the Nation promised to pay it in principal & interests; but the National Assembly has retained the faculty to redeem us from the mass of annuities, which deprive us of a part of our money, and which require a dreadful overload of contributions.[38]

For Cormeré, an immediate reimbursement of the annuities was politically expedient, because anything else would be yoking the French people to unfair tax contributions. The question of debt-reimbursement thus lay, as the author insisted, at the heart of the nation's political, as well as commercial, interest; national and social interests dictated it:

I just proved that the repayment of annuities is an operation dictated by political reason & the interest of the balance of our trade, it is advised by the interest of the Nation, commanded by the social interest, since the annuities weaken all bonds of society.[39]

That Cormeré's numbers were not an actual calculation but an expression of his political will becomes evident when we look at the point in his *Mémoire général* where he concedes that his promise of saving the French nation 50–52 million livres was based on the assumption that the National Assembly would agree to an immediate liquidation of annuities. However, he also discussed the possibility that the National Assembly might not decree such a solution and claimed that he could still save the French nation approximately 50 million. He now offered a list of further savings (made by *réconstitutions volontaires*) that also amounted to approximately 50 million.[40] These alternative calculations suggest that his arguments were political in nature rather than mathematically or fiscally sound.

Two days after Cormeré was refused permission to present his reform plans to the National Assembly, a member reminded the Comité des Finances that the Assembly had assigned them to review the *Mémoire*. It was decided that the Comité would discuss it, but without hearing the author, in order to avoid critique from outsiders. It was furthermore agreed that a simple reading of the *Mémoire* would not suffice, so it was first referred back to the baron d'Harambure.[41] After this decision was made, the proceedings of the Comité never again mentioned Cormeré's reform plans.

The explanation for why the Comité seems to have strategically outsourced the verification of Cormeré's plans (it was not rendered to the Cabinet des Finances, but to one single person, "who knew the plan quite well"), might lie in the fact that the committee was skeptical of Cormoré's calculations, and had already inquired about their reliability. Furthermore, the baron de Montesquiou, president of the Comité des Finances, had given its report (including the work by the Cabinet des Finances) to the National Assembly only a few days before, on November 18, 1789. Montesquiou had begun his exposé by stating that finding small remedies would not suffice, and that a new general plan for the fiscal regime was needed immediately.[42] Before a plan could be drawn up, though, the nation had to understand the present situation in detail: to know where the state lost and gained; to identify the amount of debts from its various credit schemes; and to comprehend its revenues in the form of tax contributions, etc. In order to grasp the extent of the debts, it was necessary to distinguish between accumulated debts (*dettes constituées*), in other words those debts that were determined by a fixed contract (perpetual annuities), and those debts "to which we dare to give the very vulgar, very trivial, but very expressive denomination of glaring debts (*dettes criardes*)."[43] Thus did Montesquiou describe the annuities with variable nominees and interest rates, and also variable duration (life annuities). According to the Comité des Finances, these debts posed the question of justice vis-à-vis all future generations, as they turned the entire nation into a "tribune to capitalists"; they were a "genuine violation of public faith [...] It is therefore a matter of national dignity and loyalty to stop this injustice."[44] The plan thus was to determine the size of the expenses and reduce them; to extinguish the accumulated debts; and to reimburse the "glaring debts."[45] The costs of these last, however, were so difficult to predict that the financial department could not entirely anticipate their amount. This had to do, in large part, with the nature of the data available from the old regime. There were three main forms of financial documents that identified revenues and expenditures. The *prospective account*, often designated with the title *mémoire* or *état*, sketched out at the beginning of the fiscal year (in October), estimated expenses and revenues for the upcoming fiscal year. Since the Seven Years' War, however, financial authorities had begun to draft prospective accounts not for the upcoming year alone, but for several years ahead. They seemed confident to project ahead because the figures in the projected accounts had not changed much. France thus "sacrificed the goal of maximizing individual revenue items to a policy of orderliness and predictability."[46] The second available document, the *preliminary retrospective account*, referred to as *état actuel* or *état abrégé*, was usually drafted at the end of the fiscal year and thus estimated (not least on the basis of past preliminary retrospective accounts) revenues and expenditures at a time when financial authorities could not have reliable data yet. This document, in turn, formed the basis for next year's prospective accounts. The third available document, the *retrospective account* (called *état au vrai* or *état actuel*) constituted "summaries of the enormously extensive records of detailed transactions that each year filled many thousands of pages and hundreds of volumes."[47] It is thus not surprising that it took many years for those summaries to be available. As James Riley has shown, the final accounts for 1758 were presented in 1771, and the accounts for the years 1776–80 were only completed in 1788. Hence, those retrospective accounts could not provide data rapidly enough for detailed calculations of the public debt. Furthermore, policy-makers were well aware that the data at hand

TABLEAUX *justificatifs et explicatifs annexés*
au présent mémoire.

Nº I. Etat comparatif des dépenses et des dettes
publiques dans l'ancien état, et suivant
le nouveau plan du comité des finances.

Nº II. Etat comparatif des revenus publics dans
l'ancien état, et suivant le nouveau plan
du comité des finances.

Nº III. Etat comparatif entre les revenus publics,
suivant le plan du comité des finances,
et les dépenses et dettes publiques, suivant le même plan.

Nº IV. Anticipation sur les revenus de l'Etat.

Nº V. Fonds d'avances et de cautionnements.

Nº VI. Offices de finances.

Nº VII. Tableau des remboursements à termes
fixes, suspendus au mois d'août 1788.

Figure 2.1 Summary of the list included in the table by the Comité des Finances.[50]

could not provide exact numbers: painfully conscious of the deficit in the
public treasury that confronted them, they readily understood that none of
these documents was trustworthy.[48]

When Montesquiou referred to the Comité's rigorous calculations, he
referred to a double-entry bookkeeping technique that separated the profit
and loss statement from the capital, which was at the time not standard pro-
cedure in public accounting.[49] The Comité's calculations offered one table
of state expenses, a second showing the revenues, and a third list that calculated the actual difference (see Figure 2.1).

Such tables represented the attempt to address the current difficulties in
obtaining reliable data and in using new accounting techniques, because "one
must devote all one's means, all one's resources; [...] Anything that leaves this
work imperfect will only be palliative, and palliatives no longer suit us."[51]
The Comité now recalculated and refined the numbers at hand, generated
by Jacques Dufresne (1732–1832), deputy at the Assembly for the clergy, presented to the Assembly on August 31, 1789. They then tried to come up with a
plan to improve the amount of state revenues, which they sought to augment
in such a way that they could save about 30 million (not 50 million as Cormeré
had suggested) and thus increase state capital.[52] The Comité assumed that
the public debts alone amounted to 228 million. Out of these 228 million,
162 million were due to annuity schemes alone: 56,796,924 million were due to
perpetual annuities; and 105,253,076 million were due to life annuities—by far
the biggest post on the list (see Figure 2.2).[53]

Voici Messieurs, l'état des dépenses que la caisse nationale serait chargée d'acquitter :

1° Les rentes viagères constituées ; elles se mon-

tent à	105,253,076 liv.
2° Les rentes perpétuelles constituées.........	56,796,924
3° Les gages actuels des charges de magistrature, jusqu'à ce que la liquidation en ait été faite.	9,355,160
4° Intérêts d'effets publics, d'emprunts à termes suspendus et autres, en ayant retranché les objets compris dans les remboursements précédents.............	31,443,082
5° Les indemnités dues à différents titres (1)..............	3,179,000
6° Emprunt national de septembre 1789...................	2,000,000
7° Dépense de la maison du Roi, ou liste civile (2).........	20,000,000
8° Dépenses concernant les provinces, savoir:	
1. Les ponts et chaussées........ 5,680,000 liv.	
2. Les primes et encouragements accordés au commerce et aux manufactures........ 3,262,000	
3. Les frais de procédures criminelles............ 3,180,000	
4. Les frais de perception ou traitement des receveurs généraux et particuliers des finances, réduits au moyen du remboursement de leurs charges............ 3,400,000	
5. Remise en moins-imposé sur les différentes généralités et pays d'Etats 7,123,000	
6. Les travaux de charité....... } 3,055,000 La mendicité..... }	
7. Construction et entretien des bâtiments publics. 1,874,000	
8. Dépenses variables dans les provinces........ 4,500,000	
9. Police et garde de Paris....... 3,985,000	
	36,059,000 liv.

Parmi les objets qui composent cette somme de 36,059,000 livres il nous a paru qu'il était nécessaire de faire une distinction entre ceux qui devait en rester à

A reporter........	228,027,242 liv.

Figure 2.2 The Comité's list of public debts.[54]

The Comité thus presented an improved list (compared to the one dated August 31, 1789), that showed ways to augment state revenues or to reduce expenses per state department (see their suggestions in Figure 2.4, compared to Figure 2.3) so that about 30 million could be saved. While they made many changes and suggestions, they left the sum of the debts caused by annuities entirely untouched.

> The tables we have just put in front of you are of the utmost accuracy, since they take things as they are (*l'état où elles sont*), and they are not based on any system. There are no suppositions or omissions; there are only existing revenues, and the totality of the expenses, we have not surrendered ourselves to any kind of speculation; we have even pushed them back, so as not to fall into any error, and to leave you your hopes for improvement in their entirety.[55]

This exemplifies the nature of the calculations. Indeed, the Comité stated the need to reimburse those onerous debts as rapidly as possible, but they did not attempt to convert these debts into alternative, and more predictable, credit schemes. Furthermore, they did not re-calculate or re-consider the amount of these debts. This points to the difficulties the members of the Comité faced. They first needed reliable data, and seemingly could not even begin to come up with mathematical formulas that would enable them to calculate all the various annuity schemes placed on several nominees, or with variable interest rates. The tables the Comité presented did not offer a new *système* of debt-conversion, as John Law's scheme once had done (the word "system" strongly recalled the years under the Scotsman's influence).[56] Furthermore, as Montesquiou admitted, the Comité's computations did not offer any *spéculations*, a term that evoked, as the next section will show, a mathematical formula that calculated with contingent (and thus uncertain) variables. The report gave tables of exclusively "existing revenues."

Calculating, converting, and liquidating the debts

Compared to the autumn of 1789, the fiscal situation had changed significantly in 1793. The Constituent Assembly had decided in the last month of 1789, as is known, to create a new currency, the *assignats*, which were backed by land-property. This was possible only through the confiscation of ecclesiastical property (decree of November 2, 1789).[59] The Constituent Assembly then agreed to issue 400 million *assignats* in January of the following year; each denomination was worth 1,000 livres and came with an interest rate of 5 percent. The *assignats* were supposed to avoid state bankruptcy, in that the state's creditors could, in exchange for the credit payments, acquire national property or sell the *assignats* for the face value of the land. The original plan thus comprised the withdrawal from circulation of those *assignats* that had been sold, thus returning those

ETAT des dépenses et des dettes publiques, arrêté le 3 août 1789, par M. Dufresne, et vérifié par le comité des finances.

Nos

1. Dépenses générales de la maison du Roi et de celle de la Reine, de monseigneur le Dauphin, des enfants de France, de madame Elisabeth, et de Mesdames tantes du Roi, avec les traitements annexés à différentes parties, et en y comprenant divers objets de dépense dans les forêts, qui étaient autrefois payés sur le produit des bois.. 25,000,000 liv.

2. Maisons de Monsieur, frère du Roi, et de Madame; maisons de monseigneur le comte et de madame la comtesse d'Artois, de monseigneur le duc d'Angoulême et de monseigneur le duc de Berry, et traitements conservés aux personnes qui ont servi les enfants de monseigneur le comte d'Artois, dans leur bas âge.. 8,240,000

3. Affaires étrangères, lignes suisses, et courses des courriers de ce département. 7,330,000

4. Département de la guerre, traitements et objets accessoires, non compris ce que les provinces s'imposent et versent directement dans les caisses militaires... 99,091,000

5. { Marine et colonies....... 40,500,000 } Supplément demandé pour indemnités et récompenses qu'exigeront les réformes déterminées dans les établissements des colonies.... 400,000 } 40,900,000

6. Ponts et chaussées............ 5,680,000

7. Haras sous les ordres de M. le grand écuyer, de M. le duc de Polignac et de M. le marquis de Polignac.............................. 814,000

8. Rentes perpétuelles et viagères........................ 162,030,000

9. Intérêts d'effets publics et d'autres créances................. 44,247,000

10. Gages de charges représentant l'intérêt de la finance................. 14,729,000

11. Intérêts et frais des anticipations qui portent sur 1790 et 1791; intérêts et frais de renouvellement des billets des fermes, des autres anticipations ou des emprunts nécessaires pour balancer le besoin de l'année 1789................. 15,800,000

12. Engagements à temps envers le clergé............................ 2,500,000

13. Indemnités à différents titres............................ 3,179,000

14. Pensions....................................... 29,554,000

15. Gages du conseil et traitement de M. le chancelier, de M. le garde des sceaux, au secrétaire d'Etat de la maison du Roi, à divers magistrats, compris leur franc salé et traitements à d'autres personnes............................ 3,161,000

16. Intendant des provinces, leurs subdélégués et leurs commis................. 1,413,000

17. Police de la ville de Paris........ 1,569,000
18. Guet et garde de la ville de Paris....... 1,138,000
19. Maréchaussée de l'Ile de France......... 251,000 } 3,985,000
20. Entretien et réparation du pavé de Paris....... 627,000
21. Travaux dans les carrières qui sont sous la ville de Paris et environs...... 400,000

22. Remises, ou moins-imposé sur la recette des pays d'élection et des pays conquis: décharges et modérations sur les vingtièmes et la capitation: remises aux pays d'Etats... 7,123,000

23. Traitements aux receveurs, fermiers et régisseurs, et autres frais de recouvrements... 19,511,000

24. Les cinq administrateurs du Trésor royal, payeurs des rentes, etc........... 3,372,000

25. Dépenses du département des mines,
26. Traitements et autres dépenses de l'administration des monnaies, de celle de la caisse du commerce; de celle du département des mines et des bureaux de l'ancienne compagnie des Indes 794,000 } 3,139,000
27. Bureaux de l'administration générale....... 2,345,000

28. Fonds réservés sur le produit de la loterie royale, et sur la ferme du Port-Louis, pour des actes de bienfaisance........................ 173,000

29. Secours à des Hollandais qui se sont réfugiés en France................. 830,000

30. Communautés et maisons religieuses; secours pour la construction d'édifices sacrés......... 2,182,000 } 5,711,000
31. Dons, aumônes, secours, hôpitaux, enfants trouvés, etc........ 3,529,000

A reporter............... 507,532,000 liv.

Figure 2.3 Table of public expenses and public depts presented on August 31, 1789.[57]

	SUITE de l'état des dépenses, arrêté le 31 *août* 1789, *par M. Dufresne, etc.*	
N°⁸	Report.....................	507,532,000 liv.
32.	Travaux de charité..	1,911,000
33.	Destruction du vagabondage et de la mendicité...............................	1,144,000
34.	Primes et autres encouragements pour le commerce...........	3,862,000
35.	Jardin royal des plantes, et cabinet d'histoire naturelle....................	130,000
36.	Bibliothèque du Roi..	159,000
37.	Universités, académies, colléges, sciences et arts...	1,004,000
38.	Passeports en exemption de droits à la marine royale, aux ambassadeurs et aux ministres étrangers..	400,000
39.	Entretiens, réparations et constructions de bâtiments, employés à la Chambre publique...	1,874,000
40.	Dépenses de plantations dans les forêts, de curements de rivières et d'autres objets dont le payement est assigné sur le produit des bois et sur le Trésor royal...	817,000
41.	Frais de procédure criminelles et de prisonniers............................	3,180,000
42.	Dépenses dans les provinces dont l'objet varie tous les ans, et qui se renouvellent de différentes manières.....	4,500,000
43.	Dépenses imprévues..	5,000,000
	TOTAL.....................	531,513,000 liv.

Figure 2.3 (Continued)

assignats to the state. In April 1790, the National Assembly transformed the *assignats* from state bonds to legal tender (decree of April 17, 1790) and lowered their interest rate from 5 to 3 percent. Furthermore, smaller denominations, more practicable for daily life, were issued. *Assignats* were thus assigned another task: they were to help with the acute scarcity of money. This, however, did not quite work out as planned either, as the *assignats* soon decreased in value, owing to the high exchange rates. In September 1790, the National Assembly gave out further *assignats* worth 800 million, and eliminated interest rates on the *assignats* altogether. The *assignats* were now definitely transformed from state bonds to paper money.[60]

After the revolutionary currency had been in use for three years, it had not remedied the financial crisis nor reduced the public debts. For that reason, the members of the Convention (now Legislative Assembly; elections to the Convention were held in September 1792) increasingly sensed that the solutions at hand (*assignats* and a new tax system) did not suffice, and therefore ordered the Comité des Finances to come up with a new plan to deal with the annuity schemes. It did so. In his capacity as current president of the committee, Pierre-Joseph Cambon gave his report to the Convention, which he opened with the following words:

> A long time ago you ordered your Comité des Finances to report to you on life annuities. The speculators (*agioteurs*) await it with impatience and despair; the egoists, the usurers, and vampires of the old regime

ÉTAT des dépenses et des dettes publiques réduites par le décret de l'Assemblée nationale du 6 octobre 1789, et par le plan du comité des finances.

Nos

1. L'offre faite au nom du Roi, et le décret de l'Assemblée nationale du 6 octobre, sanctionné par Sa Majesté, ont réduit cet article à...................... 20,000,000 liv.

2. Le décret de l'Assemblée nationale du 6 octobre, sanctionné par le Roi, avait fait un premier retranchement de 3,000,000 livres sur cet article. Monsieur ayant offert de réduire à 2,000,000 livres l'article qui le concerne ; et le traitement conservé aux personnes qui ont servi les enfants de M. comte d'Artois, dans leur bas âge, devant être renvoyé aux pensions, cet article se trouve réduit naturellement pour les deux provinces, à.................. 4,000,000

   Pensions de M. le duc d'Angoulême et de M. le duc de Berry............. 700,000

3. Le décret de l'Assemblée nationale du 6 octobre, sanctionné par le Roi, a réduit cet article à.. 6,300,000

4. Le décret de l'Assemblée nationale du 6 octobre, sanctionné par le Roi, a réduit cet article à.. 79,000,000

5. Le décret de l'Assemblée nationale, du 6 octobre, sanctionné par le Roi, a réduit cet article à.. 39,000,000

6. Le comité des finances propose de renvoyer cette dépense à la direction des assemblées provinciales, et de la réduire à moitié : ci.................. 2,840,000

7. Le décret de l'Assemblée nationale, du 6 octobre, sanctionné par le Roi, a supprimé cette dépense en totalité..................................

8. Il n'y a aucun changement à cet article, ci.......................... 162,050,000

9. En retranchant de cet article, l'intérêt des cautionnements des compagnies de finance, celui du fond d'avance des fermiers de la caisse de Poissy, et celui de 50,800,000 livres d'assignations suspendues sur les domaines et bois, cet article est réduit à.. 31,443,082

10. Après le remboursement des receveurs généraux et autres charges que le plan du comité des finances propose, jusqu'à la concurrence d'un capital de 119,000,000 livres, cet article ne subsistera plus que pour.......... 9,355,160

11. Le remboursement des anticipations fait disparaître cet article ; mais l'emprunt national de septembre 1789, subsiste pour...................... 2,000,000

12. Le décret de l'Assemblée nationale du 6 octobre, sanctionné par Sa Majesté, a anéanti cet article....................................

13. Il n'y a rien de changé à cet article, ci.......................... 3,179,000

14. Le plan du comité des finances réduit cet article à.................. 18,000,000

15. }

   { Le travail du comité des finances réduit ces deux articles à.............. 2,774,000

16. }

17. ⎧ Ces cinq articles sont considérés par le comité des finances comme des dépen-
18. ⎪ ses locales qui ne sont pas de nature à être imposées sur tout le royaume.
19. ⎨ Il pense de même sur l'article 22, l'article 32, l'article 39 et l'article 42,
20. ⎪ montant ensemble à 20,537,000 livres qui doivent être regardés comme dé-
21. ⎩ penses locales ; mais afin de pourvoir aux besoins extraordinaires que peuvent
       éprouver ces différentes parties, le comité a proposé d'y destiner une som-
       me équivalente au quart de leur montant, ci........................ 5,134,250

22. Renvoyé à l'observation de l'article 17.................................

23. Cet article, d'après les remboursements faits, la réduction du nombre des em-
    ployés, et la modération de leur traitement, ne sera plus compté que pour.. 5,700,000

24. Cet article, par les mêmes raisons, est réduit à........................ 2,330,000

25.
26. } Le travail du comité des finances, réduit ces trois articles à.............. 1,275,000
27.

28. Le décret de l'Assemblée nationale, du 6 octobre 1789, sanctionné par Sa Ma-
    jesté, supprime cet article....................................

29. Il n'y a rien de changé à cet article : ci.............................. 830,000

30. ⎧ Ces deux articles sont renvoyés par le décret de l'Assemblée nationale du
31. ⎨ 6 octobre, sanctionné par le Roi, à la charge de l'administration des biens
    ⎩ du clergé..

   A reporter................ 395,930,492 liv.

Figure 2.4 Table of public expenses and public debts according to the plan of the Comité.[58]

N**	SUITE de l'état des dépenses réduites par le décret, etc.	
	Report....................	395,930,492 liv.
32.	Renvoyé à l'observation de l'article 17..........................	
33.	Renvoyé à l'observation de l'article 17..........................	
34.	Le travail du comité des finances a réduit cet article à..............	3,262,000
35.	Le comité des finances l'a réduit à...........................	92,000
36.	Réduit par le comité des finances à...........................	69,000
37.	Réduit par le comité des finances à...........................	1,000,000
38.	Il n'y a rien de changé à cet article...........................	400,000
39.	Renvoyé à l'observation de l'article 17..........................	
40.	Le comité des finances est d'avis de la suppression de cet article.........	
41.	Il n'y a rien de changé à cet article, ci........................	3,180,000
42.	Renvoyé à l'observation de l'article 17..........................	
43.	Le comité des finances réduit cet article à........................	2.400,000
		406,333,492
	La dépense de justice gratuite dans tout le royaume.................	412,333,492 liv.
	TOTAL.....................	413,334,922 liv.

Figure 2.4 (Continued)

are alarmed by it; they have communicated their fears to the annuitants who have place the fruits of their labor in the hands of the government to ensure honest ease: but let them rest assured, the Convention having never had any other objective than to reduce the usurious rate of interest that has been granted, to thwart all combinations of the speculators (*agioteurs*), and to protect honest citizens; our work has been done on these principles.[61]

Cambon set out his committee's new agenda: those *agioteurs* and *vampires* mentioned would have no fear of the new report, unless the Comité aimed to draw up a plan for the public debts caused by life annuities. In other words— as the report would make clear later on—the yearly reimbursements of the debts would not liberate France from the yokes of these selfish creatures. Instead, the Comité argued for a liquidation of debts by converting them into a more predictable credit system, one that would, however, still be fair to all the "honnêtes citoyens."[62]

The wish to impose a new order on the public debts was not new. However, this time, in contrast to all the previous occasions, the Comité changed two things: they made use of probabilistic computations; and they also incorporated statistical data on human life expectancy into their calculations. Furthermore, they also re-evaluated all available data on the public debts delivered in the Constituent as well as Legislative Assemblies. Not surprisingly, they found the data at hand unsatisfactory:

> None of these accounts or reports ever disclosed the capital provided for the composition of life annuities, the investments that were made on one, two, three or four heads; the rate of interest that was granted; or the ages of the heads on which the annuities were placed; and consequently, they presented no basis for judging the true burden on the State from life annuities, and for preparing a fair and useful operation.[63]

As Cambon claimed, no previous study of the fiscal situation had taken into account the varying numbers of heads included in the schemes, nor the fluctuating durations of the annuity contracts, nor the different interest rates. All the studies had confused the various annuity contracts and had differentiated only two categories: namely perpetual annuities and life annuities. Furthermore, no study gave sufficient information about the *rentiers'* ages.[64] New methods of calculation were thus needed.

The analyses of two experts were particularly helpful to the Comité's new calculations: first, the statistical data on life expectancy generated by Antoine Déparcieux (1703–1768), who, in his *Essai sur les probabilités de la durée de la vie humaine*[65] from 1746, had evaluated the life expectancy of the cohort that had bought *tontines* (another form of life contingent investment) in 1696; and second, the newer approach to reforming annuity schemes that made use of probabilistic mathematics presented by the Genevan mathematician, Emmanuel-Étienne Duvillard (1775–1832). In 1786, Duvillard had submitted his *Recherches sur les rentes et les emprunts et les remboursements*[66] to the Finance Minister Calonne, and had published his work with the endorsement of the minister and the Académie des Sciences a year later.[67] Furthermore, the Comité also consulted works by "various other French, English, and Dutch authors," by which the president presumably referred to the statistical and arithmetical approaches by Paul Edme Crublier de Saint-Cyran, William Petty, and Willem Kerseboom.[68]

The mathematician Duvillard had not based his reflections on the internal operations of the various annuity schemes on arithmetical or statistical computations alone. In his *Recherches,* he had developed investment evaluation criteria, had calculated the evolution of the rate of return, the ideal term, and the future value of a loan. He had then shown that the lender's chances to increase income did not necessarily augment in time, but that the borrower's obligations did.[69] Duvillard had also generated new refinancing strategies and had furthermore promulgated that he could have saved the French state several million livres with his method,[70] which he called a "spéculation."[71]

The mathematician had exposed the (Genevan) bankers' annuity schemes. For a provision paid for by the crown, they conveyed deals with variable and high rates of return (of 8 percent or more). The schemes could offer seemingly attractive deals for the subscribers, because the annuities were placed on thirty randomly picked girls, the famous "thirty virgins of Geneva," who had survived smallpox. This meant that if one girl died, the subscribers still received 29/30 of the interest, and so on. Duvillard now argued that French people, including ministers, were fooled by the marketing strategies of the Genevan bankers, because they did not grasp how annuities operated—a critique that echoed the Comité's assessment from 1793. Duvillard had proved mathematically that, with their variable interest rates, the Genevan schemes did not necessarily increase income, but only augmented the element of chance affecting the revenues, which equaled a long-term subscription to an annuity with stable interest (thus on one head) with the same value.[72] Another misleading belief, in his assessment, was the idea that the average life expectancy indicated the moment when the annuity would yield profits.[73] Rather, in order to help the crown benefit from annuities (but in a way that did not deter lenders), Duvillard had offered a "spéculation" that consisted of a triple calculation, and this now proved very helpful to the Comité's project of liquidating the public debts. The mathematician had explained: first, the creditors should identify the maximum profit of the annuity. Second, they needed to determine the age at which they would attain this maximum.[74] And third, they should calculate the time the annuity would have to run until the creditor received the same total of money he or she would have had if he or she had purchased an annuity on one head, based on a standard rate of return. Duvillard thus calculated the interest rate at which a creditor would grant a loan to the French state in exchange for a stable annuity that would be paid at fixed term.[75] He then presented the mathematical formula for the proposed "spéculation." First, the total value of the collected annuities needed to be assessed. Second, Duvillard identified "at what compound interest rate [...] one would have had to place the original capital [...] to accumulate the preceding value during the term [...] when the annuity lasts." Hence, Duvillard could determine "the future value of the reinvested annuities [...] and the compound rate of return" and showed how to apply them to the "equivalent placement of the original capital." The mathematician then explained that the annuity placement, as he had defined it, was "equivalent to a usual placement that lasts during the same term as the annuities [...], at the same compound rate."[76] Duvillard thus had identified the optimal value of a *rente*, which he understood "as a verifiable scientific basis to evaluate the actual return of lifetime rents as financial placements."[77]

Duvillard did not fail to remind his readers of the novelty of this approach, and to underscore that it was superior to older rule-of-thumb-based calculations.[78] This was exactly what appealed to the Comité des Finances: "It is with all these instructions that we have established the real value of life annuities."[79] Accordingly, Cambon explained that such a "theory of annuity" could have spared the former government a rather serious mathematical mistake, which had led them to believe that a life annuity, with limited contract duration and an interest rate of 10 percent, was equal to a perpetual annuity with an interest rate of 5 percent. This mistake had, according to this view, serious consequences and kept the French people in ignorance of the present fiscal state: "They have made an error on which it is very important to shed light, and which experience and the calculations published by various authors should have rectified long ago."[80] Cambon understood that the reason for such a mistake lay in a misconception of the average life expectancy. Such a rule-of-thumb conception did not take into account that the life expectancy of a young child was very different to that of a middle-aged person. The Genevan bankers, however, understood this perfectly well, and so placed their schemes unto the heads of girls living in the peaceful republic of Geneva. "This is how the foolishness of our former government was played out, and huge fortunes were made without spending a single penny, but only by lending a loan."[81]

By means of these theoretical approaches, the Comité now articulated its political position. Thanks to Déparcieux's study, it understood that perpetual annuities with a 5 percent interest rate equaled life annuities with 10 percent interest only if they were placed on a nominee aged at least fifty-seven years. Thanks to Duvillard's mathematical approach, they discovered that a life annuity with 10 percent interest on one head equaled a perpetual annuity with 9 percent interest. It followed, therefore, that previous calculations of the value of French debts had all been false: the state lost more than 130 million from annuities placed on one head, aged between nine and twenty-one years, from one scheme alone.

> We could have cited even more ruinous loans, and presented you with the results of those made in life annuities on two, three, or four heads; but we thought that it would suffice for you to be aware of some of the abuses, for you to hasten to bring about a salutary reform.[82]

Cambon expressed his regret that these new calculations took so long, but he still thought that the Comité's new reform plan, following Duvillard's calculations, could put an end to such abuses. [83]

The plan that the Comité proposed also followed the directives of the Convention's decree of August 24, 1793. The new law had created a "Grand Livre de la dette publique non viagère" (which created fresh data) and converted all life annuities into perpetual annuities at 5 percent interest (which was not far from Duvillard's proposed ideal). The Comité suggested that all outstanding life annuity payments that would be due on the first day of Germinal (March 21) should be paid at the original interest rate on presentation of the original titles, birth certificates of the *rentiers,* and all heads involved in the scheme, etc. After these payments, all life annuities would be converted into perpetual annuities at 5 percent interest. All those who had not submitted their claims by the next upcoming

Vendémiaire (September 22) would lose all rights to payments. With this plan, so Cambon declared, the Convention would finally, four years into the Revolution, make a long-overdue break with the old regime:

> By this operation, you will separate the past from the future; you will know in all details the current amount of the life debt, and the extinctions that have taken place, either by death, emigration, or sequestration; you will withdraw the royal title, and you will republicanize this part of the debt, as you did for the consolidated debt.[84]

The Comité also realized that professional mathematicians were needed to undertake such calculations and indeed engaged Duvillard to determine the conversions of the life annuities into perpetual annuities. Duvillard later recalled this engagement as follows:

> This operation was without a doubt the most beautiful that has ever been done in Finance. It was the first example of a mathematically correct law of the continuous union of science with the work of administration.
> [...]
> I was pleased to have rendered a service to the state through my talents, and to the annuitants by saving them from restitution [...] or an equivalent reduction in the capital of their annuities. The financial disorder having been one of the main causes of the revolution, the salvation of the Republic required a reform of these usurious loans by consolidating the public debt.[85]

The Comité's report could now, thanks to the mathematician's calculations, give many examples for the computations of the proposed conversions and also offer tables that simplified those calculations (see Figure 2.5).

What represented for Duvillard one of the most beautiful challenges for a mathematician led others strongly to condemn those self-interested, indeed egoistic, schemes invented by bankers. The Comité finally had a plan against those "vampires" who were sucking the blood of the French state.[87] After revolutionary experience had shown that all former endeavors had not sufficed to reduce the public debts, the mathematical approach finally chosen by the Comité unraveled their true extent. Crucially, it also offered new computational tools to surmount those same fiscal difficulties. In other words, probabilistic mathematics offered a way to convert and liquidate those debts in a way that still honored the spirit of 1789. This, at least, was the political justification articulated by Cambon. However, the proposed conversion still meant a limitation of repayments, and so also needed new rhetorical legitimation strategies, which almost inevitably led to stronger condemnations of the self-interest behind those annuity schemes.

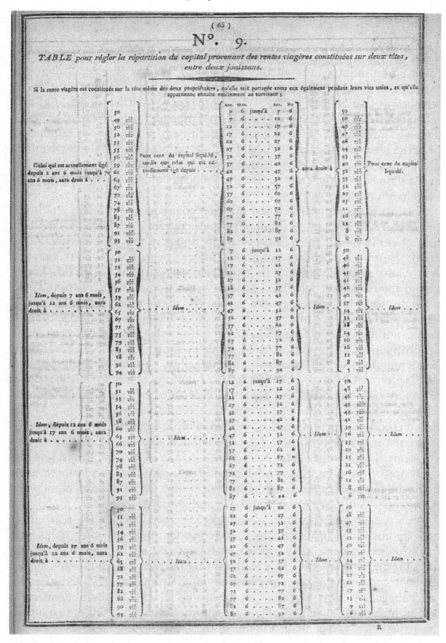

Figure 2.5 One of the many examples of conversions given by the Comité des Finances.[86]

Conclusions

This chapter began by describing how the 1789 oath to honor the pre-existing debts complicated the new fiscal regime's relation to the past. From this followed an inquiry into whether the radical fervor against self-interested "speculators" and "vampires" was inherent within the ideas of 1789, or whether we can detect a change in the different revolutionary dealings with self-interest. As has been shown, it proved difficult for the Comité to devise a plan to liquidate the debts caused by annuities that, on the one hand, honored the 1789 oath to take on the old regime's debts (which did not permit an abrupt end to be set to those debts); and, on the other hand, found ways to avoid state bankruptcy and to free the French people from an unduly heavy burden of taxation.

The question of how to address this challenge was undoubtedly a political one, but it was also, in no small part, mathematical. We need to ask, then: how could those different (self-) interests (those of private individuals and creditors of the French state; or public interest) be reckoned and reconciled? As we have seen, the Assemblies went from a declaration of defending individual interests and individual property rights, and an intention to repay all annuities (which meant a total ban on the abandonment or disruption of annuity payments or simple conversions), to a strong condemnation of those same annuity schemes as expressions of self-interest and egoism that ought, according to the Convention, to be ended as soon as possible. These strong condemnations of self-interest thus emerged at a moment when members of the Convention had realized that the solutions at hand (i.e. the issue of *assignats* and the tax reform) did not suffice to remedy the parlous financial situation of the state. For that reason, the Comité became aware in 1793 that new methods of calculation were needed in order to grasp, and also to articulate, the true extent of these very specific debts and to come up with new solutions. The Comité therefore re-evaluated the older estimations and calculations of the assemblies and committees, created new and more clearly arranged tables, and made use of statistical data about life expectancy, but more importantly, also of probabilistic mathematics.

With deeper understanding of those credit systems came the realization, and the possibility of verbalizing that realization, that the state's debts were much higher than originally anticipated. It is interesting to note that it was only after the application of the new methods that the members of the Convention began to condemn those annuity schemes more strongly as self-interested and, indeed, egoistic. This suggests that the strong increase in moral condemnation of life annuities and of individual self-interest was a result of revolutionary experience, rather than original to the ideas of 1789, or even to radical Enlightenment philosophy. Or, to put it differently, the discursive condemnation of self-interest was more urgent in 1793 than it was in 1789, as it helped to justify and to distract from the fact that the Convention had been unable to come up with earlier and better solutions to the budgetary crisis.

In his report, Cambon seems to have wanted to jolt the members of the Convention into action and to instill a new feeling of urgency. This was important after four years of discussions about the fiscal situation, and also proved useful when new grounds of legitimation were needed in order to argue for a change in the Assembly's dealings with annuity schemes. Duvillard's mathematical formulas enabled the Convention to go beyond reimbursement strategies, and to come up with a liquidation system that could finally "separate the past from the future," as the president of the Comité des Finances put it in his report to the Convention. The Comité thus advocated a solution that aimed to discontinue the fiscal practices of the old regime while, at the same time, honoring the oath taken in 1789. However, in order to legitimize the new pathway that Duvillard's calculations suggested—in other words, to finally convert the debts into more predictable credit schemes—the Convention needed to make clearer than ever before that, in setting an end to those schemes invented by "vampires," the French state was defending the interests of the nation against such egoistic blood-suckers. Statistical data, numbers, and calculations eventually produced the *one* truth Anson was demanding in 1790 and that the legislators needed to articulate to the people.

In contrast to the statements made in the early months of the Revolution, which had left a certain ambiguity about the question of intention and personal responsibility for the fiscal crisis, the Convention's assessment of those responsible for the credit schemes embodied a process of disambiguation. The new republican government now judged political actions by their impact on the nation and deduced personal intention from the outcome of an action. There were only good or bad actions, intended either for or against the republic. Accordingly, the new revolutionary *l'homme régénéré*[88] needed to be liberated from the temptation to follow his or her individual self-interest.

Notes

1 Rebecca Spang, *Stuff and Money in the Time of the French Revolution* (Cambridge, MA: Harvard University Press, 2015), 15.
2 Spang, *Stuff*, 72. The question of the old in the new regime was prominently raised by Alexis de Tocqueville in his seminal work on the French Revolution, *L'Ancien Régime et la Révolution* (Paris: Michel Lévy frères,1856) and has ever since occupied scholars. The debate reached its peak in the twentieth century in the dispute between "Marxist" and "revisionist" interpretations of the Revolution. See, for an overview of the debate: Gail Bossenga, "Origins of the French Revolution," *History Compass* 5, no. 4 (2007): 1294–1337; Robert Foster and Timothy Tacket, eds., "The Origins of the French Revolution: A Debate," *French Historical Studies* 16 (1990): 741–65; Michel Vovelle, "L'Historiographie de la Révolution française à la veille du bicentenaire," *American Historical Review* 272 (1988): 113–26; Lynn Hunt, *Politics, Culture and Class in the French Revolution* (Berkeley: University of California Press, 1984); Thomas Doyle, *Origins of the French Revolution* (Oxford: Oxford University

Press, 1980); or more recently Thomas Kaiser and Dale Van Kley, eds., *From Deficit to Deluge: The Origins of the French Revolution* (Stanford: Stanford University Press, 2011).

3 See David Weir, "Tontines, Public Finance, and Revolution in France and England, 1688–1789," *The Journal of Economic History* 49, no. 1 (March 1989): 95–124, especially 97.

4 See Gail Bossenga, "Financial Origins," in Kaiser and Van Kley, *From Deficit to Deluge*, 37–66, 38. There were three options for defaulting on public debt: The first and most recurrent option was the temporary suspension of repayments. Another alternative was what contemporaries called a "reform," which meant that all interest rates higher than 5 percent (the legal maximum interest) were reduced to this "ordinary rate," with the argument that interest payments over 5 percent were a form of "excess." The third way of defaulting included the possibility of reducing all revenues on the originally invested capital below 5 percent, which was a "much more serious attack on the rights of the government creditors." See François Velde and David Weir, "The Financial Market and Government Debt Policy in France, 1746–1793," *The Journal of Economic History* 52, no. 1 (March 1992): 1–39, 8–9.

5 See Mathilde Moulin, "Les rentes sur l'Hôtel de Ville," *Histoire, économie et société* (April 1998): 623–48, especially 624; Katia Béguin, *Financer la guerre au XVIIᵉ siècle: La Dette publique et les rentiers de l'absolutisme* (Seyssel: Edition Champ Vallon, 2012), 9–12. For the inherent risk in the trade with annuities, see especially chapter 4 of Béguin, *Financer la guerre*, 104–35.

6 See Bossenga, "Financial Origins," 44.

7 See Velde and Weir, "The Financial Market," 1.

8 "Une Nation ne peut conserver sa considération & son crédit qu'en acquittant fidèlement ses engagemens: [...] c'est du mode de liquidation que vous choisirez, que dépend maintenant le salut de l'Empire." Pierre-Hubert Anson, *Opinion de M. Anson, député de Paris, sur la liquidation de la dette publique, lue le 17 Septembre 1790*. Imprimé par ordre de l'Assemblée Nationale (Paris, 1790), 2–3. See also Edna H. Lemay, *Dictionnaire des Constituants 1789–1791* (2 vols), vol. 1 (Paris: Universitas, 1991), 22–23.

9 The minutes of the Comité des Finances make very clear how difficult it was for the Comité and its different subdivisions to gather all necessary information in order to know how much the state owed to its private debtors and how much money the various state departments actually spent. See Camille Bloch, *Procès-verbaux du Comité des Finances de l'Assemblée Constituante* (Rennes: Impr. Oberthur, 1922), especially 27.

10 "Vous avez décrété, avec raison, que les différens projets sur le mode de liquidation de la dette publique, qui pourroient vous être présentés, seroient discutés, avec la circonspection, l'étendue & la lenteur même qui conviennent à une délibération de cette importance.[...] Mais ne perdez pas de vue cependant, Messieurs, que les intérêts divers, qui se combattent, peuvent lutter contre la vérité; que c'est aux Législateurs à fixer définitivement l'opinion incertaine des meilleurs Citoyens, & qu'il n'est pas possible de différer plus long-temps le jugement de cette grande question soumise à votre décision."Anson, *Opinion*, 1–2.

11 Anson, *Opinion*, 2.

12 See, for example, Steven L. Kaplan, *Bread, Politics and Political Economy in the Reign of Louis XV*, 2nd ed. (London: Anthem Press, 2015), especially 97–163; Christine Zabel, "Challenges of Food Security: Free Trade, Distribution and Political (In)Stability in Mid 18th Century France," *European Journal for Security Research* 3 (2018): 35–50.

13 See Albert O. Hirschman, *The Passions and the Interests: Political Arguments for Capitalism before Its Triumph* (Princeton: Princeton University Press, 1977), 50.

14 See, here representatively: Richard H. Thaler, *Misbehaving: The Making of Behavioral Economics* (London/New York: Norton, 2015).
15 Keith M. Baker, "Introduction," in *Inventing the French Revolution: Essays on French Political Culture in the Eighteenth Century*, ed. Baker (Cambridge: Cambridge University Press, 1994), 1–11, here 5–6.
16 Hirschman, *The Passions*, 57–58, quotation 112.
17 See François Furet, *Penser la Révolution française* (Paris: Gallimard, 1978).
18 See Timothy Tackett, *Becoming a Revolutionary: The Deputies of the French National Assembly and the Emergence of French Revolutionary Culture (1789–1790)* (Philadelphia: The Pennsylvania State University Press, 2006), 4–5.
19 Tackett, *Becoming a Revolutionary*, 6.
20 Tackett, *Becoming a Revolutionary*, 7.
21 I am very grateful to Tilman Haug for his valuable comments.
22 See Bloch, *Procès-verbaux*, V–VII. However, Bloch confuses the dates of the decree by the National Assembly, which she mentions as August 11, 1789 (not July 1789). See also Tackett, *Becoming a Revolutionary*, 219–21.
23 See Bloch, *Procès-verbaux*, Procès-verbal du 11 août 1789, 22.
24 See Bloch, *Procès-verbaux*, Procès-verbal du 11 août 1789, 22.
25 "Ce département est très chargé, et le compte final ne peut en être rendu de quelques jours." See Bloch, *Procès-verbaux*, Procès-verbal du 28 août 1789, 27.
26 See Bloch, *Procès-verbaux*, Procès-verbal du 2 septembre 1789, 31.
27 See Bloch, *Procès-verbaux*, Procès-verbal du 4 septembre 1789, 33–34.
28 "Les bases de ses calculs, et qui s'assurera de leur exactitude." See Bloch, *Procès-verbaux*, Procès-verbal du 5 novembre 1789, 51–52.
29 See Archives Parlementaires (hereafter AP), X: Du 12 novembre au 24 décembre 1789, séance du samedi 21 novembre 1789, 159.
30 See AP, X, séance du samedi 21 novembre 1789, 170–175; and Guillaume-François Mahy de Cormeré, *Mémoire sur les finances et sur le credit, pour server de suite aux Recherches, considerations Nouvelles sur les finances* [...]. Imprimé par ordre de l'Assemblée nationale (Paris: chez l'auteur, 1789).
31 Guillaume François Mahy de Cormeré, *Mémoire général sur le crédit et sur les finances* (Paris: chez l'auteur, 1789), 29–30.
32 Cormeré, *Mémoire sur les finances*, 21.
33 See also AP, X, séance du Samedi 21 novembre 1789, 175–207.
34 "Il n'est point d'emprunts plus onéreux que ceux qui sont effectués en viager. [...] Ces appâts n'ont point échappé aux spéculateurs: leur empressement à placer dans les emprunts viagers n'est une preuve sans réplique: ces emprunts, depuis 12 ans, se sont multiplies à l'excès; leurs intérêts forment une surcharge énorme pour les peuples, & leurs extinctions [...] ne présentent qu'un moyen très-lent de libération fort inférieur à l'intérêt des capitaux [...]." Cormeré, *Mémoire général*, 30–31.
35 See also Cormeré, *Mémoire sur les finances*, 13.
36 See Cormeré, *Mémoire général*, 4.
37 Cormeré, *Mémoire général*, 32.
38 "Il suit de cet exposé, que l'intérêt de l'Etat ne sollicite pas moins puissament, que celui de la balance du commerce, un Décret qui accorde aux Administrateurs de la Caisse Nationale la faculté de rembourser les rentes viageres [...] La dette est reconnue, la Nation a promis de l'acquitter en principaux & intérêts; mais l'Assemblée Nationale ne s'est point interdit la faculté de se rédimer de cette masse d'intérêts viagers, qui nous privent d'une partie de notre numéraire, qui nécessitent une surcharge effrayante de contributions." See Cormeré, *Mémoire général*, 32–33.

39 "Je viens de justifier qu'au moyen du remboursement des rentes viagers, opérations dictée par la politique & l'intérêt de la balance de notre Commerce, conseillé par celui de la Nation, commandée par l'intérêt social, puisque les rentes viageres atténuent tous les liens de la Société." See Cormeré, *Mémoire général*, 52.

40 Cormeré, *Mémoire général*, 145–48.

41 See Bloch, *Procès-verbaux*, Procès-verbal du 23 novembre 1789, 62–63.

42 See AP, X, séance du mercredi 18 novembre 1789, 90.

43 See AP, X, séance du mercredi 18 novembre 1789, 90.

44 "Véritable violation de la foi publique [...] Il est donc de la dignité et de la loyauté nationale de faire cesser cette injustice." See AP, X, séance du mercredi 18 novembre 1789, 90–91.

45 See AP, X, séance du mercredi 18 novembre 1789, 90.

46 James C. Riley, "French Finances 1727–1768," *The Journal of Modern History* 2, no. 92 (June, 1987): 209–43, 217.

47 Riley, "French Finances," 216.

48 Riley, "French Finances," 215, 219. This was apparent also in Jacques Necker's *Compte rendu*, which offered sugarcoated numbers.

49 See Jonathan Levy, "Accounting for Profit and the History of Capital," *Critical History Studies* 1, no. 2 (Fall 2014): 171–214, especially 182–83.

50 AP, X, séance du 18 novembre 1789, 97.

51 "Le calcul rigoureux de tout ce que nous venons de comprendre sous le titre de dettes criardes est donc le premier de tous les calculs à faire; c'est à y pourvoir qu'il faut consacrer tous ses moyens, toutes ses ressources; dons patriotiques, vaisselle des églises et des particuliers, ventes extraordinaires, banque nationale, banque particulière, tout est bon s'il opère ce grand bien. Tout ce qui laissera cet ouvrage imparfait ne sera que palliatif, et les palliatifs ne nous conviennent plus." See AP, X, séance du 18 novembre 1789, 91.

52 AP, X, séance du 18 novembre 1789, 95.

53 AP, X, séance du 18 novembre 1789, 93.

54 AP, X, séance du 18 novembre 1789, 92.

55 "Les tableaux que nous venons de mettre sous vos yeux sont de la plus grande exactitude, puisqu'ils prennent les choses dans l'état où elles sont, et qu'ils ne s'appuient sur aucun système. Il n'y a ici ni suppositions, ni omissions; nous ne vous présentons que des revenus existants, et la totalité des dépenses, nous ne nous sommes livrés à aucune spéculation; nous les avons re-poussées même, afin de ne tomber dans aucune erreur, et de vous laisser VOS espérances d'amélioration tout entières." AP, X, séance du 18 novembre 1789, 95.

56 Rebecca Spang, "The Ghost of Law: Speculation on Money, Memory and Mississippi in the French Constituent Assembly," *Historical Reflections/Réfléxions Historique* 31, no. 1 (Spring, 2005): 3–25. For the various old regime interpretations of the *système Law*, see especially pp. 10–14 of the same article. See also Florence Magnot-Ogilvy, ed., *Gagnons sans savoir comment: Représentations du Système de Law du XVIIIᵉ à nos jours* (Rennes: Presses Universitaire de Rennes, 2017); and Arnaud Orain's new monograph, *La politique du merveilleux: Une autre histoire du Système de Law (1695–1795)* (Paris: Fayard, 2018); furthermore, see Antoine Murphy, "John Law and the Assignats," in *La Pensée économique pendant la Révolution française*, ed. Philippe Steiner and Gilbert Faccarello (Grenoble: University of Grenoble Press, 1990), 431–48. See also Christine Zabel, "From Bubble to Speculation: 18th Century Readings of the 1720s," in *Boom, Bust and Beyond: New Perspectives on the 1720 Stock Market Bubble*, ed. Stefano Condorelli and Daniel Menning (Berlin/Boston: De Gruyter, 2019), 303–32.

57 AP, X, séance du 18 novembre 1789, 100.

58 AP, X, séance du 18 novembre 1789, 101.

59 For a study of property during the French Revolution, see Rafe Blaufarb, *The Great Demarcation: The French Revolution and the Invention of Modern Property* (Oxford: Oxford University Press, 2016).

60 For the history of the *assignats*, see especially Spang, *Stuff and Money.*

61 "Vous avez ordonné depuis long-temps à votre comité des finances de vous faire un rapport sur les rentes viagères. Les agioteurs l'attendent avec impatience et désespoir; les égoïstes, les usuriers et les vampires de l'ancien régime en sont alarmés; ils ont communiqué leurs craintes aux rentiers qui ont placé le fruit de leur travail entre les mains du gouvernement pour s'assurer une honnête aisance: mais que ces derniers se rassurent, la Convention n'ayant jamais eu d'autre but que de réduire le taux usuraire de l'intérêt qui a été accordé, de déjouer toutes les combinaisons des agioteurs, et de protéger les honnêtes citoyens; notre travail a été fait d'après ces principes." See Pierre-Joseph Cambon, *Rapport et projet de décret sur la dette publique viagère, présentés à la Convention nationale, au nom du Comité des Finances, à la séance du 1er germinal an II de la République française. Imprimé par ordre de la Convention Nationale* (Paris: Imprimerie nationale, 1793), 1.

62 See Cambon, *Rapport*, 1.

63 "Aucun de ces comptes ou rapports n'a jamais fait connaître quel était le capital fourni pour la constitution des rentes viagères, ni les placemens qui ont été faits sur une, deux, trois ou quatre têtes, ni le taux de l'intérêt qui a été accordé, ni les âges des têtes sur lesquelles les rentes sont assises; et par conséquent, ils ne présentaient aucune base pour juger la véritable charge de l'État provenant des rentes viagères, et pour préparer une opération juste et utile." See Cambon, *Rapport*, 2.

64 See Cambon, *Rapport*, 2.

65 Antoine Deparcieux, *Essai sur les probabilités de la durée de la vie humaine: D'où l'on déduit la manière de déterminer les rentes* [...] (Paris: Guérin frères, 1746). For Deparcieux's arithmetic, see also Cem Behar and Yves Ducel, "L'Arithmétique politique d'Antoine Deparcieux," in *Arithmétique politique dans la France du XVIIIe siècle*, ed. Thierry Martin (Paris: INED, 2003), 147–61.

66 Emmanuel-Étienne Duvillard, *Recherches sur les rentes, les emprunts et les remboursemens* [...] (Paris: chez l'auteur, 1787).

67 See Cambon, *Rapport*, 3.

68 The notion of "political arithmetics" goes back to William Petty and his work with the same title of c. 1676, posthumously published in 1690. See Lars Behrisch, *Die Berechnung der Glückseligkeit: Statistik und Politik im späten Ancien Régime* (Ostfildern: Jan Thorbecke Verlag, 2016), 18. See also Will Derringer, *Calculated Values: Finance, Politics, and the Quantitative Age, 1688–1766* (Cambridge, MA: Cambridge University Press, 2018); Ted McCormick, *William Petty and the Ambitions of Political Arithmetic* (Oxford: Oxford University Press, 2009).

69 See Yuri Bondi, "The Double Emergence of the Modified Internal Rate of Return: The Neglected Work of Duvillard (1755–1832) in a Comparative Perspective," *The European Journal of the History of Economic Thought* 13, no. 3 (2006): 311–35, here 311–12, 314, 318.

70 See also Biondi, "The Double Emergence," 318.

71 Guy Thuillier, ed., *Le premier actuaire de France: Duvillard (1755–1832)* (Paris: Sans Coll, 1997), 12–13.

72 Duvillard, *Recherches*, 78–79.

73 Duvillard, *Recherches*, 80.

74 Duvillard, *Recherches*, 115.

75 See Biondi, "The Double Emergence," 314–15.

76 For explanation and translations, see Biondi, "The Double Emergence," 315–16.

77 Biondi, "The Double Emergence," 316.

78   See Duvillard, *Recherches*, Avertissement. See also Biondi, "The Double Emergence," 318.
79   "C'est avec toutes ces instructions que nous avons établi la valeur réelle des rentes viagères." See Cambon, *Rapport*, 3.
80   "Ils ont consacré une erreur sur laquelle il est très-important de l'éclairer, et que l'expérience et les calculs publiés par divers auteurs devraient avoir rectifiée depuis long-temps." Cambon, *Rapport*, 4.
81   "C'est ainsi qu'on se jouait de l'imbécillité de notre ancien gouvernement, et qu'on se préparait des fortunes énormes sans débourser un seul denier, mais seulement en prêtant un crédit." Cambon, *Rapport*, 4.
82   "Nous aurions pu vous citer encore des emprunts plus ruineux, en vous présentant les résultats de ceux faits en viager sur deux, trois ou quatre têtes; mais nous avons pensé qu'il suffirait que vous connusiez une partie des abus, pour que vous vous empressiez d'y apporter une réforme salutaire." Cambon, *Rapport*, 6.
83   The economists François Velde and David Weir emphasize that it was institutional and political circumstances, rather than individual errors, that led to the breakdown of the old regime. They contest a historiographic tradition that identifies the annuities and their allegedly excessive interest rates as disastrous policy errors. Instead, the authors assess that "money managers of the Old Regime were closely attuned to investor preferences and market conditions," and that contemporary markets did not seem to confirm that yields were too excessive, but traded annuities at similar prices to those the government offered. See Velde and Weir, "The Financial Market," 3–4, 36. These findings encourage us to rethink an over-hasty condemnation of the old regime's annuity practices, and remind us to explore further the impact of political structures and institutions on financial markets and decisions. However, certain questions remain. Why would arithmeticians and mathematicians throughout the eighteenth century attempt to reform the annuity practice and offer their expertise to policy makers, if nobody thought that there could be an alternative to the high interest rates on *rentes viagères*? Even if Duvillard's proposed reforms of life annuities were no more than a strategy to further his own career, how could he have expected to be successful if the government was not interested in reforming the practice, and planned to fall back on its default policy?
84   "Par cette opération, vous séparez le passé de l'avenir; vous connoîtrez dans tous les details le montant actuel de la dette viagère, et des extinctions qui ont eu lieu, soit par mort, émigration ou séquestre; vous retirerez le titre royal, et vous républicaniserez cette partie de la dette, comme vous avez fait pour la dette consolidée." Cambon, *Rapport*, 7.
85   "Cette opération a été sans contredit la plus belle qui se soit jamais faite en Finances. Ce fut le premier exemple d'une loi mathématiquement juste de l'union continue de la science au travail de l'administration. [...] Je me félicitais d'avoir rendu service à l'État par mes talens, et aux rentiers en les sauvant de la restitution [...] ou d'une diminution équivalente sur le capital de leurs rentes. Le désordre des finances ayant été une des principales causes de la révolution, le salut de la République exigeat une réforme de ces empruns usuraires en consolidant la dette publique." See Duvillard, "Souvenirs," in Thuillier, ed., *Le premier actuaire*, 29–43, quotation 38.
86   Cambon, *Rapport*, 65.
87   Cambon, *Rapport*, 16.
88   Mona Ozouf, "La Révolution française et la formation de l'homme nouveau," in *L'homme régénéré: Essais sur la Révolution française*, ed. Ozouf (Paris: Gallimard, 1989), 118.

Part II

Understanding, teaching, and learning about self-interest

3 Commercial sociability and the management of self-interest in Isaac de Pinto's letter on card-playing

Koen Stapelbroek

Introduction

The later seventeenth and eighteenth centuries saw the publication of a plethora of theories of self-interest. In conjunction with the main political issue of the time, that of "Jealousy of Trade" (the threat—and actual reality—that competition between states for trade could spark all-out warfare), the challenge for political writers and philosophers was to align a realistic minimal description of human nature's capacities to live in society with a prospective plan for international peace and general economic growth. The historical record of humankind and its institutions of justice, property, and inequality provided ample material to be absorbed into moral philosophical analyses of modern politics that, in turn, gave rise to numerous reformist visions, projects for peace, and commercial regulations.[1]

At the center of the range of philosophical, international political, economic, social, and institutional challenges lay the luxury debate. The topic of luxury, as it was understood at the time, concerned human passions and motivational mechanisms, governmental policies or regulations, and their social, economic, and political consequences both domestically and abroad.

Luxury was, essentially, historically contingent. It lived in the human imagination and could not be separated from subsistence, as humans were often inclined to sacrifice direct self-preservation to status, honor, or beauty, depending on circumstance. Likewise, no state could, for its own security and well-being, afford to focus its policies solely on subsistence goods and shelter in isolation from the competitive rivalry of production and trade of goods whose value was subject to the motions of the imagination. Any attempt to do so was bound to culminate not in a stable equilibrium and withdrawal from global markets and warfare, but in general poverty, revolution, depopulation, and vulnerability to foreign power. It was the desire for new goods that had caused a spirit of commerce to arise in the minds of Europe's rulers, traders, and small manufacturers, and this spirit drove the transformation of early modern societies as they adopted market-oriented practices that had to be accommodated by adequate policies.[2]

By the second half of the eighteenth century, the debate about modern commerce and its political management had evolved into discussions about the relation between public credit and the constitution and character of imaginary wealth in relation to financial markets. Still, the overarching format of the earlier luxury debate that connected state policies to moral philosophy remained. Virtually all political writers of the time were engaged in solving the puzzle of what moral motivational principles were internally consistent with sustained economic growth and global political power. The concept of "Machiavellism", as it was used at the time, in this regard served as a derogatory shorthand for a style of politics that was stuck in the past, in line with the political actions of Renaissance princes looking for territorial aggrandizement, and not suited to confront the specific challenges of modern commercial society. Especially after the publication of the *Anti-Machiavel* by Voltaire and Frederick the Great and the diffusion of that work in the 1740s, the charge of "Machiavellism" was also laid against political writers who were deemed not to have succeeded in solving the puzzle of modern politics and its underlying social psychology.[3]

This chapter focuses on the most sophisticated Dutch contributor to the luxury debate, the Amsterdam financier and political writer Isaac de Pinto. Among historians of economic thought, the name Pinto is associated with his defense of modern financial institutions in his *Traité de la circulation et du crédit*, but to contemporaries, he was known as the author of the *Essai sur le luxe*. It will be argued here that at the core of Pinto's *Traité* lay a theory of the commercial state whose historicity ran parallel to the contingencies of value and self-interest that he addressed in his minor writings, including one on the subject of the eighteenth-century fashion of card-playing. It is from these minor writings that both the nature and the political relevance of Pinto's theory of self-interest can be gleaned. Pinto's political thought formed a "system" of thought about the long-term common interest of states. Yet, the key to understanding his "system" is his idea of self-interest in relation to value.[4]

One way of engaging with self-interest and the theme of commercial sociability was through treating the theme by proxy.[5] Pinto did not solely defend the practice of credit and state debts that was part of his vision of international peace to take the sting out of "Jealousy of Trade," and in the process implicitly cast David Hume as a "Machiavellian." He also wrote small texts in which he analyzed commercial sociability and from which contemporaries would have understood Pinto's conception of self-interest. In his essay on luxury, he criticized writers such as Melon and Voltaire and theorized how individuals valued objects and how value in society could be consolidated or destroyed. Likewise, in his often-overlooked letter on card-playing, addressed to Diderot, he distinguished between the virtues of ancient and modern politics and defended card-playing as a moral interface for people's actions in the marketplace. Card-playing was frivolous, but it took the edge off human passions, just as self-interest in commercial society took the edge off virtue and vice and required a specific political mindset. Those who knew best how to manage their hand and successfully play the game of cards were

better attuned to what was beneficial to modern society than those who practiced virtue or old-fashioned patriotism. In this way, Pinto used card-playing
as a metaphor for commercial sociability and took the unusual position of
defending card-playing against its many eighteenth-century critics.

The point, however, was not about card-playing as such. By taking the
exceptional stance of defending card games, Pinto was doing something
comparable to his main work, in which he defended modern finance. By
standing up for card-playing as well as credit, and by sanctioning luxury from
a non-moralistic perspective, he framed and signaled his position as a political writer on the most important economic issues of the time, and attacked
the thinking of a number of his contemporaries. Writers such as Diderot,
or Hume, Voltaire, and Melon, whose understanding of the politics of modern commercial societies was imperfect, leaned in their different ways on
notions of ancient virtue—such as political friendship—or failed to understand credit; according to Pinto, they thus lapsed into a "Machiavellian,"
pre-modern, attitude to the value system of commercial society. In this
way, Pinto's playful critique of Diderot's judgment of the passions, applied
to card-playing, represented a fundamental attack on Diderot's political
thinking as inconsistent with the modern world and incapable of support-
ing the policies and institutions of eighteenth-century societies. For Pinto,
it was impossible to separate modern wealth from the financial mechanisms
of credit and the manners and attitudes of commercial society, which resembled those that pertained to playing games such as cards. Any continued
belief in virtue and friendship as key principles in modern politics, over-
looking the significance of credit and commercial self-interest, betrayed a
profound misunderstanding of the history of humankind.

The aim in this chapter, therefore, is to connect the realm of social
action and theoretical microanalysis of individual motives and self-interest
to the realms of financial, constitutional, and international politics. Pinto,
much like his British and Neapolitan contemporaries David Hume and
Ferdinando Galiani, was a fabulously well-connected figure both as a writer
and as a political actor. By placing him in his eighteenth-century context,
and by recognizing the challenge of understanding the requirements of
modern politics as key to the text on card-playing, it becomes possible to
see the wider polemical meaning of Pinto's argument in praise of frivolous
sociability and his critique of luxury, and also to understand their mutual
consistency. Moreover, it becomes possible to see the connection between
these moral sketches and Pinto's views on international trade, finance, and
the modern constitutional commercial state.

Dutch trade, modern wealth, and the commercial state

In Pinto's thinking, the development of new forms of wealth and that of the
modern state were two sides of the same coin. The former needed to be adequately supported by the latter, or would be destined to collapse. The first

occasion for Pinto's reflections on self-interest, luxury, and the creation
and destruction of value in commercial society was related to the rise and
subsequent decline of the Dutch trade republic. In his unpublished "Tribut
patriotique" to Stadholder William IV, from the late 1740s, Pinto sketched
how the development of American and Asian trade by European states and
their East India Companies had given rise to a system of global economic
development.[6] Appraising the general effects that modern wealth had on
the world and especially the well-being of European nations, Pinto argued
that something of a "revolution," in the classical sense of the word, had
taken place. Those philosophers and politicians who held that the gold and
silver that had entered Europe from the mines of Peru and Mexico had not
enriched Europe, but rather made subsistence goods and manual labor
more expensive, failed to see the bigger picture. The discovery of America
had set in motion a series of mechanisms that generated intercontinental
currents of capital and goods streams. Whatever criticisms could be made
of global trade, Pinto argued, it was still the case that Amsterdam's population had dramatically broken the barriers of its earlier existence and,
instead of 20,000 inhabitants, the city now sustained 220,000.[7] The "discovery" of global trade and the creation of new forms of wealth meant the world
was never going to look the same again.

This protracted revolutionary process had taken place in the space of the
past centuries, and it was crucial to understand the key role that the Dutch
state had played in it, especially in hindsight during the eighteenth century.
It was by way of the East India Company that Dutch traders had inadvert-
ently tapped into the "secret" of how a country with few natural resources
could survive and flourish in the modern world. Earlier, during the sixteenth
century, the Spanish monarchy had changed the scene of modern politics
by globalizing it in a more straightforward territorial sense. The primitive
acts of imperial expansion, which included the transport of gold and silver
to Europe, had, however, set off a chain of new developments through which
the modern commercial state took shape:

> The world seemed to enlarge under the power of the Spanish monarchy,
> and in many respects altered its form. A general opulence introduced by
> the gold and silver of the new world, the multitude of hands employed
> to supply the new wants and luxury of America, have created new
> means of subsistence. When the political machines, like the elements
> of commerce, grew more extensive, vast and complicated, they required
> springs stronger and more numerous. It became necessary to multiply
> the circulation of paper, by which the numerary wealth was increased.
> This was done as it were by instinct, but with fear and trembling. We
> scarce knew what we were doing, or for what reason. Gold and silver
> having lost three fourths of their value, a great quantity was required to
> represent so many things, and to keep the same machines going which
> money had set in motion. Means of all sorts were to be trebled. Without

an augmentation of the signs of value, which form an artificial wealth, neither commerce nor luxury could have subsisted. It is the discovery of America, which, by an extraordinary increase in the mass of gold and silver, has extended commerce, luxury, navigation, and manufactures. There required a greater rapidity of circulation; and by a singular paradox, as money multiplied and grew common, it required so many more signs to represent it. Public funds, paper, and stocks, became necessary, sometimes to absorb an excess of specie, and sometimes, like a sponge, to be pressed and give it back again.[8]

The discovery of America was not an immediate historical turning point, but would prove to be crucial in its long-term impact on global trade, the circulation of new goods, and the awakening of the imagination in the desire for these goods and the knock-on effect of creating new forms of production and exchange. The consequences could be seen in terms of growing wealth in Europe alongside the concomitant disastrous effects for indigenous populations in the development of imperial exploitation and colonialism. Yet, Pinto's real focus was not on the new economic realities in isolation, but on their interaction with politics, especially on how the new commercial reality helped to shape new state forms and institutions, and a sense of how the requirements for adequate policy-making were altering.

In this regard, it was absolutely crucial to recognize that the Dutch Republic was not just a naïve early modern trade republic, like the Italian city-states of the Renaissance, in which commerce had taken the place of agriculture as the primary sector and where it upheld an "upside-down economy." Trade, in the case of the Dutch Republic, was also related to the development of the modern state. It was the manner in which the nascent Dutch state had accommodated the functioning of new capital markets and provided a secure framework for investments in proto-colonial commercial endeavors that, in its turn, had guaranteed the state its political independence and promoted the global circulation of funds. The form and actions of the state had—in a way—followed its functions and shaped itself to fit the interest of the nation. In fact, Pinto observed that the Dutch had neglected to further cultivate their original advantage, particularly following the "*facheux*" Peace of Utrecht, when Dutch politicians failed to adapt the fiscal, financial, and commercial structures of the state to the evolving requirements of the international commercial system. And this was why by the 1740s, according to Pinto, a wholesale range of reforms were necessary to restore the Dutch state and thereby its balancing role in inter-state relations.[9]

There was something almost normative about Pinto's argument about the economic imperative to modern politics. If global trade managed to feed so many people and was capable of sustaining population growth, there was a "duty" to get the politics right. The alternative, of rejecting modern wealth, was not an option. This was so, not just for political purposes (a state that retreated from economic expansion and population growth might easily be conquered by an ambitious neighboring state aspiring to hegemony), but also for moral reasons. In line with a Dutch tradition of thought about the growth of wealth and trade in the course of the Dutch Revolt, Pinto echoed the trope that there was a divine mission or purpose to the alignment of trade with the moral goals of humankind. At an earlier period, the Dutch had wondered about their predicament and searched for models in the history of humanity, such as the Hebrew Republic, with which to compare themselves.[10] Those original ponderings, about being a chosen nation or instrument of God, had transformed into a set of moral precepts that were key ingredients in the transition from earlier discourses of natural law to political economy.

Thus, Pinto brought a traditional Dutch discourse about trade and state development into the general debate of the mid-eighteenth century about how to create a durable European system of commerce and "perpetual peace."[11] Yet, Pinto's interests lay not in praising the achievements of the Dutch state, but in building up a general perspective on the politics of modern wealth. Pinto's object of analysis here was the state, and the degree to which states should conform to a certain standard or set of dynamic requirements in order to preserve global trade and peace among the world's dominant nations. In other words, global trade and the circulation of goods created *nouvelles valeurs*, new objects of valuation, exchange, and production, that had to be made sustainable by embedding them in political infrastructures within and between states in order for people to enjoy and further cultivate them.

In his main work, the *Traité de la circulation et du crédit*, which was first published in 1771, but had circulated in Paris and London for around a decade previously, Pinto sketched the progress of the modern state's ability to manage trade, public debts, and credit. The connections that thus arose between "circulation" and "credit" acted as checks to the development of relations between states, which had consequences for public borrowing in peace and in wartime and on the development of exchange relationships between states and their relative competitive strengths in international trade. Pinto thus noted, both in his *Traité* and in his *Essai sur le luxe*, that "the public funds are a realized alchemy" and presented credit as a solvent of inequality and agent of justice. The realm of the financial imaginary assisted in keeping the physical and the directly useful on track.[12] If all commercial states subjected themselves to these mechanisms of credit and its institutions, the realm of the imaginary could be a very real promotor of peace.

The politics of luxury and the management of pleasure

In the wake of a bankruptcy during the Seven Years' War, Pinto had left Amsterdam for Paris, where he quickly built up a political and intellectual network and was involved in the peace negotiations at Fontainebleau.[13]

These years, in which he also first circulated parts of what would become his *Traité*,[14] also saw the publication of a few small works by Pinto, including a text on luxury.[15]

The starting point of Pinto's *Essai sur le luxe* was that luxury had always been criticized in history as a moral danger to the state, and yet recently had been excessively praised for its capacities to enhance economic productivity, stimulate population growth, increase circulation of goods, and level material inequalities. The standard-bearers of the latter argument were Melon, Voltaire, and Hume. The problem, in Pinto's words, was that it was impossible to "accept this system without large restrictions" and that luxury still needed to be "methodically analyzed" to understand its political effects.[16]

As part of his general philosophy of human nature, Pinto saw an evolving interplay between the realms of the physical and the moral.[17] The key concept was error: that is, the natural conflation of the consumption of physically useful objects with the sentiment of pleasure from the consumption of luxury objects. Humans, Pinto explained in a manuscript from the early 1740s, were capable of productive moral self-deceit in the field of commerce when they attributed, through interaction between them, new imagined values to previously less useful things, and nourished desires to own these items. Luxury, thus understood, was the product of error, though not in the sense of moral depravity. Luxury consumption, along with new social attitudes including *amour propre* and vanity, was a sign of a developing social system of opinion and exchange that required new forms of accommodation in order not to collapse.[18] For Pinto, shared error in and of itself essentially increased social integration. If natural self-interested behavior cultivated ideas of the imagination beyond the level of self-preservation and subsistence, it was not the case that these were artificial desires whose utility existed purely by reference to their physical effects. They had a substance, meaning, and utility in themselves that needed to be recognized and sustained. Society was more than the sum of its needs. Pinto also noted that the moral quality of motives and the social effects of spending tended to correlate. Regardless of, and often contrary to, moral precepts, people were capable of letting their judgments of value inform their market behavior in such a way that it gave rise to a just distribution of goods. Pinto thus reconciled his view of morality as grounded in error with the idea that people's own intuitions about good and bad usually were correct.[19]

This was a far cry from the moral relativism that the modern appraisal of luxury by Melon and Voltaire tended toward. Even Saint-Lambert, the editor of the *Encyclopédie* entry on "Luxe," had copied from Forbonnais, the intended author of the Luxury entry, and indeed indirectly from Melon, that "luxury is the use which we make of riches and of industry, in order to procure an agreeable existence."[20] Melon had defined it as the "business of the State to make an Advantage of" luxury.[21] Luxury was the key to economic growth and should be cultivated, explored, and exploited. Sharing this perspective of luxury as a useful vice, Saint-Lambert felt it was important to avoid "attacking luxury" fiscally or by other redistributive means and thereby risk a relapse into simplicity. Saint-Lambert offered as his solution that the task of politics was to contain the socially divisive aspects of commercial society through an "implicit reform" of new moral codes that would promote the recirculation of capital and enhance productivity.[22] In this way, the incorporation of new kinds of property, such as national debts—which Saint-Lambert valued very negatively[23]—into dangerously urbanized modern states might, he hoped, be kept from upsetting the political equilibrium. For Saint-Lambert, in other words, politically controlled or limited greed was good. It conspired with states to make the world go round.

For Pinto, luxury was an altogether different phenomenon. Human nature was not greedy, anti-social, and requiring correction, but fundamentally prone to error. But this was exactly what gave humanity the capacity to develop into increasingly hyper-social societies as the edifice of shared artificial values and desires rose. The political challenge of luxury, from this perspective, lay not in balancing the passions, but in managing the moral structures of exchange, value, and esteem. The precarious character of commercial society itself was what made luxury a danger. Wealth was built upon error, imagination, and self-interest, but "commerce and trade degenerate often into a game of chance."[24] Pinto did not call for a return to simplicity and frugality, even though he emphasized that the addictive character of excessive luxury was the prime cause of the decadence of states.[25] Politics, for Pinto, was the subtle management of the human imagination, not the exploitation or the patriotic balancing of human selfish weakness.

Pinto's conception of luxury not only resisted the neo-Augustinian notion of sinful human nature that the proponents of luxury had turned into a principle of public policy, but also led to different antidotes. The direct way to take the sting out of luxury would be to implement new social codes that made wealth accumulation and reinvestment, not spending, the object of admiration. But such projects carried the inherent risk of tending to "tyranny." A more promising approach that was "easier in practise than one imagined and prodigiously useful" lay in the legal creation of personal spending regimes to be managed by banks issuing loans to the profligate victims of luxury in order to save their honor and credit and prevent social capital leakages. Banks should not be egged on to drive individuals into debt, but be forced to shelter them from overspending and harming themselves and society. Similar to this idea of banking regulation in the wider interest of society, Pinto in the late 1740s had proposed to Stadholder William IV the establishment of a national lottery. If people were naturally inclined to gamble, it was best to place their urges under the control of the state and let the profits fall to the state. This way one could "turn vice into virtue."[26]

Beyond modern machiavellism: Credit and the enlightenment's blindspots on the prospects for peace

The manner in which Pinto understood luxury to be a fundamentally different phenomenon from how most of his contemporaries understood it runs parallel to his take on the use of modern financial institutions, credit, and state debts. Among the proponents of luxury, Pinto singled out David Hume as a worthy object of a sympathetic critique on the topic of finance.

Hume's approach to "Jealousy of Trade" in his essay of that title was highly similar to the message of Pinto's *Letter on the Jealousy of Commerce*. Hume famously criticized "our narrow and malignant politics" designed to "reduce all our neighbouring nations to [...] sloth and ignorance" and instead preferred to "pray [...] as a BRITISH subject [...] for the flourishing commerce of GERMANY, SPAIN, ITALY, and even FRANCE itself."[27] In other essays, he criticized British national rivalry and depicted France as a civilized monarchy. Much like Hume, Pinto argued that Britain and France:

> are formed to esteem each other, and to live in peace; yet, unfortunately, they quarrel about supposed interests, which at the bottom perhaps are misunderstood. Jealousy of commerce, and competition for power, create enmity between nations as well as between individuals. [...] If princes could be persuaded, that the real interests of commercial powers do not clash (as I shall endeavour to show hereafter) peace and the happiness of mankind might possibly be established on a durable foundation.[28]

Later editions and translations of the *Traité de la circulation et du crédit* contained in an appendix the *Lettre sur la jalousie du commerce*, in which Pinto related the eighteenth-century political idea of a project for perpetual peace to the realm of trade politics and finance. It is crucial to recognize that the *Traité* was written to confront this same topic, peace through financial politics, not public finance per se. This is why Pinto remarked, in its introduction, that between Hume and himself, there was "friendship and affection" and that their political writings did "both aim at the same object."[29]

Pinto agreed that Hume might "be right in a certain sense, when he foretells, that either the nation must destroy public credit, or public credit will destroy the nation." But Hume was crucially and fundamentally mistaken, Pinto suggested, when he considered the consequences of a voluntary bankruptcy for Britain, given its nature as a commercial society. The "natural death" of public credit was not a matter of sacrificing the interests of "thousands [...] to the safety of millions." The damage done to the nation through the general recession that would thus be caused would be much greater than Hume envisaged and, in the words of István Hont, amount to his own "worst-case scenario (the loss of independence through conquest by foreign powers)."[30]

However, this was not where the argument stopped. Pinto's critique of Hume's voluntary bankruptcy plan was not just a disagreement on the politics of public finance, but a comprehensive criticism of Hume's understanding of commercial society. Pinto effectively put Hume in the category of the "Machiavellians," political writers whose logic of commercial society was inconsistent and who conflated ancient and modern techniques of government:[31]

> Mr. Hume observed, that multiplying the representative signs lowered the value of specie. But he did not consider the necessity of having such signs to represent the multitude of things, which the abundance of gold and silver has in some measure rendered necessary. Let us new model our manners; let us go twenty centuries back; let us reduce human nature to its primitive condition; let us banish those factitious wants which we have changed into necessities; let us be philosophers, and with Diogenes reject the earthen vessel, and drink out of the hollow of the hand; let us be poor and virtuous, and Mr. Hume's principles may then be applied. But since there is no likelihood of such an alteration for some centuries, we may as well pursue our course, and endeavour to correct abuses. [...] We must not attempt to govern a corrupted people by the same laws which suit a virtuous people.[32]

Pinto inverted Hume's opinions on luxury, wage levels, and public credit. Hume, the excessive defender of luxury, as Pinto had exposed him in his *Essai sur le luxe*, was an "ancient" in disguise despite himself. Hume was inconsistent in his thinking about the integration of new artificial desires and new modes of property and their concomitant wage level effects. It was impossible to have Hume's luxury and high wages (which Hume himself struggled with), and *not* have modern finance. Pinto stressed that public credit was not a problem of commercial society, but a core manifestation of its full development. For this reason, Pinto called it a "necessity." Public finance was badly understood, badly managed, and therefore a potential inlet for abuse. Yet, to suggest that state debts might be eradicated was bad political reasoning that presaged a lapse back to antiquity.

The contexts of Pinto's letter to Diderot: The moral philosophy of the *philosophes*

When Pinto published his essay on luxury, its companion piece in many ways (although it was published only in 1768, and presumably written at The Hague on May 19, 1767) was his *Letter On Card-Playing addressed to Monsieur Diderot*. Diderot would meet up with Pinto (and people in his circle such as van Rijklof Michael van Goens) during his journey to the United Provinces in 1773–74 and referred to him in his *Voyage en Hollande* as "ce juif Pinto." A story, possibly told to Diderot by Pinto, about promiscuity and marital prostitution and the actions of the Dutch police in maintaining public morality made it into Diderot's *Le Neveu de Rameau*, where the name of the protagonist, a certain Vanderveld, was changed to "le juif." Diderot mentioned in his *Voyage en Hollande* that Pinto, whom he knew from his time in Paris, was still liable to get in trouble with the bailiffs and also recounted in a letter to Mme d'Épinay that Pinto, despite his age, was still, as he had been in Paris, "fort libertin."[33]

The reference to Pinto's reputation in Paris refers to the early 1760s, when Pinto lived in rue Coquillière, where he received a personal letter in response to his *Apologie pour la nation juive* from Voltaire.[34] While the literature relating Pinto to Diderot and Voltaire has focused mostly on the aspect of "libertinage" involved in Diderot's encounter with Pinto in the United Provinces and the defense of Jewishness in Pinto's *Apologie pour la nation juive* aimed against Voltaire, the analysis of the intellectual confrontations involved in these texts has often been ignored or been underdeveloped.[35]

A first context in which to place Pinto's letter to Diderot is that of the publication history of the *Encyclopédie*. Although Pinto addressed his letter to Diderot, it was never in reality a private communication, but a public text that followed fairly soon after the publication of Volumes VIII to XVII of the *Encyclopédie* in December 1765. Other than the article "Luxe" (IX: 763–71), by Saint-Lambert, which structurally ran parallel to Pinto's *Essai sur le luxe*, but conceptualized luxury as a totally different phenomenon from Pinto, Volume VIII included an entry by Diderot on "Jouer" (VIII: 884–88). Diderot concluded "Jouer" by stating that: "The passion for the game is one of the most fatal by which one can be possessed. Man is so violently agitated by play that he can no longer bear any other occupation."[36] Diderot's short entry "Jeu" in the same volume (VIII: 531–32) portrayed games as politically dangerous phenomena in all periods of history. While "the Lacedemonians were the only ones who completely banished games from their republic," it was the connection to vanity and avarice, also noted by Montesquieu, that made people prone to the double misfortune of being unfortunate in love and in games, as described in the twenty-third of Aristaenetus's *Love Epistles*.[37] Associating games with gallantry, Diderot argued that the damage that games could do to people and society needed to be stopped by wise laws that made people spend their time more usefully and that protected them from themselves. Earlier, in Volume II, the entry "Cartes (Jeux)" (II: 711–15), which is famous for its description of the fabrication of gaming cards and the accompanying illustrations, had included a few indications on the history of games. It did so with reference to the Jesuit Claude-François Ménestrier, who traced the history of the specific game of card-playing back to the time of the late Middle Ages and the reign of Charles VI of France. Diderot's later translation of Edward Moore's *The Gamester* continued his negative assessment of games as destructive of society and individual well-being.[38]

Pinto did not engage with the various entries by Diderot in the *Encyclopédie*, but instead contrasted his own ideas with those set out in one of Diderot's earliest publications. A second context for understanding Pinto's letter, then, is the moral philosophy of Diderot and potentially of the *philosophes* more generally. The one long quotation in Pinto's letter was taken from the opening sentences and first paragraphs of Diderot's *Pensées philosophiques*, published anonymously by Diderot in 1746 as a critique of Blaise Pascal's *Pensées* and an appraisal of the passions. Diderot, who had published an adaptation of Shaftesbury's *Inquiry concerning Virtue and Merit* in 1745, and whose *Pensées philosophiques* engaged with Jansenist neo-Augustinianism, wrote an addition to his *Pensées* in 1762, which circulated in the following years. Diderot's *Pensées* are mostly seen as an expression of his enlightened approach to religion, yet to Pinto they represented an engagement with sin, human nature, and self-interest.[39] For Pinto, Diderot's highlighting of the passions in relation to great virtues and vices, true friendship, and the sublime, did not form a useful foundation for the development of a moral analysis that fit with the self-interest of commercial society; it was too heroically republican. Relatedly, Pinto's *Précis des arguments contre les Matérialistes*, of 1774, in a similar way criticized d'Holbach's *Système de la nature* as overly obsessed with overcoming the philosophical idols of the past and incapable of providing a basis for dealing with the challenges of the second half of the eighteenth century.[40]

A third context for Pinto's letter is specifically political and international. At the time, Diderot and other French *philosophes* were the darlings of Frederick the Great's Prussian project to put the Enlightenment on a pedestal and justify his political schemes around the time of the Seven Years' War. Frederick was seeking large-scale domestic monarchical reform as well as an international redrawing of the map of Europe, and his collaboration with Voltaire on the *Anti-Machiavel*, and his invasion of Silesia, had turned Diderot, Voltaire, D'Argenson, and others into emblems of Frederick's Prussian politics. This was not to say the appreciation was always mutual: Diderot deliberately skipped Berlin on his trip via the United Provinces to St. Petersburg in 1774, calling Frederick "a great man [but] a mean soul."[41] Also, the thinking of the *philosophes* and the Prussian monarch often contrasted sharply and Frederick was as suspicious of materialism and any labels or concepts that had anti-authoritarian connotations as the *philosophes* were of Frederick's belligerent urges. Yet, during the 1750s and 1760s, the Prussian association was very much on the minds of a number of leading French statesmen who waged war against the political and intellectual ideas of these *philosophes* and their political allies through public opinion campaigns run though the French foreign ministry.[42]

Pinto's letter on card-playing to Diderot can also be placed in this context. It was not in any way a direct political attack on Diderot, the *philosophes*, or Frederick II, but did nonetheless contribute to the intellectual debate on commerce, morality, and the history of humankind. As such, the letter was a sympathetic critique of the foundations of Diderot's politics, similar to how Pinto's *Essai sur le luxe* criticized Hume, Melon, and Voltaire. As a review of the text in *The Monthly Review* put it:

Mr. de Pinto views the amusement of card-playing with the eye of a philosopher and a politician; and in examining the subject, endeavours to discover what influence this universal mode of pass-time hath on the manners and morals of mankind, in these later ages, – in the European part of the world, particularly.[43]

A final context of Pinto's letter to Diderot was the debate on card-playing (*jeux*) of the time, which was generally understood as a foil for a rather technical debate on the moral and philosophical transformations of commercial society, and in the end connected to rival positions in politics.

Here, as in the debate on credit and state debts, Pinto rejected the mainstream view by presenting himself as an advocate of games, seeing them as representative of the social and economic instincts that people had developed in commercial society. These instincts could not be constrained without destroying modernity as such. During most of the eighteenth century, the previous iconography of morality, gains, losses, and fortune involved in game-playing was simply continued and extended to wider cultural criticisms of conviviality and libertinage.[44]

In praise of frivolity: Card-playing as a mirror for commercial politics

Pinto's letter to Diderot was a moral philosophical provocation to the *philosophes*. It argued that the real history of humankind and progress had little to do with "Enlightenment" and deist and materialist outlooks on reason and the passions, and that the *philosophes*' continued reliance on histories written by Jesuits blanked out the proper recognition of the development of commercial sociability out of imagination, contemporaneously to the development of new goods and values in Europe.

At the outset of his letter to Diderot, Pinto made clear that the topic of his text was not just card-playing, but the history of humankind and the different ways in which this history might be understood and analyzed. In line with his perspective on the history of commerce, circulation, and the creation of *nouvelles valeurs*, Pinto declared that: "Upon the while, it appears to me that human-kind (I mean, that small part of it which occupies our Europe) is rather altered for the better."[45] Pinto's main argument was that new modes of social interaction were conducive to passions that did not fit directly with the structures of public political rationality:

Before the epoch of cards, there was less union between the sexes; I mean, they were less together, less in society or company; the men were more so: the meetings in clubs, taverns were more in vogue; convivial drinking formed more connexions, more friendship; the heaviness of time on hand, which is one of the most powerful causes of the unfolding of human perfectibility, excited men to cultivate their talents, to employ themselves, to study, to labor at the arts, to cabal, to project conspiracies: politics were the subject of the conversations which leisure, and a kind of necessity for passing away the time, produced; they censured the government; they complained of it, conspired against it; and there were on such occasions, friends to be found, who might be trusted: the great virtues and the great vices were more common.[46]

It was for this reason that Pinto disagreed with Diderot. From Pinto's point of view, Diderot's moral philosophical perspective was too republican, old-fashioned, and Machiavellian. The source for Pinto's disagreement with Diderot was a specific one.

Diderot's *Pensées philosophiques*, as quoted by Pinto, had suggested that "there is nothing but the passions, and the very great passions too, that can elevate the soul to great things."[47] Diderot had argued that the passions in their unmitigated form were the lifeblood of political "virtue," "friendship," and "the greatness and energy of nature."[48] Instead, Pinto replied, card-playing "has prepared the human head and heart for receiving the impressions which the progress of knowledge, and of the new lights thrown upon things might operate on the government, and on manners."[49] As Pinto explained:

> The magic of card-playing forms the common point of concourse of almost all the passions in miniature. They all, as one may say, find in it their nourishment. Everything indeed is microscopical, and more illusive than the common illusion. A confused idea of good and bad luck presents itself: vanity itself finds its account in it: play seems to establish a false show of equality among the players: it is the call that assembles, in society, the most discordant, the most incongruous individuals; avarice and ambition are its movements; the universal taste for pleasure flatters itself with procuring its satisfaction by this amusement; [...] the sphere of our passions becomes contracted, concentered, and confined to a petty orbit; [...] And it is from the fermentation of the great passions that there commonly results more evil than of good, humankind has gained more than it has lost. There are no longer great virtues, but then we do not see so many great crimes as formerly: assassinations, poison, and all the horrors of a civil war, are incompatible with the state of a nation, in which the men and women lose so great a part of their time at cards.[50]

Card-playing, in this manner, performed similar functions to credit.[51] It brought out one's actual status (one's hand, if you will), or the effects of one's actions. And in that way, it held up a mirror to the self that helped to shape individuals' self-knowledge and reframe their appropriate behavior in modern society. Card-playing, like credit, channeled human emotions and motivations in a society in which the rules of success and failure, for individuals as well as on an aggregate level, be it economic or political, were different from those that had determined life in earlier times.

In fact, Pinto suggested that card-playing and modern politics had grown up together. It was actually hard to define the direction of causality between them. Using Diderot's scattered observations on the history of card playing in the *Encyclopédie* article "Cartes" for his own purposes, Pinto located the beginning of the rise both of modern monarchical civilization and of card-playing to the time of the reign of Charles VI of France in the second half of the fourteenth century. If in this period European culture started to alter itself, the famous inventions and institutional and political shifts had got more than their fair share of attention, while "there may be found a cause subaltern, obscure, and imperceptible, which acting more universally, incessantly withal, may have served sometimes as a spur, sometimes as a curb to the others."[52] If a commercial culture emerged across Europe, this was not by design, but through a chain of events and a "concurrence of many causes" that lay outside of anyone's control.[53]

Furthermore, if commercial morality, such as developed in early modern times into the eighteenth century, offered new possibilities for people to express themselves, it also required politics to adjust its principles. As Pinto argued in his *Letter to Diderot on Card-playing*, "both in the natural and moral state of man"—the latter was built upon the former—"there results a new system of manners, temper, and constitution."[54] Card-playing had assisted in civilizing human manners and the comprehensive way in which it spoke to the human passions was representative of the progress of, as well as the dangers to, commercial society. It made no sense to try to separate the virtues and vices of commercial society. What mattered in comparing previous compounds of human emotions to the present was that "humankind has gained more than it has lost" and that while states could rely on patriotism no longer, the self-deceptive conditioning of the passions made humans fit for commercial society, which needed an altogether different style of politics. In "my system," Pinto reasoned, "the infatuation of a frivolous amusement, which deceives and eludes the effect of the passions [...] means the virtues are often lopped of their growth; but then the vices [...] are still more."[55] This was the essence of commercial liberty that still had to be thought through properly to "operate on the government, and on manners."[56] While the modern history of humankind had seen three crucial revolutions (the demise of feudalism, the discovery of America, and the invention of printing and progress of arts and sciences), which together conspired to the rise of civil liberty, population growth, and "a greater equality among man," the fourth was still incomplete. Even if "spiritual Machiavelism," the "abuse of the excellence of religion," had lost its supporters, there remained many "errors political and moral" that still had to be "exhausted" before human civilization would be securely lifted to a higher level.[57]

Referring to the as yet unpublished manuscripts that became the *Traité de la circulation et du crédit* and the *Letter on the Jealousy of Commerce*,[58]

Pinto declared, "I flatter myself that I have somewhere in my writings, demonstrated that the interests of states, well-understood, do not thwart each other, and I am persuaded that this is the same with private individuals."[59] If this started to be recognized more generally, it would support a more comprehensive understanding of modern politics; in fact, Pinto already observed that "even political Machiavelism begins to sink in its credit with princes."[60] And, in the final instance, he mused about a future in which these insights would become obvious and lead humankind to "favorably invert Horace's *Ætas parentum pejor avis, &c.*"[61] Pinto thus connected his positive appraisal of card-playing, as an index of how the values of commercial society had developed and needed to be politically accommodated to the concept of Machiavellism. As long as politics by European rulers was conducted based on a zero-sum "Jealousy of Trade" basis, it would remain fundamentally out of sync with how individuals in commercial societies operated, interacted, and created wealth out of their imagination and imposition of value onto goods. Pinto's message was ambivalent in this regard. He noted that most European monarchs had seen the light and that "political Machiavelism," the direct drive to go to war for territorial aggrandizement and glory, had begun to wane. Yet, it was the more fundamental "spiritual Machiavelism" that took the form of "errors political and moral," which still had to be "exhausted." Among those errors were the failure to see luxury for what it was, and to recognize the logical necessity of credit and modern finance for both modern wealth and international stability, and the preference on the part of Diderot for the passion of manly patriotic virtue over strategically playful self-interest. Pinto's point was lightly presented but highly critical and serious. If the figureheads and famous thinkers of the so-called Enlightenment really wanted to have a positive effect on the history of humankind, they had better rethink their moral philosophy and their historical understanding, and let go of moralistic intuitions and preconceptions that no longer fit with reality.

Ironically, it was the negative judgment of the contemporary translator of Pinto's text into English that hammered home the political point, which Pinto himself had left more implicit and up to the reader's interpretation. Defending the traditional set of republican virtues and rejecting Pinto's defense of card-playing, the translator contrasted "false patriotism," "false interest," "luxury," effeminacy, societies "overwhelmed with debt," and the "horrors" of Augustan Rome, with "the great virtues, on which alone the happiness of society can solidly rest" and "those stern and many virtues which were the genuine guardians of Roman liberty."[62] Apart from whether card-playing played any role or could be symbolic of the recent changes in the structure of social interactions, the translator questioned "in the totality":

> whether the human blood has lately flowed in lesser streams? Half a million of lives recently sacrificed in Germany, to the most false and futile of all motives, all paradox a-part, seem unhappily to prove that men, may be at once frivolous and sanguinary, ridiculous, and deplorable.[63]

If Pinto stopped well short of suggesting that his friend Diderot and the *philosophes* had blood on their hands and simply presented his argument to Diderot as a paradox, his translator put the matter back where it belonged and related the imperfection of modern politics to the bloodshed of the Seven Years' War. The question, put in a crudely simplistic form, was whether the management of modern societies required a revival of classical republican virtues, or a comprehensive, thoroughgoing redevelopment of politics in line with the newly developed social attitudes. Pinto's oeuvre as a whole—along with his actions as a diplomat, investor, and policy advisor—was primarily aimed against those who thought they were in the second camp, but whose views were nonetheless influenced by remnants of the politics of the past. In the face of the challenges of managing commercial society, modern politics could seem paradoxical and counterintuitive. One major aspect was the impact that commercial sociability had on the relation between the state and the value judgments of individuals. Pinto believed that writers including Melon, Hume, Voltaire, and Diderot were not yet tuned into the new ways in which self-interest created value and that had to be politically accommodated in order to prevent economic stagnation, financial crises, revolutions, and violent international conflict. And Diderot's rejection of card-playing as morally corrupt served as an example for Pinto to make this point.

Conclusion: "Harnessing" the passions?

What can one conclude from all of this in light of the theme of self-interest, as it is approached in this volume? It was no coincidence that it was a development economist with an impressively wide intellectual vision of politics who opened up the field of thinking about passions and interests in the later twentieth century. Albert Hirschman's *The Passions and the Interests* was highly influential in suggesting that the recognition of different sets of values lay at the foundation of thinking about what became capitalism before the dawn of the nineteenth century.[64] Likewise, the most refined eighteenth-century theories of self-interest and commercial sociability were put together by writers who are now often considered to have been political economists. These writers, of whom Isaac de Pinto was just one, were obsessed with how post-Roman feudal Europe gave rise to new forms of wealth, global trade, and a different kind of society and how Europe's dominant commercial monarchies conquered the world through economic exploitation. Hirschman recognized clearly that these eighteenth-century writers, who analyzed this historical transformation, generally saw human passions as the basic material for attitudes of self-interest and the motivational characteristics that helped explain the rise of global trade and modern economic exchange. Moreover, Hirschman did so within a context in which economic development was often subject to disciplinary reductionism and twinned with political ideology.[65] While Hirschman's engagement with eighteenth-century ideas of self-interest is historically most interesting when placed in its own context (of American and Western global trade politics and the geopolitics of the Cold War), it would be a mistake to adopt Hirschman's own schematic from the 1970s as the basis for understanding the eighteenth-century debates on passions and commercial society. One reason is that Hirschman's schematic was an experimental starting point (as he himself emphasized in the Preface) and does not represent the full range and differentiation of ideas that were developed at the time. The idea that the passions, famously, could be "harnessed" represents not one or a few, but a plethora of views of how this "harnessing" was done and which combinations of conditions and institutional settings over time had given rise to it. In order to understand the full variety of how eighteenth-century writers discussed the passions and their conversion into new social and cultural forms, one should not focus solely on the idea of interest, which implicitly assumes that the core of the transformation can be captured by a micro-perspective of economic action. The most promising approach to recapture the debates of the eighteenth century and make them useful for our time may not lie in the attempted reduction of historical change to an idea of interest, however refined. This was also clearly not Hirschman's project or intention. Instead, rather than focusing on the canonical texts on economic issues by a limited number of famous writers, one may learn more from widening the object of study. A further step toward the reconstruction of rival views on market society, to use Hirschman's phrase, would be to focus more precisely on ideas about the passions in relation to historical change. To do so, one could include the minor writings by the most sophisticated thinkers of the time, reconstruct their debate through comparison of their ideas and understanding of their mutual criticisms and try to appreciate the subtle differences. Going back to the eighteenth century and the original sources, also and *especially* those small curious works on card-playing, gallantry, love, social habits, cultural forms, and religious ideas might open up new perspectives and fault lines and add analytical clarity. This may not seem the shortest road to understanding the prehistory of capitalism, but then again, it might be.

Notes

1 For the best overview, see István Hont, *Jealousy of Trade: International Competition and the Nation-State in Historical Perspective* (Cambridge, MA: Harvard University Press, 2005), esp. 1–156.

2 For the range and development of the luxury debate, see István Hont, "Luxury and Commerce," in *The Cambridge History of Eighteenth-Century Political Thought*, ed. Mark Goldie and Robert Wokler (Cambridge: Cambridge University Press, 2006), 379–418.

3 For the context of Voltaire and Frederick II's *Anti-Machiavel*, see Isaac Nakhimovsky, "The Enlightened Prince and the Future of Europe: Voltaire and Frederick the Great's Anti-Machiavel of 1740," in *Commerce and Peace in the Enlightenment*, ed. Béla Kapossy, Isaac Nakhimovsky and Richard Whatmore (Cambridge: Cambridge University Press, 2017), 44–77. For the longer

history of 'Anti-Machiavellism' and some eighteenth-century charges of inherent 'Machiavellism' levied at 'anti-Machiavellians', see Ioannis D. Evrigenis and Mark Somos, "Wrestling with Machiavelli," *History of European Ideas* 37, no. 2 (2011): 85–93; and the other essays in that special issue on "Anti-Machiavellian Machiavellism."

4 For a comprehensive account of Pinto's life and career, see Ida Nijenhuis, *Een Joodse Philosophe: Isaac de Pinto (1717–1787)* (Amsterdam: NEHA, 1992); and José L. Cardoso and António de Vasconcelos Nogueira, "Isaac de Pinto (1717–1787): An Enlightened Economist and Financier," *History of Political Economy* 37 (2005): 264–92. For this "system," see Koen Stapelbroek, "From Jealousy of Trade to the Neutrality of Finance: Isaac de Pinto's 'System' of Luxury and Perpetual Peace," in *Commerce and Peace in the Enlightenment*, ed. Kapossy, Nakhimovsky and Whatmore, 78–109.

5 It was common at the time to write short recreational pieces on light subjects and use them to approach major philosophical themes. To give one example that fits with Pinto's letter on card-playing, Ferdinando Galiani wrote a text on gallantry and experimented with the idea as a replacement for earlier Christian moral values in society: see Koen Stapelbroek, *Love, Self-Deceit and Money: Commerce and Morality in the Early Neapolitan Enlightenment* (Toronto: University of Toronto Press, 2008), 133–35.

6 Ets Haim - Livraria Montezinos Amsterdam, BEH 48A19 (nos. 7, 9). Isaac de Pinto, "Tribut patriotique présenté avec le plus profond respect à Son Altesse Sérénissime Monseigneur le Prince d'Orange et de Nassau," particularly the "Essai sur le credit" and the "Essai sur les finances en général," Nationaal Archief Den Haag (hereafter NADH), 2.21.005.39, (Gogel collection), inv. 165; see also "Reflexions politiques, au sujet d'une augmentation de taxe qu'on propose de mettre sur chaque action de la Compagnie des indes orientales sous le titre d'amptgeld," NADH, 1.10.29 (Fagel collection), inv. 2204.

7 Pinto, *Tribut patriotique*, n.p.

8 Isaac de Pinto, *An Essay on Circulation and Credit: in Four Parts; and a Letter on the Jealousy of Commerce* (London: J. Ridley, 1774), 29–30. Originally published as Isaac de Pinto, *Traité de la circulation et du crédit: [...] & suivi d'une lettre sur la jalousie du commerce, où l'on prouve que l'intérêt des puissances commerçantes ne se croise point* (Amsterdam: M.M. Rey, 1771). References are to the English translation.

9 Pinto, *Tribut patriotique*, n.p.

10 See: Wyger Velema and Arthur Weststeijn, eds., *Ancient Models in the Early Modern Republican Imagination* (Leiden: Brill 2017); Koen Stapelbroek, 'The History of Trade and the Legitimacy of the Dutch Republic. In Histories of Trade as Histories of Civilization, edited by Antonella Alimento and Aris Della Fontana, Basingstoke: Palgrave MacMillan, 2021/forthcoming.

11 This tradition of analyzing Dutch trade as an embryonic case for the regulation of international commerce, inequality, and finance is the object of the present author's forthcoming study, *Carthage Must Be Preserved: The Neutrality of Trade and the End of the Dutch Republic.*

12 Pinto, *Essay on Circulation and Credit*, 44; Pinto, *Essai sur le luxe* (Amsterdam, 1762), 25.

13 Richard H. Popkin, "Hume and Isaac de Pinto," *Texas Studies in Literature and Language. A Journal of the Humanities* 12 (1970): 417–30; Richard H. Popkin, "Hume and Isaac de Pinto, II. Five new letters," in *Hume and the Enlightenment: Essays Presented to Ernest Campbell Mossner*, ed. William B. Todd (Edinburgh: Edinburgh University Press, 1974), 99–127. In 1777 Pinto became the object of a slander campaign waged by the *Gazette des Deux-Ponts*, which branded him a pro-English traitor to the Dutch (francophile) interest. Pinto's own dossier of the affair is in BEH 48A19 (nos. 5, 6, 8).

14   Pinto, *Essay on Circulation and Credit*, xv.

15   Besides the *Essai sur le luxe*, notably, Isaac de Pinto, *Apologie pour la nation juive: Réflexions critiques sur le premier chapitre du VIIe tome des oeuvres de M. Voltaire* (Amsterdam, 1762), which signaled his entrance into *philosophe* circles.

16   Pinto, *Essai sur le luxe*, 3.

17   As Pinto argued in the later chapters of *Précis des arguments contre les matérialistes* (The Hague, 1774), in which he discussed natural philosophy, religion, and free will and criticized d'Holbach's *Système de la nature*.

18   BEH 48A19 (no. 11) entitled "Paradoxe soutenu de plusieurs exemples pour prouver que la vérité nous conduit souvant à l'erreur et l'erreur à la vérité". See also no. 10, an early version of his critique of philosophical materialism.

19   The same theory, developed by his uncle Celestino, was held by Ferdinando Galiani: Stapelbroek, *Love, Self-Deceit and Money*, 56–87.

20   [Jean-François de Saint-Lambert], *Essay on Luxury written originally in French by Mr. Pinto* (London: T. Becket and P.A. De Hondt, 1766), 1. The title of the English translation erroneously suggested that Pinto, who by then was known for his own *Essai sur le luxe*, was the author of the text of the *Encyclopédie* article.

21   Jean-François Melon, *A Political Essay upon Commerce* (Dublin: P. Crampton, 1738), 194, 174.

22   [Saint-Lambert], *Essay on Luxury*, 58, 44, 80–86, 81.

23   [Saint-Lambert], *Essay on Luxury*, 52.

24   Pinto, *Essai sur le luxe*, 17.

25   Pinto, *Essai sur le luxe*, 24.

26   Pinto, *Tribut patriotique*, n.p.

27   David Hume, "Of the Jealousy of Trade," in *Essays Moral, Political, and Literary*, ed. Eugene Miller (Indianapolis, IN: Liberty Fund, 1985), 331. For context, see Hont, *Jealousy of Trade*, 75–76. Likewise, Adam Smith, *An Inquiry into the Nature and Causes of the Wealth of Nations*, ed. Roy H. Campbell, Andrew S. Skinner, and W. B. Todd, 2 vol. (Clarendon Press: Oxford, 1976), book IV chapter 7, par. 13 deemed the colonies of Spain and Portugal useful for all European states. Cf. Hume's phrasing with Pinto's, *Jealousy of Commerce*, 191 ("Our neighbours, reduced to misery [...] Such a devouring commerce would destroy itself").

28   Pinto, *Essay on Circulation and Credit*, xv.

29   Pinto, *Essay on Circulation and Credit*, xix.

30   Pinto, *Essay on Circulation and Credit*, 104–6. For the quotation from Hont, see Hont, *Jealousy of Trade*, 339.

31   Pinto used "Machiavellism" as an organizing category in his political thought. See below and also Pinto, *Letters on the American Troubles* (London: John Boosey and John Forbes Hackney, 1776), 10, where he argued that the more straightforward ancient "Machiavelism is no more—That atrocious doctrine, which at the beginning of this century still misled the ministers of a mild and just nation [i.e. France], is banished for ever. You will easily understand that I speak of those gloomy and crooked politics which tended to oppress the husbandman, the artificer, and the people in general, in order to prevent revolts, and to render them more industrious".

32   Pinto, *Essay on Circulation and Credit*, 104.

33   For these indications, see Alan J. Freer, Isaac "de Pinto e la sua 'Lettre à Mr. D[iderot] sur le jeu des cartes," *Annali della Scuola Normale Superiore di Pisa. Lettere, Storia e Filosofia, Serie II*, 33, no. 1/2 (1964): 93–117. See also: Alan J. Freer, "Ancora su Isaac de Pinto e Diderot," *Annali della Scuola Normale Superiore di Pisa. Lettere, Storia e Filosofia, Serie II*, 35, no. 1/2 (1966): 121–27;

Paul Pelckmans, "Le 'Voyage en Hollande' de Diderot," *Neuphilologische Mitteilungen* 86, no. 3 (1985): 294–306; Leon Schwartz, *Diderot and the Jews* (Vancouver: Fairleigh Dickinson University Press, 1981), 130–33, 181–82; Henri L. Brugmans, "Autour de Diderot en Hollande," *Diderot Studies* 3 (1961): 55–71; Gustave Charlier, "Diderot et la Hollande," *Revue de littérature comparée* 82 (1947): 190–229; and Madeleine van Strien-Chardonneau, *Le Voyage de Hollande: Récits de voyageurs français dans les Provinces-Unies, 1748–1795* (Oxford: Voltaire Foundation, 1992).

34 Freer, "Isaac de Pinto e la sua "Lettre"," 101–2.

35 Pinto's engagement with finance and the racial-cultural stereotyping engaged in by Voltaire fits with Francesca Trivellato, *The Promise and Peril of Credit: What a Forgotten Legend about Jews and Finance Tells Us About the Making of European Commercial Society* (Princeton: Princeton University Press, 2019). See also: Adam Sutcliffe, "Can a Jew Be a Philosophe? Isaac de Pinto, Voltaire, and Jewish Participation in the European Enlightenment," *Jewish Social Studies* 6, no. 3 (2000): 31–51; José Luís Cardoso and António de Vasconcelos Nogueira, "Isaac de Pinto (1717–1787) and the Jewish Problems: Apologetic Letters to Voltaire and Diderot," *History of European Ideas* 33, no. 4 (2007): 476–87.

36 VIII: 888: "La passion du jeu est une des plus funestes dont on puisse être possédé. L'homme est si violemment agité par le jeu, qu'il ne peut plus supporter aucune autre occupation." *Encyclopédie, ou dictionnaire raisonné des sciences, des arts et des métiers, etc.,* ed. Denis Diderot and Jean le Rond d'Alembert, University of Chicago: ARTFL Encyclopédie Project (Autumn 2017 edition), Robert Morrissey and Glenn Roe, eds., http://encyclopedie.uchicago. edu/. A case against games (especially gambling) was also made in the article "Épargne" by Joachim Faiguet de Villeneuve in Vol. V (V: 745–50).

37 *Encyclopédie* VIII: 531: "les Lacédémoniens furent les seuls qui bannirent entiérement le *jeu* de leur république."

38 Donald Schier, "Diderot's Translation of 'The Gamester,'" *Diderot Studies* 16 (1973): 229–40. On Diderot's philosophical relation to games, see Jean Mayer, "La philosophie de Diderot: une philosophie de joueur," *Le Jeu au XVIIIᵉ siècle* (Aix-en-Provence: Edisud, 1976), 203–14.

39 On these aspects of Jansenism and their social and economic consequences (including chapter 10 on lotteries), see René Taveneaux, *Jansénisme et prêt à intérêt: Introduction, choix de textes et commentaires* (Paris: Vrin, 1977).

40 Pinto, *Précis des arguments contre les matérialistes,* passim. For context on the relations between salon parlour games, politics, moral philosophy, and atheism, see Huguette Cohen, "Galiani, Diderot, and Nature's Loaded Dice," *Studies on Voltaire and the Eighteenth Century* 311 (1993): 35–59.

41 Quoted from Mme d'Épinay's correspondence in: Schwartz, *Diderot and the Jews,* 182.

42 Koen Stapelbroek, "Dal sistema di Utrecht (1713) al sistema di Vattel (1758); attraverso l'Observateur Hollandois e 'quelques arpents de neige' in America," *Rivista Storica Italiana* 129, no. 2 (2017): 495–535; Nakhimovsky, "The Enlightened Prince and the Future of Europe."

43 "Review of On card-Playing in a Letter from Monsieur de Pinto, to Monsieur Diderot, with a Translation from the Original, and Observations by the Translator," *The Monthly Review; or, Literary journal* 38 (January 1768): 28–29.

44 See: Robert *Mauzi*, "Écrivains et moralistes du XVIIIᵉ siècle devant les jeux de hazard," *Revue des sciences humaines* 90 (1958): 219–56; Thomas M. Kavanagh, "The Libertine's Bluff: Cards and Culture in Eighteenth-Century France," *Eighteenth-Century Studies* 33, no. 4 (2000): 505–21; Thomas M. Kavanagh, *Enlightenment and the Shadows of Chance: The Novel and the Culture of*

Gambling in Eighteenth-century France (Baltimore: Johns Hopkins University Press, 1993); Thomas M. Kavanagh, *Dice, Cards, Wheels: A Different History of French Culture* (Philadelphia: University of Pennsylvania Press, 2013); Luisa Messina, "Les jeux de cartes dans le roman libertin du dix-huitième siècle," *Les chantiers de la création* 11 (2019): https://doi.org/10.4000/lcc.1562; John Dunkley, *Gambling: A Social and Moral Problem in France, 1685–1792* (Oxford: Voltaire Foundation, 1985), 188–217; Francis Freundlich, *Le monde du jeu à Paris 1715–1800* (Paris: Albin Michel, 1995); Elisabeth Belmas, *Jouer autrefois: Essai sur le jeu dans la France modern, XVIᵉ–XVIIIᵉ siècle* (Seyssel: Éditions Champ Vallon, 2006); Isabelle Journeaux, "Le jeu à travers les romanciers français et anglais du XVIIIᵉ siècle," *Revue d'histoire moderne et contemporaine* 40, no. 1 (1993): 49–85; Colas Duflo, *Le jeu: De Pascal à Schiller* (Paris: PUF, 1997).

45 Isaac de Pinto, *On Card-Playing in a Letter from Monsieur de Pinto, to Monsieur Diderot with a Translation from the Original, and Observations by the Translator* (London: J. Walter, 1768), 17.

46 Pinto, *On Card-Playing*, 18–19.

47 Pinto, *On Card-Playing*, 23.

48 Pinto, *On Card-Playing*, 23.

49 Pinto, *On Card-Playing*, 24.

50 Pinto, *On Card-Playing*, 20–21.

51 This aspect was also noted by Cardoso and Nogueira, "An Enlightened Economist and Financier" and "Isaac de Pinto (1717–1787) and the Jewish Problems," but connected to the idea of the stock-market as a "jeu."

52 Pinto, *On Card-Playing*, 26.

53 Pinto, *On Card-Playing*, 25.

54 Pinto, *On Card-Playing*, 20.

55 Pinto, *On Card-Playing*, 22.

56 Pinto, *On Card-Playing*, 24.

57 Pinto, *On Card-Playing*, 25–28.

58 For an interpretation of these texts in this perspective, see Stapelbroek, "From Jealousy of Trade to the Neutrality of Finance."

59 Pinto, *On Card-Playing*, 28.

60 Pinto, *On Card-Playing*, 28.

61 Pinto, *On Card-Playing*, 28.

62 Pinto, *On Card-Playing*, 31–40

63 Pinto, *On Card-Playing*, 40.

64 Albert O. Hirschman, *The Passions and the Interests: Political Arguments For Capitalism Before Its Triumph.* (Princeton: Princeton University Press, 1977).

65 See the intellectual biography by Jeremy Adelman, *Worldly Philosopher: The Odyssey of Albert O. Hirschman* (Princeton: Princeton University Press, 2013).

4 The concept of self-interest in eighteenth-century anthropology and economic theory

From Richard Cumberland to Adam Smith

Simone De Angelis

This chapter reconstructs a line of argumentation, related to the topic of self-interest, that proceeds from the antagonism between Richard Cumberland and Thomas Hobbes and leads onto the relationship between Adam Smith and Jean-Jacques Rousseau. The crucial point, however, is that neither Rousseau nor Smith ever considered the concept of self-interest in isolation. Drawing on general assumptions in early modern natural law dating back to Hugo Grotius, both writers habitually discussed self-interest in relation to the concepts of compassion and/or sympathy. The consideration of self-interest in isolation does not appear to be an eighteenth-century phenomenon, but rather pertains to later times. In the eighteenth century, self-interest and compassion were considered two intrinsically connected sides of human nature.[1] Given this context, it proves especially urgent to review self-interest in anthropological terms and from the perspective of the history of science and medicine, as this represents a lacuna in the relevant literature (Albert Hirschman, Pierre Force, István Hont).[2] The more recent literature on Adam Smith likewise neglects the relevance of the anthropological dimension of self-interest in favor of the current debate regarding a potential continuity between Smith's writings on moral philosophy and on economics. In his 2018 essay on the development of Adam Smith's economic system, Moritz Isenmann, for example, puts forward compelling arguments to disprove the thesis which proposes a continuity between Smith's *Theory of Moral Sentiments* (1759) and his *Wealth of Nations* (1776), as this thesis evokes a notion of differentiation between Smith and modern liberalism.[3] Isenmann, furthermore, argues that the continuity thesis cannot not draw upon Smith's *Lectures on Jurisprudence* (1762–1764), as the *Lectures* were "still [in keeping with] the traditional idea of trade as an exchange of 'surplus' for 'necessities'"; and because central concepts of Smith's system were not yet included in *Wealth of Nations*.[4] Instead, Isenmann points out the impact of French *économistes* on the development of key concepts in the *Wealth of Nations*, particularly those of "concurrence" (*competition*) and self-interest. Among other things, Isenmann draws attention to the second volume of *Philosophie rurale ou économie générale et politique de l'agriculture* (1763) by the French physiocrats François Quesnay and the marquis de Mirabeau (the elder).[5] According to Isenmann, Smith develops his economic theory in *Wealth of Nations* by (critically) engaging with the French physiocrats independently of his *Theory of Moral Sentiments*. Hence, the first issue to be addressed is how and to what extent the French physiocrats relate to the idea of self-interest, as this is considered in the second section of this chapter.

The level of significance of *Philosophie rurale ou économie générale et politique de l'agriculture* (1763) held for the Scottish philosophical political economists was, in fact, already pointed out in a seminal article published in 1989 by István Hont. There, Hont discusses how Smith developed the theory of commercial society against the backdrop of the three- or four-stage theory of the development of human societies: 1. the hunter-gatherer-fishers societies; 2. the pastoral economy; 3. agriculture; and 4. commercial society. In the context of natural law, the four-stage theory is considered the natural norm for the development of societies and implies a theory of natural "progress" to which the physiocrats adhered. However, according to Hont, Smith does not assume this norm. Rather, he analyzes the historical development of social, political, and economic systems in Europe since the decline of the western Roman empire, as well as the relationship between rural and urban areas since the late Middle Ages, especially in northern Italian cities. Hont draws particular attention to the crucial third book of *Wealth of Nations*, in which Smith explicitly refers to the "retrograde and unnatural order" which he regards as having determined the development of economic systems in Europe.[6] Accordingly, Smith does not consider the emergence of "foreign commerce" and "manufactures" to be a result of the establishment of "agriculture." Rather, Smith regards "foreign commerce" and "manufactures" as having caused "agriculture" to become well established.[7] Here, Smith particularly refers to Britain's economic and political history since the seventeenth century.[8] Smith draws on the core of natural law theory when developing the "system of natural liberty": that is the human desire for self-preservation and the appropriate choice of cultural techniques necessary to safeguard human existence and lead a peaceful life within society, without requiring a form of institutionalized rule or a so-called "projector" who artificially and rationally steers economic processes in a certain direction.[9] For Smith, self-interest is to be understood, therefore, in terms of *self-preservation* as a coalescence of anthropology and history, according to which "[e]very man, as long as he does not violate the laws of justice, is left perfectly free to pursue his own interest his own way, and to bring both his industry and capital into competition with those of any other man, or order of man."[10] This poses the question: how did Smith arrive at the idea of examining economic systems based on the relationship between history and nature, or history and anthropology?

This paper generally assumes that there is a connection between Smith's *Theory of Moral Sentiments* and *Wealth of Nations*. Understanding the reciprocal relationship between the concepts of sympathy and self-interest in these significant publications, requires, first, a comparison of Adam Smith's and Jean-Jacques Rousseau's moral philosophies regarding the category of compassion, and this is addressed in the third section below. This, in turn, renders it necessary to consider the relationship between natural law, medicine, and commercial society as well as the physiological and psychological implications of self-interest and sympathy in both Cumberland and Smith. Regarding natural law, Jean Barbeyrac's translations of and commentaries on the works of Grotius, Pufendorf, and Cumberland were particularly influential during the eighteenth century and these are considered in the fourth part of the chapter. The fifth section describes Smith's pivotal notice of the changes in natural history that occurred primarily in France around 1750 (and affected Hume's and Ferguson's philosophies of history), and his implementation of them in his understanding of a "progressive state's liberal economy."

The 'Liberal' system of agriculture and the idea of self-interest in physiocratic terms

Aside from referring to Smith's stay in France between 1764 and 1766, Isenmann remains very vague on the subject of Smith's relationship to the French context and the extent to which Smith came into contact with the French ideas.[11] Neither Isenmann nor Hont gives any indication of the changes in the Enlightenment's nature-related and historical thinking that surfaced in Buffon's natural history around 1750 and are reflected in the works of various philosophers, historians, and naturalists across Europe; yet these changes affected Smith's ideas and notions concerning economy. Before discussing both the relationship between nature and history in the second half of the eighteenth century, and a model of the philosophy of history pertaining to the same period, it is helpful to sum up in four points the main positions formulated in the second volume of *Philosophie rurale ou économie générale et politique de l'agriculture* (1763) by the physiocrats François Quesnay and the marquis de Mirabeau. These four points serve to illustrate the normative basis of the economic system of agriculture that can be observed in natural law theory, the physiocrats' liberal attitude which centers on the idea of self-interest, and their criticism of governmental intervention in the natural order.

1 The *Philosophie rurale* introduces the concept of subsistence ("la subsistence"), i.e. the acquisition of minimal essential necessities as a prerequisite for society and as a basic human need.[12]
2 The physiocrats refer to the three-stage theory, to which correspond three different forms of subsistence economy or society, respectively.[13]
3 The *Philosophie rurale* lists the mistakes a political government makes when intervening in the natural order of agriculture through regulatory

measures and by favoring other economic forms, such as manufacturing. At the same time, the physiocrats elucidate their "liberal" system, which is based upon the idea of self-interest.[14]

4 The physiocrats distinguish the laws of politics (*speculations*) from the laws of nature, which include both physical causes and self-interest. The laws of nature also determine the economic system's effects (whether beneficial or unfavourable) on the public (*nation*). In this context, self-interest (*intérêts particuliers*) adjusts to the respective physical causes, corresponding to the respective varying properties of the objects and environment (*circonstances*).[15]

This renders the situation ambivalent: on the one hand, the *Philosophie rurale* formulates "liberal" principles that are compatible with key concepts of Adam Smith's economic system. On the other hand, however, Smith, rejects the physiocrats' objective to transform the French economy through great efforts that comply with the natural order. Thus, calling attention to this significant French context, significant though it is, does not suffice so as to explain Smith's position in *Wealth of Nations*. Rather, it is essential to take into consideration additional relevant contexts, such as the moral philosophy and the nature-related, as well as historical, thinking of the Enlightenment, which also influenced Smith.

Jean-Jacques Rousseau and Adam Smith: The moral category of compassion

In his posthumously published 2015 study, *Politics in Commercial Society*, István Hont identifies a number of arguments based on a comparison of Rousseau's and Smith's approaches to moral philosophy.[16]

1 Both theories of morality are based on common ground regarding the category of compassion (*pitié*), i.e. the ability to participate in and sympathize with the suffering of others. This is the case even though Smith does not draw the same conclusions as Rousseau does in the latter's *Discourse on the Origin of Inequality* of 1755: namely that law and politics are a result of self-interest (*amour propre*), which is also the cause of inequality among people.[17] The attempt to solve the so-called "Adam Smith problem"— i.e., a repeatedly implied inconsistency between *Theory of Moral Sentiments* and *Wealth of Nations*—must assume that the instinct for compassion constitutes "the archetype of morality as such."[18]

2 In *Theory of Moral Sentiments,* Smith adopts Rousseau's concept of compassion, generalizing and translating it as "sympathy," which results in a parallel structure of the respective moral systems: Rousseau: *amour propre*/compassion; Smith: self-interest/sympathy.[19]

3 The modern debate on moral philosophy originates from Thomas Hobbes's concept of self-love and his "selfish system." The moral

systems that subsequently address this issue try to offset Hobbes's position by developing the "system of sympathy."[20]

4 Smith not only generalized but also historicized the concept of compassion: in parallel to Rousseau's history of self-love (*amour propre*) as expressed in *Discourse on the Origin of Inequality*, Smith pens a natural history of sympathy or a "conjectural history of the origins of commercial society" and the "social self" in *Theory of Moral Sentiments* and thus creates a new genre of histories of humanity.[21]

5 In his definition of a commercial society, Smith draws on moral psychology, stating that the "impartial spectator" internalizes social and moral norms. In this context, Smith emphasizes the role of psychological pain which manifests itself as a quasi-punitive voice of conscience when humans break moral rules or transgress social norms.[22]

6 Ultimately both Rousseau and Smith are theorists of commercial society. Rousseau generally advocates a theory of a "closed commercial society," according to which a state need not grow externally—neither through military action nor through trade. His idea of "balanced growth" as "domestic growth" is based on the right to own property that all men and women acquire through their own work.[23]

7 The extent to which Smith actually succeeds in imitating this patriotic model remains debatable: while Rousseau is primarily concerned with the Republic of Geneva's watchmaking industry, Smith focuses on Britain's "open commercial state" and trade with the colonies in *Wealth of Nations*. Smith, however, admits that the "love of our country" is a much stronger sentiment than the "love of mankind."[24]

Hont also points out that the insight that "self-regarding and other-regarding motives were not in rigid opposition"[25] had been inherent in the natural law tradition since the seventeenth century. This observation has not as yet received the attention it deserves: Pufendorf in his 1672 *De Jure Naturae et Gentium*, and even more so his eighteenth-century commentator, Jean Barbeyrac, for instance, both assume the existence of an equilibrium between self-love (*amor sui*) and sociability (*socialitas*) as parts of the foundation of natural law (*lex naturalis*).[26] Moreover, as regards compassion, Rousseau drew a decisive stimulus from Hugo Grotius who in the seventh of his *Prolegomena* on *De Juris Belli ac Pacis* (1624) reinterpreted the *pietas* impulse in terms of a social virtue. In order for the impetus to be sociable (*appetitus societatis*) to unfold, one must restrain the instinct for self-preservation through compassion, which can also be observed in young children and irrational animals.[27] Finally, perhaps the most important source of the notion of sympathy is Richard Cumberland, who prominently addressed Thomas Hobbes's theses but goes largely unnoticed in the literature on self-interest. Since Cumberland's approach to natural law also allows for a few fundamental remarks on the relationship between the physical and moral realms of the world, his position will be explained in more detail in the following section.

Natural law, medicine, and commercial society

A central premise of early modern natural law is the parallel consideration of the physical realm of the tangible world (*physica*) and the ethical realm of human actions (*ethica*), both of which are seen to be regulated by natural law.[28] This notion leads Cumberland to realize that human actions are triggered jointly by the faculties of the soul—i.e. mental faculties—*and* those of the body.[29] The actual novelty of natural law lies in the fact that Cumberland draws upon the legal concept of Francisco Suàrez's scholastic philosophy, on the hypotheses of Descartes's physics, and on the findings of William Harvey, Thomas Willis, and Richard Lowers's anatomy as well as on the "sciences of life" (especially Harvey's and Marcello Malpighi's embryology). Moreover, Cumberland followed the debate on the "laws of nature" at the Royal Society (Christopher Wren, Christiaan Huygens), which also left its mark in the title of his main work, *De Legibus Naturae* (1672).[30] To invalidate Hobbes's hypothesis on egoism, Cumberland invokes a number of physiological arguments informed by theories about the circulatory system and the anatomy of the nerves and heart. They show that acts of mutual benevolence are also rooted in natural propensities (*propensiones naturales*) within the animal kingdom. A central observation in this context, for instance, states that all requirements of both the body and self-preservation are determined by the circulatory system: when these requirements are satisfied, self-love does not prevent individuals from helping or preserving other (related or unrelated) animals of the same species, and hoping that these others will be ready to help them in turn.[31] Cumberland thus quotes a kind of "reciprocal altruism" and thereby not only defuses Hobbes's thesis of an inherent "right to all things" in the natural state, but also exposes the Hobbesian construct of a fear of death—which, in the natural state, leads humans to inflict harm upon others—as a false presumption.[32] A central point here is that Cumberland does not confront Hobbes on the level of conscious human actions but on that of a living being's *pre-reflexive* and *pre-conscious* actions and inclinations, which arise from the body's very form and constitution.[33] Cumberland's concept of pre-reflectivity quasi-reverses Hobbes's perspective: in *Leviathan* (chapter 17), Hobbes claims that human capacities for reason and language prompt humans—unlike mindless animals—to employ these very capacities contrary to the natural law.[34] As the pre-reflexive disregards the mind (*mens*), Cumberland reveals the level of behavioral complexity already present at living nature's pre-conscious level. Cumberland, of course, assumes a higher development of human beings in terms of a scale of living entities, in which the human brain's mental capacities—especially those of imagination and memory—far exceed those of animals. In humans, these more refined mental capacities, as well as sensory perception and movement, depend not only on the structure and design of the brain and on humans' upright gait, but also on the nerves leading to the brain through the spinal cord. In *De Legibus Naturae*, Cumberland refers to chapter 26 of Thomas Willis's *De Cerebri Anatome* (1664):[35] there, the physiologist describes the sympathetic nerve (*nervus sympathicus*), which he refers to as the "intercostal nerve", a specific anatomical structure of the human body that serves as mediator between mental (i.e. relating to conceptions of the brain) and affective functions (i.e. affections).[36] Cumberland particularly highlights the passage in Willis's work where the latter describes the physiological conditions of moral sensation in the human body and the regulation of affects:

> Certainly the Works of Prudence and Vertue depend very much on the mutual commerce which happens to the Heart with the Brain: because, that cogitations about the acts of the Appetite or Judgment may be rightly described, it is behoveful for the flood of the blood to be restrained in the Breast, and the inordinations of it and of the Heart itself so be governed by the Nerves.[37]

Around 1750, the physiologists at the University of Edinburgh's Medical School—including William Cullen, a friend of Hume's and Smith's—also agreed with Willis's ideas of the sympathetic nerve and its function in the human body. Those Edinburgh physiologists agreed that sympathy constitutes a form of sensitivity and a vitally important principle.[38] The juxtaposition of the physical and the ethical realms in Cumberland's natural law also renders comprehensible, according to Evelyn L. Forget, the epistemic continuity between the physiological theories of the Edinburgh Medical School and the social theories proposed by Hume and Smith:

> The epistemological continuity between the physiological theories of the Edinburgh medical school and the social theories of Smith and Hume seems apparent. The same principle explains the action of sensation, the coordination of the organs of the body, and the "social principle" that allows "fellow-feeling" to emerge in a society.[39]

In *Theory of Moral Sentiments*, Smith likewise emphasizes both the psychosocial and the physical dimensions of sympathy: "Persons of delicate fibres and a weak constitution of body complain, that in looking on the sores and ulcers which are exposed by beggars in the streets, they are apt to feel an itching or uneasy sensation in the correspondent part of their own bodies."[40]

However, the crucial factor in further developing the notion of sympathy is that Hume and Smith also extend the "logic of reciprocity" to trade, of which they likewise consider it an underlying feature. This is to say that, in early modern state politics, the logic of trade did not always have to fall in line with the "logic of war"; rather, the aim was to reach a balance between the two.[41] Such a perspective suggests an anthropological basis for commercial society which can, in principle, already be found in Cumberland: affect regulation—to which our bodies are alerted by natural law—in practical terms refers to the distribution of goods, that is to say to strong forms of self-interest within the commercial and consumer society. However, this means that affect regulation has an influence on free actions (*actiones liberae*) that aim to establish and promote the common good (*bonum commune*) of a group. This applies to actions contributing to the fair distribution of goods and services to maintain the well-being of all people, e.g. among the members of a family or society. These free actions are regulated by the natural law and based on principles which relate, for example, to acts of mutual benevolence or reciprocal altruism.[42]

Considering Cumberland's anti-Hobbesian approach, these statements also make sense in view of the historical and political context: the actual matter at hand is thus the development of the theory of a commercial society as the seventeenth century gave way to the eighteenth. This transition results from a continuity which unfolds in the context of natural law, medicine, and economic theory. If one attributes economic interests not only to the individuals in a society, but also to states that are competing for the lead role in global trading markets, Cumberland already outlines what (with a view to David Hume) is referred to as "Jealousy of Trade": i.e., the respective changes in how social relationships as well as political ones between states are perceived.[43] The economy indeed constituted a fundamental factor in the policies of states such as England and France, who waged a global conflict around the time of the Seven Years' War (1756–1763), which was informed, among other factors, by their striving to conquer trading markets in North America and India. At the same time, the theory of a commercial society forms the basis of the post-Hobbesian developments in political theory which primarily affect the eighteenth century. Thus, the criterion that defines a political economy, from Hume and Smith's point of view, is one which includes trade in the *raison d'état*, i.e. into the practical political concerns of states and their (self-)preservation, and this did not exist during the Renaissance (Machiavelli) and the early seventeenth century (Hobbes).[44] Accordingly, trade also became the subject of early modern natural law. Hence Jean Barbeyrac's Pufendorf commentary (with which Adam Smith was familiar)[45] defines the relationship between trade, property, and price (the last understood in terms of "moral quantity" or "value of things and actions") as follows: "Trade is a result of the ownership of goods, & the price is a result of trade; both prove absolutely necessary and are coordinated through a kind of exchange, which is ultimately what trading is about."[46]

Commercial society and self-interest in terms of "philosophical history"

According to what has been stated above, it is therefore logical and plausible that:

> [T]he theory of "commercial society" developed in the course of the 18th century cannot be interpreted as a mere reflex of emerging

capitalism or of the liberalism displayed by an ascending bourgeoisie; it must rather be understood as the result of a shift within the theoretical concept of natural law towards questions of sociability, passions and interests, moral responsibility, and especially a "philosophical history."[47]

This section of the chapter will focus on the question of "philosophical history" and provide a tentative insight into how it affects the framework and interpretation of fundamental concepts in Adam Smith's economic system. Smith does not share the conclusions drawn by Rousseau in *Discourse on the Origin of Inequality* (see above), on the one hand, because he belongs to a younger generation;[48] but, on the other, because he ultimately judges self-interest in an entirely different way from Rousseau. However, the disparity between Smith and Rousseau is also linked to the fact that Smith's interpretation of history is in line with that of the Scottish philosophers David Hume and Adam Ferguson. Historical consciousness in the second half of the eighteenth century is also related to the development of the "sciences of life" around 1750. The latter provided a conceptual framework for "philosophical history," an aspect which—as far as Adam Smith is concerned— has thus far received little attention.[49] During the second half of the eighteenth century, one can basically distinguish between two types of a philosophy of history.

The first one is the prognostic philosophy of history, as is present in (for instance) Rousseau, Iselin, and Kant. This type eliminates chance from the context of historical events in order to "achieve a stable final state of historical development in which a socialized person's 'bliss' is guaranteed."[50] To a certain extent, the French physiocrats' economic thinking also pertains to this prognostic model, insofar as the physiocrats pursued the plan of the natural order according to mechanistic criteria and strove to steer the economy in this direction.

The second type—which most notably traces back to the Scottish philosophers Hume and Ferguson, while also manifesting itself in Johann Gottfried Herder's *Ideas for the Philosophy of the History of Mankind* (1784–1791)—by contrast ascribes chance a decisive role in the context of historical developments: "Here history becomes an accumulation of experiences the course of which, however, cannot derive from planned human action."[51] Moreover, the second type of philosophy of history is characterized by two issues of late Enlightenment anthropology: the naturalization of history; and the relationship between moral philosophy and history. Natural history, the "sciences of life," the natural history of humanity, cultural history, and the history of humankind thus entered into a new relationship with one another. This engendered a naturalization of concepts such as "development," "progress," "genesis," "contingency," and so on. Speaking with Peter Hanns Reill, historians adopted the language of life scientists.[52] This was demonstrated, for instance, by Adam Ferguson, who in his 1792 *Principles of Moral and Political Sciences* defined "progressive subjects" as follows:

> Progressive natures are subject to vicissitudes of advancement or decline, but are not stationary, perhaps in any period of their existence. Thus, in the material world, subjects organized, being progressive, when they cease to advance, begin to decline [...]. While subjects stationary are described by enumeration of co-existent parts [...], subjects progressive are characterized by the enumeration of steps, in the passage from one form of state or excellence to another, [...] the natural state of a living creature includes all its known variations, from the embryo and the fœtus to the breathing animal, the adolescent and the adult, through which life in all its variations is known to pass.[53]

He thereby explicitly refers to a living creature's stages of development, from embryo to death, as described by Buffon in his *Natural History of Man* in the first volume of the *Histoire Naturelle* (1749).[54] In his 1767 *History of Civil Society*, Ferguson stated, moreover, that, as to its purpose, the civilization process was open-ended and, as a matter of principle, remained not rationally plannable. Nevertheless, he stipulated—very much in the spirit of an anthropology based on natural law—that *instincts* and local *circumstances* (such as geographical or climatic conditions) shape societies and have an impact on the development of humankind.[55] This Ferguson puts as follows:

> Like the winds, that come we know not whence, and blow whithersoever they list, the forms of society are derived from an obscure and distant origin; they arise, long before the date of philosophy, from the instincts, not from the speculations, of men. The croud [sic] of mankind, are directed in their establishments and measures, by the circumstances in which they are placed; and seldom are turned from their way, to follow the plan of any single projector.[56]

The speculative plans of a so-called "projector" thus cannot control the processes of either civilization (Ferguson) or the economy (Smith). According to Ferguson, the criteria determining the process of civilization, therefore, basically result from local circumstances and instinctive motivations for action. Thus, they cannot be rationally planned and remain open in terms of preconceived results. Ferguson concludes that society's organizational forms emerge by chance and are subsequently perpetuated through the rational exercise of power. From the point of view of moral philosophy, already David Hume's 1749 *Enquiries Concerning the Human Understanding and Concerning the Principles of Morals* posed the question as to what extent human behavior can be standardized, or how human action can be judged according to the standards of evidence. Hume thus treated history as an experimental field which provides documentation of humankind's self-experiments.[57] In the chapter "Of Liberty and Necessity," Hume also noted that it was not so much a question of *uncertainty* of events and their respective causes, but rather of the random motives and conditions for human actions ("the secret operation of contrary causes")[58] which caused the supposed constancy of human nature to appear problematic. A genetic model of history, which took into consideration the diversity of the outcomes of human action and assumed heteronomy as the pre-supposition of explaining historical reality, thus lent itself as a solution to the contradiction between norm and contingency.

Adam Smith's concepts of a "progressive state" and a "system of natural liberty"

Around 1750, the discovery of the freshwater polyp triggered a change in the methodology of the "sciences of life."[59] Against the backdrop of a recognition of the limitations of mathematical methods and empiricism, leading naturalists (among them Buffon, Bonnet, and Haller) developed a new methodological approach in natural history, using thought experiments, analogies, and hypotheses as well as comparing and putting into relation apparently remote objects.[60] In this context, the "naturalization of history" meant that processes such as those relating to society and civilization, or to economic matters, were regarded as analogous to processes of living bodies; that is, as Ferguson puts it, as "progressive subjects" or "subjects organized." In *Wealth of Nations*, Adam Smith actually adopts and significantly further develops the physical and moral components of sympathy he described in *Theory of Moral Sentiments*. In a central chapter of *Wealth of Nations*, Smith combines elements of commercial society described above: self-interest, Cumberland's sociobiological theory of reciprocal altruism, and trade as the subject of Barbeyrac's Pufendorf commentary. Smith speaks of a "propensity in human nature [...] to truck, barter, and exchange one thing for another,"[61] wherein humans differ from all other faunal species: "[this propensity] is common to all men, and to be found in no other race of animals, which seem to know neither this nor any other species of contracts."[62] Moreover, Smith, in fact, applies an approach of cooperation theory by pointing out that people rely on the help of other people, which he also bases on a comparison to the animal kingdom:

> When an animal wants to obtain something either of a man or of another animal, it has no other means of persuasion but to gain the favour of those whose service it requires. [...] Man sometimes uses the same arts with his brethren, [...]. In civilized society he stands at all times in need of the cooperation and assistance of great multitudes [...]. In almost every other race of animals each individual, when it is grown up to maturity, is intirely independent [...]. But man has almost constant occasion for the help of his brethren, and it is in vain for him to expect it from their benevolence only.[63]

It is self-love which restores the balance to altruism: "He will be more likely to prevail if he can interest their self-love in his favour, and shew them that it is for their own advantage to do for him what he requires of them."[64] Hence Smith's central thesis is that it is in the self-interest of others to see that my needs are met.[65] The "bartering disposition" is, therefore, the reason for the differentiation between professions and talents within a society, for the development of a division of labor, and why in hunting or herding societies, one person or group crafted bows and arrows which they subsequently exchanged for cattle and game without having to hunt themselves.[66] Smith also explicitly compares a central principle of his economy with a characteristic of animate bodies:

> The uniform, constant, and uninterrupted effort of every man to better his condition, the principle from which publick and national, as well as private opulence is originally derived, is frequently powerful enough to maintain the natural progress of things toward improvement, in spite both of the extravagance of government, and of the greatest errors of administration. Like the unknown principle of animal life, it frequently restores health and vigour to the constitution, in spite, not only of the disease, but of the absurd prescription of the doctor.[67]

The "unknown principle" is similar to the vital principle on which the growth of organic bodies is based.[68] The use of explicative models from the "sciences of life "links Smith to Herder.[69] In *Ideas for the Philosophy of the History of Mankind* (1784–1791), Herder draws on Caspar Friedrich Wolff's two-phase law of organic growth[70] when he describes his own two-phase law of the cultural history of mankind: 1. the unfolding of the vital force in space and time; 2. organization: mass migrations, the formation of states, training in cultural techniques, etc.[71] In Smith's system, labor is, so to speak, the active economic principle in the history of mankind: "Labour [...] is the only universal [...] or the only standard by which we can compare the values of different commodities at all times and at all places."[72] Land, profit, and labor are the constituents of the social order:

> The whole annual produce of the land and labour of every country, or what comes to the same thing, the whole price of that annual produce, naturally divides itself, [...], into three parts; the rent of land, the wages of labour, and the profits of stock; and constitutes a revenue to three different orders of people; to those who live by rent, to those who live by wages, and those who live by profit. These are the three great original and constituent orders of every civilized society, from whose revenue that of every other order is ultimately derived.[73]

Smith's "progressive state," moreover, follows Ferguson's biological concept of "progressive natures." Here Smith particularly considers the situation of the "labouring poor":

It deserves to be remarked, perhaps, that it is in the progressive state, while the society is advancing to the further acquisition, rather than when it has acquired its full complement of riches, that the condition of the labouring poor, of the great body of the people, seems to be the happiest and the most comfortable. It is hard in the stationary, and miserable in the declining state. The progressive state is in reality the chearful [sic.] and the hearty state to all the different orders of the society. The stationary is dull; the declining, melancholy.[74]

In his analysis, the interest of the first two social orders—i.e., the landowners and workers—is "strictly and inseparably connected with the general interest of society."[75] However, the landowners' part, in which profits are generated without effort and labor, is characterized by a certain level of "indolence" and even ignorance of the consequences of "publick regulation."[76] These consequences, however, directly affect the worker, whose wages indeed steadily increase with increasing work, but "when this real wealth of the society becomes stationary, his wages are soon reduced to what is barely enough to enable him to bring up a family, or to continue the race of labourers. When the society declines, they fall even below this."[77] However, the interest of the third order—i.e., the merchants and manufacturers— is linked to the general interest to a different extent than the other two. The plans and projects of this third order, whose members mainly demonstrate more "acuteness of understanding" than the "country gentleman," are generally carried out in the interest of their own economic sector rather than in the interest of society.[78] Since the merchants and manufacturers have a better knowledge and understanding of their self-interest than the gentleman, the latter is persuaded "to give up both his own interest and that of the publick, from a very simple but honest conviction, that their interest, and not his, was the interest of the publick."[79] Based on this analysis, Smith now queries whether the interests of the merchants and manufacturers correspond with the general interest:

The interest of the dealers, however, in any particular branch of trade or manufactures, is always in some respects different from, and even opposite to, that of the publick. To widen the market and to narrow the competition, is always the interest of the dealers. To widen the market may frequently be agreeable enough to the interest of the publick; but to narrow the competition must always be against it, and can serve only to enable the dealers, by rising their profits above what they naturally would be, to levy, for their own benefit, an absurd tax upon the rest of their fellow-citizens.[80]

The French economic historian Daniel Diatkine recently showed that Smith argues not only in terms of economic theory, but also in terms of actual history, as he considers the political situation of Great Britain which led to the American Declaration of Independence after the end of the Seven Years' War (1763–1776). The novel aspect of the British empire's politics at this time was that it identified its own interests as congruent with those of the merchants and manufacturers; and Britain was thus transformed into a colonial empire.[81] In this context, Smith analyzes three dimensions of capitalism: as product of history (the commercial society); political and intellectual construction (the mercantilist system); and economic process (the accumulation of capital). The accumulation of capital enriches not only the merchants and manufacturers, but also the workers, even though a significant inequality remains. The mercantilist system proves unfair, however, because it is biased: it confuses the interests of merchants with the common good. Smith's analysis sets out to demonstrate this very misperception, and show that the interests of the merchants are, on the contrary, mostly opposed to the common good. In addition, the mercantilist system is responsible for the development of a large colonial empire which, in turn, threatens Britain's constitutional monarchy (as resulted from the 1688 revolution) and could thus lead to a new tyranny.[82] The comparison with the history of the Roman empire, therefore, is indeed always present in *Wealth of Nations*. Smith, moreover, pays special attention to the criterion of the political power's ("legislator's") *distance* from the merchants' and manufacturers' self-interest; a distance, which, by contrast, is lacking in the mercantilist system. Political impartiality is the distinguishing feature of a "system of natural liberty," which constitutes the counterpart of a system of commercial society as advocated by Smith.[83] Against this background, the aesthetic theory of the impartial spectator (which Smith developed in *Theory of Moral Sentiments*) can be considered as a model for the legislature's distance or political impartiality in *Wealth of Nations*.[84]

Smith's "system of natural liberty" is, nevertheless, no abstract construct, as it is based on an analysis of the actual situation in the Britain's North American colonies, to which Smith dedicates an important chapter ("Of Colonies") in Book IV of *Wealth of Nations*. There, Smith primarily criticizes the British government's "mercantile spirit" of granting privileges to merchants and manufacturers in trading with the colonies.[85] Nonetheless, Smith also considered the colonies a quasi "system of natural liberty," which he describes in broad terms by taking a comprehensive look at the colonies in North America. In doing so, he focuses on the contingent conditions of country,[86] population, geography, flora and fauna, culture,[87] economy,[88] politics,[89] relationship to the mother state,[90] etc. He then compares these conditions to those in Great Britain, Europe, and the colonies of other countries such as Spain or Portugal. Smith's analysis essentially follows the principles of Buffon's new natural history, as well as Hume's and Ferguson's naturalistic philosophy of history. Buffon proposes that one ought to integrate observations, generalize facts, and combine them by analogy so as to arrive at general overviews of natural history.[91] Buffon is explicitly mentioned in Smith's chapter on the colonies, in a statement about the *Cori* as viviparous quadrupeds in St. Domingo. In a 1755 letter to the *Edinburgh Review*, Smith speaks of a "compleat system of natural history" that Mr. Buffon and Mr. Daubenton were working on at the time.[92]

In addressing the problem of monopoly in trading with the colonies, Smith argues on two levels: that of anthropology and physiology, and that of the economy. It is no coincidence that Smith explains the problem of Great Britain's "body politick" through the analogy of a vital process, namely that of blood circulation:

> In her present condition, Great Britain resembles one of those unwhole-some bodies in which some of the vital parts are overgrown, and which, upon that account, are liable to many dangerous disorders scarce inci-dent to those in which all the parts are more properly proportioned. A small stop in that great blood-vessel, which has been artificially swelled beyond its natural dimensions, and through which an unnatural pro-portion of the industry and commerce of the country has been forced to circulate, is very likely to bring on the most dangerous disorders upon the whole body politick.[93]

In other words, Smith transfers Jean Barbeyrac's concept of the balance (*juste équilibre*) between *amour propre* and *sociabilité* in human nature[94] to the "body politick." In this context, the bloodstream analogy concerns the (im)balance of a nation's economic system: according to Smith, Britain's weight in trading with the colonies had "unnaturally" shifted towards the interests of monopolists, thus threatening the collapse of the entire "body politick." The aim is to (re-)establish the "natural balance" between trade and commerce which was broken by the "monopoly of the colony trade."[95] This is important, he claims, as a political and economic break between Britain and the colonies is impending: "The expectation of a rupture with the colonies, accordingly, has struck the people of Great Britain with more terror than ever felt for a Spanish armada, or a French invasion."[96] Therefore, the legislature must not abruptly disrupt "those overgrown man-ufactures," as this would actually cause more damage to the body politic, if not its death: if the blood "is stopt in any of the greater vessels, convulsions, apoplexy, or death, are the immediate and unavoidable consequences."[97] Instead, Smith advocates a "progressive" introduction of the "system of natural liberty" in Great Britain:

> Some moderate and gradual relaxation of the laws which give to Great Britain the exclusive trade to the colonies, till it is rendered in a great measure free, seems to be the only expedient which can, in all future times, deliver her from this danger, which can enable her or even force her to withdraw some part of her capital from this overgrown employ-ment, and to turn it, though with less profit, towards other employ-ments; and which, by gradually diminishing one branch of her industry

and gradually increasing all the rest, can by degrees restore all the different branches of it to the natural, healthful, and proper proportion which perfect liberty necessarily establishes, and which perfect liberty can alone preserve.[98]

As Smith understands his "perfect liberal system," the "open commercial state" depends on reducing privileges and on the distance or impartiality of the legislature in relation to the economic agents involved in the market. The resulting competition restores the natural balance between the various trading sectors. In the context of such a competition, everyone is completely free to pursue their own interests, provided they abide by the law. Once again, Smith derives and establishes the criterion of distance from the experiences of the North American colonies. With a view to the emerging new democracy in America,[99] he ultimately attributes the colonies' economic and civilizational progress to their political distance from Great Britain, despite the fact that he advocates the union with the colonies.[100]

Conclusion

The above explanations should have made clear that it is not sufficient to attribute Adam Smith's concept of self-interest to the French physiocrats, whose economic ideas, as well as the mercantilist system of privileges, he clearly rejected. Instead, the anthropological foundation of self-interest must be emphasized. Moreover, thinkers of the eighteenth century—prominently Rousseau, who proved influential on Smith—never applied the concept of self-interest per se, but always understood and discussed it in relation to the other central anthropological concept, that of compassion. Both concepts— *amour propre* and *sympathie* or *sociabilité*—are considered distinct, yet intrinsically linked, qualities of humans as physical and moral beings. However, both concepts have their roots in early modern natural law, and in the eighteenth century were received and discussed via Barbeyrac's influential translations of and comments on Grotius, Pufendorf, and Cumberland. In Cumberland's account of natural law, these two concepts also correlate via the analogy of blood circulation, which also plays a central role in Smith's interpretation of economic conditions. Yet, in order to understand how Smith brings together moral-philosophical and anthropological, as well as political and economic, principles in *Wealth of Nations*, it is indispensable to address Hume's and Ferguson's philosophical histories, as well as the natural history of Buffon, which has left obvious traces in Smith, particularly in the chapter on the North American colonies. Smith thus proves to have been a quintessential eighteenth-century scholar who incorporated nature and society, economic and political thought and action, and morality in his considerations. At the same time, Adam Smith makes a more general statement about the change in the concept of (self-)interest, which Albert O.

Hirschman has already formulated to some extent: Smith uses "interests" and "passions" as synonyms, not antonyms, as had been the case with previous authors writing about self-interest. Also, the concept of "self-interest" is generalized, since it no longer relates to a specific social order or a specific political actor, but to humanity as a whole.[101] This is due to the complex relationships between the anthropological and economic implications of self-interest that became relevant after 1750.

Notes

1 See, for example, Gloria Zuñiga y Postigo, "Adam Smith on Sympathy: From Self-Interest to Empathy," in *Propriety and Prosperity, New Studies on the Philosophy of Adam Smith*, ed. David F. Hardwick and Leslie Marsh (London: Palgrave Macmillan, 2014), 136–46; Agnieszka Czarnecka, "Taming Egoism: Adam Smith on Empathy, Imagination and Justice," *Cracow Studies of Constitutional and Legal History* 9, no. 2 (2016): 233–41; Robert B. Lamb, "Adam Smith's System: Sympathy not Self-Interest," *Journal of the History of Ideas* 35, no. 4 (1974): 671–82.

2 Albert O. Hirschman, *The Passions and the Interests: Political Arguments for Capitalism before Its Triumph* (Princeton: Princeton University Press, 1977); Pierre Force, *Self-Interest before Adam Smith: A Genealogy of Economic Science* (Cambridge: Cambridge University Press, 2003); István Hont, *Politics in Commercial Society: Jean-Jacques Rousseau and Adam Smith* (Cambridge, MA: Harvard University Press, 2015).

3 Moritz Isenmann, "Die langsame Entstehung eines ökonomischen Systems: Konkurrenz und freier Markt im Werk von Adam Smith," *Historische Zeitschrift* 307 (2018): 665–69.

4 Ibid., 685–86 (My translation.)

5 Isenmann, "Die langsame Entstehung eines ökonomischen Systems," 687–88.

6 István Hont, "Adam Smith and the Political Economy of the "Unnatural and Retrograde Order,"" in *Jealousy of Trade: International Competition and the Nation-State in Historical Perspective*, ed. István Hont (Cambridge, MA: Harvard University Press, 2005), 374–75.

7 Adam Smith, *An Inquiry into the Nature and Causes of the Wealth of Nations* (Oxford: Oxford University Press, 1976), vol. 1, III.iv, 422: "It is thus that through the greater part of Europe the commerce and manufactures of cities, instead of being the effect, have been the cause and occasion of the improvement and cultivation of the country."

8 Ibid., 424: "From the beginning of the reign of Elizabeth too, the English legislature has been peculiarly attentive to the interest of commerce and manufactures, and in reality there is no country in Europe, Holland itself not excepted, of which the law is, upon the whole, more favourable to this sort of industry. Commerce and manufactures have accordingly been continually advancing during all this period. The cultivation and improvement of the country has, no doubt, been gradually advancing too: But it seems to have followed slowly, and at a distance, the more rapid progress of commerce and manufactures."

9 Hont, "Adam Smith and the Political Economy," 376: "Smith violently opposed the Physiocratic plan of the forced sectoral rearrangement of the French economy according to the natural order."

10 Smith, *Wealth of Nations*, vol. 2, IV.ix, 687.

11 Isenmann, "Die langsame Entstehung eines ökonomischen Systems," 688.

12 François Quesnay and Victor de Riqueti, *Philosophie rurale ou économie générale et politique de l'Agriculture, réduite à l'ordre immuable des loix physiques & morales, qui assurent la prospérité des empires* (Amsterdam: Les Libraires Associés, 1764), vol. 2, 14: "To renounce consumption equals renouncing life. Mankind's continuity depends on this primitive requirement". (My translation.)

13 Ibid., 17.

14 Ibid., 112: "So it is necessary that they [sc. the political government of agriculture, SdeA] pervert every economic order; they lose sight of the peasants' self-interest [...]." (My translation.)

15 Ibid.,158.

16 The following points 1–7 relate to the first two chapters and the last chapter of István Hont, *Politics in Commercial Society.*

17 Hont, *Politics in Commercial Society*, 20–22.

18 Ibid., 20–21.

19 Ibid., 26–28. See also Adam Smith, *The Theory of Moral Sentiments* (London: Penguin, 2009), 15: "Pity and compassion are words appropriated to signify our fellow-feeling with the sorrows of others. Sympathy, though its meaning was, perhaps, originally the same, may now, however, without much impropriety, be made use of to denote our fellow-feeling with any passion whatever."

20 Hont, *Politics in Commercial Society*, 32–33.

21 Ibid., 35 and 42.

22 Ibid., 39–40.

23 Ibid., 124–26.

24 Ibid., 127, 130–31.

25 Ibid., 33.

26 Samuel Pufendorf, *Le Droit de la nature et des gens, ou Système général des principes les plus importans de la morale, de la jurisprudence, et de la politique* (Basel: Thourneisen, 1732), Bk. 1, ch. 3 (De la loi naturelle en général), §XV, note 5, 195–96. See also Simone De Angelis, *Anthropologien, Genese und Konfiguration einer "Wissenschaft vom Menschen" in der Frühen Neuzeit* (Berlin, New York: De Gruyter, 2010), 357–58.

27 Hugues Grotius, *Le Droit de la guerre et de la paix* (Amsterdam: Pierre De Coup, 1724), Discours Préliminaire, vol. 1, §§VI-VII, 5–6: "It is therefore not true that every animal, without exception, pursues only its own benefit. [...] There are those [animals] that neglect their own interests on behalf of their own offspring or in support of other individuals of the same species [...]." (My translation.)

28 See Simone De Angelis, "Lex naturalis, Leges naturae, "Regeln der Moral": Der Begriff des "Naturgesetzes" und die Entstehung der modernen "Wissenschaften vom Menschen" im naturrechtlichen Zeitalter,"" in 'Natur', Naturrecht und Geschichte: Aspekte eines fundamentalen Begründungsdiskurses der Neuzeit (1600–1900), ed. Simone De Angelis, Florian Gelzer, and Lucas M. Gisi (Heidelberg: Winter, 2010) 47–70; see also De Angelis, *Anthropologien*, ch. 6.

29 Richard Cumberland, *Traité philosophique des loix naturelles, ou l'on recherche et l'on établit, par la nature des choses, la forme de ces loix, leurs principaux chefs, leur ordre, leur publication & leur obligation* (Amsterdam: Pierre Mortier, 1744), Discours Préliminaire de l'Auteur, §18, 20.

30 De Angelis, *Lex naturalis*, passim.

31 Cumberland, *Traité philosophique des loix naturelles*, ch. II, §17, 138.

32 Ibid., §18, 140. On Cumberland's concepts of "reciprocal altruism" and cooperation see also De Angelis, *Anthropologien*, "Introduction", 8–11 and ch. 6.2 ("Biologie der Moral"), 363–74.

33 Cumberland, *Traité philosophique des loix naturelles*, ch. II, §20, 145–46.

34 Ibid., §22, 152–54.
35 Ibid., §23, 159–62; here, 161.
36 Thomas Willis, "The Anatomy of the Brain and the Description and Use of the Nerves," in *The Remaining Medical Works of that Famous and Renowned Physician Dr. Thomas Willis*, ed. Samuel Pordage (London: Dring, Harper, Leigh, and Martyn, 1681), ch. 26, 160.
37 Ibid., 162; Cumberland, *Traité Philosophique des Loix Naturelles*, ch. II, §26, 168–67. Cf. De Angelis, *Anthropologien*, 383–87.
38 Evelyn L. Forget, "Evocations of Sympathy: Sympathetic Imagery in Eighteenth-Century Social Theory and Physiology," annual supplement, *History of Political Economy* 35 (2003): 290–95.
39 Ibid., 292.
40 Smith, *The Theory of Moral Sentiments*, 14.
41 István Hont, *Jealousy of Trade: International Competition and the Nation-State in Historical Perspective* (Cambridge, MA, London: Harvard University Press, 2005), 6.
42 Cumberland, *Traité philosophique des loix naturelles*, ch. II, §27, 170 and 173. It is noteworthy that current empirically oriented research on altruism or economic and social actions refers to "strong reciprocity," which is considered "a predisposition to cooperate with others, and to punish (at personal cost, if necessary) those who violate the norms of cooperation, even when it is implausible to expect that these costs will be recovered at a later date." Herbert Gintis et al., "Moral Sentiments and Material Interests: Origins, Evidence, and Consequences," in *Moral Sentiments and Material Interests: The Foundations of Cooperation in Economic Life*, ed. Herbert Gintis et al. (Cambridge, MA, London: MIT Press, 2005), 8.
43 Hont, *Jealousy of Trade*, 1–6.
44 Ibid., 9: "Truly modern politics, [...], commenced when trade became the focus of political attention. Jealousy of trade was thus a post-Machiavellian development." On the subject of Machiavelli's concept of state, cf. Thomas Maissen, "Der Staatsbegriff in Machiavellis Theorie des Wandels," in *Niccolò Machiavelli, Die Geburt des Staates*, ed. Manuel Knoll and Stefano Saracino (Stuttgart: Steiner, 2010), 55–70. Hirschman also dedicates the second part of his essay to the question as to "[h]ow Economic Expansion was Expected to Improve the Political Order." See Hirschman, *The Passions*, 67–113.
45 Smith, *The Theory of Moral Sentiments*, VII, IV (on the manner in which different authors have treated the practical rules of morality), II, 390.
46 My translation. See Pufendorf, *Le droit de la nature et des gens*, Bk. 5, ch. I, §1, note 1, 1–2.
47 My translation. See Hans E. Bödeker and István Hont, "Naturrecht, Politische Ökonomie und Geschichte der Menschheit: Der Diskurs über Politik und Gesellschaft in der Frühen Neuzeit," in *Naturrecht — Spätaufklärung — Revolution*, ed. Otto Dann and Diethelm Klippel (Hamburg: Meiner, 1995), 87.
48 Hont, *Politics in Commercial Society*, 41.
49 See, however, Peter H. Reill, "Eighteenth-century Uses of Vitalism in Constructing the Human Sciences," in *Biology and Ideology: From Descartes to Dawkins*, ed. Denis R. Alexander and Ronald L. Numbers (Chicago, London: University of Chicago Press, 2010), 61–87.
50 Wolfgang Pross, "Geschichte als Provokation der Geschichtsphilosophie, Iselin und Herder," in *Isaak Iselin und die Geschichtsphilosophie der Europäischen Aufklärung*, ed. Lucas M. Gisi and Wolfgang Rother (Basel: Schwabe, 2011), 208. (My translation.)
51 Ibid. (My translation.)

52 Peter H. Reill, "Das Problem des Allgemeinen und des Besonderen im geschicht-
    lichen Denken und in den historiographischen Darstellungen des späten 18.
    Jahrhunderts," in *Teil und Ganzes: Zum Verhältnis von Einzel- und Gesamtan-
    alyse in Geschichts- und Sozialwissenschaften, Beiträge zur Historik*, ed. Karl
    Acham and Winfried Schulze (Munich: DTV, 1990), 141–68, here, 156.

53 Adam Ferguson, *Principles of Moral and Political Sciences* (Edinburgh: Stra-
    han, Cadell & Creech, 1792), vol. 1, 190–92.

54 Ibid., 190–91; Jean L. Le Clerc de Buffon, *Œuvres Complètes de Buffon* (Paris:
    Garnier, 1853), vol. 2, "Histoire Naturelle de l'Homme," 1–99.

55 Adam Ferguson, *Essay on the History of Civil Society* (London: Printed for
    Millar & Cadell, in the Strand; and Kincaid, Bell, Edinburgh, 1768), part III,
    sec. 2 ("The History of Subordination"), 187.

56 Ibid.

57 David Hume, *Enquiries Concerning the Human Understanding and Concerning
    the Principles of Morals* (Oxford: Clarendon, 1902), 83–84: "The records of
    wars, intrigues, and revolutions, are so many collections of experiments by
    which the politician or moral philosopher fixes the principles of his science, in
    the same manner as the physician or natural philosopher becomes acquainted
    with the nature of plants, minerals, and other objects, by the experiments
    which he forms concerning them."

58 Ibid., 87.

59 Marc J. Ratcliffe, *The Quest for the Invisible: Microscopy in the Enlightenment*
    (Farnham: Ashgate, 2009).

60 Simone De Angelis, "Gedankenexperimente, Analogien und kühne Hypothesen:
    Die Bedeutung der 'Wissenschaften vom Leben' für die Beziehung von Anthro-
    pologie und Geschichtsdenken in der Spätaufklärung — ein programmatischer
    Entwurf," in *Konzepte der Einbildungskraft in der Philosophie, den Wissenschaf-
    ten und den Künsten des 18. Jahrhunderts*, ed. Rudolf Meer, Giuseppe Motta,
    and Gideon Stiening (Berlin, Boston: De Gruyter, 2019), 303–21.

61 Smith, *Wealth of Nations*, vol. 1, I.ii, 25.

62 Ibid.

63 Ibid., 26.

64 Ibid.

65 Ibid., 26–27: "It is not from the benevolence of the butcher, the brewer, or the
    baker, that we expect our dinner, but from their regard to their own interest."

66 Ibid., 27–30.

67 Ibid., vol. 1, II.iii, 343.

68 This does not render Smith a "vitalist", nor does it suggest that his is a "vitalist
    system", as Charles T. Wolfe critically observed; see Charles T. Wolfe, "Smith-
    ian Vitalism?" *Journal of Scottish Philosophy* 16, no. 3 (2018): 264–271. Instead,
    the comparison between economy and animate bodies is linked to the c. 1750
    approach in natural history outlined above, which ties it to the resulting nat-
    uralization of history.

69 Peter H. Reill, "Eighteenth-century Uses of Vitalism," 61–87.

70 Caspar F. Wolff, *Theorie von der Generation in zwei Abhandlungen erklärt
    und bewiesen* [1764], *Theoria Generationis* [1759], ed. Robert Herrlinger
    (Hildesheim: Georg Olms Verlagsbuchhandlung, 1966), here, *Theorie der
    Generation*, Zwote Abhandlung, §28.

71 Wolfgang Pross, "Die Begründung der Geschichte aus der Natur: Herders
    Konzept von 'Gesetzen' in der Geschichte," in *Wissenschaft als kulturelle Praxis
    1750–1900*, ed. Hans E. Bödeker, Peter H. Reill, and Jürgen Schlumbohm
    (Göttingen: Vandenhoeck & Ruprecht, 1999), 187–225.

72 Smith, *Wealth of Nations*, vol. 1, I.v, 55.

73 Ibid., I.xi.p, 265.

74 Ibid., I.viii, 99.
75 Ibid., 265.
76 Ibid.
77 Ibid., 266.
78 Ibid.
79 Ibid., 267.
80 Ibid.
81 Daniel Diatkine, *Adam Smith, La découverte du capitalisme et de ses limites* (Paris: Seuil, 2019), 169.
82 Ibid., 139–80.
83 Ibid., 173.
84 Smith, *The Theory of Moral Sentiments*, part IV, ch. 1, esp. 215–16: "When the legislature establishes premiums and other encouragements to advance the linen or woollen manufactures, its conducts seldom proceeds from pure sympathy with the wearer of cheap or fine cloth, and much less from that with the manufacturer or merchant. The perfection of police, the extension of trade and manufacture, are noble and magnificent objects." Cf. also Diatkine, *Adam Smith*, 65–98 and 175.
85 Smith, *Wealth of Nations*, vol. 2, IV.vii, 584: "Of the greater part of the regulations concerning the colony trade, the merchants who carry it on, it must be observed, have been the principal advisers. We must not wonder, therefore, if, in the greater part of them, their interest has been more considered than either that of the colonies or that of the mother country. In their exclusive privilege of supplying the colonies with all the goods which they wanted from Europe, and of purchasing all such parts of their surplus produce as could not interfere with any of the trades which they themselves carried on at home, the interest of the colonies was sacrificed to the interest of those merchants."
86 Ibid., IV.vii.b, 565: "Every colonist gets more land than he can possibly cultivate. He has no rent, and scarce any taxes to pay. No landlord shares with him in its produce, and the share with the souveraign is commonly but a trifle. He has every motive to render as great as possible a produce, which is thus to be entirely its own. But his land is commonly so extensive, that with all his industry, and with all the industry of other people whom he can get to employ, he can seldom make it produce the tenth part of what it is capable of producing. He is eager, therefore, to collect labourers from all quarters, and to reward them with the most liberal wages."
87 Ibid., IV.vii.a, 560: "The vegetable food of the inhabitants, though from their want of industry not very abundant, was not altogether so scanty. It consisted in Indian corn, yams, potatoes, bananas, &c. plants which were then altogether unknown in Europe, and which have never since been very much esteemed in it, or supposed to yield a sustenance equal to what is drawn from the common sorts of grain and pulse, which have been cultivated in this part of the world time out of mind."
88 Ibid., IV.vii.b, 566: "The high wages of labour encourage population. The cheapness and plenty of good land encourage improvement, and enable the proprietor to pay those high wages. In those wages consists almost the whole price of the land; and though they are high, considered as the wages of labour, they are low, considered as the price of what is so very valuable. What encourages the progress of population and improvement, encourages that of real wealth and greatness."
89 Ibid., 585: "The councils, which, in the colony legislature, correspond to the House of Lords in Great Britain, are not composed of an hereditary nobility. [...] Before the commencement of the present disturbances, the colony assemblies had not only the legislative, but a part of the executive power. [...] There is

more equality, therefore, among the English colonists than among the inhabitants of the mother country. Their manners are more republican, and their governments, those of three of the provinces of New England in particular, have hitherto been more republican too."

90 Smith, *Wealth of Nations*, vol. 2, IV.vii.b, 567: "In their dependency upon the mother state, they resemble those of ancient Rome; but their great distance from Europe has in all of them alleviated more or less the effects of this dependency. Their situation has placed them less in the view and less in the power of their mother country."

91 Buffon, *Œuvres Complètes*, vol. 1 ("De la manière d'étudier l'histoire naturelle"), 26.

92 Smith, *Wealth of Nations*, vol. 2, IV.vii.c, 560 and note 9.

93 Ibid., IV.vii.c, 604–05. Cf. also Diatkine, *Adam Smith*, 143–44.

94 Pufendorf, *Le droit de nature et des gens*, Bk. 1, ch. 3, §XV, note 5, 196.

95 Smith, *Wealth of Nations*, vol. 2, IV.vii.c, 604.

96 Ibid., 605.

97 Ibid.

98 Ibid., 606.

99 Alexis de Tocqueville, *De la Démocratie en Amérique* (Bruxelles: Société Belge de Librairie, 1837).

100 Smith, *Wealth of Nations*, vol. 2, IV.vii.c, 625: "The distance of America from the seat of government, besides, the natives, of that country might flatter themselves, with some appearance of reason too, would not be of very long continuance. Such has hitherto been the rapid progress of that country in wealth, population and improvement, that in the course of little more than a century, perhaps, the produce of American might exceed that of British taxation. The seat of the empire would then naturally remove itself to that part of the empire which contributed most to the general defense and support of the whole."

101 See Hirschman, *The Passions*, 111–12.

5 The problem of embeddedness revisited

Self-interest as a challenge in ethnographic and historical research

Christof Dejung

How universal is *Homo Oeconomicus*? And how should we envision the relationship between the economy and the rest of society within the context of intercultural comparisons? These questions have been the focus of ethnological research since the early twentieth century. Many ethnologists had lingering doubts about the allegedly timeless model of humans as actors driven solely by self-interest; a model which, with the advent of neoclassical theory, had achieved its significance largely because it abstracted itself from its cultural and historical contexts and was based on the simple premise of maximum utility.[1] Such an approach met with bitter resistance from certain circles of ethnologists; as a matter of fact, the emerging academic discipline of ethnology was founded upon the very supposition that the so-called "primitive" cultures of Africa, Tierra del Fuego, and Polynesia functioned according to fundamentally different rules than modern societies. Consequently, researchers were convinced, the exchange of goods and services was also organized differently than in Western industrial societies. These ethnologists contended that basic assumptions of modern economic theory were to be "provincialized"[2] and considered an integral feature of Euro-American modernity in the first place. These models were, in their view, not universal at all and thus unsuitable for developing an understanding of the economies of non-Western civilizations. Furthermore, they argued that exchanges of goods and services in such civilizations did not serve individual maximum utility, but were instead socially embedded and primarily pursued with the aim of stabilizing the societies in question. However, such views were hotly contested even within the field of ethnology: other researchers were convinced that people in all cultures endeavored to realize their self-interest. These researchers postulated that the models of modern economic theory were universally valid and thus could also be applied to colonized indigenous peoples.[3]

This essay aims to show that these debates offer valuable insights for the field of economic history and ultimately challenge the notion of "the economy" as a clear-cut social subsystem. By questioning the limits of the use of economics to explain certain phenomena, and by scrutinizing the relationship between economics and society, the ethnological debate highlighted issues that were also often addressed by historians.[4] The concept of social embeddedness, which was developed within the scope of the economic anthropology debate, was often at the heart of these discussions. Ever since 1985, when the sociologist and economist Mark Granovetter published his groundbreaking article "Economic Action and Social Structure"[5] and introduced the concept of social embeddedness to the general social-scientific theoretical debate, the problem of embeddedness has become a key aspect of many economic-sociological and economic-historical works that seek to overcome the limitations of neoclassical theory. Granovetter's idea was that the exchange of goods and services should no longer be interpreted as a purely economic relationship between isolated buyers and sellers. Instead, he argued that serious consideration should be given to the fact that economic actors are invariably embedded within a social context, and that their actions are influenced not only by individual utility expectations, but also by cultural codes, social expectations, and possible sanctions.[6] Despite the undeniable fruitfulness of this concept, the ubiquitous use of the term "embeddedness" has been repeatedly criticized of late. Don Robotham, for example, notes that economists who work with the tools of institutional economics primarily view social embeddedness as a means of reducing transaction costs. In accordance with the notion of market players who behave in a rational and calculating manner, Robotham contends that the respective institutional frameworks are used to achieve the smoothest possible exchange of goods and services. By contrast, he says that many ethnologists see the institutional framework as a source of reciprocity and trust, and thus as an actual counterpart to the market, which is considered basically a domain driven by self-interest.[7]

These diverse notions of the relationship between the market and social contexts open the floodgates of the theoretical debate.[8] The matter is rendered even more complicated because the concept of embeddedness emerged during a debate that raged for decades over the nature of the modern market economy in relation to archaic economic systems. Granovetter's essay also responded to the aforementioned ethnological research controversy, which had been sparked by Karl Polanyi. In his book *The Great Transformation*, published in 1944, Polanyi had postulated the theory that, starting in the nineteenth century, the European economy had emerged as an autonomous realm during the process of modernization, whereas the economic activities of traditional societies—particularly in the ostensibly primitive tribal cultures of non-Western civilizations—were determined by social and family-related constraints.[9] In doing so, Polanyi sought to counter such views as those introduced by Adam Smith, who had maintained that even people in traditional societies had a quasi-natural tendency to optimize their individual gain through economic exchanges.[10] Granovetter, on the other hand, assumed an intermediate position in his article. He was of the opinion that utility-maximizing economic action also occurred in traditional societies (a position that had been disputed by the substantivist school of thought that strongly identified with Polanyi). Granovetter also argued that economic exchanges have always been socially embedded, even in modern societies (a circumstance that was generally viewed as of only secondary importance by the formalists, who were the rivals of the substantivists).[11] Granovetter's proposed solution was to interpret economic action as social action, whereby, by definition, it could not exist outside of social networks, but instead was embedded in them and thus constituted an integral component of these structures. He pointed out that social behavior was always intentional, and thus automatically rational, although this rationality need not necessarily be oriented toward economic profit: "[I]t aims not only at economic goals but also at sociability, approval, status, and power." Granovetter went on to say that most economists adopt a narrow interpretation of rationality because they draw an arbitrary line between social and economic intentions.[12]

Although the concept of embeddedness put forward by Granovetter sought to demonstrate a way out of the cul-de-sac that the field of economic anthropology had maneuvered itself into with the dispute between the substantivists and the formalists, his proposal was unable to bring a definitive conclusion to the debates concerning the relationship between modern industrial capitalism and the rest of society that had been pursued since the late nineteenth century. Indeed, if every social action can also be understood as an economic one, it undermines the very notion that economics is a clearly definable social subsystem. It is highly symptomatic of this state of affairs that Granovetter opted to give his article the subtitle "The *Problem* of Embeddedness." The fact that, despite decades of debate, economic anthropologists have ultimately failed to reach a consensus about how to envision the relationship between economy and society suggests that there exists a highly complex and paradoxical relationship between these two analytical categories that—and this is the case for historical analyses as well—cannot easily be reduced to a common denominator.

This contribution sets out to describe this ongoing conflict by tracing the genealogy of the concept of embeddedness. This entails expanding the economical and historical theoretical discussion to include post-colonial theory, because economic anthropologists have, while disputing over the concept of social embeddedness, also heatedly debated the limits of Western explanatory models of the world. The contentious issue concerned the question whether the economy as a sphere of activity distinctively characterized by self-interest was a universal feature that could be detected in all human societies, or whether such a utility-driven system was particular to modern Western societies: according to the latter view, economic transactions were always socially embedded and thus mitigated with regard to the cohesion of society as whole in, respectively, pre-modern and non-European societies.

The chapter is subdivided into four parts: the first section shows how during the late nineteenth and early twentieth centuries social scientists postulated a dichotomy between a socially nonembedded modern economy and a socially embedded premodern economy. They cited primitive non-European economies, which were described by contemporary ethnologists as prime examples of such embedded economic forms. The second section traces the debate between the substantivists and the formalists. Based on descriptions of non-European economic systems, researchers such as Bronisław Malinowski, Marcel Mauss, and Karl Polanyi openly criticized the ostensibly timeless figure of the utility-maximizing *Homo Oeconomicus*. At the same time, however, a number of economic ethnologists argued that non-European actors were bound to an economic rationality that was similar to what had been observed in modern Western economies, leading these researchers to conclude that the postulates of modern economic theory could indeed claim universal validity. The third section describes how the purported dichotomy between modern Western and primitive non-Western economies lost plausibility after the end of colonial rule and the rise of structuralist approaches in ethnology. Economic ethnologists also began to use ethnographic methods to describe the modern economy as socially embedded. Nevertheless, a number of critics argued that, due to its complexity, modern capitalism could not be adequately described using ethnological approaches that had been developed primarily to document small-scale, traditional economies. The fourth section suggests a possible way out of this dilemma that does not involve seeing the economy as a highly differentiated social subsystem that can be adequately described only with the aid of genuine economic approaches. Instead, the quest to understand the nature of the economy should be understood as a heuristical strategy that delves into the question of how societies cope with shortages and organize relationships based on trade, without necessarily resorting to the theoretical arsenal of the field of economics. The chapter thus aims to show that the question of whether self-interest can be historized—or whether it is a human universal—lies at the heart of this debate.

The modern age and its reflection

The quest to understand the nature of the economy has captivated a multitude of sociological theoreticians since the late nineteenth century.[13] In view of the sweeping upheaval that European society experienced during industrialization and the establishment of capitalism, these researchers began to explore what was characteristic of the "economy" under these new circumstances. Many were of the opinion that the modern economy was influenced by development processes in two respects: in terms of quantity—since industrial means of production made it possible to produce astonishing amounts of goods—and in terms of quality. Economic activities increasingly appeared to have been removed from their social embeddedness, and were now governed by a specific rational and utility-maximizing logic of their own. Max Weber, for example, was of the opinion that entrepreneurs in the capitalist world allowed themselves to be guided solely by the "objective interests of modern rational management," adding that this was by no means identical to their private or family interests, which were characterized by "feelings of mutual solidarity" and rested on an "affectual basis." Hence, these private interests "stand in direct conflict with the rational [...] economically specialized organization of their environment."[14] Werner Sombart presented similar arguments and was of the opinion that, in modern capitalism, economic activity is disassociated from its social context and becomes an end in itself. He argued that it is precisely this self-referentiality that gives capitalism its enormous dynamism.[15] Georg Simmel contended that the modern economy was characterized by "the elimination of the personal element" and that this made money "the ideal representative of such a condition since it makes possible relationships between people but leaves them personally undisturbed."[16]

All of these researchers were convinced that the capitalist economy was so overwhelmingly productive precisely because it had escaped the restraints of social embeddedness and gave economic actors free rein to realize their self-interest. According to Weber, this was a specifically Western phenomenon. Societies in India and China were, in his opinion, incapable of forging a capitalist economy because they were too rooted in their religious traditions.[17] Such arguments set the capitalist economy entirely apart from "the other," both in a temporal and a geographical sense: temporally in that a pre-modern form of economy is juxtaposed with a modern one, and geographically in that capitalism is portrayed as a purely Western achievement. This is an indication of how reflections on social modernizations often involved drawing a line of demarcation with the non-Western world, irrespective of the geographical location or period in history.

Particularly during the colonial era, the reshaping of the world map also led to a reorganization of temporal notions; non-Western peoples were viewed as primitive or backward, in other words, they were denied "coevalness."[18] The field of ethnology established itself in the late nineteenth century as an academic discipline that dealt with the so-called primitive cultures of the colonial periphery. However, in the eyes of cultural scientist Erhard Schüttpelz, the fact that ethnologists turned their attention toward peoples who lived on the "dark side of earthly progress" resulted in a paradox. In his opinion, ethnology constitutes the only academic discipline that is capable of voicing consistent empirical and theoretical criticism of social evolutionism. In order to develop this criticism, though, Schüttpelz emphasizes that the field of ethnology requires the "primitive" as a figure that translates between evolutionary models of progress and approaches that could be used to challenge these models. Nevertheless, he notes that this "primitive" is not an actual, identifiable form of society, but rather a cultural projection of "the other" that modern Western society has contrived to bolster its own sense of self-assurance.[19] Accordingly, ethnological studies inevitably exhibit a certain degree of self-referentiality.

And in fact, after the mid-nineteenth century, numerous ethnologists, economic geographers, and economists aimed to gain insights into the development of human civilization and modern societies by studying colonial and indigenous peoples. For instance, the German ethnologist Max Moszkowski postulated that "the study of how primitive people live is essentially always based on the assumption that this endeavor will allow us to recognize the foundations of our own development." He went on to say that "we believe that these peoples, who we also refer to as indigenous peoples, have remained relatively close to the original state of mankind, and we hope that what our studies reveal about their lives will produce a mirror image of our own past." Even though ethnologists based their research on the premise of the civilizational and—more importantly—technological superiority of Western society, they still strove to emphasize the cultural competence of indigenous peoples and stressed over and over that even "the primitive races of Southeast Asia and Australia [...] can gaze back on thousands, if not tens of thousands, of years of developmental history that doubtlessly has left its mark on them."[20]

Not surprisingly, many ethnologists were outraged over the work of economist Karl Bücher who, in his sweeping account of economic history, *Die Entstehung der Volkswirtschaft*, had set about compiling the character traits "of the lowest-standing people to form an impression of the origins of the economy and the development of society" and, in doing so, had disputed that such persons possessed any economic acumen whatsoever beyond "the individual search for food."[21] One of Bücher's harshest critics was Wilhelm Koppers, a Catholic priest who was appointed professor of economics in Vienna in 1928. He contended that Bücher not only "viewed the entire world of indigenous peoples as a largely homogeneous mass," but also that his theory about primitive societies having no economies whatsoever stood in stark contrast to the entire body of ethnological research, which had encountered "no people anywhere or at any point in history who completely lacked a culture and an economy." Consequently, Koppers concluded that "wherever there is any type of culture, some form of economy can also be found."[22] Similar arguments were presented by Hungarian legal scholar Felix Somló in his 1909 book on the exchange of goods in primitive societies, *Der Güterverkehr in der Urgesellschaft*, in which he characterized what he called the "lowest level" of primitive economy in a manner that has startling similarities with the description of the modern economy that Mark Granovetter published three-quarters of a century later:

> We may not assume that either an economically isolated individual or a group of economically fully integrated individuals occupies the lowest level; rather we have encountered, at the lowest level that is accessible to us, an assembled economic group that consists of mutually dependent economic individuals and smaller economic groups, which represents for us the earliest system for the circulation of goods.[23]

The pre-modern economy as a socially embedded phenomenon?

All of these studies were, of course, produced within a colonial context. They were, however, not pursued with the primary goal of facilitating the economic exploitation of overseas territories and possessions. Instead, the ethnological discourse can be interpreted as an effort to use the non-Western world as a mirror that allows modern society to reflect upon itself and explore whether or not conventional Western ways of thinking are universally applicable.[24] Ethnologist Bronisław Malinowski was one of the first researchers to use the economies of primitive societies to challenge the paradigms of the economy of the day. In an article published in the *Economic Journal* in 1918, he argued that a self-interested figure such as the utility-maximizing entrepreneur and a system "with the interplay of supply and demand determining value and regulating all economic life" did not exist on the Trobriand Islands, which he had studied.[25] He went into greater detail in his main work *Argonauts of the Western Pacific*, published in 1922, which specified that economic transactions on the Trobriand Islands fell into three categories. first, there was bartering, in which Melanesian traders were interested in making the best possible deal. Second, there were transactions within one's own family. And, third, there was the Kula ring, *i.e.* the regular exchange of bracelets and necklaces across the Trobriand Islands, which stabilized alliances with other tribes.[26]

During the 1930s, Berlin-based ethnologist Richard Thurnwald voiced the opinion that applying "our current rationalist point of view and our modern economic thinking [...] to primitive cultures" was "an invalid approach."[27] Although Thurnwald explicitly referred to the enormous diversity of non-Western forms of economy—noting in the process that China had an organized banking system and a highly effective merchant class—he was convinced, nevertheless, that he could identify certain commonalities among them. In his opinion, two characteristics were emblematic of the primitive economy: first, the fact that people often got along without money and that achieving the greatest possible amount of profit was not an end in itself; second, that transactions were often influenced by social rank and that all aspects of life—and thus also economic activities—were part of a coherent social whole.[28]

Such views were popularized during the 1940s and 1950s with the publication of works by Karl Polanyi and Marcel Mauss that are today regarded as seminal texts in the field of economic anthropology. It was ultimately the shockwaves from the economic crisis of the inter-war era and the rise of fascism that prompted Karl Polanyi in his work *The Great Transformation* to conclude that an economy that had shed its social embeddedness—like the economies that had formed during the nineteenth century in the Western world—takes on self-destructive tendencies, as actors are merely driven by self-interest, and finally drags the remaining society down with it.[29] Polanyi thus dismissed the views of such great philosophers of the Enlightenment as Adam Smith, David Hume, and Georg Wilhelm Friedrich Hegel, who had postulated that economic exchanges compelled social actors to be honest, self-sufficient, and reliable, leading these great minds to conclude that the market was governed by the same moral laws as civil society.[30] As far as Polanyi was concerned, the political and economic turmoil of the early twentieth century had exposed such hopes for what they were: nothing but wishful thinking. According to Polanyi, the antithesis of the modern age, in which the market represented the central authority and all other social spheres merely functioned as its appendages, was to be found in pre-capitalist social formations, in which the economy did not constitute its own sphere, but was instead always embedded within social contexts.[31] He cited diverse non-European peoples as prime examples of such pre-modern societies, in which people had little interest in monetary gain, and supported his assertions in particular with references to the research of Malinowski and Thurnwald.[32]

Shortly thereafter, Marcel Mauss published his book *The Gift*, in which he also seized upon Malinowski's studies and questioned his distinction between gifts that served as payment for goods and gifts that stabilized social relationships. In Mauss's view, this distinction was irrelevant because ritualized economic transactions in archaic societies—such as those practiced by the Melanesian Kula ring and the potlatch ceremony of the Native Americans of the Northern Pacific Coast—always served to stabilize social relationships.[33] In fact, he pointed out that it was a distinguishing characteristic of these societies that economic exchanges never took place between individuals, but were instead always interactions among collectives.[34] Mauss thus also contrasted primitive societies with modern industrial societies, in which the actions of economic players were primarily characterized by the cold and calculated pursuit of individual profit. Although he admitted that moral considerations also played a role in industrial societies, he argued that such factors invariably conflicted with the world of business and commerce. By contrast, in archaic societies there was no contradiction between morals and economy. Mauss's book was more than just an analytical study. It was a polemic work and a critique of modern societies being purely driven by self-interest—not to mention the pretense that *Homo Oeconomicus* could transform from an abstract economic concept to an actually existing aspect of everyday normality.[35] Mauss also adopted decidedly teleological arguments. In his view, socioeconomic development appeared, almost inevitably, to end in the "iron cage" of capitalism (in the words of Max Weber).[36]

The latent tension between the universal rationality assumptions of modern economic theory and the ethnological endeavor to demonstrate the limits of this theory—by describing traditional tribal societies—eventually erupted in a bitter debate between the so-called formalists and their rivals, the substantivists. Already by the early 1940s, ethnologist Melville Herskovits and economist Frank Knight were clashing over the question of whether it was better to use inductive or deductive methods to conduct a sociological analysis of the economy.[37] Herskovits's view of the matter was that people of all cultures engage in utility-maximizing behavior—even if their preferences may vary from culture to culture—leading him to conclude that it would also be expedient in economic anthropology studies to start out by examining the choices made by individual actors.[38] But this methodological individualism, which was explicitly oriented toward the model of modern economic theory, was fiercely criticized one and a half decades later. The dispute was sparked by Polanyi's essay, "The Economy as an Instituted Process." Polanyi revisited the arguments put forward by Malinowski and Mauss and differentiated between two forms of economic activity. On the one hand, there were formalistic types of economic activity, in which transactions were devoid of social embeddedness and driven by pure self-interest. He said that such pursuits were most common in industrial societies. On the other hand, there was a substantivist form of economy that was typically found in pre-industrial societies. Here, he pointed out that it was the interactions between people and their social environment that were the focus of attention.[39]

The culture-relativistic position adopted by Polanyi and other researchers, who were subsequently referred to as substantivists, was fundamentally questioned by such ethnologists as Herskovits and Raymond Firth.[40] They noted that people of all cultures have to deal with a scarcity of resources, and they behave rationally when searching for a solution to the ensuing problems; hence, the suppositions of modern economic theory could claim to be universally valid. These formalists, as they were called, alleged that Polanyi had adopted a romantic view of pre-industrial societies that was ultimately hostile toward the market. Furthermore, they pointed out that ancient kingdoms and archaic cultures had also engaged in trade and maintained markets, and that this was not a specifically modern phenomenon, as Polanyi would lead people to believe. They went on to say that the concept of self-interest was not limited to monetary matters, and could also be applied to other social areas. Finally, they expressed regret that Polanyi refrained from applying the substantivist approach to modern society.[41]

Formalist ethnologists adopted a universalistic approach when they rejected the idea of a fundamental difference between economic forms in Western and non-Western societies and, instead, searched for commonalities.[42] Already back in the 1930s, British economist D. M. Goodfellow had voiced the opinion that modern economic theory should rightly be considered universal, since it would be absurd to assume that primitive cultures and Western industrialized societies operate under their own individual economic laws: "[I]f we turn our attention to these [...] differences we shall find at the very outset that we are robbed of our hard-and-fast line between the savage and the civilized." In Goodfellow's view, there are societies in every corner of the world that endeavor to control economic exchanges through traditional practices and the threat of sanctions, and everywhere there are individuals who seek to utilize resources as efficiently as possible and strive to maximize their earnings from business relationships. He also noted that among colonial peoples and modern Europeans alike it is common to allow relatives to have a stake in one's own businesses to strengthen social ties.[43]

The explosive nature of the question of how best to study the economies of pre-modern societies was also reflected by the fact that the economic anthropology dispute was closely linked to debates in the field of history. Polanyi was also strongly influenced by Karl Bücher's study on the history of the economy, *Die Entstehung der Volkswirtschaft,* first published in 1893, in which the author had voiced the opinion that not only were there no organized exchanges of goods among colonial indigenous peoples, but that the economies of ancient European cultures were also primarily oriented toward individual self-sufficiency. Bücher maintained that it was not until the Middle Ages that a market economy gradually emerged.[44] Many historians disagreed. Eduard Meyer, an expert in the study of antiquity, argued at the Conference of German Historians in 1895 that ancient economies were undoubtedly market-oriented, and could lay claim to certain similarities with the economic structures of the modern age. The decades-long dispute between modernists and primitivists that marked the study of the economic history of the ancient world only came to a conclusion when British historian Moses Finley drew upon economic anthropology approaches to give a completely new twist to the debate in the 1990s. Finley conceded to Bücher that there was, in fact, no profit-oriented entrepreneurialism in the ancient world that was comparable with modern-day capitalism. In contrast to Bücher, however, he considered it as relatively unproductive to explore the degree of modernity in ancient economies or their lack of development toward a market economy. Instead, he argued with reference to Malinowski and Polanyi that it was misleading to analyze ancient economies based on the concepts of modern economic theory. He maintained that the ancient world had no economic system in the modern sense of the word. Monetary profits were viewed not so much as an end in themselves, but rather as an opportunity to acquire political influence and status.[45] Finley argued that ancient economies were but one component of a macrosocial order that revolved around acquiring positions of power. He thus took a similar position to the one assumed by the substantivist economic anthropologists.[46] In effect, both ethnologists and historians remained, at least to a certain degree, similarly skeptical over whether approaches from the field of economics were actually suitable to the study of societies that differed from modern Western civilization in a temporal and/or geographical sense.[47] This can be seen as an indication that the interests of historians and ethnologists share similarities to the extent that researchers in both disciplines attempt to reveal structures and cultural paradigms of societies that are fundamentally different from their own.[48]

In the field of economic anthropology, the dispute between the substantivists and the formalists ended with an overwhelming sense of fatigue at the turn of the twenty-first century, without these adversaries having achieved any consensus on key issues. The heated nature of the dispute was largely a reflection of the fact that this was a conflict over fundamental questions about human nature: about whether people are primarily selfish or altruistic, whether they are able to make decisions based on their own free will, or whether their actions are determined by their social surroundings. The different camps also disagreed over whether the most effective path toward a social science analysis should be based primarily on observations of the relevant society, i.e. an inductive approach, or built on universally valid premises derived from theory, i.e. a deductive method of investigation. However, the conflict remained largely gridlocked because these very fundamental positions were almost never empirically verified. To make matters worse, the rivals often had only a superficial knowledge of the conceptual systems and epistemological positions of the opposing side, ultimately leading the debate to drift into fruitless polemic. Nevertheless, this made for the formation of economic anthropology as a separate subdiscipline, and economic analyses became an integral part of the ethnological arsenal of methods after the mid-twentieth century.[49]

Post-colonial reversals

The establishment of economic anthropology took place at a time when ethnology was forced to reorient itself fundamentally in response to the geopolitical turmoil in the wake of World War II. After the end of colonial rule and amid increasing criticism of the exploitation of the Third World, ethnological narratives that attempted to depict non-European cultures as primitive lost their persuasiveness. Such arguments were now seen as Eurocentric and, at best, as "exoticizing."[50] Thanks to the work of Claude Lévi-Strauss, structural anthropology became the new paradigm in which research now primarily focused on the relationships between specific cultural elements in the societies under consideration.[51] The use of structuralist methods made it possible to call into question the ostensibly clear dichotomy between primitive and modern societies. Lévi-Strauss argued that the act of thinking in modern societies was characterized by an engineering approach that aims to alter existing conditions, whereas "savage thinking" in primitive societies could be viewed as a "tinkering" approach that is oriented toward pre-existing conditions and seeks to adapt them in new and creative ways. Even though this approach continued to underscore the differences between modern and primitive societies, Lévi-Strauss explicitly denied that one way of thinking was superior to the other, and he pointed out that it was virtually impossible to make an absolute distinction between the two.[52]

As a result of these developments, ethnologists increasingly sought to escape the narrowness of the Western self-image by scrutinizing modern society from an ethnographic perspective. Back in the late 1930s, for instance, Malinowski contended that contemporary ethnology had "to break down the barriers of race and cultural diversity [...] to find the human being in the savage [... and] to discover the primitive in the highly sophisticated Westerner of today."[53] Consequently, after the 1970s, cultural anthropologists such as Mary Douglas and Victor Turner began to apply ethnological approaches to Western societies.[54] The same trend can be observed in the field of economic anthropology, in which such researchers as James Carrier, Chris Hann, and Richard Rottenburg have demonstrated that social relationships and networks also play a key role in the capitalist economy.[55] Embeddedness was now no longer the signature trait of pre-modern economies, as it had been in Polanyi's heyday, but instead, thanks to the work of Granovetter, it could now be used as a concept to study the social embeddedness of the modern capitalist economy.

However, the use of ethnographic concepts to study industrial societies did not remain undisputed. Critics pointed out that when studying modern cultures, it was often impossible to do justice to the macrosocial vision that constitutes one of the main pillars of classic ethnology. In Bruno Latour's work *We Have Never Been Modern*, the author notes that social anthropologists who strive to rid their discipline of all exotic connotations by studying Western societies end up losing what constituted the very originality of their research. Although in tropical regions they succeeded in observing the totality of these cultures from a vantage point at the margins of society, when they returned home these same researchers limited themselves "to studying the marginal aspects" of their own culture and thus lost "all the hard-won advantages of anthropology."[56] This is hardly surprising, since the complexity of capitalist economies, which are characterized by constant innovation and far-reaching, often global chains of impact, can be far less effectively interpreted as a "total social fact"[57] than the small-scale economies of traditional societies.[58]

A major accomplishment of the ethnographic study of Western economies, however, was that it demonstrated the great difficulty in maintaining an absolute division between pre-modern and modern economies, or rather between gift economies and market societies—as Polanyi, Mauss, and other substantivists had postulated. This also called into question conventional rationality assumptions of economic theory. Ethnologist Malcolm Chapman and economist Peter J. Buckley, for example, noted during an ethnographic study of modern companies that professional managers did not always make commercial decisions based on numerical calculations and the evaluation of their self-interest. Although they accepted that their companies had to make a profit to survive, no managers were willing to sacrifice their own corporate divisions in a bid to make a profit for the overall company. Furthermore, the managers in question never made any calculations of transaction costs. During daily operations, they carefully considered who they intended to do business with and who to avoid. Yet intuition and experience often played a larger role here than rational calculations. Based on these observations, Chapman and Buckley questioned the attempt by Oliver Williamson to render corporate decisions quantifiable based on calculations of transaction costs. In their opinion, such an approach was outdated and resembled those used by ethnologists during the nineteenth century. In both fields, economics and social anthropology, researchers examined their objects of study with the help of observer-defined categories, instead of inquiring about how the actors they studied interpreted their worlds. It should be noted that Chapman and Buckley had not set out to abandon the concept of rationality in favor of other categories, such as the level of emotional response. Instead, they were of the opinion that the decision-making of the managers could indeed be interpreted as rational. But they said that this rationality differed from what was postulated by modern economic theory. As a matter of fact, managers did not aim solely for monetary profit but made decisions with regard to their work environment as well.[59]

It is hardly surprising that Chapman and Buckley chose institutional economics as an ideal approach to reflect on a reconceptualization of economic activity. Starting in the 1990s, institutional economics was increasingly described as a possible means that helped to link economics with the general field of social sciences.[60] At the core of institutional economics is the assumption that economic transactions never take place in a vacuum, but that they are governed by institutional conditions, which offer actors a certain guarantee that contractual agreements will be respected. In other words, there were rules (or institutions) that made sure that economic actors were not misled by contractors whose self-interest induced them to behave opportunistically. In addition to formal rules, such as legal regulations, authors like Douglass North also pointed to the importance of informal institutions. North underscored that these informal institutions included concepts of honor and social conventions. In fact, in the literature there is often an emphasis on the importance of family and ethnic networks.[61] What is problematic about this approach is the implication that economic players use the relevant social networks merely to make their businesses as profitable as possible. Studies on the history of family-owned firms have come to the conclusion, though, that the owners of family firms were above all interested in maintaining their respective businesses in order to safeguard the well-being of their families as social entities. Making short-term profits was, at most, a means to ensure the continuity of the family.[62] As the abovementioned study by Chapman and Buckley shows, the findings on the history of family firms can also be adapted to publicly traded and professionally managed modern companies. Harold James similarly pointed out that it would be "endlessly naïve" to assume that entrepreneurs were "simply driven by a quest for profit."[63] Numerous micro-historical studies confirm the observation that the owners of modern companies were sincerely concerned about the well-being of their employees and business partners, and supported them during times of crisis, without calculating the costs and potential benefits of these actions. This, in turn, does not necessarily mean that their generosity was devoid of any economic considerations. As a matter of fact, such behavior could enhance the social relationships between owners and employees, thereby minimizing in-company transaction costs, even if historical actors rarely formulated this in such explicit terms. Instead, it appears that entrepreneurs did not see social and economic spheres as clearly separate areas of interest, and viewed their concern for the social surroundings of their business as a natural part of their company-specific habitus.[64]

The close intertwining of social and corporate spheres even in the modern business world is one of the reasons why the repeated attempts—based on the criterion of social embeddedness—to differentiate between various types of capitalism in diverse countries and regions of the world should be viewed with a certain amount of skepticism.[65] For instance, it is often postulated that the Chinese economy differs from Western capitalism in that economic relationships in China primarily came into existence based on networks that engendered personal relationships (*guanxi*) and trust, while it is said that Western economies are characterized by cost-benefit calculations, the pursuit of self-interest, and the presence of formal institutions.[66] Such a dichotomization can be traced at least as far back as Weber's *Protestant Ethic*.[67] However, a number of researchers have raised objections to such "orientalizations." Instead, they argue that social relationships also play a pivotal role in Western economies. They furthermore point out that, even before the arrival of Europeans, Asia had highly effective trading and banking networks of remarkable institutional stability.[68] Furthermore, historical studies have shown that European and Asian merchants observed very similar cost-benefit calculations at least since the early modern period, and that social networks were of equally fundamental importance in both regions.[69] Hence, the category of embeddedness can be used to help identify slight variations between economic systems in different countries and parts of the world, but it appears less suitable for pinpointing more clear-cut differences between socially embedded and non-embedded economies.

"The economy" as a heuristic concept

What insights does the genesis of the concept of embeddedness offer for our understanding of the economy as a social system? For starters, it is striking that the clear definitions and dichotomies that formed the basis for the development of this concept have been gradually dispelled during the course of the debates on the social embeddedness of the economy. When it comes to the relationship between the economy and society, there do not appear to be any clearly discernible boundaries between modern industrial capitalism and the economies of traditional societies. Instead, it is possible to identify many areas of overlap, fluid transitions and, at best, minor variations. All economic systems, regardless of whether they are classified as modern or pre-modern, appear to have complex relationships between the economy and society, and the actors within these systems generally endeavor both to maintain social relationships and to realize their self-interest. The dispute over whether the economy is a separate social sphere can thus ultimately be interpreted as a debate over the self-image of modern societies, in which all participants have knowledge of the basic possible distinctions between a multitude of social subsystems; this self-image only emerged in modern, diverse societies.

Interestingly, although the economic anthropology debate revolved around the relationship between the economy and society, even staunch substantivists such as Malinowski, Mauss, and Polanyi did not believe that they could entirely dispense with the term "economy." Even if they assumed that the economy should be viewed as an embedded process and that gift economies were primarily governed by the rule of reciprocity, it still seemed appropriate to qualify certain forms of trading and of coping with scarcity as economic activities. The latter had so many similarities with our understanding of modern economic activities that a comparison could easily be drawn to a capitalist economy. This is highly remarkable because it would have been conceivable for these researchers to view such phenomena as the Kula ring and the potlatch ceremony as purely social in nature, and to forgo all use of the semantically overloaded concept of the "economy" when describing these traditions. Nevertheless, the substantivists decided to describe such practices as economic activities, but still insisted that these actions were organized according to rules that differed from those postulated by modern economic theory. However, they neglected to discuss where the exact line could be drawn between economic and non-economic spheres, or, whether such a differentiation was in any way useful at all.[70] A similar degree of vagueness could be noted in the works of Mark Granovetter, who, although referring to the social embeddedness of economic activities, does not discuss how economic activities can be recognized as such, nor how they differ from other social activities, nor where precisely the line is to be drawn between the economy and the society in which it is embedded.[71] By the same token, economic approaches that do not limit cost-benefit calculations to the monetary sector quickly find themselves in need of clarification. As Gary Becker has shown, it is possible to use a microeconomic approach to explain such social phenomena as marriage behavior, crime, altruism, and birthrates.[72] Such an approach, however, quickly becomes tautological: according to this view, social behavior can be explained best by assuming that, when presented with alternative options, people will attempt to maximize their utility. When one seeks to determine, however, what utility is, the answer will be: what people try to maximize. The more the model of *Homo Oeconomicus* is used to explain political, social, cultural, and psychological circumstances, the more it loses its elegance and persuasiveness. In the words of Maurice Godelier in 1965: "If the production of services is economic, then the economic sphere absorbs and explains the whole of social life, religion, kinship, politics, the acquiring of knowledge. [If] everything becomes 'economic,' by rights [...] nothing actually remains as economic."[73]

This sense of ambiguity can hardly be avoided without resorting to economic-theoretical definitions, whose limitations are exposed with the concept of embeddedness. However, conceptual vagueness need not necessarily be a disadvantage and can actually be put to productive use. In a bid to move the field of ethnology beyond the impasse of the substantivism-formalism debate, Richard Wilk has proposed to develop pragmatic solutions for the conceptualization of economic anthropological studies. In his opinion, there are many good reasons to view economics not so much as a subsystem that is characterized by a specific form of rationality that should be described using the approaches of modern economic theory, but rather to use the term "economics" as a heuristic concept instead.[74] Following from this, social activities can be studied from an economic perspective without anticipating the result of this work based on the premises of economic theory. Or, as Plattner put it: "The relevance of market theory to tribal society must be demonstrated, not assumed."[75]

This approach exhibits interesting parallels to Niklas Luhmann's proposal that an analysis of the economic sphere should make it possible to make certain assertions about society as a whole.[76] The productive nature of this approach is that the economy can be described as a special social subsystem, in which scarcity and bartering are handled. This understanding of the economy, however, is explicitly identified as a perspective selected by the observer and not as something that inevitably results from a natural economic cost-benefit calculation. The term economy thus assumes the function of a "transcendental signifier," in other words, a concept that, in the opinion of Philipp Sarasin, paves the way for a productive "way of questioning and thinking" and can serve as a "requisite speculative guiding concept" that "offers us an epistemological perspective from which our descriptions are organized."[77]

Such an economic history based on self-reflection would tie in with the observations of Michel Foucault, who saw the figure of *Homo Oeconomicus* as a subject of governmental rationality. According to Foucault, the concept of an economic actor who only seeks to satisfy his self-interest is a necessary response to the challenge faced by every modern-day government, namely reconciling individual freedom of action and state controlling mechanisms. For even if governmentality strives for control, it still requires free subjects, because only their "desires" can provide the driving forces required to keep society running.[78] This would mean that the modern economic actor is not the autonomous, self-aware, and self-interested individual that is portrayed by the field of economics, but rather the result of a modern-day subjectivization process. Accordingly, this actor would not be the result of social disembeddedness at all, as Polanyi and Mauss believed; instead, he would be just as embedded as the primitive described by ethnologists. In fact, the economic actions of modern people were not embedded in an archaic tribal culture, but instead in the institutional order and the cultural system of capitalism,[79] which they perpetuate through their actions.[80]

Such a position, which is supported by Maurice Godelier, among others, resolves the alleged contradiction between a formalist and a substantivist economy that fueled a bitter dispute in the field of economic anthropology for several decades.[81] According to this view, all economies are socially embedded, and modern industrial capitalism differs only slightly (by dint of its technological prowess), but not substantially, from archaic economic systems. However, even such a view derived from neo-Marxist and post-structuralist approaches fails to avoid the fundamental pitfall, namely that the economy can never be distinctly differentiated from other social spheres, and instead must always be considered in relation to political circumstances and cultural interpretations. The differentiation between the economy and other social subsystems thus remains the result of social self-interpretation processes and analytical classifications.

Conclusion

The debate about the social embeddedness of economic exchange, which kept economic anthropologists busy for so long, thus also is a true challenge for economic history. As a matter of fact, it problematizes the very object of investigation of the subdiscipline, i.e. the economy. This incertitude, however, can also be used to devise a research program. The question of whether the pursuit of reciprocity and the stabilization of networks were of paramount concern for historical actors, or whether they consciously ignored such social ties to realize their self-interest, or whether this distinction was of any relevance to them whatsoever, cannot be resolved based on theoretical assumptions, but instead should be made the starting point of empirical studies.[82]

The quest for self-interest would thus be at the core of economic history. Scholars might want to refrain from a dichotomic approach (such as characterized the debate about embeddedness in economic anthropology). Neither would they aim to prove that self-interest was a universal trait that could thus be considered the foundation of any economic activity (which has been the paradigm of neo-classical theory, but might be a statement too general to be suitable for empirical research in history). Nor would they choose to argue that self-interest is a feature of modern economies that replaced an earlier consideration for societal cohesion, as such a notion (guided by modernization theory) has been refuted by numerous studies. Rather, historians might wish to historicize self-interest by examining the extent to which economic actors had to reconcile individual motives with social expectations when they strove for the maximization of utility. By placing the focus of the analysis on exploring the extent and limits of economics and the various facets in which economic activity appears in diverse historical and cultural contexts, it is possible to outline more clearly both the associated social structures that were relevant in the historical past, and the patterns of interpretation adopted by today's scholars for their examination. Hence, it is ultimately not so much a matter of *finding* the economy, but rather the search in itself, i.e. the journey, which is the actual goal of economic-historical analysis.

Notes

1 Hansjörg Siegenthaler, "Geschichte und Ökonomie nach der kulturalistischen Wende," *Geschichte und Gesellschaft* 25 (1999): 276–301; Jakob Tanner, "Die ökonomische Handlungstheorie vor der 'kulturalistischen Wende'? Perspektiven und Probleme einer interdisziplinären Diskussion," in *Wirtschaftsgeschichte als Kulturgeschichte. Dimensionen eines Perspektivenwechsels*, ed. Hartmut Berghoff and Jakob Vogel (Frankfurt a.M.: Campus, 2004), 69–98.

2 Dipesh Chakrabarty, *Provincializing Europe: Post-colonial Thought and Historical Difference* (Princeton: Princeton University Press, 2000).

3 See, for an overview on this debate: Stuart Plattner, "Introduction," in *Economic Anthropology*, ed. Stuart Plattner (Stanford: Stanford University Press, 1989), 1–20; Richard Wilk, *Economies and Cultures: Foundations of Economic Anthropology* (Boulder: Westview Press, 1996), 4–13; Chris Hann, *Social Anthropology* (London: Hodder & Stoughton, 2000), 55; Gertraud Seiser, "Neuer Wein in alten Schläuchen? Aktuelle Trends in der ökonomischen Anthropologie," *Historische Anthropologie* 17 (2009): 157–77

4 See, for example: Hartmut Berghoff and Jakob Vogel, eds., *Wirtschaftsgeschichte als Kulturgeschichte, Dimensionen eines Perspektivenwechsels* (Frankfurt a.M.: Campus, 2004); Christof Dejung, Monika Dommann, and Daniel Speich Chassé, eds., *Auf der Suche nach der Ökonomie: Historische Annäherungen* (Tübingen: Mohr Siebeck, 2014).

5 Mark Granovetter, "Economic Action and Social Structure: The Problem of Embeddedness," *The American Journal of Sociology* 91, no. 3 (November 1985): 481–510.

6 Mitchel Y. Abolafia, "Markets as Cultures: An Ethnographic Approach," in *The Laws of the Market*, ed. Michel Callon (Oxford: Blackwell, 1998), 69–85.

7 Don Robotham, "Afterword: Learning from Polanyi," in *Market and Society: The Great Transformation Today*, ed. Chris Hann and Keith Hart (Cambridge: Cambridge University Press, 2009), 272–83.

8 Ironically, in his essay Granovetter distanced himself from the notion that the embeddedness concept could be viewed as a guaranteed rational solution to the problems of transaction costs, in other words, a solution that is abstracted from social realities and immune to what he referred to as personal "motives for integration [that are] unrelated to efficiency": Granovetter, "Economic Action and Social Structure," 504.

9 Karl Polanyi, *The Great Transformation: The Political and Economic Origins of Our Time* (1944; repr., Boston: Beacon, 2001).

10 Adam Smith, *An Inquiry into the Nature and Causes of the Wealth of Nations*, vol. 1 (1776; repr., London: J. M. Dent, 1954), 12–13.

11 Granovetter, "Economic Action and Social Structure," 482.

12 Ibid., 506.

13 Dejung, Dommann and Speich Chassé, *Auf der Suche nach der Ökonomie*.

14 Max Weber, *Economy and Society: An Outline of Interpretive Sociology*, vol. 1 (Berkeley: University of California Press, 2013), 98 and 153.

15 Werner Sombart, *Der moderne Kapitalismus: Historisch-systematische Darstellung des gesamteuropäischen Wirtschaftslebens von seinen Anfängen bis zur Gegenwart* (Munich: Duncker & Humblot, 1928).

16 Georg Simmel, *The Philosophy of Money* (1900; repr. London: Routledge, 2011), 327.

17 Max Weber, *The Protestant Ethic and the Spirit of Capitalism,* trans. Talcott Parsons (London: Allen & Unwin, 1930), 25–27.

18 Johannes Fabian coined the term "denial of coevalness" to illustrate that nineteenth-century ethnologists often viewed their travels to the colonial periphery as journeys through time to earlier periods of human history: Johannes Fabian, *Time and the Other: How Anthropology Makes its Object* (New York: Columbia University Press, 1983).

19 Erhard Schüttpelz, *Die Moderne im Spiegel des Primitiven: Weltliteratur und Ethnologie (1870–1960)* (Munich: Wilhelm Fink, 2005), 392–93.

20 Max Moszkowski, *Vom Wirtschaftsleben der primitiven Völker (Unter besonderer Berücksichtigung der Papua von Neuguinea und der Sakai von Sumatra)* (Jena: Gustav Fischer, 1911), 1.

21 Karl Bücher, *Die Entstehung der Volkswirtschaft* (Tübingen: Laupp, 1913), 7–8 and 26.

22 Wilhelm Koppers, "Die ethnologische Wirtschaftsforschung: Eine historisch-kritische Studie," *Anthropos. Internationale Zeitschrift für Völker- und Sprachkunde* 10 (1915): 617; Wilhelm Koppers, "Die ethnologische Wirtschaftsforschung: Eine historisch-kritische Studie," *Anthropos. Internationale Zeitschrift für Völker- und Sprachkunde* 11 (1916): 1027.

23 Felix Somló, *Der Güterverkehr in der Urgesellschaft* (Brussels: Misch & Thron, 1909), 177.

24 Such approaches could also be found in other academic disciplines, such as biology: Alessandro Duranti, "Mediated Encounters with Pacific Cultures: Three Samoan Dinners," in *Visions of Empire: Voyages, Botany, and Representations of Nature*, ed. David P. Miller and Peter H. Reill (Cambridge: Cambridge University Press, 1996), 328.

25 Bronisław Malinowski, "The Primitive Economics of the Trobriand Islanders," *Economic Journal* 31 (1921): 1–16, quote: 15.

26 Bronisław Malinowski, *Argonauts of the Western Pacific: An Account of Native Enterprise and Adventure in the Archipelagoes of Melanesian New Guinea* (London: Routledge, 1922).

27 Richard Thurnwald, *Die menschliche Gesellschaft in ihren ethno-soziologischen Grundlagen*, vol. 3, *Werden, Wandel und Gestaltung der Wirtschaft* (Berlin: De Gruyter, 1932), 45–47 and 204–5.

28 Richard Thurnwald, *Economics in Primitive Communities* (London: Oxford University Press, 1932), xiii-xv.

29 Polanyi, *The Great Transformation*.

30 For more on this topic, see Albert O. Hirschman, *The Passions and the Interests: Political Arguments for Capitalism before Its Triumph* (Princeton: Princeton University Press, 1977); Emma Rothschild, *Economic Sentiments: Adam Smith, Condorcet, and the Enlightenment* (Cambridge, MA: Harvard University Press, 2001); Werner Plumpe, "Die Geburt des "Homo oeconomicu"": Historische Überlegungen zur Entstehung und Bedeutung des Handlungsmodells der modernen Wirtschaft," in *Menschen und Märkte: Studien zur historischen Wirtschaftsanthropologie*, ed. Wolfgang Reinhard and Justin Stagl (Vienna: Böhlau, 2007), 319–52.

31 Polanyi, *The Great Transformation*, 45 and 72–76.

32 Ibid., 45–55 and 276–80.

33 Marcel Mauss, *The Gift: The Form and Reason for Exchange in Archaic Societies* (New York: Norton, 1990), 5–7 and 73.

34 Marilyn Strathern also concurs that the people of New Guinea do not see themselves as individuals, but rather primarily as part of a social organization. This means that work is never an individual endeavor, but always a joint effort that is influenced by the achievements of other people: Marilyn Strathern, *The Gender of the Gift: Problems with Women and Problems with Society in Melanesia* (Berkeley: University of California Press, 1988), 13–15.

35   Mauss, *The Gift*, 65–76.

36   Weber, *Protestant Ethic*, 181.

37   Frank Knight, "Anthropology and Economics," *Journal of Political Economy* 49 (1941): 247–68; Melville Herskovits, "Economics and Anthropology: A Rejoinder," *Journal of Political Economy* 49 (1941): 269–78.

38   Melville Herskovits, *Economic Anthropology: A Study in Comparative Economics* (New York: A. Knopf, 1952).

39   Karl Polanyi, "The Economy as an Instituted Process," in *Trade and Market in Early Empires: Economies in History and Theory*, ed. Karl Polanyi, Conrad Arensberg, and Harry Pearson (Glencoe, IL: The Free Press, 1957), 243–70.

40   Raymond Firth, ed., *Themes in Economic Anthropology* (London: Tavistock, 1967).

41   For more on this debate, see: Granovetter, "Economic Action and Social Structure," 482; Plattner, "Introduction;" Wilk, *Economies and Cultures*; Hann, *Social Anthropology*, 55; Seiser, "Neuer Wein in alten Schläuchen?;" Jens Beckert, "The Great Transformation of Embeddedness: Karl Polanyi and the New Economic Sociology," in *Market and Society: The Great Transformation Today*, ed. Chris Hann and Keith Hart (New York: Cambridge University Press, 2009), 38–55.

42   The cliché of a premodern economy that is naturally embedded in everyday life, and in which exchanges and work cannot be clearly differentiated from activities in other social spheres, such as those pursued in family and religious activities, is also called into question by Georg Elwert, "Sanktionen, Ehre und Gabenökonomie: Kulturelle Mechanismen der Einbettung von Märkten," in *Wirtschaftsgeschichte als Kulturgeschichte*, 119–42.

43   David M. Goodfellow, *Principles of Economic Sociology: The Economics of Primitive Life as Illustrated from the Bantu Peoples of South and East Africa* (London: Routledge, 1939), 4–5 and 15–17.

44   Bücher, *Die Entstehung der Volkswirtschaft*.

45   Moses Finley, *The Ancient Economy* (Berkeley: University of California Press, 1999).

46   Harry W. Pearson, "The Secular Debate on Economic Primitivism," in *Trade and Market in the Early Empires*, 3–11; Thomas Gross, "From Karl Bücher to the Formalist-Substantivist Debate," in *Karl Bücher: Theory – History – Anthropology – Non Market Economies*, ed. Jürgen G. Backhaus (Marburg: Metropolis 2000), 245–74; Beate Wagner-Hasel, "Hundert Jahre Gelehrtenstreit über den Charakter der antiken Wirtschaft. Zur Aktualität von Karl Büchers Wirtschaftsanthropologie," *Historische Anthropologie* 17 (2009): 178–201.

47   See, for example, the problems associated with studying the economy of the early modern era: Martin Dinges, "Wandel des Stellenwertes der Ökonomie in Selbstzeugnissen der Frühen Neuzeit," in *Menschen und Märkte*, 269–90.

48   Edward E. Evans-Pritchard, "Anthropology and History," in *Essays in Social Anthropology*, ed. Edward E. Evans-Pritchard (London: Faber & Faber, 1962), 172–263; Keith Thomas, "History and Anthropology," *Past and Present* 24 (1963): 3–24.

49   Wilk, *Economies and Cultures*, 4 and 12.

50   Richard Rottenburg, "Von der Bewahrung des Rätsels im Fremden," in *Neue Perspektiven der Wissenssoziologie*, ed. Dirk Tänzler, Hubert Knoblauch, and Hans-Georg Soeffner (Konstanz: UVK, 2006), 119–36.

51   Claude Lévi-Strauss, *Anthropologie structural* (Paris: Plon, 1958).

52   Claude Lévi-Strauss, *La Pensée sauvage* (Paris: Plon, 1962). The concept of *bricolage* (tinkering) developed by Lévi-Strauss could thus also be used to describe modern phenomena such as the emergence of nationalist topos in Switzerland during the nineteenth and twentieth centuries: Guy P. Marchal,

"Das "Schweizeralpenland". Eine imagologische Bastelei," in *Erfundene Schweiz: Konstruktionen nationaler Identität*, ed. Guy P. Marchal and Aram Mattioli (Zurich: Chronos, 1992), 37–49.

53 Bronisław Malinowski in his introduction to Julius E. Lips, *The Savage Hits Back* (New Haven: Yale University Press, 1937), vii.

54 Mary Douglas, *Natural Symbols: Explorations in Cosmology* (London: Cresset, 1970); Victor Turner, *From Ritual to Theatre: The Human Seriousness of Play* (New York: Performing Arts, 1982).

55 José Mulder van de Graaf and Richard Rottenburg, "Feldforschung in Unternehmen. Ethnografische Explorationen in der eigenen Gesellschaft," in *Teilnehmende Beobachtung: Werkstattberichte und methodologische Reflexionen*, ed. Reiner Aster, Hans Merkens, and Michael Repp (Frankfurt a.M.: Campus, 1989), 19–34; James G. Carrier, "Maussian Occidentalism: Gift and Commodity Systems," in *Occidentalism: Images of the West*, ed. James G. Carrier (Oxford: Clarendon Press, 1995), 85–108; Chris Hann, "Tradition, sozialer Wandel, Evolution. Defizite in der sozialanthropologischen Tradition," in *Rationalität im Prozess kultureller Evolution: Rationalitätsunterstellungen als eine Bedingung der Möglichkeit substantieller Rationalität des Handelns*, ed. Hansjörg Siegenthaler (Tübingen: Mohr Siebeck, 2005), 283–301.

56 Bruno Latour, *We Have Never Been Modern* (Cambridge, MA: Harvard University Press, 1993), 100.

57 Mauss, *The Gift*, 3 and 71–73.

58 In his monumental three-volume study *Civilisation matérielle, économie et capitalisme,* Fernand Braudel argued that market structures are also a universal characteristic of premodern societies, whereas capitalism is a highly specific economic form whose roots date back to overseas trading during the fifteenth century. Braudel noted that there was a certain amount of friction between this capitalistic economy and local and regional market economies: Fernand Braudel, *Civilisation matérielle, économie et capitalisme, XVe–XVIIIe siècle*, 3 vols. (Paris: Armand Colin, 1979).

59 Malcolm Chapman and Peter J. Buckley, "Markets, Transaction Costs, Economists, and Social Anthropologists," in *Meanings of the Market: The Free Market in Western Culture*, ed. James G. Carrier (Oxford: Berg, 1997), 225–50.

60 For more on this topic, see, for example, Karl-Peter Ellerbrock and Clemens Wischermann, eds., *Die Wirtschaftsgeschichte vor der Herausforderung durch die New Institutional Economics* (Dortmund: Gesellschaft für Westfälische Wirtschaftsgeschichte, 2004).

61 Douglass C. North, *Institutions, Institutional Change and Economic Performance* (Cambridge: Cambridge University Press, 1994); Avner Greif, "Institutions and International Trade: Lessons from the Commercial Revolution," *The American Economic Review* 82 (1992): 128–33.

62 See, for example: Sylvia J. Yanagisako, *Producing Culture and Capital: Family Firms in Italy* (Princeton: Princeton University Press, 2002); Christina Lubinski, *Familienunternehmen in Westdeutschland: Corporate Governance und Gesellschafterkultur seit den 1960er Jahren* (Munich: Beck, 2010); Christof Dejung, "Worldwide Ties: The Role of Family Businesses in Global Trade in the 19th and 20th Century," *Business History* 55 (2013): 1001–18.

63 Harold James, *Krupp: A History of the Legendary German Firm* (Princeton: Princeton University Press, 2012), 3 and 178.

64 Christof Dejung, *Commodity Trading, Globalization and the Colonial World: Spinning the Web of the Global Market* (New York: Routledge, 2018), 147 and 159–60.

65 Peter A. Hall and David Soskice, *Varieties of Capitalism: The Institutional Foundations of Comparative Advantage* (Oxford: Oxford University Press, 2001).

66 Susanne Rühle, *Guanxi Capitalism in China: The Role of Private Enterprises and Networks for Economic Development* (Marburg: Metropolis, 2012).
67 Weber, *Protestant Ethic*.
68 Christopher A. Bayly, *Rulers, Townsmen and Bazaars: North Indian Society in the Age of British Expansion 1770–1870* (Cambridge: Cambridge University Press, 1983); Rajat K. Ray, "Asian Capital in the Age of European Domination: The Rise of the Bazaar, 1800–1914," *Modern Asian Studies* 29 (1995): 449–554.
69 Jack Goody, *The East in the West* (Cambridge: Cambridge University Press, 1996); Dejung, *Commodity Trading, Globalization and the Colonial World*.
70 Polanyi, *The Great Transformation*; Mauss, *The Gift*.
71 Granovetter, "Economic Action and Social Structure".
72 Gary S. Becker, *The Economic Approach to Human Behavior* (Chicago: The University of Chicago Press, 1976).
73 Maurice Godelier, *Rationality and Irrationality in Economics* (New York: Monthly Review Press, 1972), 22. See, for a critical account of the paradigms of neoclassical economics, among others: Robert Skidelsky, *Money and Government: The Past and Future of Economics* (New Haven: Yale University Press, 2018).
74 Wilk, *Economies and Cultures*, 31.
75 Plattner, "Preface," in his *Economic Anthropology*, ix–xii, quote: x.
76 Niklas Luhmann, *Die Wirtschaft der Gesellschaft* (Frankfurt a.M.: Suhrkamp, 1988), 8–10.
77 Philipp Sarasin, "Replik," *Internationales Archiv für Sozialgeschichte der deutschen Literatur* 36 (2011): 183–85, quote: 183.
78 Michel Foucault, *Security, Territory, Population* (Basingstoke: Palgrave Macmillan, 2007), 72–74.
79 Arjun Appadurai, "Introduction: Commodities and the Politics of Value," in *The Social Life of Things: Commodities in Cultural Perspective*, ed. Arjun Appadurai (Cambridge: Cambridge University Press, 1986), 48.
80 See: Nina Verheyen, "Gemeinschaft durch Konkurrenz. Georg Simmel und Ellenbogenmenschen des Kaiserreichs," *Merkur* 10/11 (2013): 918–27.
81 Godelier, *Rationality and Irrationality in Economics*.
82 Wilk, *Economies and Cultures*, 5 and 11.

Part III
Embodying, feeling, and practicing self-interest

6 Commercial desires in a web of interest

Dutch discourses on (self-) interest, 1600–1830

Inger Leemans

In 1778, the Dutch-Frisian nobleman Onno Zwier van Haren (Figure 6.1) gave his son Duco instructions for his future life in commerce. Duco had laid aside his aristocratic training in the military for a different line of service to his country, as a trader. According to his father, there was no shame in this career shift:

> No, Duco, there's no need for shame
> That you, though trained in soldiery
> Play, in warehouses, a different game
> In equal service to our dear country.
> That you, of coffee, sugar, spice
> Help to determine the right price,
> Establish what place is most fit
> To grow the cotton. Better by far
> Than what you could do in the war.[1]

In line with the Enlightenment tradition of explaining phenomena in the context of their historic origins and evolution, Van Haren then describes the birth of commerce, and how it was developed in humanity's primitive natural state. After being evicted from Paradise, humans had to obtain food, shelter, and clothing. After a while, they started to seek to improve their living conditions. In the first phase, this was mostly done by the violent capture of other people's produce ("heroism was robbery"), but later they learned to innovate and exchange—the cornerstones of civilization. Van Haren goes on to describe the affective economy that underlies civilization:

> For the people of all times,
> Of every nation, of each clime,
> are ever wont to shun pale dearth
> and love self-interest from birth.
> The passions, always man's companions,
> and industry, fruit of ambition,
> prosperity, which is industry's yield.[2]

Figure 6.1 Portrait of esquire, politician and author Onno Zwier van Haren, by Philippus Velijn (around 1800).

Source: Courtesy of Rijksmuseum Amsterdam RP-P-1911-2880.

The poem states that humanity is driven by desires and that the wealth of nations depends on a chain of passions, which starts with self-interest (*eigenbaat*). Interestingly enough, Van Haren completely ignores the religious distrust of greed and uncontrolled desires. In fact, the poem does not refer to religion at all. Van Haren explains that human beings, in their urge to outgrow their state of poverty, are self-interested. Through this urge, they become industrious and prosperous, obtaining such commercial virtues as modesty, gentleness, and prudence. This affective commercial web is juxtaposed to the violent world of noblemen, which is driven by vainglory: "What is the nobility on this earth?/Why should we think so high of it?"[3] Van Haren compares the rather useless aristocracy unfavorably to the merchant class, who serve their country and help to improve its welfare and strength. With self-interest as its foundation, commerce enriches the commonwealth, bringing peace, prosperity, and industriousness, thus furthering the arts and sciences.

These mercantile verses, written by an aristocratic regent, present a revealing preview of Dutch early modern cultural discourses on self-interest. This chapter will show that Van Haren's poem should be understood in a longer tradition of Dutch-language texts that addressed the virtues of commercial drives.[4] During the seventeenth and eighteenth centuries, the Dutch Republic produced an impressive body of texts discussing commerce, trade, and interest. Most economic concepts and theories were formulated in pamphlets commentating on contemporary events, in political-economic tractates, or in literary texts (theater plays, poems, songs, satires). Also, visual imagery (e.g. paintings of markets and exchanges, cartoons, or prints depicting commercial negotiations) played an important role in the conceptualization of markets and market behavior.[5] Yet, this rich cultural discourse did not generate a term comparable to the English concept of self-interest. We currently lack a history of the Dutch discourse on self-interest,[6] and there are few monographs or textbooks on early modern Dutch economic theory.[7] This chapter can be, therefore, no more than a first exploration of the conceptualizations of self-interest. It will start with a brief introduction to the Dutch terminology relating to self-interest, and then trace some of the transitions that these terms went through during the seventeenth and eighteenth centuries.[8]

Van Haren's advice to his son Duco to forgo the glory and horror of a noble career and embrace the virtues of commercial life seems to fit in with the fundamental shift from passions to interest, as described in Hirschman's seminal study *The Passions and the Interests*.[9] During the eighteenth century, according to Hirschman, the vehement and violent passions, such as ambition, the pursuit of glory and the urge for honor, were discredited in favor of the commercial concept of self-interest, which was projected to be a rational drive, with the ability to check vehement passions. Pierre Force, in *Self-interest Before Adam Smith*, pays more attention to the notion of interest as human self-love.[10] Force and Hirschman thus present the story of self-interest before it became a key concept in economic theory: that is, in the sense of pecuniary interest as a self-regulating economic balance.

As this chapter will show, early modern Dutch discourse invested strongly in analyzing commercial drives. Already in the seventeenth century, Dutch discourse started to adapt the contemporary moral economy to the developing modern economy, describing the urge for personal gain as a dominant motive for human behavior and a productive impulse for stable (Republican) states. However, these early conceptualizations of self-interest differed in some essential points from our modern-day notion of self-interest. Dutch discourse tended to describe the urge for profit as an *embodied* passion. Furthermore, the commercial drives were not (solely) regarded as individual passions; rather, they were seen as a productive and positive force within the social fabric of society. Self-interest became strongly connected to the interest of the Dutch Republic, which was perceived as commercial in nature.

Interest, *hebzucht*, *winzucht*, *eigenbaat*, and *eigenbelang*

The early modern Dutch language does not seem to have had a specific word for "self-interest": that is, a term that provides a combination of financial gain or debt, interestedness (i.e. being interested in a product), investment (i.e. being invested in a cause), and a prioritizing of the individual.[11] In the early modern period, the Dutch word *interest* functioned above all as a financial term, indicating accrual-money paid for the use of borrowed money, or forbearance of a debt according to a fixed ratio (Figure 6.2).[12] The term *interest* was, therefore, also used in the negative sense of damage: "Behold, what damage, interest and loss the Beggars have caused our city!"[13]

Interest could also be used to express concern for something (to be interested in), or possible advantage (to have an interest in, to gain from). This sense of *interest*, essential for the later interpretations of self-interest in economic theory, seems to have been deduced from French and Italian

Figure 6.2 Frontispiece of Jacques Le moine de L'Espine, *Nieuw interest-boek* (Amsterdam, Widow of J. van Dijk & J. Ratelband, 1702).

intérêt and *interesse*. Most Dutch-language books published in the first half of the seventeenth century with *interest* in the title are accountancy and arithmetic books; in the same period, however, Dutch publishers also started to sell the duc de Rohan's *De l'interest des princes et estats de la chrestienté* (1639). From the 1650s onwards, Dutch-language texts started to discuss "the interest of the seven provinces."[14] The most famous example of this moral-political interpretation of *interest* (the stakes a state or person may have in a specific cause) was *Interest van Holland, ofte gronden van Hollands-Welvaren* (1662), by the brothers Pieter and Johannes de la Court. Apart from the work of the De la Courts, the financial interpretation of the word *interest* remained dominant in the early modern period. Furthermore, the usage of *interest* in the sense of "self-gain" is rare.[15] The word *zelf-interest* does not exist in Dutch, despite the effort of the De la Courts to introduce the term *eigen-interest*. The De la Courts' work will be discussed below.

The meaning of interest in the sense of "advantage, ensuring one's own benefit" could be addressed in Dutch through the words *eigenbaat* (advantage to oneself), *eigenbelang* (self-interest/concern), *zelfzucht* (the urge for the self), or *eigenliefde* (self-love). Of these three, *eigenbaat* was used most often up to the end of the eighteenth century. At the beginning of the nineteenth century, *eigenbelang* took over as the most prominent term, with *zelfzucht* gaining importance later in the century. The transition from *baat* to *belang* seems indicative of a shift from a more utilitarian (usage, profit) term, used in the realm of accountancy (the opposite of *baat*, "gain," is "cost" or "loss, damage"), to a more general indication of concern, weighing the pros and cons of a situation: "It is in my best *belang* (interest) to [...]"; "it is our *belang* (concern) [...]" As will be shown below, *eigenbelang* took the accountancy aspect out of *eigenbaat*. *Eigenliefde* remained in steady use all through the early modern era and the nineteenth century, primarily in moralistic literature and religious instruction.

If one wanted to highlight the financial urge underlying self-interest, one would probably turn to a term such as *winzucht* (the inclination or urge for profit), *geldzucht* (the urge for money), *goudzucht* (the urge for gold), or *baatzucht* (the urge for personal gain). Of these three, *baatzucht* had the weakest link to finance: it would more often be used in the context of the realm of power, where it went hand-in-hand with *staatszucht*—the urge for honor, status (*staat*), and glory. *Winnen* (to gain) and *geld* (money) were used within the realm of finance. However, their etymology shows no connection to *interest* in its sense of "concern," or "have an interest in." The *-zucht* words operated within the context of terms that had a firmer base in moral theory and theology: *heblust* and *hebzucht* (the urge to possess) connected strongly to the realm of greed (*gierigheid*), gluttony (*gulzigheid*), and misery (*vrekkerigheid*).[16] It is interesting to note that the variety of terms indicating a drive to gain and to accumulate (*win, baat*) seems to have expanded in the early modern period, while the usage of terms indicating the urge to have, guard, and keep for oneself (*hebzucht, gierigheid*) did not increase.

The short lexicographical exploration above shows that in the Dutch language no term existed that can be seen as comparable to our modern concept of self-interest. The components of financial profit, vested interest (*belang*), and the individual or the self were not strongly connected. They could not be combined in one term. Another interesting observation is that the terms primarily used to indicate the urge for financial gain (*winzucht, geldzucht, goudzucht*) originally had a strong pejorative undertone: *zucht* (sigh, inclination, urge) indicates a strong passion, a dishonorable yearning. The interpretations of such words as *eigenbaat, winzucht,* and *geldlust* were strongly informed by the Protestant discomfort with usury and luxury. However, as will be described below, this changed over the course of the seventeenth century, when more neutral and positive interpretations of these words came to the fore. The new commercial economy also required a new moral economy. By zooming in on this transition, focusing on texts in which terms relating to interest took on a more neutral, positive, and productive meaning, this chapter aims to enrich existing (art) historical research which has highlighted the moral and religious interpretations of the early modern discourses on commerce and wealth.[17]

A commercial republic

During the early modern period, most of the semantic field described above witnessed shifts in interpretation and valuation, informed by political and economic developments. In the course of the seventeenth century, the Dutch Republic managed to acquire a dominant position in the European political realm. To achieve this, it had to invent the nation as a republic within the context of the European monarchies, and to find unity and stability, in spite of the recurring threat of civil unrest and the constant power clashes between the stadtholders and the regents of the different states. A second challenge was posed by the development of the Dutch Republic into one of the first modern economies.[18] The shift toward a market-based economy took extensive sociocultural engineering in order to bring the commercial system in line with dominant moral economies. This was achieved, among other means, through the development of a remarkable positive discourse on the advantages and virtues of commerce.[19]

The republic started to produce a stream of texts and images that celebrated trade and commerce as vital to its economic growth and central to its self-image. The Dutch Virgin—the allegorical personification of this new, prosperous nation—was regularly portrayed with Mercury, the God of Trade, by her side.[20] Amsterdam canal houses chose Mercury for façade decorations and house names (Figure 6.3). Famous Dutch authors, such as Joost van den Vondel, wrote odes to navigation and trade, to the Amsterdam Stock Exchange, and to the tradesmen who had "wrested" the Dutch polders from the sea.[21] Merchants and trade started to be perceived as essential components of civic life and the body politic.[22]

Figure 6.3 Plaque of canal house "Zeevrucht", singel 36 in Amsterdam, displaying Mercury trying to rest while being awakened by a rooster, signifying vigilance and the dawn of a new day.

While in other countries trade was often discredited as an occupation unsuitable for distinguished persons, the Dutch Republic early on started to project commerce as central to the prosperity of the young nation.[23] This was not accomplished without effort. The concerns transmitted by the classical Christian tradition about the corrupting influence of trade, lurking in the temptation to succumb to greed and luxury, were also deeply felt within the republic.[24] From the 1580s onward, in mercantile discourses, the moral challenges facing profit-seeking merchants were avidly debated, while the importance of philosophical, literary, and moral education for Christian merchants were stressed.[25]

Winzucht

A famous example of this development is *Mercator sapiens*, the inaugural lecture by the Dutch poet and scholar Caspar Barlaeus on the occasion of the opening of the Amsterdam Athenaeum Illustre in 1632.[26] In the lecture, Barlaeus puts forward a commercial philosophy with rules that merchants should abide by, in order to keep to a virtuous path.[27] Although Barlaeus was not the first humanist to take up this topic,[28] he was innovative because of his appraisal of commercial life as essential to the prosperity of the nation, and of merchants as resourceful and persevering citizens. He calls the Dutch Republic a *winst-gierige Natie* (profit-greedy nation), and praises the Dutch as "a people always seeking advantage, surrounded by the sounds of clinking gold and silver, in a city that strives only for profit."[29] He acknowledges how the urge to make profit drives traders to extraordinary efforts, such as leaving their wives and children in order to explore new horizons.[30] Barlaeus praises commercial virtues, such as wisdom, cautiousness, carefulness, and usefulness.

However, only in a few instances does Barlaeus discuss the impulse that drives mercantile behavior, and he does not single out a specific term for it. Mostly, Barlaeus praises trade in general, and where he discusses the drive for profit, he leans on the classics—on Aristotle and Cicero—and on Christian teachings, to state that a merchant should control his passions for riches with his rationality and senses, by regarding wealth as unimportant, and by making sure he does not become too greedy and eager.[31] In these instances, Barlaeus turns to biblical and pejorative terms such as *begerig* (covetous), *winst-gierig* (profit-greedy), *geldzuchtig* (money-thirsty), and *wellustigheyt* (lechery), underlining the Protestant norm that commercial passions could turn into vices. Honesty and wisdom should curtail the mercantile affective economy.

With the growing prosperity of the Dutch provinces, specifically after the Peace of Münster in 1647, Dutch poets seem to have felt the urge to rewrite the chapter on *winzucht*. One of them was Jan Vos, who was not only a poet and playwright, but also a glazier by profession, well-connected to the Amsterdam regents, whose patronage he cherished.[32] In various instances Jan Vos used the term *winzucht* in a positive way, freeing it from its traditional connection with greed and usury. In 1662, at the occasion of the fourth extension of the city of Amsterdam, Jan Vos composed a *tableau vivant* that was shown several times in the Amsterdam theater.[33] The accompanying poem praised the city for its *winzucht*:

> A well-directed city will gain power everywhere.
> Here, the bold profit drive finds many beaten paths
> Vigilant commerce is highly esteemed at the river Amstel.[34]

Here, the pejorative connection of *winzucht* with uncontrolled lust and greed is downplayed, moving the term more toward "acquisitiveness." The drive for profit is seen as bold and enterprising, something to be esteemed, not to be frowned upon.

Two years later, in a poem in praise of Amsterdam's social welfare system—"On the immigrant's orphanage"—Jan Vos reflects on how Amsterdam is taking in streams of immigrants who all want to be at the place where they can get rich: "*Winzucht* pulls people from far-away places." Instead of crying out to close the city gates against these gold diggers, Vos urges the city to persevere in its aim to be open to people from all different denominations.[35] In a poem on a ship captain, Vos stresses—like Barlaeus before him—that *winzucht* urges men to press on beyond boundaries. As ships are built to carry cargo, so commerce guards the state.[36] *Winzucht* thus comes to be seen as not only an esteemed, but also a necessary, drive for commercial enterprise, which in itself is projected to be a cornerstone of the Dutch state. Vos contrasts *winzucht*, which is a basis for prosperous and stable states, with *eigenbaat* or *hebzucht*, which forms a threat to society by piling up goods (taking them out of the system): "Do not give usurious self-interest and acrimonious jealousy the opportunity to pierce your bosom."[37]

The famous Dutch poet Joost van den Vondel used *winzucht* in a comparable way. In a poem composed on the occasion of the opening of the new city hall in Amsterdam in 1655, Vondel takes the reader on a walk from the city hall to the stock exchange, just around the corner. He describes this famous commercial building as the pounding heart of the international economy and as a beehive of *gewinzucht*:

> Cupidity fills up the ample galleries
> Around the square, that hive of bees,
> An excellent smell, won from the land.[38]

The beehive metaphor, a symbol of virtuous productivity, and the pounding heart, turn *gewinzucht* into a necessary and productive force in society. Here, we are reminded that the beehive parable by Bernard Mandeville, portraying how private vices may render public benefits, is embedded in Dutch contemporary thought (although most studies largely overlook this background).[39]

In 1663, Vondel used the story of Phaeton to stress that the West would never have explored the East and taken silver, gold, and diamonds from those regions, if it had not been for *gewinzucht*, which makes men bold and prepared to face all kinds of challenges: heat, cold, cannibals, or storms: "Profit softens labor, and will always sell itself for a higher gain."[40] In this view, acquisitiveness helped to found the Dutch empire. Vondel's poems might thus also serve as an argument in recent re-readings of Dutch imperialism and the Dutch Republic's self-representation through the mutual promotion of empire building and modern state capitalism.[41]

The true interest of the Republic of Holland

In the same years in which Vondel and Vos tried to detach the term *winzucht* from its original connotation of vice and lust, elevating it to a powerful and productive drive for Dutch commerce and empire, the term *interest* was also put into play to help explain the economic and political success of the Dutch Republic. *Interest* features in the title of one of the first, and certainly the most internationally acclaimed, political-economic treatises of the Dutch Republic: *Interest van Holland, ofte gronden van Hollands-Welvaren* (1662), written by the brothers Pieter and Johannes de la Court, successful cloth merchants from Leiden (Figure 6.4).[42] The treatise was translated

Figure 6.4 Portrait of Pieter de la Court (1667), by Abraham van den Tempel.

Source: Rijksmuseum Amsterdam, SK-A-2243.

into German (1665 and 1671) and French (1709). It was also translated into English, probably in the 1660s, although this first translation circulated only in manuscript form. In the end, *Interest van Holland* would have to wait until 1702 before it was published in English by the London publisher John Darby under the title *John de Witt, and other Great Men in Holland.*[43]

As stated above, traditionally the term *interest* in the Dutch language was mainly used in the realm of finance and accountancy. The De la Courts' work was essential in bringing in a second interpretation of *interest*, namely as a moral and political term, balancing common interest and the passion of self-love.[44] This tension combined classic (Epicurean/Neo-Stoic) and Christian (Augustinian) thinking about self-love with Machiavellian theory on *raison d'état* (reasons of state). The term *interesse* was used in this manner by the Florentine republican Francesco Guicciardini, who argued that human nature is essentially selfish. This selfish behavior, however, could be justifiable as long as it was directed toward aristocratic honor and public interest, instead of pecuniary advantage.[45] Guicciardini thus connected personal *interesse* to the reason of state.

The De la Court brothers introduced the term *interest* with its double meaning to Dutch discourse, along with the term self-interest (*eigen-interest*). In line with Thomas Hobbes and others, they stressed that, "Self-interest is the most important, if not the only aim of all human endeavor"; "one has to acknowledge that the self always comes first."[46] The use of the accountancy term *interest* may have helped to suggest that the interests of persons and of the state could be calculated, or predicted in some way. This is also highlighted by Hirschman: one of the aspects which made self-interest useful as a concept for regulating the state and its economy was that it made actions predictable.[47]

Along with the introduction of *interest* and *self-interest* as moral-political terms, the De la Courts also brought in the tension between the passion of self-love and the needs of the state, the "interest of Holland." Arthur Weststeijn has argued that "the core of the moral thought of the brothers De la Court involves an attempt to alleviate this very tension."[48] This could be done by advocating "true" self-interest, an ambitious self-love that seeks for honor and approval from others, but not to rule others (the latter was seen by the brothers as false self-love). True love of the self should extend to embrace family, neighbors, fellow-citizens, and all of humanity.[49] The approval of others could be obtained by aligning private advantage with the common good. The De la Court brothers thus rerouted the meaning of self-interest toward a positive connection between the well-being of subjects and rulers alike: a harmony of interests. This interest is regarded as a virtue—as something to strive for, improving the person.[50]

The De la Courts occasionally used the word *eigen-interest*, but this term never gained currency, although it would appear in Dutch discourse now and again, mostly when people wanted to stress that the intended gain was private. It was the term *interest*, or *true interest*—interpreted as interdependent well-being—that gained traction, sometimes accompanied by the term *belang*.[51]

It should be noted that for the De la Courts, *true interest* is not commercial in nature: the profit people strive for is not financial, but socially directed self-love. However, it is important to stress "that the brothers De la Court never rebuke the pursuit of riches. On the contrary: in their commercial logic, wealth generally proves to be the result of sincere self-love and civil ambition. It is therefore not riches that corrupt, but power."[52] One of the main goals of the De la Courts was to discredit monarchies in favor of republicanism. As monarchies do not curb the passions, but will corrupt true self-love, they can offer no sound basis for rule. The ideology promoted the "True Freedom" with which the Dutch Republic, under the guidance of state pensionary John de Witt, had "freed" itself from the rule of the Orange family. Only a republic without a stadtholder could control the passions in order to secure the wealth of the state. Dutch republicanism thus moved away from classical republicanism, which regarded trade and luxury as undermining the civic virtues needed to underpin a stable state. Hence, Weststeijn has labeled the Dutch ideology as "commercial republicanism," and Jonathan Israel has stressed that it was a major influence on the eighteenth-century revolutionary period.[53]

Eigenbaat

In the project to develop a commercial republican ideology, directed against the influence of the stadtholders, *interest* received help from *eigenbaat*. *Eigenbaat* could have been a good candidate for the role of the Dutch version of self-interest, as it entailed both the self (*eigen*) and personal gain (*baat*), which was also used in financial contexts (*de cost ende baet*). One could even say that *eigenbaat* therefore qualified above *interest*, which remained a somewhat "foreign" term, without the connotation to the self, and which seems to have had trouble interlocking its two separate strands of meaning— financial accrual/damage and self-love/reasons of state. However, the negative connotations carried by "disgraceful *eigenbaat*" were probably too strong to allow it to be turned into a more neutral, or even positive, term. This became even more true from the 1670s onwards, when *eigenbaat* was politicized, after which it was too "tainted" to be turned into a neutral term for rational and financial profit-seeking behavior. What happened?

Traditionally, *eigenbaat* was a general term, used to describe how individuals organized their lives so that they could obtain benefit. The first frame of reference would be a monarch, or any person of power, using his power to his own advantage. This kind of *eigenbaat* clearly was a vice, which could fester like a weed, or spread like a cancer (*woekeren*). In one of his dramatic *tableau vivants*, depicting hell, Jan Vos staged Eigenbaat as an allegorical character side-by-side with Avarice, Theft, Drunkenness, Perjury, Deceit, and Lasciviousness.[54] In literature, *eigenbaat* often featured in this way—enumerated alongside all kind of general vices, without specific reference to the economic realm.

In 1679, *eigenbaat* became uniquely connected to the ambition of the Dutch Orangist faction and to the "tyranny" of the stadtholders. This was done in the theater play *Tieranny van Eigenbaat* (Tyranny of Self-interest), produced by the classicist art society Nil Volentibus Arduum (Figure 6.5).[55] *Tyranny of Self-interest* was an adaptation of the Italian republican opera-play *La Tirannide dell' Interesse* (1653) by Francesco Abarra. It was adapted by Andries Pels, one of the leading members of Nil Volentibus Arduum, at the request of the society. He was commissioned in 1671, but the play was not published until 1679, and was staged for the first time in 1680. This was probably due to the political troubles that broke out in 1672, the Disaster Year, in which the Dutch Republic was attacked by four foreign powers, and the republican regime of the "True Freedom" was overthrown through the horrid slaughter of the brothers Johan and Cornelis de Witt, and the restoration of the stadtholder. The Amsterdam theater was closed for a while.

The Dutch play was obviously written as a comment on the political situation of the Disaster Year of 1672. One of the copies of the play also has an added "key," which provides an explanation of the main characters, who represent key political figures of the Dutch Republic. Commonwealth (Gemeenebest) and Good Nature (Goedaard) embodied state pensionary Johan de Witt and his brother Cornelis de Witt. In the play, they are overthrown by Self-interest

Figure 6.5 Frontispiece of *tieranny van eigenbaat* (1679), by the classicist art society Nil Volentibus Arduum. This frontispiece was added to the 1705 edition.

(Eigenbaat), who is obviously an allegory for stadtholder William III. Eigenbaat, assisted by Evil, Deceit, and Vice (William's friends Odijk, Fagel, and Bentinck), and by Hypocrisy (the Voetian orthodox Calvinists), competes with King Ratio (the republican state of Holland), who has Virtue on his side. The play is set "on the Isle of Free Choice." Probably because of this coded attack on the stadtholder, the play was staged only once in 1680. However, it circulated in print, and was vehemently discussed. In the second stadtholderless period (1702–47), it could once more be performed, and thus gained notoriety. The fact that *Tieranny van Eigenbaat* gained sort of a cult status is indicated by the fact that three "sequels" to the play were written: *The Death of Self-interest* (1707) by Jan Pook, *The Downfall of Self-interest* (1707) by Enoch Krook, and an adapted version of the latter, *The Downfall of Self-interest in the Isle of Free Choice* (1707) by Ysbrand Vincent.[56]

These plays organized fierce attacks on Orangist, egotistic self-interest that lacked rational control. In the allegorical play *Tieranny van Eigenbaat* (1679), King Ratio is married to Virtue, but is threatened by the usurping ambitions of Self-interest (Eigenbaat), supported by the Sins. The editors of the play, Holzey and Van der Haven, argue that the neo-Stoical ideology of the Italian play is aligned with the Spinozist inclinations of Nil Volentibus Arduum. In the Dutch adaptation, the idea is put forward that self-interest—or rather Spinoza's *conatus*, the urge to persevere—is an essential condition for human happiness. Self-interest is thus not seen as a threat to moral behavior as such, as long as it is curbed by reason or by other passions.

An interesting feature of self-interest in this play is that it is depicted as luxurious and effeminized. The allegorical character of Eigenbaat is dressed as an Amazon, in a lush mantle of tiger and ermine fur, covered with gold crowns and scepters. He enters the court of King Ratio in disguise, dressed as a queen named Reason of State (Redenvanstaat). This masquerade triggers all kinds of interesting homosexual scenes in which both female Will and the male King Ratio fall in love with Eigenbaat in female disguise. The play ends with Self-interest as the victorious new ruler over the Isle of Free Choice.

We might be inclined to interpret the play in light of the eighteenth-century shift described by Hirschman in *The Passions and the Interests*, in which the "softer," effeminizing commercial self-interest takes over from the vehement and violent passions such as ambition, lust for glory, and the striving for honor. However, self-interest in these plays is hardly a commercial drive. It is strongly connected to stadtholderian rule, which was opposed to the commercial interests of the state of Holland and the republican factions. *Eigenbaat* embodied tyrannical egotism. As such, the character Eigenbaat remained popular throughout the second stadtholderless period (1702–47), and was revived in the 1780s, when a patriotic resistance started to form against William V, eventually causing his downfall in the Batavian Revolution of 1795. *Eigenbaat* thus remained strongly connected to the uncurbed political ambition of the house of Orange, and even the direct opposite of commercial interests. [57]

It is, therefore, interesting that Onno Zwier van Haren chose the term *eigenbaat* when he sang the praises of commercial self-interest to his son: "For the people of all times,/Of every nation, of each clime,/are ever wont to shun pale dearth/and love self-interest (*eigenbaat*) from birth." It is probably to be explained by the date he wrote the poem: in the early 1770s, and thus during the years that *eigenbaat*, for a short while, seems to have lost its strong connection with tyranny (the *Eigenbaat* plays appear to have been forgotten after the restoration of the Orange family in 1747), and just before that connection would be restored in the 1780s.

We can conclude that the term *eigenbaat* was too strongly tied to unfettered monarchical rule to be used as a neutral term to describe commercial interest. This point is underlined by the fact that in the series of poems in praise of commerce published after Van Haren wrote "The Merchant," different terms were used to indicate self-interest. The last part of this chapter will discuss these "trade poems" in order to see how they bring together different connotations of self-interest around the concept of *belang*. *Belang* is used to spin a web of interest between the individual and society, moving away from the question of the drives of the individual to the interest of the commonwealth. [58]

Belang

Between 1770 and 1830, around a few peak moments (1775, 1815, and 1825), some fifteen remarkably long Dutch poems were published, varying from 350 to 700 lines, and devoted exclusively to the theme of trade.[59] Most of these poems were written by merchants, clerks, or regents. They originated from the context of sociability and the decline of the Dutch economy in the eighteenth century. To fight the economic stagnation which had plagued the Dutch Republic during the eighteenth century, learned societies held prize competitions to address pressing questions such as: "What is the foundation of Dutch trade, of its growth and flourishing? What causes and events have exposed it to changes and decline?"[60] Art and literary societies pressed authors to produce poems in praise of Dutch trade. Dutch poets eagerly employed their pens to help revitalize Dutch society.[61] The fifteen long poems that sprang from these efforts put trade forward as a central economic force and the wellspring of prosperity, happiness, equality, and the global commonwealth. Poets paint a picture of *La doux commerce*, a power which, because of the necessity of contacts between people, brings about peaceful collaboration.[62] Trade is described as a civilizing power and as both the start and the engine of human civilization.

In order to explain the origin and growth of commerce, the Dutch poets turn to self-interest. Only Van Haren does so through the term *eigenbaat*. The others choose different terms: *winzucht* (desire for profit), *begeerte* (desire), *begeerzucht* (yearning), *begeervermogen* (ability to yearn), and, most importantly, *belang* (interest). The drive for profit is valued as a positive force of civilization. It is not a rational interest, but an embodied passion, an emotionally charged desire for wealth. In these poems, commercial enterprise is imagined as a process of lovemaking, and, in the end as a marriage, a "velvet bond" between commerce and the Dutch Republic, and between the republic and its colonies. Wealth is the love child of this union.[63] This embodied interpretation of interest might also explain why the poets do not employ the Dutch term *interest*: that term, borrowed from accountancy, would have recalled rationality.

Most "trade poets" try to explain the birth of commercial society, starting with humankind in its state of nature. They describe the circumstances that confronted original humans, the "wild peoples." According to the Dutch poets, original humanity was *verdierlijkt* [animalized] and wandered around "misshapen, dulled, and naked."[64] In this beastly state, original humans were without will or initiative, helplessly subject to the forces of nature. The poet Petronella Moens paints a particularly gruesome image of this "state of weeping," in which she describes how the savage "in bloody animal skins/ devours the quivering flesh, and hides in caves."[65] Several poems stress that Rousseau was incorrect to presume that the noble savage is the best state of humanity.[66] God gave humans *begeerzucht*, the urge to desire, to strive for improvement. As a rule of nature, *begeerzucht* will come to blossom.[67] *Begeerte* will provide people with the strength to escape their pitiful state and to engage in trade: "Trade supplies us with what nature may deny us."[68] Here, poets use the term *belang*. This term can be used at the level of the individual—indicating the desire for profit and improvement. More importantly, however, the term also indicates what happens at the next level— when individual interests create a web of interdependencies through trade. Trade connects people from all over the world, and urges individuals to calculate each other's interests. "You make, O Trade! the world one commonwealth/that links south to north, east to west."[69]

Markets are balancing not simply demand and supply, but also the interests of different cultures. Commerce, therefore, helps to build civilized, sociable societies. It connects the nations in a "web of interest."[70] Individual self-interest (*belang*) thus results in common interest (*belang*), which is described as a new religion:

Citizens of the world all gather together
Here, the partition walls of religion, law and rank are taken down.
Here, rich and poor all kneel before the altar of interest.[71]

Some Dutch authors even go one step further, addressing trade as a god: "O, Thou great God of Trade!"[72] As the *primum movens* behind all civilization, trade is promoted to the force that controls the whole cosmos. God may have created human beings, but it was trade that made them truly human, made them reasonable: "Thou hast formed man, he can reason because of thee."[73]

Strangely enough these poets, devout believers as they no doubt were, hardly hesitated to hail interest and trade not just as possible means for benefit, but as Godlike powers, as the forces that formed humanity and civilization. At moments when trust in the future of trade was precarious in the Netherlands, such interpretations may have helped to shift attention away from the fact that practical solutions to restore the economy were hard to find. The God of Trade would come to the rescue in the hour of need. Thus, the self that never really materialized in Dutch discourse as the equivocal problem, in these trade poems, was woven into a great web of interest, of God's or Nature's great commercial scheme.

Conclusion

It is quite a challenge, maybe even impossible, to write a history of a concept in a specific cultural domain when this concept did not originate from that domain and the word itself is not used. This is even more true for a concept as complex as self-interest, which was first employed as a category of analysis, used to understand the workings of a combination of phenomena (self-love, pecuniary gain, and the interest of states), but which consolidated into a category of practice within one specific domain—economic theory— where it gained a more fixed meaning.[74] As the cornerstone of the efficient market theory, the rational drive of self-interest came to be viewed as a constant impulse in market processes.

This volume turns self-interest back into a category of analysis, by historicizing the concept and by researching it in different national discourses and cultural realms. Here, we enrich Hirschman's and Force's work, as they mainly focused on the eighteenth century and on English and French discourses (rooted in classical and theological traditions). The first exploration of Dutch self-interest discourses presented in this chapter shows that no Dutch equivalent of the modern, economic concept of self-interest can be found. Why, then, struggle to write a history of a non-existent concept? The present author's answer would be that the concept of self-interest helps us to analyze the discourses on the role of commercial drives in the interplay of the individual, society, and the economy. This chapter has provided some first observations toward this point. It should be stressed, however that, although an attempt has been made to describe some overall, long-term trends, they are based on a limited amount of case studies, and remain in need of further, and broader, investigations.

The Dutch Republic, as the first modern economy, at a very early stage acknowledged commerce to be a pillar of society, and embraced commercial drives as central forces for human behavior. The commercial drive, which could have multiple labels (*baatzucht, hebzucht, winzucht, eigenbaat, eigenbelang, gierigheid*, etc.), was often viewed as an embodied passion (*zucht*), not as a rational motive. More importantly, the "self" of self-interest seems to have been less dominant than in other cultural domains. In Dutch discourses, interest was often described as a *social* drive, an essential force for the fabric of society, specifically those of republics.

It can be convincingly argued that the early moderns had a strong point here: capitalism would never have gained such strength if it had targeted only individuals and their personal gain. Markets connect people, as they function on the basis of exchange and reciprocity. For the Dutch Republic, this might have been all the more urgent. The unstable, young Dutch Republic, constantly challenged by threats from other states and by civil unrest from within, was bound together partly by commercial interests and by the advancement of a capitalist economy. To further stimulate these developments, the commercial republic developed a national discourse in which commerce and interest were hailed as the fabric of society, connecting citizens in a web of interest, founded on passionate drives. Cultural discourse thus played an essential role in the construction of a commercial imagined community, entangled in a *web van belang*.[75]

Notes

1 "Neen, Duco, neen, 't is geene schande, / Dat Gy, tot Krygsman opgevoed, / Nu and're diensten aan den Lande, / In Pakhuis, of Comptoiren doed. / Dat Gy de wigt van Coffy-Baalen, / Of prys van Suyker, helpt bepaalen, / Of waar 't Catoen werd best geteeld. / Die moeyte zal U beeter loonen, / Dan 't geen de Kryg U zoude toonen." Onno Z. van Haren, "De koopman, (The Merchant)," in *De koopman, De staatsman en De schimmen* (Zwolle: S. Clement, 1778), 2. Pieter van der Vliet, *Onno Zwier van Haren (1713–1779): Staatsman en dichter* (Hilversum: Uitgeverij Verloren, 1996). The poems are translated by poet Han van der Vegt. The translations are not literally word for word, but aim to convey both the general content and the rhetoric of the verses. All the Dutch original texts are given in the notes.
2 "De menschen zyn in alle tyden, / In ieder Land, in elk Climaat, Geneegen / 't bleek gebrek te myden, / Geneigd te minnen eygenbaat. / De Driften, zyn gevolg van menschen, / De Nyverheid, gevolg van wenschen, / Het Welzyn, vrucht van Nyverheid." Van Haren, "De koopman," 4.
3 "Wat is dog d'Adel thans op Aarde, / Waar door verdiend s'ons achting hier?". Van Haren, "De koopman", 6. Gert-Jan Johannes and Inger Leemans, "'Van den handel zou hij zingen'. Nederlandse koophandelsgedichten 1770–1830," *De Negentiende Eeuw* 40, no. 1 (2016): 1–33.
4 Gert-Jan Johannes and Inger Leemans, "O Thou Great God of Trade, O Subject of my Song!" Dutch Poems on Trade 1770–1830," *Eighteenth-Century Studies* 51, no. 3 (2018): 337–56. This chapter focuses on Dutch-language texts, leaving neo-Latin discourses aside.
5 Inger Leemans and Wouter de Vries, "Why Wind? How the Concept of Wind Trade Came to Embody Speculation in the Dutch Republic," *Journal of Modern History* (forthcoming); Alex Preda, "In the Enchanted Grove: Financial Conversations and the Marketplace in England and France in the 18th Century," *Journal of Historical Sociology* 14, no. 3 (2001): 276–307, here 281.
6 Weststeijn's article on the passion of self-love in the works of the brothers De la Court provides a good introduction to the topic, although it analyzes the concept of self-interest primarily from the perspective of political history: Arthur Weststeijn, "From the Passion of Self-love to the Virtue of Self-interest: The Republican Morals of the Brothers De la Court," *European Review of History: Revue européenne d'histoire* 17, no. 1 (2010): 75–92. DOI: 10.1080/13507480903511934. See also: Arthur Weststeijn, *Commercial Republicanism in the Dutch Golden Age: The Political Thought of Johan & Pieter de la Court* (Leiden: Brill, 2012).
7 Jan van Daal and Arnold Heertje (eds.), *Economic Thought in the Netherlands, 1650–1950* (Aldershot: Avebury, 1992), 34; Irene Hasenberg-Butter, *Academic Economics in Holland, 1800–1870* (Den Haag: Nijhoff, 1969), 145–47. See also: Paul C. H. Overmeer, "De economische denkbeelden van Gijsbert Karel van Hogendorp (1762–1834)" (PhD diss., Tilburg University, 1982); Karel Davids,

"Economic Discourse in Europe between Scholasticism and Mandeville: Convergence, Divergence and the Case of the Dutch Republic," in *Departure for Modern Europe: A Handbook of Early Modern Philosophy (1400–1700)*, ed. Hubertus Busche and Stefan Heßbrüggen-Walter (Hamburg: Felix Meiner Verlag, 2011), 80–95.

8 I am very grateful to Christine Zabel for inviting me to the conference "Knowledge(s) of Self-Interest," and for her very helpful comments on the earlier draft of this chapter.

9 Albert O. Hirschman, *The Passions and the Interests: Political Arguments for Capitalism Before Its Triumph* (Princeton: Princeton University Press, 1977).

10 Pierre Force, *Self-Interest Before Adam Smith: A Genealogy of Economic Science* (Cambridge: Cambridge University Press, 2003). Although Force provides a long-term analysis of interest, relating it back to the classic (Epicurean, Stoic) and theological (Augustinian) traditions, his main focus is on the eighteenth century, reading Adam Smith in the context of Mandeville, Hume, and specifically Rousseau's *amour de soi* and *amour-propre*. Gilbert Faccarello, "A Tale of Two Traditions: Pierre Force's Self-interest before Adam Smith," *European Journal of the History of Economic Thought* 12, no. 4 (2005): 701–12.

11 The observations in this paragraph are based on a combination of etymological / lexicographical research in historical dictionaries (e.g. *Woordenboek der Nederlandsche Taal*: https://ivdnt.org), etymological dictionaries (http://www.etymologiebank.nl), and an analysis of the digitized early modern text corpora in the DBNL (*Digitale Bibliotheek voor Nederlandse Letteren*: www.dbnl.nl), Nederlab (www.nederlab.nl), and the STCN (*Short Title Catalogue of the Netherlands*: www.stcn.nl).

12 *Oxford English Dictionary* s.v. *Interest*, 10A.

13 Zegher van Male, *Lamentatie behelzende wat datter aenmerkensweerdig geschiet is ten tyde van de Geuserie ende de Beeldenstormerie binnen ende omtrent de stadt van Brugghe*, ed. Charles L. Carton (Gent: Vanderhaeghen-Hulin, 1859), 42.

14 Hend. Spindelius, *Rechtmatige defensie van't interest der Vereenigde Nederlanden, tegen het eygen-batigh ende onredelijck Oldenborgs tollgesoeck op de vrye Weser-stroom* (Amsterdam: C. Jansz, 1647).

15 In 1646, Jesuit Adriaen Poirters stated that good friends are hard to come by: "most of them have their fundament in self-gain and interest" ("het meeste-deel leght den grondt-steen al op eyghen baet ende interest"). Adriaen Poirters, *Het masker van de wereldt afgetrocken* (1646), ed. Joseph Salsmans and Edward Rombauts (Oisterwijk: Uitgeverij Oisterwijk, 1935), 201.

16 In the Dutch States Translation of the Bible (1637) *interest* is not used, nor is *hebzucht, geldzucht, winzucht*, or *eigenbaat*. When Paul writes to Timothy on how the love of money is the root of all evil, the Dutch translation uses *geldgierigheid*. 1 Timotheus 6:10: "Want de geldgierigheid is een wortel van alle kwaad."

17 Max Weber, *Die protestantische Ethik und der Geist des Kapitalismus* (Tübingen: Mohr, 1934). In his seminal study *The Embarrassment of Riches: An Interpretation of Dutch Culture in the Golden Age* (London: Collins, 1987) Simon Schama analyzed the unease of Dutch society with its accumulating wealth. The body of research on luxury debates is too vast to cover in one note. See for inatsance Maxine Berg and Elizabeth Eger, *Luxury in the Eighteenth Century: Debates, Desires and Delectable Goods* (Basingstoke: Palgrave, 2002); István Hont, "The Early Enlightenment Debate on Commerce and Luxury," in *The Cambridge History of Eighteenth-Century Political Thought*, ed. Mark Goldie and Robert Wokler (Cambridge, NY: Cambridge University Press, 2006), 379–428.

18 Jan de Vries and Ad van der Woude, *The First Modern Economy: Success, Failure, and Perseverance of the Dutch Economy, 1500–1815* (Cambridge: Cambridge University Press, 1997); Jonathan Israel, *The Dutch Republic: Its Rise, Greatness and Fall, 1477–1806* (Oxford: Clarendon Press, 1998); Maarten Prak, *The Dutch Republic in the Seventeenth Century: The Golden Age* (Cambridge: Cambridge University Press, 2005); Catherine Secretan and Willem Frijhoff, *Dictionnaire des Pays-Bas au siècle d'or* (Paris: CNRS, 2018).

19 Deirdre McCloskey, *Bourgeois Dignity: Why Economics Can't Explain the Modern World* (Chicago, IL: University of Chicago Press, 2010).

20 The Dutch Virgin is herself a central personification of the profits of commercial life. Poems glorify the riches the Dutch Virgin is able to take in, bringing prosperity and fertility to the young nation. Arie-Jan Gelderblom, "De maagd en de mannen. Psychokritiek van de stadsuitbeelding in de zeventiende en achttiende eeuw," in Arie-Jan Gelderblom, *Mannen en maagden in Hollands tuin. Interpretatieve studies van Nederlandse letterkunde 1575–1781* (Amsterdam: Thesis Publishers, 1991), 78–93.

21 Joost van den Vondel, *Inwydinge van 't Stadthuis t'Amsterdam* (Amsterdam, Wed. A. de Wees, 1665).

22 Dorothee Sturkenboom, *De ballen van de koopman: Mannelijkheid en Nederlandse identiteit in de tijd van de Republiek* (Gorredijk: Sterck & De Vreese, 2019).

23 John G. A. Pocock, *The Machiavellian Moment: Florentine Political Thought and the Atlantic Republican Tradition* (Princeton: Princeton University Press, 1975); Steven Pincus, "Neither Machiavellian Moment nor Possessive Individualism: Commercial Society and the Defenders of the English Commonwealth," *The American Historical Review* 103 (1998): 705–36; Martin van Gelderen and Quentin Skinner, *Republicanism: A Shared European Heritage*, 2 vols (Cambridge, NY: Cambridge University Press, 2002).

24 Schama, *The Embarrassment of Riches*; Margaret C. Jacob and Catherine Secretan, eds., *The Self-Perception of Early Modern Capitalists* (New York, NY: Macmillan, 2008).

25 Sturkenboom, *De ballen van de koopman*.

26 Caspar Barlaeus, *Mercator sapiens* (Amsterdam, 1632), Dutch translation by Wilhelmus A. Buyerius: *Verstandighe Coopman* (Enkhuizen: W. Buyserius, 1641). http://www.let.leidenuniv.nl/Dutch/Latijn/BarlaeusBuyseriusCoopman1641. html; Catherine Secretan, ed., *Le "Marchand philosophe" de Caspar Barlaeus. Un éloge du commerce dans la Hollande du siècle d'or. Étude, texte et traduction du Mercator Sapiens* (Paris: H. Champion, 2002); Caspar Barlaeus, *The Wise Merchant*, ed. Anna-Luna Post, trans. Corinna Vermeulen (Amsterdam: AUP, 2019); Clé Lesger, "Merchants in Charge: The Self-Perception of Amsterdam Merchants, ca. 1550–1700," in *The Self-Perception*, ed. Jacob and Secretan, 75–97; Harold J. Cook, *Matters of Exchange: Commerce, Medicine and Science in the Dutch Golden Age* (New Haven, CT: Yale University Press, 2007).

27 Barlaeus specifically targets the merchant, providing examples from his trade and challenges specific to his daily practices. Dirk van Miert, *Humanism in an Age of Science: The Amsterdam Athenaeum in the Golden Age* (Leiden: Brill, 2009), 228.

28 Famous early examples are *De Koopman* by Dirck Volkertsz Coornhert (1580) and the extensive tractate *Geestelijck Roer van 't Coopmans-schip* (1638) by the reformed minister Godefridus Cornelisz Udemans. Marijke Spies, *De koopman van Rhodos: Over de schakelpunten van economie en cultuur*, *De zeventiende eeuw* 61 (1990): 166–73; Schama, *The Embarrassment of Riches*.

29 "een winst-gierige Natie, onder het gestadigh gerammel van geldt, ende in een Stadt diewelcke seer tot winninge genegen is," Barlaeus, *Verstandighe Coopman.*

30 "zy schromen al evenwel niet om daarheen te trekken, zo daar maar winst te doen is, ja zy verlaten Vaderlant, Wyf, en Kinderen, om een stuiver te winnen en profijt te doen," Barlaeus, *Verstandighe Coopman.*

31 "niet, dat ick de rijckdommen liefde verwerpe, maer op dat ick de selve door hulpe van bescheydenheyt ende redelijckheyt soude temmen ende matighen;" "dat hy daer op behoort te letten, dat hy, te weten, niet al te begeerigh zy," Barlaeus, *Verstandighe Coopman*, fol. B3r.

32 For an excellent study on Jan Vos, and how he combined his artistic with his professional career, see Nina Geerdink, *Dichters en verdiensten: De sociale verankering van het dichterschap van Jan Vos (1610–1667)* (Hilversum: Verloren, 2012).

33 Geerdink, *Dichters en verdiensten*, 111–12; 143–44.

34 "Een welbestierde stadt krijgt overal gezagh. / De stoute winzucht vindt hier veel gebaande spooren. / De wakkre Neering wordt aan d'Amstel groot geacht," Jan Vos, "Vergrooting van Amsterdam" (1662), in *Alle de Gedichten*, vol. 2 (1672), 835.

35 "Elk poogt te weezen daar men rijkdom weet te haalen./ De winzucht trekt het volk uit veergeleege paalen.. Volhardt, ô Stadt! volhardt in d'armen by te staan," Jan Vos, "Op 't Weeshuis van d'arme vremdelingen," in *Alle de Gedichten*, vol. 1 (1664), 157.

36 "De scheepen zijn gebouwt om koopmanschap te laaden: / Zoo houdt de rijke Beurs de Staat der Staaten staan. / De winzucht vreest noch windt, noch Thetis diepe paaden." Jan Vos, "Op 't glas in 't huis van Symen Willemsen, Schipper op d'Eendracht," in *Alle de Gedichten*, vol. 1 (1664), 177.

37 "Laat woekrend eigenbaat noch overbitse nijdt, / Nooit toegang krijgen om uw boezem te deurbooren." Joost van den Vondel, *Alle de Gedichten*, vol. 2 (1672), 198.

38 "Gewinzucht propt de breede en lange galerijen, / Die brommen in 't vierkant, gelijck een korf, vol byen, / En uitgelezen geur, gewonnen op het velt," Vondel, *Inwydinge van 't Stadthuis t'Amsterdam*, C1. *Winzucht* and *gewinzucht* are comparable terms with different spelling.

39 Hans Blom, "Decay and the Political Gestalt of Decline in Bernard Mandeville and his Dutch Contemporaries," *History of European Ideas* 36 (2010): 153–66.

40 "Zoo zal het westen 't heldere oosten/ Gaen aendoen, over zee en zant, / Om purper, gout, en diamant, / En zich Charibd en Scyl getroosten. / Gewinzucht ziet geen rampen aen, / Geen hitte, noch bevrozene assen. / Geen waterhonden haer verbassen, / Geen storm, noch bulderende Orkaen. / Zy vreest geen wilde menschevreeters. / De winst verzacht den arrebeit, / En veilt en vent zich om wat beters." Vondel, *Faëton Of Reuckeloze stoutheit* (1663), scene II.

41 Susan Legêne, "The European Character of the Intellectual History of Dutch Empire," *BMGN—Low Countries Historical Review* 132, no. 2 (2017): 110–20; Elizabeth A. Sutton, *Capitalism and Cartography in the Dutch Golden Age* (Chicago, IL: University of Chicago Press, 2015).

42 Pieter de la Court, *Interest van Holland, ofte gronden van Hollands-Welvaren* (Amsterdam: Joan C. van der Gracht, 1662).

43 New editions would follow in 1743 and 1746. Weststeijn, *Commercial Republicanism*, 350–53.

44 Weststeijn, *From the Passion of Self-love.*

45 Weststeijn, *Commercial Republicanism*, 173.

46 "*Eigen-Interest* is het voornaamste, indien niet eenigste oogwit aller mensche-like uitwerkingen." [Pieter de la Court], *Sinryke Fabulen*, 192; "vermits men gelooven moet dat eygen altijds voorgaat." De la Court, *Interest van Holland*, Preface 2r.

47 Hirschman, *The Passions*, 48–56.

48 Weststeijn, *Commercial Republicanism*, 176.

49 Rudi Verburg, "The Dutch Background of Bernard Mandeville's Thought: Escaping the Procrustean Bed of Neo-Augustinianism," *Erasmus Journal for Philosophy and Economics* 9, no. 1 (2016): 32–61.

50 Ibid. Rudi Verburg has persuasively demonstrated the influence of the *Interest* of De la Court on Bernard Mandeville's work.

51 For instance, in the work of Lambert van Velthuysen (1622–1685). Hans Blom, *Morality and Causality in Politics: The Rise of Naturalism in Dutch Seventeenth-Century Political Thought* (Utrecht: H. W. Blom, 1995); Wiep van Bunge, *From Stevin to Spinoza: An Essay on Philosophy in the Seventeenth-Century Dutch Republic* (Leiden: Brill, 2001); Karel Davids, "From De la Court to Vreede: Regulation and Self-regulation in Dutch Economic Discourse from c. 1660 to the Napoleonic Era," *The Journal of European Economic History* 30, no. 2 (2001): 245–89.

52 Weststeijn, *Commercial Republicanism*, 193.

53 Jonathan Israel, *Radical Enlightenment: Philosophy and the Making of Modernity, 1650–1750* (Oxford: Oxford University Press, 2001), 22.

54 "Gierigheidt, Eigenbaat, Roovery, Dronkenschap, Meineedigheidt Bedrogh, Onkuisheidt". Jan Vos, "Beschryving der Vertoningen [...] op de vrede tusschen Engelandt en Neederlandt in 't Jaar 1654," in Jan Vos, *Alle de gedigten* (Amsterdam: Gerrit en Hendrik Bosch, 1726), 585.

55 *Nil Volentibus Arduum. Tieranny van eigenbaat (1679). Toneel als wapen tegen Oranje*, ed. Tanja Holzhey, Kornee van der Haven, and Rudolf Rasch (Zoeterwoude: Astraea, 2008).

56 Jan Pook, *De dood van Eigenbaat: of de herstelde Wil in het Eiland van Vryekeur* (Amsterdam: M. van Heems, 1707); Enoch Krook, *De Ondergang van Eigenbaat* (Amsterdam: Erven J. Lescaille, 1707); Ysbrand Vincent, *Ondergang van Eigenbaat in het eiland van Vryekeur* (Amsterdam: Erven J. Lescaille, 1707).

57 Bernardus Bosch, *De Eigenbaat* (Amsterdam, M. de Bruyn, 1785), a patriotic play in which Self-interest has turned into a relentless female (a reference to Wilhelmina van Pruisen). Gert-Jan Johannes and Inger Leemans, *Worm en Donder. Geschiedenis van de Nederlandse Letterkunde 1700–1800* (Amsterdam: Prometheus, 2013), 668–69, 691–92.

58 This section of the chapter is based on a previous publication: Gert-Jan Johannes and Inger Leemans, "O Thou Great God of Trade, O Subject of my Song!": Dutch Poems on Trade, 1770–1830. *Eighteenth-Century Studies* 51, no. 3 (Spring 2014): 337–356." While that article provides a general description of the commercial ideology of these poems, here the focus is on *belang* as a form of self-interest.

59 The Dutch word *koophandel* incorporates both the English words "trade" and "commerce." *Koophandel* emphasizes the use of money (*kopen* = to buy). In the twentieth century the term would be replaced by the more general term *handel* [trade].

60 Koen Stapelbroek, "The Haarlem 1771 Prize Essay on the Restoration of Dutch Trade and the Economic Branch of the Holland Society of Sciences," in *The Rise of Economic Societies in the Eighteenth Century*, ed. Koen Stapelbroek and Jani Marjanen (Basingstoke: Palgrave Macmillan, 2012), 257–84.

61 Marleen de Vries, *Beschaven!: Letterkundige genootschappen in Nederland, 1750–1800* (Nijmegen: Vantilt, 2001); Joost J. Kloek and Wijnand W. Mijnhardt, *1800: Blueprints for a National Community* (Assen: Van Gorcum, 2004).

62 Anoush F. Terjanian, *Commerce and its Discontents in Eighteenth-Century French Political Thought* (Cambridge: Cambridge University Press, 2013).

63 "Bloei duurzaam, hartsvriendin! / Door regt en trouw en koopgewin; / Weer schraapzieke eigenbaat en wulpsche dartelheden." Adolph H. Hagedoorn, "De lof van den Nederlandschen Koophandel," *Proeven van poëtische mengelstoffen* [...]V (Leiden: Kunstliefde Spaart Geen Vlijt, 1777), 195–215, here 214.

64 Helmer Helmers, "De handel," in *Nagelaten gedichten*, 3rd ed. (The Hague: J. Allart, 1823), 77–103, here 93.

65 "in bebloede beestenvachten / Het lillend vleesch verslindt, en in spelonken schuilt." Petronella Moens, "De koophandel beschouwd als een voornaam middel van volksbeschaving," in *Verhandelingen en prijsverzen uitgegeven door de Gendsche Maatschappij van Nederlandsche Taal en Letterkunde* 1 (Gent: A. B. Steven, 1826), 171–84, 173.

66 Although the Dutch were critical of Rousseau, his ideas did set the intellectual agenda. Helen Paul, "Rousseau in de Republiek: Nederlandse reacties op de burgerlijke godsdienst van Jean-Jacques Rousseau," *Groniek* 3 (1999): 103–13; Walter Gobbers, *Jean-Jacques Rousseau in Holland: Een onderzoek naar de invloed van de mens en het werk (ca. 1760–1810)* (Gent: secr. KVATL, 1963).

67 Kerkhoven sees *begeerte* as the "eedle zucht om altijd voort te streven" (the noble urge to strive further). Theodorus J. Kerkhoven, "De koophandel," in Theodorus J. Kerkhoven, *Gedichten*, 2 vols. (Amsterdam: M. Westerman, 1825), vol. 1, 101–4. See also: Theodorus J. Kerkhoven, "De koophandel, dichtstuk," in ibid., vol. 2, 1–2.

68 Moens, "De koophandel," 183.

69 "Dus vormt ge, o Handel! de Aard' tot één Gemeenebest, / En hecht het Zuid aan 't Noord, en 't Oosten aan het West". Helmers, "De handel," 87.

70 Lambrecht van den Broek, "Nederlands koophandel," in *Gedichten* (Rotterdam: Wed. J. Allart, 1828), 21–42, 31.

71 "Des werelds burgerij is hier te zaam vergaderd./ Hier valt de scheidsmuur weg van Godsdienst—wet en rang; / Hier knielen arm en rijk voor 't outer van 't belang". Van den Broek, "Nederlands koophandel."

72 Willem H. Warnsinck, "De koophandel," *Vaderlandsche Letteroefeningen* 2 (1816), 309–18.

73 "Gij hebt den mensch gevormd, door u is 't dat hij denkt." Helmers, "De handel," 92.

74 For the distinction between contested concepts used as category of practice or as category of analysis, see: Chris Lorenz and Stefan Berger, *The Contested Nation: Ethnicity, Class, Religion and Gender in National Histories* (Basingstoke, New York: Palgrave Macmillan, 2008).

75 In a follow-up project, in collaboration with Frans-Willem Korsten (Leiden University), we will further investigate this claim of the Dutch Republic finding unity through commercial *imagineering*.

7 Practical knowledge of self-interest

The disembedding of agency in rural areas, eighteenth and early nineteenth centuries

Ulrich Pfister and Friederike Scholten-Buschhoff

Introduction

This study explores the relationship between the development of knowledge regarding self-interest in the eighteenth and early nineteenth centuries, and contemporary practice guided by self-interest. It focuses on two major processes that are usually related to a spread of self-interested behavior. These are: first, the increase of personal autonomy with respect to the management of the household economy in the wake of the so-called "Industrious Revolution";[1] and second, the tendency to orient the management of rural estates toward maximizing short-term income in the context of the "Great Transformation" and the rise of market culture.[2] The paper investigates the ways in which practices that can be described as financially self-interested relied on practical knowledge; and whether such practical knowledge informing self-interested behavior was anchored in propositional knowledge of self-interest that emerged and circulated among members of the learned elite. The evidence suggests that practices of self-interest spread without an intellectual foundation. Rather, the emergence of learned discourses that provided arguments for the moral legitimacy of self-interested behavior, and produced knowledge useful[3] for its practical implementation, may have constituted a posteriori rationalizations of processes that were unfolding in society at large.

The first, shorter part of this chapter combines information on the "Industrious Revolution"—that is, developments in labor effort and consumption patterns—in various parts of Europe, and confronts it with the emergence of discourses legitimizing self-interested economic behavior, in particular in the wake of the publication of Mandeville's *Fable of the Bees* (1705/14). The second part focuses on the management of rural estates in western Germany and relates practices of self-interest to Polanyi's concept of the "Great Transformation." It appears that practical knowledge of practices that can be linked to self-interest developed mostly without any connection to learned discourse on the topic. Particularly at the household level, this was due to the fact that self-interested behavior was easy to develop and to adopt. At the level of estate management, practical obstacles against disembedding everyday transactions from their social context rendered the transition to self-interested behavior a piecemeal and often erratic process.

The "Industrious Revolution" and Mandeville's beehive

The core idea of the "Industrious Revolution" thesis, as developed by Jan de Vries,[4] is that from the late seventeenth century households worked more because they wanted to increase their consumption of traded goods. This broadened the markets for manufactured goods, and—by increasing the number of potential users—also increased the potential profits from research and development of technologies to raise labor productivity in manufacturing.[5] Hence, the Industrious Revolution constituted a major force that triggered the Industrial Revolution and the transition to modern economic development.

A simple economic model of the Industrious Revolution thesis starts from the assumption that households have love-of-variety preferences, meaning that they prefer differentiated goods to non-differentiated ones.[6] Relevant historical examples that are intimately linked to self-presentation include fashion goods, which produce utility through social distinction, and differentiated domestic goods, which contribute to the construction of personal identity. The improvements in trade organization and business techniques that took place from the second half of the seventeenth century lowered trading costs, and massively increased the supply of consumer goods contributing to variety, such as Indian textiles ("fashion's favorite" in much of eighteenth-century Europe), Chinese porcelain, and colonial goods.[7] The resulting rise in product variety increased the utility of consuming traded goods relative to that derived from using undifferentiated goods originating from domestic subsistence production, such as coarse gray woolen cloth. Consequently, households reallocated labor from subsistence to the production of items for trade (manufactured goods in particular), thus generating disposable income that could be spent on consumption. This mechanism constituted a major force underlying the development of regional export industries or proto-industries.[8] Moreover, because the utility of total consumption rose relative to the utility of leisure, households increased their labor supply; that is, they were prepared to work longer hours and more days per year for given wages.

Scholarship remains divided over the Industrious Revolution thesis. Indeed, one author has argued that major parts of inland Europe failed to participate in this process, mainly for institutional reasons.[9] Nevertheless, classic inquiries into the history of consumption demonstrate that in the course of the late seventeenth and eighteenth centuries post-mortem inventories in northern France and England contained an increasing number of traded products, characterized by heightened variety. A recent estimate of the number of working days per year in English agriculture suggests a massive expansion of the labor effort between the early seventeenth and nineteenth centuries. Finally, evidence from a number of European regions on the allocation of household labor between agricultural and non-agricultural activities, and to different types of proto-industrial work, is consistent with an income-maximization strategy.[10] Whereas the issue of the empirical relevance of the Industrious Revolution thesis is certainly far from settled, what follows presumes that at least some parts of Europe were characterized by patterns of development that are consistent with this concept.

In cultural terms, the Industrious Revolution involves a heightened concern on the part of individuals and households for self-management, self-presentation, care of the self,[11] and personal autonomy. All these phenomena can be considered as manifestations of self-interest in everyday behavior. In particular, the consumption of populuxe fashion goods—such as silk ribbons, printed handkerchiefs, and stockings—as well as accessories for tea- and coffee-drinking, which all constituted important elements of rationalized self-presentation, could spread informally through the emulation of role models.[12]

A similar argument holds for the spread of utility-maximizing household management. From the late eighteenth century, it became common to associate self-interested household behavior with calculations of maximum profit. A traveler's guide published in 1794 characterized the milieu in the vicinity of Zurich, a major early textile district of inland Europe, with a mixture of deprecation and admiration: "Soon these villages will be ruled by the sole consideration: which activity generates the highest weekly return?"[13] Yet, no testimonies survive that provide information on the practices that produced behavior that can be related to self-interested household management. Nothing is known about methods of calculation, simple heuristics providing smart approximations to optimum solutions,[14] or habitualized routines of household management. This holds in particular for personal documents such as the diary of Cornelius Ashworth, a farmer and weaver from the West Riding of Yorkshire writing in the 1780s, or the autobiography of the "Poor man in Tockenburg," a cotton weaver and small textile entrepreneur living in the textile district of northern Switzerland.[15] At times, however, such texts do give us glimpses into the relevance of practical knowledge relating to particular activities. The "Poor man," for instance, notes in a self-ironic tone that, most of the time, he and his wife would buy and sell yarn at the wrong moment. Strategies of trial and error seem to have constituted an important means to explore and acquire practical techniques of self-interested behavior. However, nowhere are there descriptions of ways of household management per se. It must be concluded, therefore, that knowledge underlying a style of household management guided by self-interest remained entirely in the sphere of practical knowledge, was acquired by trial and error or by imitating models, and possibly remained in the sphere of tacit knowledge.

This implies a second conclusion, namely, that propositional knowledge—that is, knowledge expressed in declarative sentences or indicative propositions—regarding self-interested economic behavior at the level of individuals and households had little connection with actual practices regarding the choice of traded consumer goods and household management, and developed essentially in the form of a posteriori rationalizations of processes unfolding in society at large. Bernard Mandeville, the major contemporary herald of the Industrious Revolution, illustrates this point in his principal work, the *Fable of the Bees*. As is well known, the *Fable* develops the paradox that individual characteristics held in low esteem (passions, vices) may inform actions that contribute to public welfare in a systematic way. The subtitle of the editions from 1714—*Private Vices, Publick Benefits*—catches this idea. In a central passage, Mandeville argues that vices such as Luxury, Pride, and Inconstancy (linked with the mutability of fashion) employed millions of the poor. Envy and Vanity became "Ministers of Industry" because "Their darling Folly, Fickleness/In Diet, Furniture and Dress,/[...] was made/the very Wheel that turn'd the Trade." Through the stimulation of trade, "Vice nurs'd Ingenuity, Which join'd with Time and Industry" and increased material welfare, that is, "Life's Conveniences [...] To such a Height, the very Poor/Liv'd better than the Rich before."[16] By connecting the consumption of fashion and domestic goods with trade, innovation, and industriousness, Mandeville developed a narrative on empirical phenomena that occupies center stage in ongoing research on the Industrious Revolution thesis.

Mandeville played a pivotal role in the development of a learned discourse on self-interest for two main reasons. First, he broadened the discussion of the relationship of interest and political order to include individual and household behavior, and aggregate material welfare: that is, the material side of the common good. Second, he threw into sharp relief the contingent nature of the relationship between individual virtue and the common good. This set him notably in opposition to the Dutch tradition of commercial republicanism, which studied the conditions under which private passions can be tamed and channeled into virtuous behavior contributing to the common good.[17] Mandeville's highly controversial claim concerning the importance of human passions in economic matters stimulated an inquiry into the human motives underlying economic behavior. The most prominent positions were developed by Jean-Jacques Rousseau and Adam Smith, from their critiques of Mandeville's discussion of selfish passions as a driver of human conduct in the neo-Augustinian tradition of the French moralists.[18] Of central importance was a careful distinction between love of oneself (*amour de soi*), considered as a prime motive of all beings to care for their own welfare, and self-love (*amour-propre*), a relational sentiment guiding humans to engage in actions that heighten their individual honor and diminish that of others. Commercial society contributed to a greater prominence of self-love, yet this derived from love of oneself, which both authors considered as the first principle of human action. At the same time, love of oneself could also provide the basis for virtue and reason. In Adam Smith's work in particular, this laid the basis for fashioning self-interest as a human motive amenable to reasonable deliberation and oriented mainly toward guiding market exchanges.[19]

To fully appreciate Mandeville's role in the development of the concept of self-interest, it is important to consider his theory of knowledge.[20] As a physician, Mandeville was an avowed empiricist following an antirationalist tradition as epitomized by Locke. He was convinced that human knowledge of the world is derived wholly from sense experience. According to him, all our knowledge comes a posteriori and it is imprudent to reason from any basis other than from facts.[21] While this epistemic position on knowledge undoubtedly helped Mandeville to develop statements that appear to anticipate the later principle of laissez-faire, it also buttresses a reading of the *Fable* as a rationalization of commercial society based on sensual experience. He employed the genre of satiric fable to hold up a mirror to a conservative society occupied with restoring the moral standards of a time long past,[22] and to reflect the standards that actually existed at his time of writing. As the above sketch of the transition from selfish passions to economic self-interest in Adam Smith shows, the foundations of learned discourses on self-interest cannot be reduced to an observation of ongoing processes in societies at large, however; the frameworks employed by the *res publica* of the literati developed in considerable autonomy. Still, the example of the relationship between the Industrious Revolution and Mandeville's *Fable* seems to turn the implications of Albert Hirschman's *The Passions and the Interests*[23] upside down. Hirschman argued in the 1970s that the intellectual concept of self-interest as it emerged in the eighteenth century provided a foundation for new ways of behavior at the level of households and individuals. By contrast, the foregoing suggests that learned discourse on self-interest reflected on and rationalized forms of behavior that had become increasingly common and demanded little theoretical knowledge on the part of individual actors.

Estate management and the Great Transformation: Western Germany around 1800

This section analyzes the management of grain revenues and leasehold contracts on noble estates, in order to track the emergence of practical knowledge of self-interest in the context of the "Great Transformation." This term refers to the relationship between markets and societies that Karl Polanyi first introduced (1944).[24] He shows that until the end of the era of feudalism, markets and economic transactions were part of processes of reciprocity, redistribution, and household organization. Accordingly, economic activities were usually embedded in social relationships. The establishment of individual property rights and formal markets in the course of the nineteenth century had the effect of disembedding economic transactions from social relationships: this is what Polanyi terms a "Great Transformation."

The evidence is drawn from the account books of five rural estates owned by nobles situated in present-day North Rhine-Westphalia, Germany, over the time period c. 1650–1850.[25] In the context of estate management, contemporaries documented every administrative activity, which enables us to trace the processes of decision-making and their results.[26] All of the estates analyzed in this study are representative properties that include a castle. However, the size, scope, and structure of these estates vary greatly from one to the other and depend upon the local conditions, family history, and business management of each one. The estate of Nordkirchen, close to the Ruhr area (Dortmund), represents the region of Westphalia. The other four estates are spread across the lower Rhineland. The estates of Dyck and Wissen lie in fertile zones of the Lower Rhine, whereas the estates of Heltorf and Schönstein are located in areas less suited for arable farming and showing a relatively higher degree of commercial development (see Figure 7.1). In addition, Heltorf

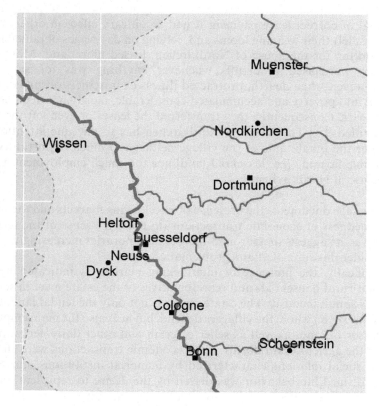

Figure 7.1 Map showing the locations of the estates of Nordkirchen, Dyck, Wissen, Heltorf, and Schönstein

and Dyck in particular are located close to urban centers of trade: that is, Neuss and Düsseldorf.

Written documents preserved in the archives of these estates, and originating roughly from the last third of the eighteenth and first third of the nineteenth century, sometimes make use of the word "interest," mostly in conjunction with the entitlements and the income of the estate. None of these passages is particularly explicit about the semantic connotation of the term, however. This holds in particular with respect to the potential opposition between the common good vs. private self-interest. Nevertheless, a memorandum written in 1800 by the administrator of the estate of Nordkirchen sheds an indirect light on the increasing awareness of a particular interest of the estate as distinct from the common good of the rural community:

> The poor inhabitants of the parish have always gained some income from employment at the house of Nordkirchen. One has seen it as a necessity to employ them all the time, because—apart from weaving—there are only few or no possibilities to earn money in this region. Whereas in some cases this good arrangement helped to achieve the goal of correct lease payment it had a contrary effect in other cases: most left their weaving looms and, relying on day wages obtained from working for the house of Nordkirchen, leased more land. Moreover, they purchased foodstuffs whenever anything was for sale. [...] However, when dearth, protracted illness or mischiefs occurred, they fell into poverty and accumulated considerable, mostly non-recoverable arrears. Consequently, they transferred the leases or even left the land untilled. [...] The house of Nordkirchen has to pay due attention to offer the inhabitants of the village neither too much opportunity for arable farming [i.e. leasehold land] nor too much employment at the house of Nordkirchen.[27]

This passage documents the presence of interlocking markets and the social embeddedness of economic transactions (in Polanyi's sense of the term).[28] Moreover, it suggests that, around 1800, contemporaries increasingly began to consider this state of affairs problematic.

Specifically, the presence of interlocking markets is indicated by the fact that rural households and representatives of the estate meet in several markets simultaneously. The estate owner is not only the feudal landowner (*Grundherr*)[29] on whom the villagers depend, but he is also the main employer and lessor of land, as well as seller of grain and other daily necessities.[30] Before the agricultural reforms, these economic transactions were embedded in social relations characterized by manorial institutions and noble paternalism. Elite behavior was driven by the desire to represent and to maintain social status, specifically, *Adeligkeit* ("nobility," in its social and cultural meaning).[31] Being noble required appropriate landed and financial wealth; therefore, the noble estate as such, as well as its management, served the preservation and expansion of *Adeligkeit*. Moreover, noble status relied on social superiority and required the exercise of power. However, *Grundherrschaft*—the manorial system—was far from a bipolar relationship in which the patrimonial, all-powerful landlord faced the subservient peasant. The asymmetrical relationship between peasants and lords was much more complex and characterized by consensus, cooperation, loyalty, and conflict. As the noble landlord strove to maintain his dominant position in society, he found himself in constant negotiations for cooperation.

Because of these cooperative efforts, self-interest remained of limited relevance in the social strategies of noble estate owners until c. 1800. Rather, paternalism played a decisive role in shaping the asymmetrical relationship between peasants and lords. Following E. P. Thompson, paternalism provides the social framework and ideology for authority in a society where there is a close physical proximity, as well as a great social distance, between the ruled and their masters.[32] Paternalistic rule implies an acceptance of the superior position of the elite by the subordinates, in exchange for the elite's obligation to protect the livelihood of the lower classes. In the passage quoted above, this reciprocal relationship is made explicit in the perceived obligation of the estate to provide employment for the poor. In a world governed by a culture of paternalism, the elite can maintain their social position only through the well-being of the common people. Hence, there was very little room for strategies oriented toward the self-interest of estate owners before c. 1800. This is confirmed, for example, by the fact that non-paternalistic behavior (e.g. selling grain at a high price, regardless of the buyer's options) was punished directly: buyers and thus also lessees and employees refused to purchase. Pursuing self-interest regardless of social embedding was hardly possible, therefore.

In order to see how contemporaries engaged with a strategy of self-interest, and to identify the kind of knowledge they required to do so, some basic information is required about how estates operated in the region under study. Rural estates owned by nobles usually comprised two organizational levels: the *Ökonomie* and the so-called *Rentei*. The *Ökonomie* related to the personal household of the owner and his family. The *Rentei* administered the estate's income, mostly in the form of grain and money rents. In particular, its activities involved the storage and processing of grain in the estate's bakery and brewery, decisions regarding the magnitude and timing of grain sales, and the donation of stocks to the local poor relief administration. The scope of the activities of the *Rentei* varied and depended mainly on the size of an estate's possessions.

Until the early nineteenth century, a major portion of an estate's income was generated through the manorial system, that is, the *Grundherrschaft*.[33] At its center stood the noble house, and peasants transferred a multitude of dues, fees, and payments[34] to the manor on an annual basis. These revenues of money and goods (such as eggs, cattle, and—mainly—grain) formed the financial backbone of the landed estates and the basis of their owners' wealth. In addition, as noble estates west of the river Elbe engaged in farming only to a very limited extent, an increasing portion of the farmland was leased out to peasants, for a certain period of time, for a monetary rent on a time-limited level. Thus, already by the end of the eighteenth century, rent from leases had become the second major source of estate income, representing about 40 percent of the total. To summarize: large early modern estates constituted complex households, important land lessors, centers of grain and animal farming, and included workshops that processed agricultural products.

All the income streams and transformative activities of an estate were managed by an administrator, a so-called *Rentmeister*. These officials were in charge of the collection, organization, and documentation of all dues, leases, and additional payments, and therefore held an important place in the estates' organization. According to the records, the sale of grain surpluses, in particular, and the leasing of land made up a considerable part of their work.[35] The role of these *Rentmeister* was crucial because, in the area under study, most proprietors of rural estates were absentee landowners. Thus, the estate management was completely in the administrators' hands; they were not only responsible for collecting duties and organizing the estate, but also wielded authority over the local peasant community on behalf of the owners. They thus acted as mediators of *Grundherrschaft*.

After about 1800, it is possible to identify three changes in the management of estates that can be linked to endeavors that sought to disembed transactions of goods such as grain or land, and orient them toward the self-interest of the owner. First, grain sales were organized on a more formal basis. Until the late eighteenth century, estates sold grain stocks mostly in an informal way that required little organization. Grain was sold whenever the opportunity arose, regardless of price fluctuations and internal cycles of grain revenues. From about 1800, grain sales increasingly took the form of public auctions held on pre-announced days. For this purpose, administrators disseminated information on planned sales in newspapers and through public announcements in order to attract more potential buyers, especially from outside the local community. In particular, these efforts served to attract grain traders from nearby towns, for this group purchased in large quantities. To maximize revenues, owners and administrators fixed limits on minimum prices, and they explored suitable selling dates in advance. One technique relied on the observation of urban prices to project and exploit price increases for the sales of a particular estate.[36]

Second, leasehold contracts relating to farmland were formalized and made subject to regular re-negotiation. During the early modern period, leasehold contracts, while being of fixed duration, were mostly prolonged informally with the rent remaining unaltered. In the course of the eighteenth century, the proportion of contracts with a fixed duration increased, and over the first half of the nineteenth century, rents were less constant. Between the 1780s and 1810s, between 15 and 80 percent of all contracts concluded during a particular decade resulted from auctions. The administrator of Nordkirchen explicitly used the threat of auctioning off the lease of a particular plot to maximize revenue. In 1814, he wrote to the owner's representative:

> I believe that another try [i.e., another negotiation round] might increase the *surplus* [original term] a bit more. [...] As soon as I have received your reply I will ask the leaseholders to increase the offer they made yesterday, and should they disagree, I will set a date to auction the lease to the highest bidder.[37]

Consequently, negotiations conducted without the instrument of an auction usually led to an increase in rent.

Third, estates developed new activities apart from grain farming, and in which interaction with the local community was much looser. Nearly every estate examined in this study turned to forestry as a principal activity. The agrarian reforms (c. 1808–50), which terminated the obligations of the farmers toward manors and thereby diminished the estates' grain revenues, was pivotal in this process. The parallel dissolution of the commons increased the supply of land suitable for silviculture, and the high wood prices prevailing during the early stages of industrialization offered large profits. Thus, estate owners frequently used the proceeds from the payments effected by peasants for the redemption of feudal rights to develop important activities in forestry. Some estate owners also sought to develop industrial activities. For example, Count August von Spee (Heltorf) erected a paper mill near Ratingen,[38] and already at the end of the eighteenth century, Count Johann Franz Wilhelm von Salm-Reifferscheidt (Dyck) started to commercialize the mineral water from his own well.[39]

All these new activities reduced the multiplex interactions between estates and villagers and thereby disembedded economic transactions from social relations. This enabled the rural elite to pursue the perceived self-interest of their estates by attempting to maximize their profits from grain sales and the leasing of land. In that sense, self-interest here expresses itself in the pursuit of higher profits. Apart from the know-how required to run business ventures or to engage in commercial forestry, these efforts might require dexterity in exploiting competition among peasants for land, the identification of suitable channels to publicize information on planned auctions, or the ability to access information about the grain prices prevailing in urban markets.

Above and beyond all this, the reorientation of estate management toward a higher concern for the self-interest of the owner rested on a trend toward more systematic record-keeping. Account books surviving from the seventeenth and eighteenth centuries are poorly structured and omit details. For example, in the context of sales or leases, there is often little information about the identity of the buyers or the tenants, the terms of the contract,

Figure 7.2 Account book page comprising revenues and expenditures of Nordkirchen for the years 1842–43 to 1843–44.

Source: LWL Archivamt, Nor. Ak 3542 (1845).

relevant prices, and the negotiations in general. From the early nineteenth century onward, commercially oriented book-keeping practices became more common in the management of *Grundherrschaften* (rural estates), at least in the region under survey here. This change is first recognizable by the introduction of a uniform structural scheme. Incomes and expenditures were no longer aggregated according to their spatial provenance but according to functional criteria (see Figure 7.2).

As can be seen in the sources of the revenues and expenditures in Nordkirchen for the years 1842–43 and 1843–44[40] shown in Figure 7.2, the accounts now distinguish between the different legal foundations of revenues. Column 5, for example, refers to revenues and expenditures relating to tithes, and Column 7 from the grain economy of the estate. Arrears were increasingly listed separately, and a consistent division between actual payments and outstanding claims was introduced as well. Finally, business operations, such as grain sales or leasing land, became much more transparent and structured over time. Previously they had been documented only occasionally, but they now became an integral part of record-keeping.[41]

More systematic record-keeping resulted in part from closer supervision of administrators by estate owners. This is reflected in the expansion of the correspondence between the two groups. Operational issues were often discussed—self-interest was put into practice by reflecting upon what was best for the profit of an estate, and by drawing on the experience of past operations, which could be easily tracked thanks to the more systematic record-keeping.[42]

The development and deployment of practical knowledges of self-interest raise the question: to what degree were these actions informed by propositional knowledge? The catalog of the library held by the estate of Heltorf (Düsseldorf) provides a representative answer, as it is one of the few aristocratic book collections surviving to the present day that is both well-documented and extensive.[43] Over the early modern period, successive owners built an impressive library covering multiple fields of learning, and purchases of books accelerated in the course of the eighteenth century. In that century alone, the library shows annual increases of 12 to 13 percent, which is far above the average for book purchases of that period.[44] However, no direct correlation is discernible between knowledge gained from books and the changes in estate management noted above. Books newly acquired in the second half of the eighteenth century mainly dealt with such topics as language, geography, religion, history, and general entertainment. Works on agriculture and household management (*Kamerlistenliteratur*, *Hausväterliteratur*), which may indicate an increasing interest in affairs concerning rural estates, remained rather rare by comparison.[45]

In addition, administrators do not seem to have received any formal training before the middle of the nineteenth century. Of those serving on the estates studied here, none attended a specialized agricultural school. Their biographies[46] suggest that they acquired basic skills in other administrative offices, by running a private farm, or simply by helping their predecessors. The disembedding of estate management and its subjection to self-interest certainly required more elaborate practical knowledge than did the same processes in household management, and on estates these processes were, to some degree, amenable to reflection by the actors involved. Nevertheless, there seems to be no relationship between the development of learned understanding of self-interest and the spread of practical knowledge enabling its implementation in everyday practice.

In concluding this analysis, it is also important to stress that the efforts of estate owners and managers to detach their operations from multiplex interaction with villagers, subject them to self-interest, and render them more profitable, were only moderately successful at first. In 1824, for instance, the administrator of Nordkirchen discussed whether the grain sale that had just taken place (and that had fetched only a low price) should be approved by the owner. Ultimately, he recommends approval, with the argument that non-approval would result in a high risk of losing market access in the future:

> I'm really embarrassed whether to recommend the approval of the sale or not. There are a range of aspects which speak against the approval: the low [grain] prices in general, as well as the lack of prospect of a higher rise of prices in the future, the difficulty of storing the old and new grain simultaneously which will result in high storage costs, furthermore the loss of the capital that can be gained from grain sales and finally the fact that the refusal of ratification could have a detrimental effect on future sales and reduce competition. These reasons speaking for the ratification are probably pre-dominant.[47]

This example from Nordkirchen shows that contemporaries were well aware of their (self-)interests (that is, higher profits from sales), but achieving those

Table 7.1 The origin of rye buyers in Nordkirchen, 1700–1850, and Heltorf, 1680–1832 (n = number of observations)

		Parish	Vicinity (< 8km)	Distant region (> 8km)	Town
Nordkirchen n=644	% share of total buyers	77.5	20.8	1.7	–
	% share of transaction volumes	73.2	19.7	7.1	–
Heltorf n=438	% share of total buyers	25.3	71.9	0.7	2.1
	% share of transaction volumes	22.7	71.8	1.7	3.8

Source: Account books Nordkirchen and Heltorf.

outcomes in reality proved significantly more difficult. There are multiple reasons for this.

First, an analysis of the structure of the buyers of grain sold by estates shows that the estates discharged themselves from their social responsibilities only very gradually. Although administrators strove to attract grain merchants from nearby towns, the majority of their buyers continued to come from their own parish or the surrounding area. In Heltorf and Nordkirchen, more than 95 percent of the buyers lived less than eight kilometers from the estate (Table 7.1). Further analysis shows that this proportion did not increase over time.[48]

Although estate owners gradually lost their manorial claims of dominance over the peasants, they continued to be the main lessors and employers in each parish because they still possessed huge properties, so that their dealings with the local population remained embedded in interlocking markets and paternalist obligations.[49]

Second, profit motives were thwarted by uncertainties and a lack of appropriate information. The estate's grain could be sold to outsiders only if the roads were passable, but high prices did not necessarily go together with good weather. In addition, the trajectory of grain prices was difficult to predict. Consequently, the administrator of Dyck wrote to the owner in May 1820: "Since, therefore, no one can say anything definite about the further rise or fall of the price, I want to ask your Highness obediently whether I should sell the fruits [i.e. grain] now."[50] It also turns out that the rural estate holder's attempts to align rural grain prices with urban ones[51] was helpful only to a limited extent. Prices behaved differently between town and countryside, given the poor state of market integration due to limited market access (higher distances, lack of infrastructure) and a limited market liquidity.[52]

In sum, the full development of the self-interest of noble estate owners required a considerable detachment from their social function, meaning that their economic operations were no longer embedded in interlocking markets and paternalist obligations. This required several conditions to hold (such as availability of information, and suitable infrastructure rendering possible frequent interactions with non-locals), and these remained difficult to fulfill during the early part of the nineteenth century.

Conclusion

The growth of practical knowledge concerning practices that can be linked to self-interest was mostly unconnected with the development of learned discourse on the topic. Particularly in the case of household management and consumption, this was because the knowledge intensity of new practices was low, and relevant know-how could be obtained by imitating models, by trial and error, and by learning by doing. The transfer of the notion of interest from the realm of politics to economic behavior, which Albert Hirschman has traced, and which took place during the first half of the eighteenth century, may well have been informed, as this paper's findings suggest, by intuitive observation of the ongoing Industrious Revolution. The slowness of the spread of a profit-oriented management style in rural estates in western Germany was due not so much to poor knowledge transfers as to practical and social constraints that limited the capacity of estate owners and administrators to disembed their operations from paternalist obligations and interlocking markets. In sum, our analysis stresses the multiplicity and the protracted nature of the development of a culture of knowledges relating to self-interest.

Notes

1 Jan de Vries, *The Industrious Revolution: Consumer Behaviour and the Household Economy: 1650 to the Present* (Cambridge: Cambridge University Press, 2008).
2 Karl Polanyi, *The Great Transformation* (New York: Farrar & Rinehart, 1944); William Reddy, *The Rise of Market Culture: The Textile Trade and French Society: 1750–1900* (Cambridge/Paris: Cambridge University Press/Editions de la Maison des Sciences de l'Homme, 1984).
3 Joel Mokyr, *The Gifts of Athena: Historical Origins of the Knowledge Economy* (Princeton: Princeton University Press, 2002).
4 De Vries, *The Industrious Revolution*.
5 Nicholas F. R. Crafts, "Explaining the First Industrial Revolution: Two Views," *European Review of Economic History* 15, no. 1 (April 2011): 153–68, here 57–58.
6 Avinash K. Dixit and Joseph E. Stiglitz, "Monopolistic Competition and Optimum Product Diversity," *American Economic Review* 67, no. 3 (June 1977): 297–308; for an application to the spread of the consumption of colonial goods during the period under study, see Jonathan Hersh and Hans-Joachim Voth, "Sweet Diversity: Colonial Goods and the Rise of European Living Standards after 1492," *CEPR Discussion Paper* 7386, no. DP7386 (July 2009).

7 In addition to Hersh and Voth, "Sweet Diversity," see: Beverly Lemire, *Fashion's Favourite: The Cotton Trade and the Consumer in Britain: 1660–1800* (Oxford: Oxford University Press, 1991); Maxine Berg, "In Pursuit of Luxury: Global History and British Consumer Goods in the Eighteenth Century," *Past and Present* 182 (February 2004): 85–142; Giorgio Riello and Tirthankar Roy, eds., *How India Clothed the World: The World of South Asian Textiles 1500–1850* (Leiden: Brill, 2010).

8 Peter Kriedte, Hans Medick, and Jürgen Schlumbohm, *Industrialization before Industrialization: Rural Industry and the Genesis of Capitalism* (Cambridge/Paris: Cambridge University Press/Maison des Sciences de l'Homme, 1981).

9 Sheilagh C. Ogilvie, "Consumption, Social Capital, and the Industrious Revolution in Early Modern Germany," *Journal of Economic History* 70, no. 2 (June 2010): 287–325.

10 Daniel Roche, *The Culture of Clothing: Dress and Fashion in the "Ancien Régime"* (Cambridge: Cambridge University Press, 1994), 127–38; Lorna M. Weatherill, *Consumer Behaviour and Material Culture in Britain: 1660–1760* (London: Routledge, 1996); Jane Humphries and Jacob Weisdorf, "Unreal Wages? Real Income and Economic Growth in England: 1260–1850," *Economic Journal* 129, no. 623 (October 2019): 2867–87; Ulrich Pfister, *Die Zürcher Fabriques: Protoindustrielles Wachstum vom 16. zum 18. Jahrhundert* (Zürich: Chronos, 1992), ch. 5; Ulrich Pfister, "The Proto-industrial Household Economy: Toward a Formal Analysis," *Journal of Family History* 17, no. 2 (April 1992): 201–32.

11 In the sense of how Foucault introduced the term, see Christine Fertig and Ulrich Pfister, "Coffee, Mind and Body: Global Material Culture and the Eighteenth-Century Hamburg Import Trade," in *The Global Lives of Things: The Material Culture of Connections in the Early Modern World*, ed. Anne Gerritsen and Giorgio Riello (London: Routledge, 2016), 221–40.

12 Cissie Fairchilds, "The Production and Marketing of Populuxe Goods in Eighteenth-century Paris," in *Consumption and the World of Goods*, ed. John Brewer and Roy Porter (London: Routledge, 1993), 228–48; Hans Medick, *Leben und Überleben in Laichingen 1650–1900: Lokalgeschichte als Allgemeine Geschichte* (Göttingen: Vandenhoeck & Ruprecht, 1996), ch. 5.

13 Pfister, *Zürcher Fabriques*, 264, quoting Hans R. Maurer, *Kleine Reisen im Schweizerland* (1794).

14 Gerd Gigerenzer and Peter M. Todd, *Simple Heuristics that Make Us Smart* (New York: Oxford, 1999).

15 Edward P. Thompson, "Time, Work Discipline and Industrial Capitalism," *Past and Present*, no. 38 (December 1967): 56–97, here 71–72; Pfister, *Zürcher Fabriques*, 240, discussing Ulrich Bräker, *Lebensgeschichte und Natürliche Ebenteuer des Armen Mannes in Tockenburg* (original publication in 1788/89).

16 Frederick B. Kaye, ed., *The Fable of the Bees: Or, Private Vices, Public Benefits: by Bernhard Mandeville* (Oxford: Clarendon Press, 1924), 25–26.

17 Rudi Verburg, "The Dutch Background of Bernard Mandeville's Thought: Escaping the Procrustean Bed of Neo-Augustinanism," *Erasmus Journal for Philosophy and Economics* 9, no. 1 (Spring 2016): 32–61. On Dutch commercial republicanism, see Arthur Weststeijn, *Commercial Republicanism in the Dutch Golden Age: The Political Thought of Johan & Pieter de la Court* (Leiden: Brill, 2012).

18 See Thomas A. Horne, *The Social Thought of Bernard Mandeville: Virtue and Commerce in Early Eighteenth-Century England* (London: Macmillan, 1978), ch. 2.

19 Pierre Force, *Self-interest before Adam Smith: A Genealogy of Economic Science* (Cambridge: Cambridge University Press, 2003), esp. ch. 2; see also Albert O. Hirschman, *The Passions and the Interests: Political Arguments for Capitalism before Its Triumph* (Princeton: Princeton University Press, 1977).

20 Alfred F. Chalk, "Mandeville's Fable of the Bees: A Reappraisal," *Southern Economic Journal* 33, no. 1 (July 1966): 1–16, here 1–6.

21 Paraphrased from passages in the second volume of the *Fable*, following Chalk, "Mandeville's Fable of the Bees," 1–3.

22 E.g. Horne, *The Social Thought of Bernard Mandeville*, ch. 1.

23 Hirschman, *The Passions*; the sub-title reads: *Political Arguments for Capitalism before Its Triumph*.

24 Polanyi, *The Great Transformation*.

25 The material presented in this section is analyzed extensively in two monographs: Friederike Scholten-Buschhoff, "Die Bewirtschaftung adliger Güter in Rheinland und Westfalen: 1650–1850," Manuscript PhD dissertation (Münster: University of Münster, 2020); Johannes Bracht and Ulrich Pfister, *Landpacht, Marktgesellschaft und agrarische Entwicklung. Fünf Adelsgüter zwischen Rhein und Weser, 16.–19. Jahrhundert* (Stuttgart: Steiner, 2020).

26 In total, around 820 account books and 388 correspondence volumes (in which contemporaries discuss issues of estate management via letters) were analyzed.

27 "Die Dorf- und geringen Kirchspielseingesessenen haben zwaren von jeher immer einige [...] Verdienste mit allerhand Arbeiten am Hause Nordkirchen gehabt. Und man hat es sogar für eine Notwendigkeit angesehen, ihnen für beständig Arbeit geben zu müssen, da sie in hiesiger Gegend außer mit Weben, wenig oder nicht verdienen konnten. Wenn aber auch bei einigen der bezielte Endzweck einer richtigen Pächten Zahlung dadurch erreichet wurde, so brachte dennoch diese an sich sonst so gute Veranstaltung bei vielen anderen eine entgegen gesetzte Würkung hervor. indem die mersten ihre Weberstühle verließen, und auf ihre tägliches Verdienst am Hause Nordkirchen sich verlassend mehrere Ländereien anpachteten, allenthalben, wo nur etwas am lebensbedürfnissen verkauft wurde, mitkauften [...], nach einigen Jahren aber, wenn theure Zeiten langwierige Krankheiten oder Unglücksfälle eintraten, in Armut gerieten, ganz beträchtliche mehrenteils unerzwingliche Rückstände hatten, und dann die angepachteten Ländereien entweder anderen übertrugen, oder gar unbestellt liegen ließen [...]. Wie sehr von Seiten des Hauses Nordkirchen darauf der Bedacht zu nehmen sei, dass den mersten der Dorfeingesessenen in der Folge nicht zu vielen Ackerbau, und auch nicht so häufige Arbeit mehr am Hause Nordkirchen gegeben werde." See LWL Archivamt, Nor. Ak 13427.

28 Polanyi, *The Great Transformation*; Pranab K. Bardhan, "Interlocking Factor Markets and Agrarian Development: A Review of Issues," *Oxford Economic Papers* 32, no. 1 (March 1980): 82–98.

29 See also note 33.

30 LWL Archivamt, Nor. Ak 6535 documents annual settlements of labor services, rent payments, credit, and purchases of grain and linen between the estate and about fifty households from the 1780s to the 1810s.

31 This concept, developed in contrast to the cultural–historical concept of the "bourgeoisie," includes a special understanding of the family, a special closeness to nature, and the practice of rule and leadership. Common habitus, a connecting mentality, a common cultural model, and key concepts such as honor, service, order, duty, decency, and chivalry are closely linked with it. See Heinz Reif, ed., *Adel und Bürgertum in Deutschland: Entwicklungslinien und Wendepunkte im 19. Jahrhundert* (Berlin: Akademie, 2001), 199–203. Heinz Reif, "Adel, Aristokratie, Elite: Sozialgeschichte von Oben: Elitenwandel in der Moderne," *Historische Zeitschrift* 13, no. 2 (2016): 323–330; Otto G. Oexle, "Aspekte der Geschichte des Adels im Mittelalter und in der Frühen

Neuzeit," *Geschichte und Gesellschaft, Sonderheft* 13, (1990): 19–56; Gerhard Dilcher, "Alteuropäischer Adel: Ein verfassungsgeschichtlicher Typus?" *Geschichte und Gesellschaft, Sonderheft* 13 (1990): 57–86.

32 Edward P. Thompson, "The Moral Economy of the English Crowd in the Eighteenth Century," *Past and Present* 50 (February 1971): 76–136.

33 Until the first third/middle of the nineteenth century the *Grundherrschaft* constituted a central social institution in most parts of rural Germany; it has also been designated as "lordship over land and people." It mainly means that the peasants were legally subordinate to a landowner. They did not own the land they farmed and were dependent on the landowner throughout their life cycle. In addition, they were subject to the local jurisdiction of the landlord and liable to pay levies. However, research shows that there were substantial differences in the actual form of the system between different regions. Cf. Reiner Prass, *Grundzüge der Agrargeschichte*, vol. 2, *Vom Dreißigjährigen Krieg bis zum Beginn der Moderne (1650–1880)* (Cologne: Böhlau, 2016), here 46–52; Michael Sikora, *Der Adel in der Frühen Neuzeit: Geschichte Kompakt* (Darmstadt: WBG, 2009), here 7–8; 32–36.

34 See Friedrich-Wilhelm Henning, *Dienste und Abgaben der Bauern im 18. Jahrhundert*, in *Quellen und Forschungen zur Agrargeschichte*, ed. Wilhelm Abel and Günther Franz (Stuttgart: Fischer, 1969), here 70–77; Friedrich Lütge, *Deutsche Sozial- und Wirtschaftsgeschichte: Ein Überblick*, 3rd ed. (Berlin/Heidelberg/New York: Springer, 1979), here 102; 112–114; 166–170.

35 For more information, see Scholten-Buschhoff, *Die Bewirtschaftung adliger Güter*, ch. 7.

36 In May 1832, for instance, the steward of Crottorf observed monthly averages of grain prices in 1831 from the official newspaper (*Amtsblatt*) of the regional government in nearby Koblenz. The author marked price maxima in red. Prices of rye and oats reached their highest level in July.

37 LWL Archivamt, Nor. Ak 2357, Lakesche Verpachtungsprotokolle Nr. 45, 23.10.1814. The passage draws on Bracht and Pfister, *Landpacht, Marktgesellschaft und agrarische Entwicklung*, chs. 4 and 7.1.

38 Peter K. Weber, "Adeliges Unternehmertum im Rheinland: Aktivitäten und Mentalitäten," in *Europäischer Adel als Unternehmer im Industriezeitalter*, ed. Manfred Rasch and Peter K. Weber (Essen: Klartext, 2017), 57–72, here 65.

39 He did not operate the well himself, however, but rather leased it. See Florian Schönfuß, *Bewirtschaftung des Roisdorfer Mineralbrunnens, in Netzbiographie—Joseph zu Salm-Reifferscheidt-Dyck (1773–1861)*, ed. Martin O. Braun, Elisabeth Schläwe, und Florian Schönfuß, last modified Janary 24, 2017, accessed April 16, 2018, http://www.historicum-estudies.net/epublished/netzbiographie/preussische-zeit/mineralbrunnen/.

40 These are harvest years, starting in autumn and finishing at the end of the summer (October–September).

41 There is direct evidence of this in the account books of the houses. In addition, especially for grain management, contemporaries introduce additional accounting books referring solely to grain or cattle, for example.

42 This is documented in two types of sources: documents that support the account books, in the form of letters between administrator and owner; and in protocol books, in which administrator and owner discuss individual items of the account books in more detail systematically. Both types of document occur more frequently from the 1820s onwards. For more information also see Scholten-Buschhoff, *Die Bewirtschaftung adliger Güter*, ch. 7.1.1.

43 According to Reinhard Feldmann, "Gräflich von Spee'sche Bibliothek Schloß Heltorf," in *Handbuch der historischen Buchbestände in Deutschland*, ed. Bernhard Fabian, vol. 4 (Hildesheim/Zürich/New York: Olms, 2003), 272. For more information, also see Scholten-Buschhoff, *Die Bewirtschaftung adliger Güter*, ch. 5.3.2.

44 For this purpose, the number of new acquisitions at Heltorf was compared with available information on book production in Germany in the eighteenth century (Joerg Baten and Jan L. van Zanden, "Book Production and the Onset of Modern Economic Growth," *Journal of Economic Growth*, no. 13 (2008): 217–35). See also Scholten-Buschhoff, *Die Bewirtschaftung adliger Güter*, ch. 5.3.2.

45 Both in the libraries examined here and in research in general, it can be seen that explicit literature on agriculture and administration appears only occasionally and does not seem to have been acquired systematically.

46 For this purpose, the biographies of around sixty administrators were examined. None of them received special training for their activities.

47 "Ich bin wirklich in Verlegenheit ob ich die Genehmigung des Verkaufs in Antrag bringen soll, oder nicht. Gegen die Genehmigung spricht die Niedrigkeit der Preise, für dieselbe die geringe Aussicht auf ein höheres Steigen der Preise, die Schwierigkeit neben dem alten Korn zugleich das dieses Jahr neu einkommende zu lager und gut zu konservieren, was wenigstens nicht ohne ziemlich beträchtliche Kosten geschehen kann, ferner die Entbehrung des aus dem Korn zu lösenden Kapitals und endlich der Umstand daß die Versagung der Ratifikation wohl auf künftige Verkäufe nachtheilig einwirken und die Konkurrenz vermindern könnte. Diese Gründe für die Ertheilung der Ratification möchten wohl überwiegend sein." See LWL Archivamt, Nor. Ak 12069, #24 (19.9.1824).

48 See Scholten-Buschhoff, *Die Bewirtschaftung adliger Güter*, ch. 8.3.2.

49 It has been found that landlords even expanded their ownership of land after the agrarian reforms (funded by redemption payments by peasants); see Friedrich Keinemann, *Vom Krummstab zur Republik: Westfälischer Adel unter preußischer Herrschaft 1802–1945* (Bochum: Brockmeyer, 1997), 160-170. Heinz Reif discovered that in Westphalia the nobility began a policy of land acquisition in the 1820s: Reif, *Westfälischer Adel 1770–1860: Vom Herrschaftsstand zur regionalen Elite*, Kritische Studien zur Geschichtswissenschaft 35 (Göttingen: Vandenhoeck & Ruprecht, 1979), here 227. For a discussion of this topic, also see Bracht and Pfister, *Landpacht, Marktgesellschaft und agrarische Entwicklung*, 94.

50 Dyck A 513, #97.

51 For example in Crottorf where the administrator observed grain prices in Koblenz, see note 36.

52 The analysis of average monthly prices at Heltorf and in Cologne shows that price fluctuations differed; see Scholten-Buschhoff, *Die Bewirtschaftung adliger Güter*, ch. 8.3.4.

8 Pursuing self-interest

Stock market speculation in the early twentieth-century United States

Daniel Menning

Around 1900, numerous medical doctors and social psychologists became intrigued by the ways in which individuals could completely abandon their self-interest. They discovered that this neglect had two different, though interrelated, causes: the formation of a crowd or mob; and hypnosis. With regard to the first, researchers considered "shared feelings" of "animal nature" to be the reason for the formation of mobs, in which "collective popular emotion threatened the high values of consciousness and the acquisition of individuality."[1] As to the second cause, medical tests, but also performances in front of large audiences, testified to the limiting effect that hypnosis could have on an individual's exercise of free will, but also to how it could potentially result in hysterical behavior.[2] According to social psychologists, economists, journalists, and authors of how-to manuals, one place (among many) in which particular kinds of hypnosis, as well as the formation of crowds, could regularly be witnessed was the stock market, with its recurrent financial crazes and manias.[3] However, in contrast to other events—such as violent mobs, or hypnosis for the sake of medical research and treatment—the loss of one's self-interested consciousness in a Wall Street panic usually had a double negative impact. Not only did individuals lose the ability to pursue their personal aims, but they also oftentimes lost money while in a state of trance.

The relationship between financial markets, crowds, hypnosis, and the preservation of self-interest around 1900 has been touched upon in a number of studies.[4] What is curious about late nineteenth- and early twentieth-century social psychologists' descriptions of stock market manias, though, is that their accounts quite frequently remain abstract and evocative in their treatment of the matter, relying on the reader to draw parallels between the general narrative and particular events.[5] In contrast, the sociologist Urs Stäheli has studied in depth the effects of hypnosis and mass psychology, as well as various ways to preserve individuality, in stock market speculation in early twentieth-century discourses.[6] Unfortunately, however, his reading of advice manuals is at times truncated. In addition, he suggests too much coherence in advice manuals' usage of crowd discourse, and misrepresents the self-positioning of "educated" speculators.[7] A similar criticism can be voiced against the economist and philosopher Kristian Bondo Hansen's research. Comprehensive analysis of advice manuals contradicts his claims that their authors picture crowd behavior as devoid of order.[8] Again from a sociological point of view, Alex Preda has offered readings of panics around 1900, though at times it seems that for him mob psychology requires, or builds upon, a dispersed and not yet gathered crowd. This awkward definition once more tends to obscure a full understanding of the phenomenon.[9] Finally, David A. Zimmerman has looked at the problem from the perspective of literary studies. According to him, the authors of novels that included narratives of panics "were fascinated and flustered by the ways market crowds bedeviled, even disabled, causal explanations; [...] how their [the panics'] sociological and psychological dynamics unmoored individuals' psychological and ethical autonomy."[10] But the novels' authors also provided solutions for preserving self-interest. Although the findings of Zimmerman are quite stimulating, they apply to fictional accounts only.

Thus, the aim of this chapter is to take a fresh look at stock advice manuals, the autobiographies of early twentieth-century speculators, and other scattered primary sources, and to analyze the precise impact of discourses about crowds and hypnosis on advice manuals for stock market speculation. The following pages thereby attempt to study understandings of and threats to self-interest that were created by the concomitant rise of Wall Street and new ways of psychological reasoning. It thus contributes to research on what defines self-interest in particular periods in history and the conditions that appeared to enable or inhibit it.[11] The first section of this chapter considers discourses on hypnosis and mob psychology, trying to define the concept of self-interest in these works. It then moves on to the connections drawn between these debates and stock market speculation. The third section studies the ways in which, according to the authors of advice manuals, crowds were intentionally created in Wall Street, with insiders profiting from the lay speculators' inability to pursue their own self-interest. Finally, it looks at three market participants: Larry Livingston, Edward Neufville Tailer, and Thomas Lawson. These cases highlight different ways in which the Self could be positioned vis-à-vis (discourses on) financial market crowds and panics.

Mobs, hypnotism, and self-interest

When reading accounts intended to popularize the new research fields of hypnotism and mob psychology, one must keep in mind that these were not really concerned with the concept of self-interest. It seems, rather, that the ability purposefully to pursue one's personal aims was taken as the normal state of the waking conscious brain. As Professor G. T. W. Patrick from the University of Iowa briefly explained: under normal circumstances, humans are "perceiving, remembering, associating, judging, reflecting, reasoning being[s]." Their actions are "more or less deliberative" and can be described as "the result of a set of motives determined by the man's character."[12] Such abilities, he explained, had developed over the course of human evolution, which had resulted in a "change from the imitative and impulsive to the reasoning man."[13] Instead of further dwelling on these aspects, however, much more space was devoted by researchers to those moments in which people lost these abilities. For example, the crowd psychologist Boris Sidis observed that in a state of hypnosis, humans were devoid of rationality and moral sense. "Anything is accepted if sufficiently emphasized by the hypnotizer."[14] Instead of following their own free will, the hypnotized became imitative slaves of their master's commands. "To be a law unto one's self, the chief and essential characteristic of personality, is just the very trait the subwaking self so glaringly lacks."[15] The same thing seemed true of the individual in a crowd or mob. As members of large congregations and under stimuli that directed everyone's attention to a person, an event, or a thing, Patrick wrote, "men become imitative beings and their actions are determined by suggestion from the actions of others."[16] The result was, as Sidis explained, that in a mob, people "lose their will, their personality" and become completely obedient to "external command."[17] Furthermore, to these authors it seemed that women were more prone than men to become part of a mob or to be hypnotized. Thus, reading accounts of mobs and hypnotized subjects, one needs to consider their underlying assumption, mostly unspoken, that the conscious human pursuing its self-interest in a rational way was the (male) counterimage to hypnotized humans and mobs. This is also true when one looks at the application of discourses about hypnotism and crowd psychology to stock markets.

Self-interest at risk: hypnotized speculators and mob psychology

The ideal speculator, according to advice manuals, was an independent, thoughtful, educated, consciously reflecting man, free from emotional impulses and focusing on his self-interested acquisition of money. However, as Patrick proclaimed, "[b]oth in panics and in speculative manias, we observe [...] a species of hypnotization."[18] And he continued:

> In the case of the latter [i.e. manias] the ordinary business shrewdness [...] is to a large extent lost. [...] The psychology of the speculative mania is very simple. There is first, greed, furnishing the necessary emotional excitement; then imitation; then precipitate, unreasoning action. In the panic, the psychological sequence is the same, except that fear takes the place of greed.[19]

According to stock market speculation manuals, there were numerous ways, all in line with Patrick's reasoning, in which share traders could hypnotize themselves and thereby turn into senseless automatons losing sight of their own self-interest. "One of the greatest difficulties encountered by the active trader," according to George Selden, "is that of keeping his mind in a balanced and unprejudiced condition when he is heavily committed [... to] the market."[20] Having made the decision to buy shares, most lay speculators started adjusting all new facts to fit their prior decision, not allowing themselves to think that they had made a wrong choice at the outset. A typical example of such false thinking, Selden opined, was to expect the future to be a continuation of the present.[21] Yet, whereas in real life it might be possible to convince others that one's (erroneous) opinion was actually correct, the stock market could not be persuaded by false thinking. Many lay speculators appeared ignorant of that, however. Instead, as they thought constantly about their personal investments, their judgment would be even further distorted and they could be relied upon to disregard anything contradictory to their convictions.[22] In the end, speculators would become "unreasonable," "influenced and supported by the illusions of hope."[23] Even experts supposedly ran the risk of interpreting the information they studied in a way that supported their preconceived opinions, ignoring any data that contradicted them.

Hypnosis could, however, also be the result of outside influences, as Sidis pointed out on a more general level. In such cases, a particular "instigator, a leader" was necessary "who shall ferment the crowd and give it an impulse."[24] The easiest way to form a mob was to hypnotize individuals first by a period of monotony, followed by one repetitiously presented "suggestion." After a sufficient number of people had been affected, the result would be large-scale "mental contagion":[25]

> At first a crowd is formed by some strange object or occurrence suddenly arresting the attention of men. Other men coming up are attracted by curiosity: they wish to learn the reason of the gathering, they fix their attention on the object that fascinates the crowd, are fascinated in their turn, and thus the crowd keeps on growing. With the increase of numbers grows the strength of fascination; the hypnotization increases in intensity, until, when a certain critical point is reached, the crowd becomes completely hypnotized, and is ready to obey blindly the commands of its hero; it is now a mob.[26]

With regard to the stock market, numerous advice manual authors claimed to know the trigger that would pull the speculator out of monotony into sudden action. It was the stock ticker—a printing telegraph reporting the volume and price of every single transaction on the official trading floor of the exchange.[27] A sudden increase in the price of a share would attract attention and, as Humphrey Neill explained to his readers, "the faster stock prices surge upward, the hungrier the public becomes for stocks."[28] Occasionally, he continued, one can find on the tape "a signal which was flashed following a long period of dullness and inactivity."[29] And he concluded: "It is mob psychology: human nature reflecting its desire to follow."[30]

Numerous scientists, novelists, and artists also testified to the seductive, "mesmerizing" quality of the ticker.[31] However, such hypnosis was not only a state of mind that implied watching; it also involved other senses and parts of the body. For example, the noise of the machine could acquire an addictive quality. In a short story by Bracebridge Hemyng from 1885, the "click of the tape" became "a kind of music in [the main character's] ears that he had got to like."[32] The medical doctor J. Howe-Adams was convinced that the "constant ticking of the instruments in the broker's office"—thus the sound in the ears of the speculator—"throws the majority of traders into a state of self-hypnosis, in which they become automatons."[33] In addition, the bodies' positions mirrored a state between attentiveness and mental absence. George Rutledge Gibson described in 1889 that "dealers [would] hover over, and intently watch the 'ticker' as it rapidly unwinds the tangled web of fate."[34]

To be sure, such trance-like states were not always perceived critically. Though it seemed that the waking consciousness was lost and individuality surrendered for the moment, many contemporaries were convinced that such states could also clear the path to subconscious readings of the ticker tape that would enhance a person's ability to speculate.[35] Thus, it appears that it could be in the speculators' own self-interest to surrender their self-consciousness to the ticker—to become senseless, hypnotized subjects. Such behavior remained a risk, nevertheless. Because "[i]n hypnosis," as Patrick explained to his readers, "there is a temporary paralysis or sleep of the higher brain centers, upon which depends deliberative, rational action, and, the lower (older) centers alone being active, the subject becomes a mere ideo-motor machine acting out every suggestion."[36] Being hypnotized could, therefore, also be a preliminary step to hysteria, which might be activated by the medium transmitting the necessary messages, namely the ticker reporting a stimulating price development. And in this case, the monetary self-interest of the speculator was clearly at risk.

Furthermore, when people succumbed to such hypnotism and hysteria, their behavior could lead to mimesis by others, resulting in a market panic and a rule of the mob.[37] According to social psychology, such mobs might form within a single location, which by extension could mean a broker's room or the trading floor in Wall Street. The trader Larry Livingston talked (with regard to the cotton market) about the "contagion of example that makes a man do something because everybody around him is doing the same thing." Though he added cautiously: "Perhaps it is some phase or variety in the herd instinct."[38] Boris Sidis considered, on a general level, "a dense crowd, [in which] not only is our body squeezed and pressed upon, but also our spirit" as the ideal breeding ground of a mob. Once it prevented voluntary movement, "[t]he individual self sinks sensibly in the crowd."[39] And he furthermore states that "[a] large crowd, on account of the cramping of voluntary movements, easily falls into a state of fascination, and is easily moved by a ringleader, or hero."[40] Contemporary images of the stock market or broker's offices frequently emphasized such close proximity of investors when congregating on the trading floor, around the ticker, or in front of the price board.[41] Yet, crowd action, according to social psychologists, might also originate with people in dispersed locations, who were connected through some sort of media to a shared event. In the case of the stock market, the ticker was seen as such a medium, linking scattered speculators to market swings at the stock exchange. In this case, too many similar signals appearing on the tape could result in mimesis by dispersed speculators, causing further cascades of action and imitation.

The fact that the "psychology of the crowd" "was nourished by the sacred terror aroused by the anonymous mob, considered as governed only by emotions escaping the control of reason and common sense,"[42] also did not leave early mathematical economists untouched. Even as they developed theories of a "random walk" of stock market prices around the beginning of the century, they were not completely convinced by their own theories. As Irving Fisher stated in *The Nature of Capital and Income*: "Were it true that each individual speculator made up his mind independently of every other as to the future course of events, the errors of some would probably be offset by those of others. But, as a matter of fact, the mistakes of the common herd are usually in the same direction. Like sheep, they all follow a single leader."[43]

It is interesting to see that for authors describing the stock market, the new "mob psychology" also highlighted the momentary permeability of the dividing line between male and female sexual characteristics.[44] In his 1880 memoirs of *Twenty Years of Inside Life in Wall Street*, William Worthington Fowler was still convinced that a female presence in the share market was undesirable, as "[o]ne can easily imagine the effect produced by several hundred women interested in stocks, being present at a panic and giving way with feminine impulsiveness to the feelings of the hour."[45] Such comments evoked contemporary belief in a natural male rationality and ability to pursue their monetary self-interest that contrasted with the inferior ability of emotion-driven women to do the same. This distinction, however, became more difficult to uphold from the 1890s onwards, because social scientists discovered that women in general showed close parallels to the behavior of men as part of crowds. In fact, the impulsiveness and impressionability that the stock market trader Henry Clews ascribed to women were key concepts of "mob psychology."[46] However, the tension created by the new psychological readings of crowds could be solved (and male dominance thus preserved) by the interpretation that men might lose their masculine rationality in the market at certain times, whereas women never actually possessed it.[47] The "threat" posed to male equanimity by feminine behavior could, at least under normal circumstances, also be countered by separate brokers' offices or special rooms for female traders that were established in New York as early as 1870.[48] Yet, the market being integrated via the ticker, "female" or crowd panic could always spread, because the price transmitter did not gender transactions.

Fortunately, social psychologists and economists thought there were lessons to be learned from their studies of crowds more generally, but also from stock market crazes and panics.[49] According to Patrick, the disappearance of mobs was only a matter of time: "The inference which we seem compelled to draw from studies in social psychology is that social man is, in his ethical and intellectual development, many stages behind the individual man." In contradistinction to a rational individual, "the mind of society [...] is an imitative, unreflective, half-hypnotic, half-barbaric mind."[50] But this, Patrick hoped, would change through evolutionary development, though it might take a long time. Edward Ross, on the other hand, did not want to wait. Instead, he believed in self-interested rationality. He suggested that there was a need to "discredit the mass [, ... to] break the spell of numbers. [... L]et us cultivate a habit of doubt and review."[51] Finally, Edward Jones, thinking about economic crises more generally, hoped that "[i]f we could cultivate other interests sufficiently to right the intellectual balance, the crisis period might lapse indefinitely."[52] For him, the solution lay in directing the individual away from the self-interested pursuit of wealth. However, as long as such changes had not taken place, the ideal self-interested male speculator was constantly at risk of becoming part of a senseless mob and thereby losing his self-control. Yet, these were not the only lessons that could be drawn from observations of the proneness of speculators to turn into suggestible mobs.

Professionals, lay speculators and the creation of a market crowd

While all speculators were at risk of being hypnotized or becoming part of a crowd, according to the writers of advice manuals on speculation, not everyone had to do so. Rather, these authors claimed that, understanding the interrelationship of market mechanisms and crowd psychology, professionals were better able to pursue self-interested money-gaining strategies than lay investors and, what is more, they were consciously doing so at the latter's expense. Advice manuals, therefore, did not hold back in describing the threats that hypnosis and crowd action could cause to stock market speculators. Rather, according to George Selden, "One question is, what effect do varying mental attitudes of the public have upon the course of prices? How is the character of the market influenced by psychological conditions?"[53] The resulting explanations evidence, as Zimmerman phrases it, attempts "to gain cognitive and narrative control over price movements, to convert them into stories that promised aesthetic, if not financial value."[54]

The key was to connect the crowd behavior in the stock market described above with a series of stages in a boom-and-bust cycle.[55] In his *Psychology of the Stock Market* from 1919, Selden described a typical momentum investing cycle. Everything starts with "dullness" and minor price fluctuations by which "the public is still unmoved."[56] Though financial journalists call the public to action in such moments, lay speculators usually do not react yet.[57]

Only as prices slowly increase, does the number of adventurers grow, owing to the expectation of further increases.[58] If no significant reactions to the price upswing appear, many willing to buy upon short price depreciations of a share are left behind: a typical problem of "suckers," as Larry Livingston opined.[59] As prices, thus, keep going up, Selden further explains, those short in the market (i.e. betting on decreasing prices by selling shares they do not own) begin to cover en masse by buying stock. Now "the market 'boils,' and to the short who is watching the tape, seems likely to shoot through the ceiling at almost any moment."[60] With the thick-skinned pessimistic bear traders running for safety, "the outside public begins to reach the conclusion that the market is 'too strong to react much,' and that the only thing to do is to 'buy 'em [the shares] everywhere.'"[61] This results in even further price increases. "[C]onfidence and enthusiasm keep reproducing each other on a wider and wider scale until the result is a sort of hilarity on the part of thousands of men."[62] The result is a "pyramid of mistaken impressions."[63] Once the boom approaches its apparent top, bears start selling short and professional investors begin feeding their holdings to a public still eager to participate in a rising market. The weight of (short) sales, however, sooner or later pushes share prices downward, at which moment the small investors will scramble to get rid of their investments at a loss, panicking after having overstayed the cycle.[64] Selden showed himself convinced that "[t]he fact will at once be recognized that the above description is, in essence, a story of [...] an unwarranted projection by the public imagination of a perceived present into an unknown though not wholly unknowable future." Thus, the argument runs that in trying to pursue a self-interested money-winning strategy at the outset, lay investors became part of a crowd no longer able to anticipate the future correctly. While such a development may be observable for an individual stock, there could also be large-scale market panics. These formed special events in which, slowly but surely, fear spread from one speculator to the next "in increasing and decreasing waves, but growing a little greater at each successive wave." In such a "panicky market," at some point even minor sales could result in major price collapses.[65] Nevertheless, according to Selden and others, the unruly crowd or mob behaved in a very orderly fashion in the stock market.

Such regular patterns, then, made lay investors easy victims for the self-interested strategies of those professional speculators who understood the "public's mind and [... knew] how the public acts in the market."[66] To emphasize this point, Humphrey B. Neill described the boom-and-bust cycle as the result of the activities of two different groups: the professionals; and the large group of small-scale, short-term speculators. The market was, in effect, tilted in favor of the former group: "The speculatively-minded public hopes to make money by trading in stocks in a hit-or-miss manner, while the professional strives for his profits through engineering his maneuvers scientifically that the public will take from him property which he has acquired at lower prices."[67] As part of their plans, "[s]chooled market operators and pool managers realize th[e] fondness of the average investor to 'get in on rising prices,' and they use this powerful tool in their operations."[68] First, they would buy up a sufficient number of a company's shares at bargain prices. Then, the easiest way to catch the lay speculators' attention was to create movement by buying and selling simultaneously for a while.[69] As "the public is attracted by price changes," "the principal medium used in [...] advertising [... shares] is the ticker tape."[70] The attention of the "unwary" was usually caught by particularly impressive transactions that flashed out on the tape, created gossip, mesmerized the small fish, and made them join the crowd and thus lose their rational decision-making capacities.[71] In the meantime, tips would be given out to those willing to listen and stories of expected price increases were spread by professionals and made their way into newspapers.[72] The aim was additionally to stimulate the lay speculators' thirst for action and to induce them to purchase stock at ever higher prices, believing in still further increases. Once the price ascent appeared to have reached its maximum, professionals would sell out, while the public were still picking up overvalued shares. The lay speculators in the end were left with these shares on a declining market, finally "dumping stock without rhyme or reason,"[73] thereby preparing the ground for the next accumulation by professionals. As simple as it was for professionals to utilize crowd psychology, their moves were not as easy to observe in practice. Because, as Neill admitted, "[n]o pool manager is going to operate a stock in exactly the same manner each time; nor is he going to allow the stock of its own accord to rally and react in uniform movements,"[74] since all this would make the forces behind price swings too transparent and would allow freeloaders to profit or competitors to counter the moves. In Neill's view, professionals were able to change their tactics, but the crowd was not.

Such accounts were certainly not unfounded. Exchange governor Frank Sturgis openly admitted in front of a Congress Committee investigating the stock market in 1913 that simultaneous buying and selling was a way of "making a market" and of advertising a stock.[75] In another case, the shares of Hocking Coal and Iron Company had been driven up from $20 to $90 in only a few months in 1909, when the speculator James R. Keene managed the buying and selling for a pool of insiders. By January 19, 1910, the share price broke and in a short time went back down to $25.[76] Also, most investment banks underwriting securities' issues in the early twentieth century did not have distribution systems that went beyond a small number of colleagues, insurances, and rich investors. They relied, therefore, on the help of brokers who would carefully feed the new shares to the market, making sure that bankers earned a healthy profit.[77]

Thus, it seemed that while all speculators started out with a self-interested strategy for making money, the amateurs were usually not successful, being drawn into the crowd and losing their reflecting capacities and self-control along the way. But, as Neill claimed, lay speculators could learn to read the actions of the professionals and the reactions of the public using the ticker tape. As the former's moves were based, it was claimed, on crowd psychology, a trained speculator could "[t]ell from the tape what is likely to happen,"[78] and get in at the accumulation stage as well as out during the distribution phase. In the meantime, the lay speculators would carry the share price upwards. Once the amateurs were able to see the patterns in the digits, they would no longer be drawn into a crowd destined to fail, but be empowered to profit for their own monetary self-interest from the professionals' self-interested insider actions. Understanding crowd psychology was declared to be the key to successfully pursuing self-interest in the market. Applying its theories, it seemed possible to learn how to dodge the crowd that regularly lost control of its conscious Self.

Preserving the self against the crowd: Larry Livingston

The necessary learning process, however, consisted of more than simply acquiring knowledge about the market and crowd psychology. As the necessary pre-condition to pursuing self-interest, the Self had to be trained so the individual would not lose control of it. An example of a speculator who trained himself and in the end was able to preserve his Self against the crowds can be found in Edwin Lefèvre's semi-fictional autobiography of Larry Livingston, *Reminiscences of a Stock Operator*. The narrative was modeled on the "Boy Plunger" Jesse Livermore, who was one of the major speculators on Wall Street between the late nineteenth century and the 1930s, winning and losing fortunes, before eventually committing suicide in 1940. In the early 1900s, "[m]arket leaders [like Livermore] became titans in the newspaper accounts and in the literature of the time."[79]

Lefèvre's *Bildungsroman*-style narrative allows the reader to witness Livingston's evolution from a bucket shop patron, betting against the establishment's operator on short-term price fluctuations of shares, to a large-scale operator. To become a successful speculator, Livingston had to learn numerous lessons. For one thing, he discovered that many wanted to profit from his (perceived) ignorance: owners of bucket shops, considering him to be a young and inexperienced man; fake brokers not executing his orders; people offering false investment advice; and speculators convincing him of their trading techniques, which turned out to be unsuccessful. For another thing, the preservation of self-interest pre-supposed strict self-control during trades: "Whenever I read the tape by the light of experience, I made money, but when I made a plain fool play, I had to lose." This was especially the case when he "let the craving for excitement get the better of my judgement."[80] Oftentimes this was stimulated by the exciting atmosphere around him.[81] However, as *Reminiscences* made clear, impatience and doubts were the greatest enemies even to a speculator employing correct market analysis.[82] In the end, Larry Livingston learned "to study general conditions, *to take a position and stick to it*."[83] Such self-positioning was not a personal matter: "I never fight either individuals or speculative cliques. I merely differ in opinion—that is, in my reading of basic conditions."[84] This insight resulted in Livingston's claim to always *"move along the line of least resistance."*[85] There appeared to be no point in opposing major market forces, even if they were wrong in a technical sense.[86] He was convinced that "no manipulation can put stocks down and keep them down."[87] Aside from taking such a reflexive relationship to the crowd, the completion of Livingston's educational journey was marked by the realization that he not only needed "to learn [...] to follow my own inclinations. *It was that I gained confidence in myself."*[88] Such independence of mind allowed for the successful pursuit of self-interest in the market.

The explanations come alive in a story relating to Livingston's speculations in a company called Tropical Trading (TT). According to the narrative, the company's directors regularly encouraged traders to sell company shares they did not possess. Simultaneously, they limited the available supply of purchasable shares for these short-traders, so that a moment would come when more stock had been sold than could be bought—a move that was called a corner. Directors would afterwards demand exorbitant prices for shares from those who needed them to cover their short trades, "squeezing them with business-like thoroughness."[89] Reading the news during a holiday in Florida, Livingston realized that the TT insiders had once more run up the share price to $155, even though the general market tendency was downward. Fairly quickly Livingston was short in the market by 10,000 shares, before returning to New York. Bolstering his belief in the untenably high price of TT by means of statistics, Livingston sold another 20,000 shares short. Along the way, the share price had decreased to $133. As other traders had gone short as well, the company insiders decided that the floating supply was limited enough and commenced the squeeze, driving the share up to $150 with the help of the public which had considered the earlier price reaction to $133 a good moment to buy. As the price once more sagged from $150 to $140, the insiders, not willing to support it above the latter mark themselves, handed out "a flood of bull rumors about the stock" to encourage lay investors to buy.[90] Livingston explained:

> The manipulation did not seem particularly dangerous to me but when the price touched 149, I decided that it was not wise to let the Street accept as true all the bull statements that were floating around. Of course, there was nothing that I or any other rank outsider could say that would carry conviction either to the frightened shorts or to those credulous customers of commission houses that trade on hearsay tips. The most effective retort courteous is that which the tape alone can print.

To send this message, Livingston could not sell more TT, however, as this would have opened up the risk of getting cornered. He therefore chose a different tactic and started selling stock of Equatorial Commercial Corporation (EC) short—a company closely linked to TT. As the price of

EC proved soft and declined swiftly, other traders realized as well that "the strength of TT was merely a smokescreen—a manipulated advance obviously designed to facilitate inside liquidation in Equatorial Commercial."[91] By this attack from the wings, Livingston "took the wind out of the manipulators' sails."[92] Faced with generally difficult economic surroundings anyway, the insiders finally gave up their operations and TT's share price fell below $90. "I stood pat throughout because I knew my position was sound. I wasn't bucking the trend of the market or going against basic conditions but the reverse, and that was what made me so sure of the failure of an over-confident inside clique."[93]

After years of training (according to the autobiographical narrative, at least), Livingston thus sees himself as capable of successfully pursuing his self-interest in the face of a predictably behaving crowd and professional manipulators. His own Self no longer succumbs to the attractive forces of the crowd.

Panic and the construction of the self: Edward Neufville Tailer

While Livingston is described as someone who has trained his Self to be a counterpart to the crowd, Edward Neufville Tailer (1830–1917), originally a New York wholesale merchant of woolen goods and a long-time speculator, illustrates the case of a lay investor experiencing panics in the New York stock market.[94] His diaries provide insights into his everyday life as well as into his stock market activities and his attempts to reconstruct panic days in Wall Street together with his personal experiences and actions.[95] Three qualifications are necessary when trying to understand Tailer's diaries, however. First, they are ex post accounts. The notes were not written down while trading, but in the evening or during the next day(s). Second, those studying the history of emotions have emphasized that it is impossible for people to capture the "true" feelings they had in a certain situation in the past. The memory of emotions in a given moment is frequently transformed either by time and reflection or by the intention of the author.[96] Third, authors of critical biographies acknowledge the fact that individuals constantly try to make sense of their lives.[97] These qualifications, however, do not mean that the material cannot be used to understand the potential for pursuing self-interest in market panics.

Interestingly, Tailer's diary consists of two different parts: newspaper clippings of events on the one hand, and short personal notes on the other. This collage can be interpreted as an attempt to draft a narrative of days on which Wall Street panicked—the newspaper articles providing details of general events. These, of course, consist of reports about the market's actions, but for the same panicky days Tailer also included news about New York's high society and his participation in it. The clippings are often complemented by short notes about personal actions and emotions during the day. The diary, thus, contains the conscious reconstructions of the Self's comportment and its feelings of the day within a larger socioeconomic framework. Within the personal text, Tailer's emotional stress has its place. Writing about the panic of 1884, he remarks that events on May 14 "will long be remembered." He also characterized his actions two days later with intense feelings, when he states:

> [T]he great struggle back yesterday and today has been to get the ready cash to perform the usual functions of settling differences in financial transactions. The Union Trust has called in a call loan which I have with them for $50,000, but I hope to convince Mr. Edward L. Strong to let it remain on Monday should the market let off.[98]

How should such remarks be interpreted? Did Edward Tailer become part of a struggling crowd or was he a self-controlled actor on a panic day? To conclude either one or the other from his diary is dangerous. By its very nature, a diary is intended to rationalize events and a person's place in the world ex post. In these sources, people do not describe themselves as behaving irrationally, and if they do, they necessarily resort to rationalizing language. Therefore, even if Tailer had been submerged within the market crowd during the day, he still attempted to reconstruct his Self within society and vis-à-vis the economic events afterward. The Self was thus something that had to be presumed and/or created and narrated before it could be described pursuing its self-interest on panic days. Therefore, it should be acknowledged that humans who have taken part in a crowd or mob will, when looking back on the events, still tend to reconstruct some story of their pursuance of self-interest.

A benign leader: Thomas Lawson

Did an individual as part of a crowd necessarily have to be a loser in moments of panic? If malicious professionals possessed the ability to move the market at will by stimulating the masses via the ticker and other kinds of news, could not a well-meaning individual do the same for the benefit of the investing crowd? Could it thus be in the self-interest of an individual to abdicate his or her reasoning faculties and become a member of a mob? These questions were posed shortly after 1900 by Thomas Lawson, a stock market professional, author, and social reformer.[99] Coming from a background of share promotion, he had a career as a muckraking journalist after the turn of the century. In a revelatory series called "Frenzied Finance," he claimed to expose the dealings of the "System"—that is, investment bankers and brokers fleecing the small speculator on a regular basis by means of selling overvalued stock and share price manipulation.[100]

Combining his will to reform and his knowledge about trading, Lawson had the idea to intentionally cause stock market panics. These, as Zimmerman points out, were intended as "deliberate attempts to subvert the System [of investment bankers and brokers] that held a vise grip on the public's money. In financial cataclysms, he [Lawson ...] argued, lay the answers to financial tyranny"[101] and the path to a re-empowerment of the public. Lawson first attempted to influence investors' sentiments via revelations in his series "Frenzied Finance." According to his critics, it was written in an emotionally addictive, novelistic style, constantly keeping readers in suspense. Second, he expended significant amounts of money on advertising campaigns and newsletters sent to investors and financial editors. Using these media, Lawson tried to have an immediate effect on market sentiment, pushing share prices up or down. His readership may have gone into the hundreds of thousands. A third means to build a crowd in support of his plan to overturn the financial hierarchy reigning on Wall Street was a romantic novel that emotionally engaged its readers, arousing their interpersonal as well as market sympathies in a mob-psychological sense, and, thus, prepared them for action.[102]

Lawson's opponents in their turn questioned the truth and accuracy of his muckraking accounts and the sincerity of his intentions in enlisting the crowd for his stock market maneuvers. It was suggested that he personally profited from instigating lay investors into action, distributing his previously acquired shares to the ignorant during self-manufactured booms and buying them back after the inevitable busts—just as the professionals did. Therefore, rather than empowering the masses, critics claimed, he exploited them. His dubious motives were further highlighted when he returned to more traditional share price manipulations after the crash of 1907,[103] which had pre-empted a bust that Lawson was organizing himself. The reasons he gave for this reversal were that he needed to recoup personal expenses from his public media campaigns and had decided to reform Wall Street from an insider's position as a sole operator. Yet, his critics' perceived need to highlight Lawson's questionable behavior indicates the influence they considered him to have upon investors and readers. Though in the end Lawson was not successful, he did occasion the panic of 1904—according to the New York Times, "the worst freak panic that ever struck Wall Street."[104]

Overall, Lawson attempted to break the power of professionals who created market crowds for their personal gain by copying their methods. Lay speculators would once more necessarily be part of a senseless mob, but this time under Lawson's control and in their "true" self-interest. As followers of his benign leadership, they would help to ruin the professionals. This victory of the masses over manipulation, Lawson claimed, would inaugurate a new era in which every investor would be able successfully to pursue his monetary self-interest without the threat of being turned into a hapless crowd member.

Conclusion

The decades around 1900 witnessed the entry of the masses into the stock market, where men and women pursued self-interested strategies to earn easy money.[105] Their frequently unsuccessful endeavors, as well as the numerous larger and smaller panics of the time, posed new questions to observers and speculators, who wondered how price movements came about, which causal dynamics they followed, and why some persons grew incredibly wealthy through share trading, whereas many others lost. As contemporaries of the early twentieth century saw it, hypnosis and crowd action were two possible answers to account for these phenomena. Both explanations placed the collective of lay investors and their susceptibility center stage. In both ways, individuals would become submerged in a senseless unreasoning mob, making people incapable of pursuing their self-interest. But, while contemporaries were fascinated and/or terrified by both hypnotism and mobs, the loss of individual reasoning in a crowd did not necessarily imply a disappearance of order more generally. Rather, for the crowd psychologists, the advice manual writers, and the professional speculators, the stock market transactions of the captivated mass followed a specific pattern. For those such as Livingston, who had learned correctly to interpret the behavior of market participants, Wall Street opened up the possibility of gigantic gains—the pure pursuance of self-interested capital accumulation. Those caught up in the crowd, as happened to Tailer, might still reconstruct ex post the ways in which they had tried to follow their self-interest. Finally, in the case of Lawson, becoming a member of a crowd at a critical turning point could be presented as a way to overcome the vicious professionals ruling supreme at the stock exchange. Thus, the end result was permanent empowerment of lay investors after the crowd had done its job one last time. However, one had to believe in a benign leader who would take care of the self-interest of the senseless mob members. The examples demonstrate that, while the pursuit of monetary gains appears to be a timeless essence of share speculation, the reasons for the (lack of) success of self-interested individuals need to be explained with reference to the implicit or explicit beliefs about the Self's characteristics at a certain point in history. Speculation is thus a culturally embedded phenomenon.

Notes

1 Piroska Nagy, "History of Emotions," in *Debating New Approaches to History*, ed. Marek Tamm and Peter Burke (London: Bloomsbury Academic, 2019), 189–202, here 191; David A. Zimmerman, *Panic! Markets, Crises, & Crowds in American Fiction* (Chapel Hill: University of North Carolina Press, 2006), 30.

2 Zimmerman, *Panic*, 30–31, 126–49. For an introduction to the history of hypnotism that remains valuable, see also Henry F. Ellenberger, *Die Entdeckung des Unbewussten* (Stuttgart: Verlag Hans Huber, 1973).

3 The idea of mob psychology leading to stock market bubbles has a longer history, going back at least to Charles Mackay, *Memoirs of Extraordinary Popular Delusions and the Madness of Crowds* (London: Richard Bentley, 1841). On the interpretation of it, see Urs Stäheli, *Spektakuläre Spekulation: Das Populäre der Ökonomie* (Frankfurt: Suhrkamp, 2007), 154–72.

4 For a more general overview of the cultural history of the stock market around 1900, see: Stuart Banner, *Speculation: A History of the Fine Line Between Gambling and Investing* (Oxford: Oxford University Press, 2017), 56–163; Richard

Cochrane, "The Tape Readers: Financial Trading as a Visual Practice," *Philosophy of Photography* 8 (2017): 109–17; Cedric B. Cowing, *Populists, Plungers, and Progressives: A Social History of Stock and Commodity Speculation, 1890–1936* (Princeton: Princeton University Press, 1965); Ann Fabian, *Card Sharps and Bucket Shops: Gambling in Nineteenth-Century America* (London/ New York: Routledge, 1999), 153–202; Ryan Gillespie, "Gilders and Gamblers: The Culture of Speculative Capitalism in the United States," *Communication, Culture & Critique* 5 (2012): 352–71; David Hochfelder, "'Where the Common People Could Speculate': The Ticker, Bucket Shops, and the Origins of Popular Participation in Financial Markets, 1880–1920," *Journal of American History* 93 (2006): 335–58; David Hochfelder, *The Telegraph in America, 1832–1920* (Baltimore: Johns Hopkins University Press, 2012), 101–37; Jonathan Levy, *Freaks of Fortune: The Emerging World of Capitalism and Risk in America* (Cambridge, MA: Harvard University Press, 2012), 231–63; George Robb, "Ladies of the Ticker: Women, Investment, and Fraud in England and America, 1850–1930," in *Victorian Investments: New Perspectives on Finance and Culture*, ed. Nancy Henry and Cannon Schmitt (Bloomington: Indiana University Press, 2009), 120–40. For an introduction to the history of Wall Street, see: Steven Fraser, *Wall Street: A Cultural History* (London: Faber & Faber, 2006); Mike Wallace, *Greater Gotham: A History of New York City from 1898 to 1919* (Oxford: Oxford University Press, 2017), 61–104.

5   Edward D. Jones, *Economic Crises* (New York: Macmillan, 1900), 180–218; George T. W. Patrick, "The Psychology of Crazes," *Popular Science Monthly* 18 (1900): 285–94; Boris Sidis, "A Study of the Mob," *The Atlantic Monthly* 75 (1895): 188–97; Boris Sidis, *The Psychology of Suggestion: A Research into the Subconscious Nature of Man and Society* (New York: D. Appleton, 1903), 343–49.

6   Stäheli, *Spektakuläre Spekulation.*

7   See, e.g., Stäheli, *Spektakuläre Spekulation*, 238–43. The contrarian could better be described as a freeloader who takes advantage of public opinion than as someone adapting him- or herself to that opinion and thereby becoming a leader of the masses. Also, the professional (who will be discussed below) is missing from Stäheli's discussion.

8   Kristian B. Hansen, "Contrarian Investment Philosophy in the American Stock Market: On Investment Advice and the Crowd Conundrum," *Economy and Society* 44 (2015): 616–38, here 635.

9   Alex Preda, *Framing Finance: The Boundaries of Markets and Modern Capitalism* (Chicago: Chicago University Press, 2009), 213–21. In addition, considering charts to be effective tools to visualize a panic in the early twentieth century makes little sense (Preda, *Framing Finance*, 223), because the preparation of these charts was time-consuming and they were, therefore, not practical in a quickly developing market.

10   Zimmerman, *Panic*, 4.

11   For nineteenth-century transformations, see Jeffrey Sklansky, *The Soul's Economy: Market Society and Selfhood in American Thought, 1820–1920* (Chapel Hill: University of North Carolina Press, 2002). For an early twenty-first-century perspective, see Fiona Allon, "The Wealth Affect: Financial Speculation as Everyday Habitus," in *Bodies and Affects in Market Societies*, ed. Anne Schmidt and Christoph Conrad (Tübingen: Mohr Siebeck, 2016), 109–25.

12   Patrick, "Psychology," 285.

13   Patrick, "Psychology," 286.

14   Sidis, "Psychology," 295.

15   Sidis, "Psychology," 296.

16 Patrick, "Psychology," 286.
17 Sidis, "Study," 189.
18 Patrick, "Psychology," 292.
19 Patrick, "Psychology," 293.
20 George C. Selden, *Psychology of the Stock Market* (1919; repr., Mansfield Centre: Martino Publishing 2012), 55. On a more general level, these effects are described by Jones, *Economic Crises*, 186–91, 198–207.
21 Selden, *Psychology*, 45. On selective reading, see also Neill, *Tape Reading*, 106.
22 Selden, *Psychology*, 59.
23 Selden, *Psychology*, 59, 60.
24 Sidis, "Study," 188.
25 Edward A. Ross, "The Mob Mind," *Popular Science Monthly* 51 (1897): 390–98, here 391. On suggestion, see also Sidis, *Psychology*, 297–308.
26 Sidis, "Study," 190; Ross, "Mob," 392.
27 On the technical functioning of the ticker, see also Stäheli, *Spektakuläre Spekulation*, 315–20.
28 Neill, *Tape Reading*, 107. See also: Wyckoff, *Studies*, 87, 145. On the ticker as a stimulus to speculation, see Stäheli, *Spektakuläre Spekulation*, 312, 327–28.
29 Neill, *Tape Reading*, 67.
30 Neill, *Tape Reading*, 107.
31 Frank Knight, Reading the Market: Genres of Financial Capitalism in Gilded Age America (Baltimore: Johns Hopkins University Press, 2016) 127–35, quote 130. More generally see also Preda, *Framing Finance*, 132–35. He, however, somewhat overemphasizes the degree to which advice manual authors required their readers to pay attention to the ticker.
32 Bracebridge Hemyng, "Time and Tide Wait for No Man: A Tale of the Tape," in *The Stockbroker's Wife and other Sensational Tales of the Stock Exchange,* ed. John Shaw (London: John and Robert Maxwell, 1885), 170.
33 Jedediah Howe-Adams, "Concerning the Physician's Finances," *Medical Times* 32 (1908): 161–68, here 162.
34 An example of such positioning can be found in Edwin Lefèvre's novel, *Sampson Rock of Wall Street* (New York: Harper & Brothers, 1907). See Robbie Moore, "Ticker Tape and the Superhuman Reader," in *Writing, Medium, Machine: Modern Technographies*, ed. Sean Pryor and David Trotter (London: Open Humanities Press, 2016), 137–52, here 138. Quite similar is the description of the master speculator James R. Keene reading the tape. Knight, *Reading*, 91.
35 On such positive perceptions of hypnosis, see Zimmerman, *Panic*, 136–37.
36 Patrick, "Psychology," 285.
37 Zimmerman, *Panic*, 123–49; Moore, "Ticker Tape," 144–45.
38 Lefèvre, *Reminiscences*, 111.
39 Sidis, "Study," 190; Sidis, "Psychology," 299–300.
40 Sidis, "Study," 190; Ross, "Mob," 392.
41 For examples, see: Zimmerman, *Panic*, 25–26; Knight, *Reading*, 135.
42 Nagy, "History of Emotions," 191.
43 Irving Fisher, *The Nature of Capital and Income* (New York: MacMillan, 1906), 296. See also: Justin Fox, *The Myth of the Rational Market: A History of Risk, Reward, and Delusion on Wall Street* (New York: Harper Business, 2009), 13. Similarly, Henri Poincaré criticized Louis Bachelier's PhD thesis on the grounds that it disregarded an individual's behavior when part of a group. See Fox, *Myth*, 7.
44 On the following, see also Stäheli, *Spektakuläre Spekulation*, 265–301.
45 Quoted after Robb, "Ladies of the Ticker," 125.
46 On Clews, see Robb, "Ladies of the Ticker," 134. In addition, see Sidis, "Study," 196–97.

47 Anne L. Murphy, "'We Have Been Ruined by Whores': Perceptions of Female Involvement in the South Sea Scheme," in *Boom, Bust, and Beyond: New Perspectives on the 1720 Stock Market Bubble*, ed. Stefano Condorelli and Daniel Menning (Munich: De Gruyter, 2019), 261–84; Robb, "Ladies of the Ticker," 131–40.
48 Stäheli, *Spektakuläre Spekulation*, 280; Robb, "Ladies of the Ticker," 123.
49 Stäheli, *Spektakuläre Spekulation*, 198–99.
50 Patrick, "Psychology," 294.
51 Ross, "Mob," 398.
52 Jones, *Economic Crises*, 194–95.
53 Selden, *Psychology*, 8.
54 Zimmerman, *Panic*, 226–27.
55 For the following, see also Stäheli, *Spektakuläre Spekulation*, 229–44.
56 Selden, *Psychology*, 10.
57 Knight, "Reading," "(Baltimore: Johns Hopkins University Press, 2016)," 38. The importance of insider professional behavior for minor fluctuations of share prices is also attested to in Lefèvre, *Reminiscences*, 3.
58 Selden, *Psychology*, 11.
59 Lefèvre, *Reminiscences*, 46–48.
60 Selden, *Psychology*, 12.
61 Selden, *Psychology*, 12.
62 Selden, *Psychology*, 74, 77.
63 Selden, *Psychology*, 77.
64 The belief that a small number of actors stood behind panics was also put forward in parts of contemporary panic fiction. See Zimmerman, *Panic*, 16–17, 32–34.
65 Selden, *Psychology*, 16, 70, 73.
66 Neill, *Tape Reading*, XI, 117. For a contextualization of such conspiracy theories, see Knight, *Reading*, 191–251.
67 Neill, *Tape Reading*, 6; Wyckoff, *Studies*, 18–19, 144.
68 Neill, *Tape Reading*, 107.
69 For an example, see Preda, *Framing Finance*, 137. Financial journalists also regularly complained about professionals moving the market manipulatively. Knight, *Reading*, 33–44.
70 Neill, *Tape Reading*, 31, 9; Wyckoff, *Studies*, 145; Knight, *Reading*, 86–87. For a specific case of a demand for shares artificially created by a broker, see Mike Wallace, *Greater Gotham: A History of New York City from 1898 to 1919* (Oxford: Oxford University Press, 2017), 74–75. Criticism of the practice was voiced by journalists. See Cedric B. Cowing, "Market Speculation in the Muckraker Era: The Popular Reaction," *Business History Review* 31 (1957): 403–13, here 409. The role of the professional in "making" the prices also contradicts Stäheli, *Spektakuläre Spekulation*, 241–43, who considers the market itself as the producer of prices.
71 Neill, *Tape Reading*, 67. For a somewhat different reading of the ticker and hypnosis see also Stäheli, *Spektakuläre Spekulation*, 338–39.
72 On the larger implications of tips and confidence tricks, see Knight, *Reading*, 144–90.
73 Neill, *Tape Reading*, 37. See also Wyckoff, *Studies*, 61, 84.
74 Neill, *Tape Reading*, 78.
75 See Cowing, *Populists*, 53.
76 Cowing, *Populists*, 53. See also the remarks in Wyckoff, *Studies*, 42–43, 113.
77 Carosso, "Investment Banking," 92–93.
78 Neill, *Tape Reading*, IX, 17.
79 Cowing, "Market Speculation," 412.
80 Lefèvre, *Reminiscences*, 12.
81 Lefèvre, *Reminiscences*, 62–63.

82 Lefèvre, *Reminiscences*, 52.
83 Lefèvre, *Reminiscences*, 53. Emphasis in the original.
84 Lefèvre, *Reminiscences*, 153.
85 Lefèvre, *Reminiscences*, 96. Emphasis in the original.
86 Lefèvre, *Reminiscences*, 99.
87 Lefèvre, *Reminiscences*, 158.
88 Lefèvre, *Reminiscences*, 63.
89 Lefèvre, *Reminiscences*, 184–85.
90 Lefèvre, *Reminiscences*, 187.
91 Lefèvre, *Reminiscences*, 188.
92 Lefèvre, *Reminiscences*, 189.
93 Lefèvre, *Reminiscences*, 189–90.
94 For more details on Tailer, see Preda, *Framing Finance*, 133–35, 224–26, 232–33.
95 They have been studied by Preda, *Framing Finance,* though the current text diverges from his interpretation significantly.
96 As an introduction, see Nagy, "History of Emotions."
97 Pierre Bourdieu, "Die Biographische Illusion," in *Praktische Vernunft: Zur Theorie des Handelns* (Frankfurt: Suhrkamp, 1998), 75–82.
98 Diary notes, May 14 and 16, 1884. In: New York Historical Society, Mss. Edward Neufville Tailer Diaries.
99 Zimmerman, *Panic*, 81. For the following see ibid., 81–122.
100 The articles were published as Thomas Lawson, *Frenzied Finance: The Crime of Amalgamated* (New York: Ridgway, 1905).
101 Zimmerman, *Panic*, 88.
102 Zimmerman, *Panic*, 107.
103 On the panic of 1907, see Robert F. Bruner and Sean D. Carr, *The Panic of 1907: Lessons Learned from the Market's Perfect Storm* (Hoboken: John Wiley & Sons, 2009).
104 Quoted after Zimmerman, *Panic*, 90.
105 Hochfelder, "Common People."

Part IV

Taming self-interest, self-interest as limitation

9 Interest as an enduring political problem in early modern France

Rafe Blaufarb

Since the 1970s, scholars have become interested in the history of the concept of "self-interest." They have mainly pondered how this idea became dominant in modern times, not just as the basic axiom of economics, but also as the supposed key to understanding human behavior. The founding father of this area of scholarship, Albert O. Hirschman, proposed in his *The Passions and the Interests* a powerful intellectual genealogy of the concept.[1] According to Hirschman, the modern idea of self-interest originated in the realm of early modern political theory, where it was applied to rulership. From there, it migrated to the sphere of political-economic thought during the eighteenth century. The proposition that individuals are motivated by self-interest soon became a fundamental paradigm of the new discipline of economics and a major force in the social sciences more broadly. Since the publication of Hirschman's book, scholars have added nuance to his argument, but have accepted both his genealogy of the concept of self-interest and his overall research goal—to understand how self-interest became the "first principle" of economics and a virtually universal explanation for social behavior.

Unlike most of the existing literature, this chapter is not concerned with how the concept of self-interest moved from the political to the economic sphere and how it operated in that sphere, nor how it became a universal model for understanding human agency. It engages neither with Hirschman's main concern, the intellectual roots of what he called "the spirit of capitalism," nor with what Pierre Force called the "genealogy of economic science."[2] Rather, it is concerned with how early modern political theorists addressed the relationship between interest and sovereignty in the context of monarchy. This was where Hirschman began his pioneering study. But after a few pages, he concludes that the "concept of interest became fairly bogged down in its original domain," and shifts his analysis from the political realm, leaving his readers unclear how and why early modern political reformers "harnessed," "repressed," and "counteracted" the sovereign's passions.[3] In fact, the extension of the concept of interest to the economic domain did not lessen its political importance, nor did it "bog down" (whatever that means) in the realm of constitutional theory. In his effort to emphasize the novelty of interest thinking in the economic sphere, Hirschman has unfortunately obscured the continuing salience of the concept of self-interest to political thought—and this during a period which saw not only the rise of the modern state, but also a great flourishing of political theorization. Pace Hirschman, the problem of the sovereign's interest remained a major concern of political theorists and practitioners even as such canonical writers as Hume, Montesquieu, Rousseau, and Smith began exploring the concept's extra-political implications, changing its meanings, and broadening its potential applications. Interest, in short, remained a political challenge long after it had moved beyond the confines of the political realm and long after princes had given way to other kinds of sovereigns. Indeed, nothing in contemporary political life suggests that the issue of self-interest in the political sphere has lost any of its salience.

Nowhere was the problem of self-interest in politics more apparent than in absolutist France. There, the most "absolute" of rulers, Louis XIV, lauded the benefits of royal interest. "Kings are men," he wrote, but "they are a little less so when they are truly kings, because only one passion masters and dominates [them]—that of their interest."[4] Nothing highlighted the issue of the ruler's self-interest as sharply as the question of the monarch's property rights. By the sixteenth century, the notion that the king's material interest could be made to work for the common good if his property rights were wisely defined had become a central feature of French political theory and practice. Between 1560 and 1620, a legal framework was constructed to harmonize the monarch's proprietary interest with public well-being. The most important measures were the Edict of Moulins (1566), which prohibited the king from alienating Crown properties, and the edict of 1607, which barred the king from owning personal immovable property. Unable to dispose freely of the Crown domain or to possess property as a private individual, monarchs from Henri IV through Louis XVI found themselves—at least in regard to their proprietary interest—"worse off than private individuals."[5] Their capacity for property was almost entirely eliminated; only the right (or rather, obligation) to superintend the Crown domain and pass it on improved to their first-born sons remained. This approach to dealing with the king's material interest is close to the early modern strategy of "repressing and harnessing" or "counteracting" the passions discussed by Hirschman, but it is not identical.[6] Instead, royal property right was crafted to abolish the potentially harmful ways in which the king could exercise that right so that his proprietary interest would flow all the more vigorously through the beneficial channels left open. Prohibited from alienating Crown property (1566) and owning personal property (1607), the king had to express his passion for wealth and grandeur by carefully administering the Crown domain. This would benefit the entire kingdom for, in addition to ensuring political stability and territorial integrity, a flourishing royal domain ideally meant that the king could pay for his government and household without resorting to taxation. Considered part of the kingdom's "fundamental law," these regulations remained in force until the French Revolution.

The particular problem of monarchical interest

Before examining the strategies implemented in early modern France to produce a community of interest between king and people, we should note the special salience of the problem of interest to the monarchical system. Self-interest was a concern for all early modern political systems, republics no less than monarchies, but monarchy distilled the problem of interest in a particularly direct, focused way. The existing literature on interest glosses over the question of how different forms of government engage the problem of self-interest. Writing abstractly of "government" and "state," such scholars as Hirschman and Force do not consider how different forms of political organization may have elicited and responded to the sovereign's interest in quite different ways. From a contemporary perspective, it seems obvious that the perils of self-interest in politics must be greatest where sovereignty is exercised by a single individual. But this was not necessarily what early moderns thought. Louis XIV claimed that monarchy generated natural synergy between the ruler's interest and that of his subjects. The king alone, he wrote, "has no fortune but the State's, nothing for which to strive but the grandeur of the monarchy, no authority but that of law, no debts except public expenses, no friends but the people to enrich." "When we keep the State in view, we work for ourselves."[7] Thomas Hobbes agreed: "Where the publique and private interest are most closely united, there is the publique most advanced. Now in Monarchy, the private interest is the same with the publique. The riches, power, and honour of a Monarch arise only from the riches, strength, and reputation of his Subjects."[8]

French thinkers understood the superiority of monarchical government in a similar way. But they were not willing to risk the kingdom's prosperity on the king's ability to understand that his and the kingdom's interest were one. Leaving nothing to chance, they would build mechanisms to ensure this perfect community of interest.

Since they understood interest primarily in material terms, they focused their efforts on the king's right to own and dispose of property.[9] They strove for a seemingly minor goal: to restrict his discretionary power over the Crown domain. This was the proprietary endowment attached to royal sovereignty. From the fourteenth to the sixteenth century, it emerged as a category of property distinct from what belonged to the king personally.[10] This resulted in the bifurcation of the king's property right—one domanial and integral to the royal office, the other patrimonial and belonging to the man—and reinforced the doubling of his person characteristic of both English and French monarchy.[11]

The domain comprised both physical and non-physical properties, from the power of taxation to landholdings. In addition, all properties deemed insusceptible of private ownership, such as rivers and intestate inheritances, also belonged to the domain. This basic description does not even begin to hint at the legal distinctions—forming at least seven distinct categories of goods and powers—*domanistes* (domanial jurists) invented to classify the domain's different components. And in the seventeenth century, Louis XIII and Louis XIV asserted a new right, universal royal feudal superiority, which sought to subject all allodial property in the kingdom to the Crown's lordship.[12] All of these diverse physical and incorporeal elements were considered Crown property and inherent to royal sovereignty. By simultaneously working to style the king as an absolute sovereign and a proprietary feudal lord, the domain placed the problem of self-interest at the heart of France's monarchical constitution. How could the will of the monarch—not just a "mystical" or "sacred" body, but also a "natural" man with all the virtues and vices of other mortals—be made to work for the public good?

The *domanistes'* solution lay in a metaphor: the kingdom was a family, and the king its father. This metaphor had many ideological uses, not least to promote the notion of paternal government under a father-king to whom the subject-children owed filial obedience. If the "well-conducted family" was, as Bodin claimed, "the true image of the republic" and "domestic power mirrored sovereign power," then it followed that "the natural reverence of children for their parents is the bond of legitimate obedience of subjects toward their sovereigns."[13] But perhaps the main reason why the *domanistes* embraced this metaphor is because the family, as a social institution central to holding, exploiting, and transmitting property, was a versatile and familiar model easily applied to the Crown domain. Their efforts to construct a domanial regime to make the king's interest work for the public good focused on three questions: the legal status of royal succession; the monarch's relationship to the domain; and the king's right to additional, personal property. The metaphor of the family provided the matrix the *domanistes* used to formulate solutions to each.

Succession[14]

It is not at all obvious why the *domanistes* would turn to the metaphor of the family to define monarchical succession. According to the Roman law with which they were imbued, the father of the family wielded *patria potestas*—virtually absolute authority over the people and goods in his household. Among its attributes was the power to designate his successor(s) and apportion his succession. According to Roman law, a father could disinherit any or all of his children, pick new successors at will, divide his earthly goods as he pleased, or even alienate, dilapidate, and squander them during his lifetime. This was entirely incompatible with what the early modern French understood as the fundamental goal of monarchical succession—to ensure that Crown and kingdom were transmitted integrally from father to eldest son, from generation to generation. A system in which the king was free to disinherit the dauphin, choose an heir outside his lineage, or divide the kingdom into several parts was intolerable. True patrimonial succession was not a suitable model for the transmission of the French Crown.

There was, however, another model of succession available to the *domanistes*. Roman law distinguished between succession to private things, which was governed by patrimonial succession (and, thus, at the discretion of the father) and succession to public things such as offices. The latter was termed "simple succession" by Jean de Terre Rouge, the jurist whose treatise *Contra Rebelles suorum regum* (1529) would establish it as the mode of royal succession in France. In contrast to patrimonial succession, simple succession required that the inheritance (here, the Crown and its domain) pass intact to the heir. In addition, it privileged prevailing legal custom over the father's will in designating that heir.[15] In France, custom followed feudal tradition, which held that, whenever possible, the fief would go to the first-born son. Extended to the Crown, this meant that the royal office and its domain would pass integrally and automatically by primogeniture from generation to generation. The great advantage of this successoral regime was to eliminate the central feature of patrimonial succession—the wild card of *patria potestas*—and ensure the integrity and stability of the kingdom. Thanks to simple succession, the actions of "the father of the family, or rather father of the State, [would be] regulated more by the common good than by movements of [his] will."[16] Through this mechanism of succession, the Crown of France shed some of its patrimonial character to assume the status of a public office. This was an important step in the depersonalization of the concept of the state. Through the distinction between patrimonial and simple succession, the *domanistes* had discovered a way to reconcile the monarchical claim to absolute sovereignty (à la Bodin) with his absolute subordination to the Crown and the public good.[17]

Nonetheless, the French royal succession still resembled a patrimonial one. Unlike true offices, which were generally held by a succession of unrelated individuals, the Crown was passed down in the family line like that most solid and patrimonial of all properties—the fief.[18] Even Jean de Terre Rouge acknowledged the similarity, admitting that the French royal succession was *quasi hereditaria* and suggesting that it represented a hybrid *tertia species successionis* combining features of the two other forms. In the sixteenth century, *domanistes* began to compare it to special types of successoral mechanisms—the *fideicommis* and the *substitution perpétuelle*—that families used to preserve their estate intact from generation to generation.[19] For the *domaniste* Bosquet, the reigning monarch was "encumbered" by a "*substitution perpétuelle*" which "obliged [him] to transmit to his successors all the domains and properties specially designated for the good of the State and utility of the public."[20] For Charles de Lorry, an inspector of the domain, the Crown more closely resembled a "perpetual masculine legal *fideicommis* that defers the Crown and its patrimony from eldest son to eldest son, from male to male."[21] Although these two successoral devices were technically different, they had the same effect—to transmit a family estate intact, down through the generations.

These legal analogies reinforced the doctrine of simple succession in perpetuating the unity of Crown and kingdom. The *domanistes* were explicit about this. These fictions served, Inspector Lorry stated baldly, to ensure "inalienability and indivision."[22] While it may be self-evident, it is worth remembering why this was important. Inalienability and indivision of the Crown meant that parts of the country would not be transferred to foreign rulers and that there would be no internal strife between feuding lords. Life, property, and local customs would be preserved. Memories of the disasters that could ensue if the kingdom were fragmented were not just derived from histories of Frankish times. More recent examples, such as the Hundred Years' War, and events from living memory, such as the sixteenth-century Wars of Religion and seventeenth-century Fronde, made clear the existential imperative of maintaining undivided royal sovereignty and territorial integrity. Every subject's peace and prosperity depended on it. The guarantee the *domanistes* proposed was paradoxical but effective: to deprive the king of his discretion over the designation of his successor and prevent him from all involvement in the transmission to him of Crown and kingdom. To make royal sovereignty absolute, the *domanistes* absolutely deprived the king of all power over its disposition.

The domain of the crown

The *domanistes* also found familial metaphor useful in constructing a mechanism to guide the king's interest toward cultivating and preserving the Crown domain. By comparing the relationship between the king and his Crown to a marriage, they were able to assimilate the domain to a dowry. It was common in the sixteenth century to compare the sovereign's bond to the kingdom to a marriage. Elizabeth of England famously equated her relationship with the kingdom to a marriage, describing to Sir John Harrington "my good people" as "my husbands."[23] The French went further than rhetoric. They institutionalized the marriage metaphor in the *Sacre*, the elaborate coronation ceremony which sanctified the accession of a new king to the throne.[24] Among its many rituals was the placing of a ring on the new king's finger. The king received the ring, one chronicler observed, "because on the day of his *Sacre*, the king solemnly marries his kingdom and, through the sweet, gracious, and loving bond of marriage, is inseparably united with his subjects, so that they mutually love each other like spouses."[25] Different authors described differently the question of the precise nature of this marriage and the exact identity of the king's spouse. The marriage was variously called "mystical," "political," "moral and political," "holy and political," "civil, moral, and political," "mystically political, holy, and sacred," and possibly by other terms as well. The king's spouse was identified as "the Crown," "the kingdom," "the state," "the *chose publique*," and, most frequently, "the republic."[26] One might speculate that these different choices in terminology reflected different views on the nature and location of sovereignty in early modern France. For the *domanistes*, however, the key was the marriage metaphor itself, for it allowed them to impose on the Crown domain all the strictures of the dowry and thus prevent the king from disposing of it freely as he would of patrimonial property. Once again, the marriage metaphor accentuated the king's public character by limiting one of the main outlets for expressing his self-interest as a natural man: his property rights.

> The elevation of the Prince to the Throne is a consecration of his person, a marriage [...] by which his private person, extinguished and confused with the public person he wears, only continues to exist in the physical sphere and no more in the order of law. He is King or State, the terms mean the same thing. Thus, the private person can no longer exercise rights of either possession or property. The Prince sacrifices himself without reserve and for eternity.[27]

The comparison of the domain to a dowry was first proposed in the mid-fourteenth century by the Neapolitan jurist, Luca de Penna.[28] Handwritten copies of his writings began to circulate in France in the 1400s, and French jurists had begun to employ the dowry metaphor by the 1470s, if not earlier. Michel Pons, the *procureur-général* of the *parlement* of Paris, was one of the first to use it. "Just as the dowry in a charnel marriage is declared inalienable by the law, so too is the domain of the Crown, given to kings in dowry for the moral and political marriage between the king and the *chose publique*."[29] The appearance in print in 1509 of Penna's *Super tres libros* sparked an explosion in the use of the metaphor to assert domanial inalienability and describe its nature.[30] The Toulousain jurist Pierre de Belloy described the "domain that the king takes" as "the republic's dowry, which he [the king] truly administers and uses for support, service, and the public good." René Choppin, one of the first *domanistes* to write a comprehensive treatise on the domain, described it in more technical legal terms. "Just as the Julian Law renders inalienable the dowry the wife brings in marriage to her husband, so too is the patrimony and domain of the crown inseparable from the public State." Jean Bodin agreed that the domain was the "dowry that the republic brings to her spouse [the king] for her upkeep, defense, and maintenance," but went even further than the others in limiting the king's access to it. "Kings cannot appropriate it in any way [for] [...] the domain belongs to the republic." The king did not even enjoy the usufruct of it (the position of most jurists), but was only a "simple *usager*."[31]

These citations make clear the purpose of the dowry metaphor—to provide ideological and legal grounds to foreclose the king's ability to treat the domain as his personal property. The dowry was a special kind of property, subject to rigorous legal restrictions. Although the husband could use the revenue it generated to pay for legitimate household expenses, he had a moral obligation to augment its capital and a legal one to pass it on intact to the couple's children. If the marriage was childless, it would return to the wife's paternal lineage upon her death. The dowry could never become the property of her husband. This was the reason why the metaphor was so useful for describing the domain of the Crown. Since it worked like a dowry, Choppin concluded, "kings are not so much lords and proprietors as they are guardians and conservators."[32] At most, kings enjoyed "a form of usufruct" over the domain and, "no matter how long they possessed it, they could never acquire the property of it."[33] They most emphatically did not enjoy the paramount right—*abusus*, the right to alienate—of the triad which composed full property under Roman law.

The principle of domanial inability appeared in French public law at least as early as the fourteenth century. From 1364, with the accession of Charles V, kings took an oath to maintain the inalienability of the domain of the Crown as part of the *Sacre*. Although the oath disappeared from the coronation ritual in the 1490s, the fact that it had been sworn in the past was cited by jurists as evidence that domanial inalienability was a fundamental law of the kingdom.[34] They also noted that other European kingdoms—and even the republic of Venice—observed the same principle.[35] They also identified pragmatic reasons for domanial inalienability. Originally granted to the king to support the upkeep of the royal household and fund government services, it was intended to allow the king to live off his own resources rather than have to tax the people.[36] This is why Bodin characterized the domain as "the most honest [respectable] and dependable way" of funding the state.[37] As the domain diminished, so too would taxes increase. The principle of inalienability was intended to ensure that this did not happen, and that the king never had to resort to such a painful alternative.

That was the ideal. In practice, however, kings frequently alienated parts of the domain. The temptation, even need, to do so became irresistible in the early 1300s, as the burden of funding the Hundred Years' War led to significant alienations, and a corresponding diminishing, of it.[38] To stem the hemorrhage, kings began to issue ordonnances banning domanial alienations. But the fact that at least eighteen such ordonnances appeared between 1316 and 1559 suggests just how futile these efforts were.[39] Rapidly violated, the formal prohibitions on alienation were just as rapidly reissued. Although the ordonnances had little effect, they did set a legal precedent that would justify what would be prove to be lasting anti-alienation legislation over a century later.

This was the Edict of Moulins (1566), which elevated domanial inalienability to the status of an irrevocable, "fundamental law" of the kingdom. The demand to enshrine inalienability in a law of such stature was first formulated in the Estates of Pontoise of 1561.[40] Five years later, that demand was granted by Charles IX's issuing of the edict. Citing legal precedent and the pragmatic justification that a healthy domain meant low taxes, the edict

declared the domain of the Crown perpetually and irrevocably inalienable. It permitted only two partial exceptions. The first was for apanages—
proprietary endowments created for the princes of the royal family from
domain lands. These would continue to be granted, but would return to
the domain of the Crown if the prince died without male issue or if he himself became king. The second exception allowed emergency wartime alienations. But such alienations would be subject to perpetual reimbursement
by the Crown and reintegration into the domain. Together with the regime
of succession, the Edict of Moulins formed an essential part of the French
monarchical constitution. Although kings found ways of bending (although
not directly violating) its strictures on alienation in the years after 1566, the
edict remained in effect until the French Revolution.[41] From 1566 until the
end of the Old Regime, not a single new fief was created by the Crown. This
is a significant sign of the edict's impact, because infeudation was the most
solemn and absolute form of property alienation permitted in France before
1789.[42] Thus, the Edict of Moulins succeeded in eliminating virtually all of
the king's freedom to dispose of the Crown domain. With simple succession and inalienability now consecrated as fundamental laws, the monarch's
ability to express his material interest was reduced to a sole activity: super-
intending and nurturing the domain of the Crown so that his son would
inherit a thriving establishment when he became king in his turn.

Community of goods

There remained, however, a glaring exception. Although it made the domain
of the Crown inalienable, like a dowry, the Edict of Moulins did not apply
to the king's right to own personal property—goods he already possessed
before his coronation and those he acquired through purchase, gift, inheritance, or other means during his rule. What the edict had done was to draw
a legal distinction between two types of royal property right: 1) a tightly-
regulated domanial one which left no outlet for the pursuit of interest except
to build a rich inheritance for the future; and 2) a completely unregulated
personal one through which the ruler was free to express all the same passions, including selfishness and greed, as any mortal man. This bifurcation of royal property right was common to other European monarchies.[43]
Pufendorf considered it the norm wherever legislation did not determine
otherwise. He even went so far as to claim that, in general, "the King has
full and entire usufruct of the Domain of the Crown, so that he can dispose
absolutely and according to his whim of the revenues it produces, and even
augment his own *particular patrimony* with the savings he accumulates."[44]
This remained the case in England and much of Europe throughout the
eighteenth century. And it would briefly become the case in France again,
under Napoleon. But in early modern France, where domanial jurisprudence was already becoming "more precise and definitive" (read, "restric-
tive") than elsewhere, the existence of bifurcated royal property right was

extremely tenuous.[45] Born in 1566 when the Edict of Moulin assigned the king distinct rights over his domanial and personal goods, this bifurcation would end several decades later with a series of legal decisions that extinguished the king's personal property rights and foreclosed the very possibility of a royal private domain.

This shift was accomplished between 1590 and 1607 by the highest court in the land, the Paris *parlement*.[46] What prompted the *parlement*'s campaign against royal personal property was the extinction of the Valois line and the accession to the throne of a member of the related Bourbon family, Henri IV. Before becoming king in 1590, Henri had not only been one of the greatest landholders in France; he had also been—and remained—king of the sovereign state of Navarre. Henri wanted to keep both his kingdom and his estates in France separate from the domain of the French Crown in order to retain them as private property. Many jurists, however, argued that he had a constitutional duty to incorporate his personal goods into the domain. Leading the charge was Jacques de La Guesle, *procureur général* (chief prosecutor) of the Paris *parlement*.[47] In a lengthy brief, he sought to topple the reigning view that there were "two Domains, one public and royal which comes to kings through the right of their Crown, the other private and individual [which kings acquire] by succession, acquisition, donation, or other particular title." (95) Instead, the French constitution knew only the "confusion and mélange of the two domains" (96) or, more accurately, the absorption of the king's private properties into the domain of the Crown. "In France, the public Domain attracts, joins, and unites to itself the personal domain of kings even more than the magnet attracts iron; for it is an indissoluble mélange of all into all, like two liquors poured into the same vase." (114) To support this view, La Guesle cited the example of the founder of the Capetian dynasty (and Henri IV's distant ancestor), Hugues Capet. Like Henri IV, Hugues had been a great landholder upon his accession to the throne, but, unlike Henri, he had incorporated all of his properties with the Crown when he became king. In fact, it was Hugues' sacrifice of his personal properties that had recreated the domain of the Crown after its virtual destruction by the dissipations of the Merovingians and Carolingians. Thus, the doctrine of "reunion or unity of the private domain of kings to the public one of their Crown," was as old as the dynasty itself and thus a fundamental law of the kingdom (206). Moreover, it was a political necessity, as many historical examples, as well as the still-simmering religious troubles of the country, demonstrated. The fragmentation of the Crown domain meant impotent government, lordly rebellion, feuding, and civil war. It was only the unity of the domain which had "made the state a monarchy rather than the aristocracy (not to mention oligarchy, polyarchy, or other worse sort of government) it had tended to become." (114) Maintaining the absolute oneness and inalienability of the domain was essential to both interior stability and exterior strength. Ultimately, not only the grandeur of the Crown, but also the well-being of the kingdom and its people depended upon it.

For many years, Henri IV resisted the *parlement,* but in 1607 he finally agreed to incorporate his French properties into the domain of the Crown.[48] His edict of July 1607 not only confirmed this renunciation, but also upheld the domanial principles articulated years before by La Guesle and the Paris *parlement.* Because kings "dedicate and consecrate themselves to the public," its preamble explained, they "wanted to have nothing distinct and separate from it." In a surprising reversal of the dowry metaphor, the edict asserted that, through the "holy and political" marriage kings contracted with their Crown, "they dowered it [the Crown] with all properties belonging to them by personal title."[49] By shifting the gender identities that had been implied previously by the marriage metaphor, the king could now match the Crown's inalienable dowry with an inalienable dowry of his own.

This mutual sacrifice of property by each spouse (the king and the republic) to their marriage created a perfect and absolute "community of goods" between them.[50] Whereas English monarchs retained (and still retain) extensive personal property rights and thus legal existence as private individuals, domanial inalienability and what became known as "reunion" almost entirely abolished the private existence of the French king. Almost, but not quite. Although he could neither own private property nor freely dispose of domanial goods, inalienability and reunion still allowed the king one channel through which to express his material interest: the preservation, augmentation, and transmission of the Crown domain to his son. There were powerful motives—paternal love and Janus-faced force of lineage pride—for him to do so. The desire to avoid dishonoring his forefathers by diminishing the Crown and the equally powerful desire of transmitting it, enhanced, to his son and further posterity, would make the king's interest work for the kingdom's prosperity. This regime of royal property right produced the "Artificiall Eternity" Hobbes considered essential to political stability and ensured that considerations of familial or dynastic interest would always be the driver of royal action.[51]

At the same time as they were putting in place France's domanial regime, jurists such as Bodin and Le Bret were also laying the foundations of expanded royal power—often referred to as absolutism.[52] One may well wonder why French kings would accept limits on their personal property rights at the same moment when they were seeking to augment their political power. If it is clear what the subjects got from the new domanial regime—some sort of guarantee of responsible royal administration—it is less obvious what the king gained from the new arrangements. The quest for "Artificiall Eternity" embedded in the domanial regime suggests a possible answer. If kings could no longer alienate the domain, it followed that they and their successors could not be dispossessed either. By giving up personal property rights, kings confirmed their dynasty's eternal title to the kingdom itself. Domanial inalienability and eternal dynastic succession were two sides of the same coin.

Conclusion: the timelessness and selflessness of self-interest

Notions of interest as temporally unbounded, as hereditary or family-based, continued to influence French political theory down to the French Revolution. Even the most "modern" of pre-revolutionary political economists, the physiocrats or *économistes*, made it a pillar of their constitutional reforms. It is well known that they recommended giving the ruler an interest in encouraging national prosperity by granting him a share in the production of all new agricultural wealth—what they called the "co-property of the net product." This broke sharply with the *domanistes*' strategy of confining the ruler's property rights to a distinct and tightly-regulated Crown domain. Yet, in another way, the physiocrats were traditional: they insisted that the ruler's co-property would backfire unless accompanied by hereditary sovereignty. It was only "hereditary sovereignty [that] made the sovereign co-proprietor of the net product," for without hereditary succession, he would be a mere officeholder with every reason to enrich himself at the public's expense while still in power.[53] All forms of government but one-man, hereditary rule suffered from this fatal vice. Aristocracy was dangerous because it empowered "individuals with domains and families whose particular, exclusive interest can often come into conflict with the interest of the other landowners." Representative assemblies were equally problematic because "each of their members is an individual property-holder who, by different illegitimate means, can gain great riches for himself at the expense of his fellow citizens."[54] Even lifetime-monarchs had "particular, exclusive interests" that would lead them to "employ the power entrusted to them to ameliorate and extend their own properties." They would be "strongly interested in profiting from their temporary position to increase the grandeur of their family and fortune." In contrast, a hereditary, co-proprietary monarch "could only impoverish his subjects by impoverishing himself and only augment his revenue by augmenting their own."[55] Hereditary succession would ensure that "all the present and future interests of the holder of sovereign authority were intimately linked to those of society."[56] Hereditary sovereignty was "an essential condition" of the physiocratic constitution, for it alone could achieve "the common interest of sovereign and subjects."[57]

Concerns that self-interest, if bounded by temporal limits, would foster an exploitative, slash-and-burn mentality if let loose in the political sphere were hardly limited to France or the physiocrats. In Number 72 of *The Federalist*, writing on the question of whether the president should be eligible for re-election, Alexander Hamilton argued that only open-ended re-eligibility could ensure the prospect of "duration" necessary for good government. To prohibit it would result in a "diminution" of even the most virtuous man's "inducements to good behavior":

> There are few men who would not feel much less zeal in the discharge of
> a duty when they were conscious that the advantages of the station with

which it was connected must be relinquished at a determinate period, than when they were permitted to entertain a hope of OBTAINING, by MERITING, a continuance of them [...].

Worse, for a man of lesser moral fiber, the requirement to step down after just one term would be a positive invitation to indulge his own interest at the expense of the common good:

> An avaricious man, who might happen to fill the office, looking forward to a time when he must at all events yield up the emoluments he enjoyed, would feel a propensity, not easy to be resisted by such a man, to make the best use of the opportunity he enjoyed while it lasted, [...] to make the harvest as abundant as it was transitory.

However, the same man, with the hope of re-election before him "might content himself with the regular perquisites of his situation."[58] For Hamilton, re-eligibility would serve a purpose similar to that of hereditary succession: by removing the certainty of a firm temporal boundary, it would create the illusion of the "Artificiall Eternity" that early modern political theorists believed necessary to make self-interest tend toward the good.

The notion that self-interest can only function optimally in the absence of a clearly bounded temporal horizon is present in Adam Smith's work as well. He wrote that indefinite temporality was why merchants honored contracts. A merchant who made "20 contracts a day," he reasoned, understood that "he cannot gain so much by endeavouring to impose on [their] neighbors as the very appearance of a cheat would make him loose." Because he was "afraid of losing his character" and forfeiting future business opportunities, he would be "scrupulous in observing every engagement." However, a man without regular business dealings, one who did not expect every tomorrow to bring new commercial transactions, would be "somewhat disposed to cheat, because [he] can gain more by a smart trick than [he] can lose by the injury which it does [his] character." In both cases, the men were following their "self-interest, the general principle which regulates the actions of every man, and which leads men to act in a certain manner from views of advantage."[59] What determined the different business practices of the two kinds of merchants—whether or not they honored contracts—was the temporal context in which their self-interest was operating. Self-interest alone could not be relied on to produce beneficial outcomes, even in the commercial sphere. It required the illusion of unbounded time to achieve such outcomes.

Paradoxically, the main effect of temporal unboundedness—whether in the form of hereditary succession, re-election, or the prospect of future gain—on self-interest was to constrain the individual's freedom of maneuver. It did this by fixing the individual's will on an object of desire that might be obtained in the future only by observing certain prescribed forms of behavior in the present. The paradoxical constraining of free will apparent in the schemes of *domanistes*, Smith's analysis of merchant contracts, and Hamilton's plea for electoral re-eligibility reveals an even greater paradox at the heart of self-interest discourse and institution-building: that for true self-interest to emerge, the self must recede toward effacement. One is tempted to conclude that this reflects the displacement of an older passion-driven Rabelaisian self by an Enlightenment-style self of discipline and rationality. But the fact that the self-constraining domanial laws were products of the age of Rabelais casts doubt on this simplistic linear evolution. That the royal-domanial self of the sixteenth century depends on the effacement of free will no less than the eighteenth-century self of Smith and Hamilton seems as significant as it is puzzling. The strangeness of this selfless self-interest suggests that the concept that defined the "spirit of capitalism" in the eighteenth century has continued to change—and change considerably—in the centuries since Smith published *The Wealth of Nations*.

Notes

1 Albert O. Hirschman, *The Passions and the Interests: Political Arguments for Capitalism before Its Triumph*, (Princeton: Princeton University Press, 1977).
2 Hirschman, *The Passions*, 3, and Pierre Force, *Self-Interest before Adam Smith: A Genealogy of Economic Science* (Cambridge: Cambridge University Press, 2003). Another economically oriented work on self-interest is Steven G. Medema, *The Hesitant Hand: Taming Self-Interest in the History of Economic Ideas* (Princeton: Princeton University Press, 2009).
3 Hirschman, *The Passions*, 35. "One might also wonder what it might mean to say that a concept "became bogged down."
4 Louis XIV, *Mémoires et divers écrits*, ed. Bernar Champigneulles (Paris: Le Club Français du Livre, 1955), 16.
5 The phrase is from the sixteenth-century jurists, Choppin and Bacquet, cited in Robert Descimon, "Les Fonctions de la métaphore du marriage politique du roi et de la république, France, XVè–XVIIIè siècles," *Annales. Économies, Sociétés, Civilisations*, no. 6 (November–December 1992): 1127–1147, 1138.
6 Hirschman, *The Passions*, 14–20.
7 Louis XIV, *Mémoires*, 47 and 217.
8 Thomas Hobbes, *Leviathan, or the Matter, Forme & Power of a Commonwealth, Ecclesiasticall and Civill*, ed. Alfred R. Waller (Cambridge: Cambridge University Press, 1904), 131.
9 Why they conceived of interest in primarily material terms is a question worth pursuing. Hirschman notes that "some process" was narrowing the understanding of interest in this way, but offers only a few speculations as to what that process might have been. Hirschman, *The Passions*, 38–39.
10 Emile Chenon, "De la transformation du domaine royal en domaine de la Couronne du XIVe au XVIe siècle," *Revue historique du droit francais et etranger* 4, no. 4 (1925): 528–30.
11 On this phenomenon in the English context, see Ernst H. Kantorowicz, *The King's Two Bodies: A Study in Medieval Political Theology* (Princeton: Princeton University Press, 1957).

12 Universal royal overlordship had been established in England with the Norman Conquest. French kings' attempts to extend their proprietary superiority over the entire kingdom faced sustained resistance (all the way until 1789) and were never entirely successful. On the English axiom, "every acre of land is 'held of' the king," see Sir Frederick Pollock and Frederic W. Maitland, *The History of English Law before the Time of Edward I*, 2nd ed. (Cambridge: Cambridge University Press, 1968), 232–33. The relationship between this legal axiom, which is still in effect, and the development of capitalism in England has yet to be explored.

13 Jean Bodin, *Les Six livres de la République* (1583; repr., Scientia Aalen: Amsterdam 1961), 11, and "Déclaration sur les formalités de marriage, les qualités requises, le crime de rapt, etc., du 26 novembre 1639," cited in André Burguière, "L'État monarchique et la famille (XVIᵉ–XVIIIᵉ siècle)," *Annales. Histoire, Sciences Sociales*, no. 2 (March–April 2001): 313–335, here 313. The prevalence of the kingdom-family metaphor also explains why princes and princesses were called "sons of France," "children of the French people," and "true children of the *chose publique* of France." Aurélie du Crest, *Modèle familial et pouvoir monarchique (XVIᵉ–XVIIIᵉ)*, vol. 1 (Aix-en-Provence: Presses universitaires Aix-Marseille, 2002), 81.

14 Unless otherwise noted, this section is based on Ralph E. Giesey's powerful, "The Juristic Basis of Dynastic Right to the French Throne," *Transactions of the American Philosophical Society*, n.s., 51, no. 5 (1961): 3–47.

15 According to Bodin, the Crown "is not deferred by paternal succession, but rather in virtue of the law of the kingdom." *Les Six livres de la République* (Paris: Gabriel Cartier, 1599), 160.

16 Jacques de la Guesle, "Remonstrance prononcée le 29 juillet 1591 au parlement lors séant à Tours, la grande Chambre et Tournelle assemblées, sur le sujet des lettres patentes du 13 avril 1590 concernant la disunion que le feu Roy Henry IIII vouloit estre de son Patrimoine d'avec le Domaine Public et Royal," in *Les remonstrances de Messire Jacques de la Guesle, procureur general du Roy* (Paris: Pierre Chevalier, 1611), 189.

17 I thank Christine Zabel for noticing this and sharing her insight with me.

18 Of course the fief was not "absolute" property because it was held from a superior who retained a kind of property right in it and also because its owner was obliged to perform certain public services. But with the very rare exception of the allod, all real property in early modern Europe was held in dependent tenure.

19 The jurists employed two slightly different comparisons. One was to *fideicommis*—transmission of a hereditary property which imposed on the heir the obligation to bequeath it intact to a third person. The other was to *substitution perpétuelle*. Under this arrangement, the father was the administrator and usufructuary of a good, but the "naked property" (*propriété nue*) of it was permanently deferred to the next generation. In practical effect, both functioned like the English entailment.

20 Bosquet, *Dictionnaire raisonné des domains et droits domaniaux*, vol. 2 (Rouen: Jacques-Joseph Le Boullenger, 1762), 90.

21 Charles de Lorry, "Introduction," to Lefèvre de la Planche, *Mémoires sur les matières domaniales, ou traité du domaine*, vol. 1 (Paris: Desaint et Saillant, 1764), xxxviii.

22 Ibid.

23 Quoted in Cheryl Glenn, *Rhetoric Retold: Regendering the Tradition from Antiquity through the Renaissance* (Carbondale and Edwardsville: Southern Illinois University Press, 1997), 168.

24 Du Crest, *Modèle familial*, 34–43.

25 Theodore Godefroy, *Le Ceremonial de France* (Paris: Abraham Pacard, 1619), 661.
26 Descimon, "Les Fonctions de la métaphore," 1135–36; and Du Crest, *Modèle familial*, 54.
27 Charles de Lorry, Preface to Lefèvre, *Mémoires*, 83.
28 Descimon, "Les Fonctions de la métaphore," 1128.
29 Cited by Du Crest, *Modèle familial*, 57.
30 Du Crest, *Modèle familial*, 33. It was printed six times and continued to be copied by hand throughout the sixteenth century.
31 Pierre de Belloy, *Recueil de quelques plaidoyez notables* (Tolose: R. Colomiez, 1613), 59; René Choppin, *Trois livres du domaine de la couronne de France* (Paris: Michel Sonnius, 1613), 171; Jean Bodin, *Les Six livres*, 859; and Jean Bodin, "Recueil journalier de tout ce qui s'est negocié en la chamber du Tiers-Etat de France, en l'assemblée générale des trois états," in *Recueil de pieces originales et authentiques concernant la tenue des Etats Généraux*, ed. Duval and Lalourcé, vol. 3, (Paris: Barrois, 1789), 347.
32 Choppin, *Trois livres*, 180.
33 Cardin Le Bret, *De la souveraineté du Roi* (Paris: Toussaincts du Bray, 1632), 338. "None can call themselves masters and proprietors of it, but the Crown to which it belongs."
34 Anne Rouselet, *La Règle de l'inaliénabilité du domaine de la couronne: Étude doctrinale de 1566 à la fin de l'ancien régime* (Paris: LGDJ, 1997), 58–59.
35 They were also aware of other European countries that observed inalienability. Bodin, *Les Six livres*, 658.
36 This was also what was expected of English monarchs. Frederick W. Maitland, "The Crown as Corporation," in *Maitland: Selected Essays*, ed. Harold D. Hazeltine, Gaillard Lapsley, and Percy H. Winfield (Cambridge: Cambridge University Press, 1936), 108.
37 Bodin, *Les Six livres*, 856.
38 The tenuous political situation of fourteenth-century France may have also made domanial inalienability a priority. The extinction of the Capetian line and the fraught succession of their Valois cousins, as well as rival English and Burgundian claims to the throne, placed the continued existence of a unified French kingdom in doubt. It was no coincidence that this same period saw the invention of the myth of Salic Succession, which elevated succession by male primogeniture to a constitutional principle.
39 That certain monarchs issued anti-alienation ordonnances on multiple occasions, sometimes in rapid succession, is even more telling. For example, Charles VI issued four (1388, 1401, 1403, and 1413) and the warlike François I five (1517, 1519, 1521, 1539, and 1540). Isambert, Decrussy, and Taillandier, *Recueil des anciennes lois françaises*, vol. 14 (Paris: June 1829), 185.
40 Adhemar Esmein, "L'Inalienabilite du domaine de la Couronne devant les Etats Generaux du XVIe siècle," in *Festschrift Otto Gierke zum Siebzigsten Geburtstag*, ed. (Weimar: Hermann Bohlaus Nachfolger, 1911), 361–382, here 370–73.
41 Perhaps the success of the edict, relative to its ineffectual predecessors, was due more to a fundamental shift in the way the Crown raised money, rather than to any special qualities of the edict itself. Simply put, from the last decades of the sixteenth century, the Crown increasingly turned to credit (including indirect borrowing through revocable domanial concessions such as the venal office and the *engagement*) to finance its operations.
42 Again, with the exception of allods. See note 18.
43 Ernst Kantorowicz thought this public/private bifurcation of royal property right so telling that he opened his classic study of medieval political theology with an example of King George III of England's manipulation of it to illustrate

the main point of his book—that the king had "two bodies." Although Kantorowicz emphasized the ritual aspects of the public/private division of the king's person in his study, he probably would have reached identical conclusions had he focused on royal property right instead. Kantorowicz, *The King's Two Bodies*, 3.

44 Samuel von Pufendorf, *Le Droit de la nature et des gens*, vol. 2, trans. Jean Barbeyrac (Paris: Briasson, 1734), 547.

45 Esmein, "L'inalienabilite du domaine," 365. French domaine law, he notes, was "plus precis et plus definitifs qu'en Angleterre." The proprietary rights of English monarchs differed from those of their French counterparts in two important ways. First, in addition to their "ancient desmesne" which, like the French domain of the Crown, was supposed to be inalienable, they had a more recently acquired royal domain which they could—and did—freely alienate. Alongside these two different domanial rights, they also had extensive personal property rights which British monarchs still enjoy. Their principal private possession is the Duchy of Lancaster, which includes valuable stretches of land in central London, as well as goods sheltered offshore in the Cayman Islands and Bermuda. The Duchy generates about £16 million per year for the Queen's privy purse. In addition, she owns several castles, including Balmoral and Sandringham, as private property. On the historical property rights of the English monarchs, see Sir Robert Chambers, *A Course of Lectures on the English Law, Delivered at the University of Oxford, 1767–1773*, vol. 1 (Madison: University of Wisconsin Press, 1986), 167–76.

46 This paragraph draws heavily on Robert Descimon's brilliant article, "L'Union au domaine royal et le principe d'inaliénabilité. La construction d'une loi fondamentale aux XVIᵉ et XVIIᵉ siècle," *Droits* 22, no. 1 (January 1995): 79–90. See also the classic article by François Olivier-Martin, "La Reunion de la Basse-Navarre à la couronne de France," *Anuario de historia de derecho español* 9 (1932): 249–89.

47 "Remonstrance prononcée le 29 juillet 1501 [sic] au Parlement lors séant à Tours, le grand Chambre et Tournelle assemblées sur le sujet des lettres patentes du 13 Avril 1590 concernant la disunion que le feu Roy Henry IIII vouloit estre de son Patrimoine, d'avec le Domaine Public et Royal[...]" in Jacques de La Guesle, *Les Remonstrances de Messire Jacques de la Guesle, procureur général du Roy* (Paris: Pierre Chevalier, 1611), 92–212. Page numbers of quotations are given in parentheses in the text.

48 Du Crest, *Modèle familial*, 74–81. Navarre was only incorporated in 1620.

49 "Edit sur la réunion à la Couronne de l'ancien patrimoine privé du Roi" (July 1607), in Isambert, Decrusy and Taillandier (eds.), *Recueil general des anciennes lois francaises depuios l'an 420 jusqu'a la Revolution de 1789*, vol. 15, no. 191 (1829): 330.

50 Belloy, *Recueil*, 55.

51 Hobbes, *Leviathan*, 135.

52 I am grateful to Tom Kaiser for sharing his insights on the question of what French kings gained from the regime of domanial inalienability. This paragraph does little more than paraphrase his reflections on this question.

53 Pierre-Paul Lemercier de la Rivière de Saint-Médard, *L'Ordre naturel et essentiel des sociétés politiques* (London: Jean Nourse, 1767), 147–48.

54 Pierre-Samuel Dupont de Nemours, *De l'origine et des progrès d'une science nouvelle* (London: Desaint, 1768), 65–66.

55 Lemercier, *L'Ordre naturel*, 43 and 148. Pierre Force (*Self-Interest*, 238–39) notes Adam Smith's distrust of politicians and deliberative bodies. The physiocrats' critique of the various forms of government is similar to that of Thomas Hobbes. See his *Leviathan*, 131.

56 Dupont de Nemours, *Progrès d'une science nouvelle*, 77.

57 Lemercier, *L'Ordre naturel*, 66 and 202.

58 John S. Bassett, ed., *Selections from the Federalist* (New York: Charles Scribner's Sons, 1921), 2701–1. Hirschman cites this document at length to demonstrate how even the early American republicans integrated the idea of using one interest to check another into their constitutional framework. However, he does not mention the temporal dimension of Hamilton's argument. Hirschman, *The Passions*, 29.

59 Adam Smith, *Lectures on Justice, Police, Revenue, and Arms*, ed. Edwin Cannan (Oxford: Clarendon Press, 1896), 253–54.

10 Self-interest, speculation, and gambling in nineteenth-century America

Cornelius Torp

In his influential monograph *The Passions and the Interests*, German-American economist Albert Hirschman makes us see the ideological and behavioral roots of capitalism in a new light. Reconstructing an important transformation of dominant economic ideas in the seventeenth and eighteenth centuries, he argues that during this period the pursuit of material self-interest—previously condemned as the sin of avarice—was increasingly assigned the role of taming the destructive passions of man.[1] Thinkers such as Steuart, Montesquieu, and Hume normatively favored self-interest as an antidote to the more unruly passions because it allegedly led to predictability and consistency of human behavior. Adam Smith was most influential in propagating the idea that the free pursuit of self-interest, "led by an invisible hand," would result in beneficial effects for society, even if the individual had no intention to promote the public interest.[2] In the nineteenth century, the idea of the superiority and the societally benevolent repercussions of self-interested behavior eventually became common currency. The construction of the acquisitive self was at the normative center of the bourgeois capitalist project and at the heart of the fundamental transformation it entailed.

Whereas the drive to make profit became the cherished core of the pursuit of self-interest in the form of legitimate economic activity, attempts to make money by gambling were castigated. At first sight, it seems paradoxical that, at the very same time that the profit motive moved center stage in the Western world, the crusade against gambling reached its apogee and resulted in the prohibition of legal gambling opportunities on a large scale. In the nineteenth century, more or less every government in Europe and North America succumbed to the growing anti-gambling pressure by prohibiting or severely restricting lotteries, casinos, and betting. This paper will argue that these two developments, even if they might appear contradictory at first glance, are in fact causally related. The strong anti-gambling discourse served as a foil for the kind of self-interest that could be considered societally acceptable in economic operations. What is more, the need to legitimize speculative financial practices by dissociating them from gambling propelled the condemnation of gambling as the counter-image of "normal" economic activity and as deviant behavior.

The conceptualization of legitimate material self-interest and its interrelation with the anti-gambling movement of the nineteenth century can best be traced by focusing on the contested gray area between "normal" economic practices and gambling. This chapter will concentrate, therefore, on the debates about the legitimacy of particular forms of speculation, which were accused repeatedly of being inseparable from pure gambling. At the same time, exploring this conflict zone makes it possible to point out that the definition of self-interest has varied historically and that the dividing line between speculation and gambling has shifted substantially. Drawing on material from nineteenth-century American history means focusing on a case in which the controversy about speculation and gambling gained considerable political importance. Similar or related discussions and conflicts, however, were simultaneously under way in Great Britain and in most of the industrially developed countries of continental Europe. In this respect, the case of the United States is treated as *pars pro toto* of a broader development which the Western world experienced in the course of the nineteenth century. The paper starts with an overview of the American anti-gambling campaign from around 1800 until the beginning of the twentieth century, its legal accomplishments, and its underlying motives. The second section turns to the growing importance of speculative practices in the first half of the nineteenth century, and asks how this development changed the definition of economic self-interest. The final section focuses on the period after 1870 when the leading institutions of speculation, such as the New York Stock Exchange or the Chicago Board of Trade, were challenged from different sides. In the ensuing debates about the legitimacy of speculation, the question of its demarcation from gambling was the most important bone of contention.

Gambling and anti-gambling trends in the nineteenth century

Both gambling and the attempts to contain it have a long pedigree in American history, reaching back far into the colonial era. In the nineteenth century, the anti-gambling movement reached a new climax and left a considerable mark in the law books. Lotteries had been extremely popular in the Thirteen American colonies and in the early times of the republic. Initially, private citizens organized lotteries to sell high-cost property and goods. By the middle of the eighteenth century, colonial authorities had been successful in taking over the control of lotteries and used them as a way to raise additional funds. Lotteries were licensed to pay for a variety of public works such as streets, canals, bridges, churches, schoolhouses, or colleges with Yale, Harvard, and Princeton among them. In 1776, the Continental Congress, with limited success, decided to set up a grand lottery to finance the Revolutionary War. In the first decades of the young republic, states and local governments were confronted with a tax system that was shaky at best and repeatedly turned to lotteries in order to acquire the money for diverse public projects. Between 1820 and 1830, however, the wind changed. Beginning in New York and the northeastern states, organized opposition appeared and started to campaign against the "vice" of lottery play. The reformers succeeded in influencing state legislation after several cases of "abuse" had popped up. Private companies (to which the organization of the lotteries for public purposes had been turned over) exploited the schemes on their own behalf or embezzled the money. By 1860, all states of the union except Kentucky and Missouri had banned lotteries.[3]

The picture is less clear-cut with regard to those games that today we would call casino games, and particularly with regard to games played with cards and dice. On the one hand, it can be argued that these games became ubiquitous wherever the white man set foot in nineteenth-century America. On the other hand, the nineteenth century was a time characterized by continuous and strengthening attempts to stamp out gambling at all levels of society. After the Louisiana Purchase, New Orleans was the gambling capital of the United States with hundreds of gambling houses in operation, even if here, too, the opponents of gambling gained the upper hand and succeeded in suppressing it temporarily. With the westward expansion of the United States, the frontier became the new hotspot for gambling, which took place in saloons and other public places largely undisturbed by the often still absent law enforcement. Gambling flourished throughout the mining frontier during the days of the Gold Rush, making San Francisco famous for its multiple gaming opportunities by the middle of the century. But even in San Francisco, the backlash set in as early as 1855, when the state legislature outlawed most forms of public gaming. In an effort to leave behind their frontier past and to reform themselves, Californians strengthened the laws against gambling several times until 1885 when all kinds of gaming were made illegal. On occasion, the fight against gambling could turn violent, as was the case in San Francisco in 1856, when a well-known gambler died at the hands of vigilantes; or in 1835, when five gamblers were lynched by an anti-gambling mob in Vicksburg, Mississippi. In the established states on the East Coast, on the contrary, gambling was already illegal at the beginning of the century. This, however, did not prevent the rise of a wide variety of gambling businesses in the big cities. In New York City, the hub of illegal gambling in the East, allegedly around six thousand gaming establishments operated by 1850. It was this widespread antagonism between the success of anti-gambling initiatives on the legislative level, and the reality of a thriving gambling business protected by corrupt politicians, judges, and police, that ran like a golden thread throughout the history of New York in the nineteenth century.[4]

What were the motives behind the fierce fight against gambling which succeeded in its—at least official—condemnation and in making the practice increasingly illegal over the course of the nineteenth century? It was less a coherent building of ideas than a layering of a couple of diverse strands of anti-gambling sentiments which stemmed from different periods of time.

It was only from about 1800 onwards that they were fully developed and intertwined, ushering in a powerful crusade against gambling. The oldest tradition of the movement against gambling was its condemnation as a sin by the Christian religion. In the Christian cosmic order there was no place for chance—everything was predetermined by God's will. Abusing divine providence to decide the distribution of profane stakes in a game, therefore, was nothing other than sacrilege. At the same time, the perceptions and practices related to gambling, ranging from the supposedly magical qualities ascribed to objects to superstitious beliefs, formed a dangerous threat to the Christian claim to sole representation in the world of sacrality and transcendence.[5]

Even more than the Catholic Church, Protestantism denounced gambling as a dangerous vice because it ran counter to the Protestant postulate of a systematic and ascetic manner of life geared toward work. This was particularly true for the United States, where Protestantism experienced its Second Awakening between 1800 and 1830. The religious revival placed the moral conduct of the individual (exercising freedom of choice and self-control) at the center of its spiritual order. The strict moral code to which evangelical believers had to adhere firmly excluded gambling. Moreover, diverse congregations taught that, in order to reach salvation, evangelical converts not only had to avoid sinful activities themselves, but also contribute to the purification of society by eradicating vice in all its forms. Accordingly, Protestant activism loomed large among the abolitionists, but also played an important role in the growing antivice movement, which targeted alcohol as well as prostitution, drugs, and gambling.[6]

The second layer of ideas on which the anti-gambling movement could build was Enlightenment rationalism. To be sure, leading mathematicians of the Enlightenment era were fascinated by games of chance and used them to develop the foundations of probability theory and statistics. The ultimate aim of probabilistic thought, however, as Ian Hacking has shown, was "The Taming of Chance."[7] Mathematicians aspired to demystify randomness and to prove that everything was determined by eternal laws of nature. Deeply convinced of a deterministic conception of the world, they believed uncertainty to be a quality not of reality but of consciousness, less an ontological than an epistemological category. Far from the existential uncertainty that confronted gamblers when they played, probability theory's "law of large numbers" tended to rein in randomness and could be used to demonstrate that they could only lose in the long run.[8] Against this backdrop of Enlightenment rationalism, the gambler was the embodiment of irrationality. By gambling, he made a choice which no sensible individual could make: Chasing after an experience of contingency, he deliberately abandoned the very quality that defined him as a human being: reason. "The essence of gambling consists in an abandonment of reason, an inhibition of the factors of human control," as the British economist and gambling opponent John A. Hobson summed it up. At the same time, the gambler denied the success of the process of civilization as rational control over brutish instincts and wild emotions, which constituted the difference between civilized humans and savages: "The practice of gambling is thus exhibited as a deliberate reversion to those passions and that mental attitude which characterise the savage or pre-human man in his conduct and his outlook."[9]

Closely connected with these two clusters of ideas, the model of the "bourgeois working subject"—a notion the sociologist Andreas Reckwitz has recently coined—was the third important motive behind the anti-gambling movement. Having evolved in the seventeenth and eighteenth centuries and reaching a hegemonic position in North America and in European societies alike, the ideal of the bourgeois working subject combined the orientation toward an autonomous and purposeful economic activity with the norm of a disciplined and moderate conduct of life. Within bourgeois culture, work was considered to be the "place of the moral formation of the subject as a modest, moderate, and disciplined one."[10] At the same time, the bourgeois work ethic sharply distanced itself from all forms of behavior that violated the norms of purposefulness and sobriety and that raised the suspicion of being excessive and undisciplined. This, together with a prodigal life-style and idleness, placed gambling at the very center of bourgeois critique. Gamblers not only lacked the necessary seriousness of conduct; they also wasted two precious resources, the purposeful use of which was considered to be crucial for the bourgeois working subject. First, gambling meant a waste, or as Reverend Eli Hyde from New York put it in 1812, a "sinful mispense," of time—time which should have been spent on disciplined work and the pursuit of professional objectives.[11] The second central resource of capitalism the gambler sinned against was money. The illegal lotteries in New York, for instance, "absorb[ed] a vast capital," Edmund Crapsey contended in his 1872 survey of crime and vice in the City. By frittering away their money, gamblers not only took "bread from the mouths of hungry children," but they also withdrew it from "productive industry."[12]

Located at the intersection of evangelical revival, Enlightenment rationalism, and the ascent of bourgeois capitalism, these three discourses of the moral condemnation of gambling were fully developed at the beginning of the nineteenth century and ushered in a tide of anti-gambling pamphlets, the tenor of which was that one could hardly "conceive any vice more hateful than Gambling because none can be conceived more diametrically opposite to the very end of our creation!"[13] Closely related to these ideas, but unfolding only gradually over the course of the nineteenth century (partly as a result of the social reform movement), a fourth and last motive for opposition to gambling focused particularly on its social consequences. The urban working classes were at the core of this line of argument. Gambling, its critics claimed, had the potential to ruin not only individual gamblers, but also their whole families. It "beggar[ed] the rich and convert[ed] poverty into pauperism."[14] Together with alcohol it was a hotbed of criminality and "the inspirer of countless forgeries and embezzlements."[15]

There were even bigger issues at stake here. According to Anthony Comstock, the founder of the New York Society for the Suppression of Vice, gambling was a threat to virility. "The wild excitement" provoked by gambling, he stated, resulted in a total loss of self-discipline and thus would "unman" the gambler.[16] Ultimately, the manhood and the strength of the nation were in danger. "The vice of gaming," reformed gambler and Chicago anti-gambling activist John Philip Quinn stated, was a "viper which has buried its fangs deep in the very vitals of the body politic." "A nation of gamblers," he was sure, was "a nation whose course is already turned towards the setting sun."[17] Not only in nineteenth-century America, but also in Europe and in other parts of the world such as in Siam (Thailand), reformers campaigned against gambling as irreconcilable with civilization per se. As a consequence, the crusade against gambling became a part of the Western civilizing mission—aiming at uplifting the working classes, the uncultivated American West, and the "savages" all around the globe.[18]

The rise of speculation

Stemming originally from a philosophical background, the term "speculation" acquired a financial meaning only in the late eighteenth century. In *Wealth of Nations*, published in 1776, Adam Smith referred to the "[s]udden fortunes" which were "sometimes made [...] by what is called the trade of speculation." For him, however, the "speculative merchant" was a "bold adventurer" who "may sometimes acquire a considerable fortune by two or three successful speculations, but is just as likely to lose one by two or three unsuccessful ones."[19] The speculator, thus, was the antipode to Smith's cherished capitalist figure, the manufacturer. Whereas the latter was innovative, skilled, and the embodiment of a long-term-oriented self-interest working toward the good of society, the former was a rootless capitalist mercenary without intimate knowledge of a particular business, transforming "self-interest into selfishness."[20] For Smith as well as for his contemporaries, the difference between speculation and gambling was barely discernible. In many cases, it was the same traders who sold lottery tickets and shares.[21] Both the London and the New York Stock Exchanges grew out of coffee houses where trading in securities and gambling with dice and cards took place at the same time.[22] Around 1800, the numerous speculative crises of the eighteenth century—from the Mississippi and South Sea Bubbles at its beginning to the financial crisis of 1791–92 and the panic of 1796–97—still haunted public memory and seemed to underline the haphazard nature of financial markets and the gambler-like attitude of their participants. Accordingly, a common critique of speculation was that it was simply gambling by another name. Among many others, clergyman and social reformer Henry Ward Beecher in 1844 strongly believed that:

A Speculator on the exchange, and a Gambler at his table, follow one vocation, only with different instruments. One employs cards or dice, the other property. The one can no more foresee the result of his schemes, than the other what spots will come up on his dice; the calculations of both are only the chances of luck. [...] both depend more upon fortune than skill; they have a common distaste for labor.[23]

Despite their bad reputation, speculative practices expanded rapidly in antebellum America. Visitors from Europe repeatedly highlighted the ubiquity of speculation which they encountered during their travels in the United States and which was unfamiliar to them from their home countries. "Every body is speculating," French economist and politician Michel Chevalier noted with wonder in 1835, "and every thing has become an object of speculation. The most daring enterprises find encouragement; all projects find subscribers."[24] The prime object of speculation in the early republic was real estate. With the frontier moving west, millions of acres of new land were sold at auction and then often transferred several times.[25] Noah J. Major, an early settler from Morgan County, Indiana, tried to portray the spirit of the first decades of the nineteenth century when he wrote: "The love of speculation seems inherent in the minds of men, and there has been no greater field for its operation than land sales in new districts and in and about towns and cities."[26] Land as the primary commodity of speculation was soon accompanied by government debt securities. Within a few years, a lively market for shares in private business corporations developed. People started trading in diverse types of derivatives. As early as 1812, the trading in options on government bonds and shares of banks and other companies seems to have reached such a magnitude that the authorities in New York started to legislate against it.[27] Jonathan Levy has argued convincingly that the development of new financial instruments and the speculation in them should be understood largely as an attempt to come to terms with the new risks that capitalism brought about.[28] The development of an entire continent, the building of a transcontinental railroad network, the production for an expanding national and global market—all these entailed investments and risks which the traditional social safety nets such as family, friends, or the local context increasingly were not able to shoulder. Corporate stocks, railroad bonds, options, but also insurance—all were responses to the new challenges and shared a capitalist approach to risk: they commodified it. Functioning as instruments of risk management, they simultaneously made up the elements of a new financial reality which created its own forms of radical uncertainty and insecurity.

The rise of speculation in antebellum America was accompanied by diverse attempts at legitimizing it as a normal business activity and at differentiating it from gambling. One important line of argument centered around the liberal idea of self-ownership and linked it to the acceptance of risks. "A man has the right to risk his own capital," stated Edwin T. Freedley in 1853 in his widely read *Practical Treatise on Business*. The taking of risks and even "great risk[s]" from this perspective was considered to be a facet of self-ownership and rightfully rewarded with financial "gain." What set speculation apart from gambling was "study and calculation," the self-discipline of the speculator paired with "judgment."[29] Even Freedley himself, however, had to admit that success in speculation had a lot to do with luck and that for the outside observer it had "all the risk of lottery dealing."[30] A second line of defense, which stressed the commonality of all business operations, met the same problem of the insufficient dissociation of speculation from gambling. Apologists of speculation argued that risk was an inherent part of all economic transactions and that thus trade, investment, and speculation were closely related. "In the first place," as Thomas Corbet summed it up in 1841, "trade and speculation seem to be, to a certain extent or in a certain manner, unavoidably connected."[31] This position, however, ran the risk of inviting very general critiques of commercial life in which more or less all economic activities became tainted by the suspicion of resembling gambling. Already in 1815, "A Republican" in Portland argued along these lines:

> Merchandize, insurance, and gambling, are intoxicating in proportion as they depend more or less on *chance* [...] A *merchant* is in some sense a *gambler*—If his chance be unfortunate he will speculate again, hoping that his "luck will turn!" If fortunate, he will double that hazard, that he may double the profits. In this way, the passion for speculation becomes unconquerable and absorbs every correct and virtuous principle.[32]

A demarcation line between speculation and gambling, therefore, could only be drawn in other ways. Very much in line with the re-evaluation of self-interest in the eighteenth century, proponents of speculation highlighted its positive effects on the public good which were, in this view, absent in the case of gambling. In particular, there were two outcomes of speculation that were considered beneficial for the economy and the country. First, speculation helped to provide the American economy with the vast amount of capital required for the development of its infrastructure and the expansion of its production capacities. Michel Chevalier, who was more than skeptical regarding the consequences of speculation in France, cherished its impact on the United States:

> In the midst of all this speculation, whilst some enrich and some ruin themselves, banks spring up and diffuse credit, railroads and canals extend themselves over the country, steamboats are launched into the rivers, the lakes, and the sea [...] Some individuals lose, but the country is a gainer; the country is peopled, cleared, cultivated; its resources are unfolded, its wealth increased.[33]

Second, an increasing number of economists argued that speculation stabilized prices over time. Since "[s]peculation is [...] really only another name for foresight," as J. R. McCulloch put it, and speculators were experts in the anticipation of future events, they smoothed the fluctuation of prices by buying when they thought that prices were low and selling when they were high.[34] This had not only the "effect of limiting the vibrations of price within narrower extremes," but also served "to distribute over a certain period the actual supply of any article in the most advantageous manner, without any counterbalancing public disadvantage."[35]

Over the course of the first decades of the nineteenth century, the rise of speculation in the United States increasingly was accompanied by its emancipation from gambling and its slowly growing acceptance as a regular business activity. This tendency can be corroborated by a change in jurisdiction. At the end of the eighteenth century, American courts had still tended to enforce wagers on the outcome of horse races, whereas they had repeatedly ruled against plaintiffs who tried to sue for the debts resulting from commercial contracts involving a certain amount of speculation, such as on the future development of prices or currencies. Fifty years later, it was the other way around. Now, numerous laws against gambling were in place and judges annulled contracts they assumed to be wagers. Commercial transactions with a speculative content, on the contrary, were regularly enforced.[36]

Drawing a line between gambling and speculation in the struggles at the end of the "long" nineteenth century

At the end of the nineteenth century, just when speculation was becoming widely accepted as a regular business activity quite different from gambling, its reputation was challenged once again. The background of this development was the massive expansion of the organized trade in stock options and particularly in commodity futures in the decades after the Civil War. The growth of futures speculation itself was the result of tremendous changes in the trade in wheat and other agricultural products which took place after 1850, when such trade became increasingly global in scope. As late as the 1840s, the Midwest farmer or the local merchant had sacked up the grain and shipped it down the river to St. Louis or Chicago, where it was sold to the miller who had inspected the individual quality of the bagged product beforehand. Thus, the price of grain as a commodity still depended on its individual qualities as a physical object which could be traced back from the mill to the original producer. Only a few years later all this had changed. From around 1850 onward, the rapid expansion of the US railroad system revolutionized the grain trade. Train after train now unloaded its freight in Chicago, which increasingly outranked its competitors as the most important hub for agricultural trade. Here, the grain was sucked into one of the huge grain elevators—gigantic warehouses fed by steam-powered conveyor belts. After having been resold, the grain left the storehouses by ship and went to one of the big cities on the American East Coast. The tremendous economies of scale which were brought about by this handling of grain, however, could be realized only if the grain arrived not in sacks but in train loads, and if diverse batches from different producers were allowed to be mixed in the grain elevator. Inevitably, this undermined the emphasis that the traditional grain trade put on the identity of the individual product. The Chicago Board of Trade overcame the problems this posed by introducing a grading system for splitting grain into standardized quality classes and by implementing a corresponding system of inspections.[37]

At the same time, when the standardization of trade transformed wheat and other agricultural products from concrete physical objects into abstract salable commodities, the telegraph was responsible for decoupling business transactions from geographical space. Price notations and business decisions could cross thousands of miles within minutes—first across the continent and, from the 1860s onward, increasingly worldwide. After the closing of the contract, however, the shipment of the actual commodity still took days or weeks. In the meantime, the prices for grain could change dramatically, thus constituting a considerable financial risk for both the buyer and the seller. The way out of this problem were the "to arrive" contracts which determined the delivery of a certain amount of the commodity at a fixed price by some specified date in the future. In principle, "to arrive" contracts were not new and had been in use at the Antwerp Exchange as early as the second half of the sixteenth century.[38] In the first place, they worked toward significantly reducing the financial risk for both buyers and sellers of grain. At the same time, and particularly in combination with the highly standardized commodity market in Chicago, however, they served as the starting point for a new universe of risk-taking. More and more speculators now started to bet on future price movements without any goods being delivered. In most cases traders in forward contracts, or "futures," as they were called, closed their transactions simply by "setting off" the price difference between the commodity's contracted price and its actual market price in the pit.[39] According to the historian Morton Rothstein, cynical contemporaries considered futures markets to be places where "men who don't own something are selling that something to men who don't really want it."[40] From the Civil War onwards, futures trading at the Chicago Board of Trade and other commodity exchanges exploded. It did not take long before the amount of futures trading by far surpassed the trade in actual commodities. At the end of the 1880s, the dollar value of futures contracts traded at the major produce exchanges was regularly estimated to exceed the value of spot sales of actual grain by a factor of twenty.[41]

The massive increase in futures trading became a prominent target of agrarian critique when the prices for wheat and other crops started their long-term decline at the end of the 1880s. The sharp drop in prices was the result of the increasing supply of agricultural commodities on the world market, which was not met by a similar rise in demand. At the same time,

American farmers had to endure an inexorable loss in economic and societal importance compared with the booming industrial and urban areas. Confronted with falling prices and a considerable loss of income, however, the farmers did not blame the anonymous forces of the global market but rather the speculators at the Chicago Board of Trade, the New York Produce Exchange, and similar exchanges in other cities. Above all, the farmers contended, the practice of short selling (i.e. selling commodities for future delivery without owning them yet) was responsible for the depression in prices. Short sellers, they argued, used "all their force and power [...] to put prices down, because they make money by it."[42] Since the late 1880s, the agrarian protest movement—which even led to the foundation of a third political party, the People's (or Populist) Party, in 1892—vigorously campaigned against futures speculation. One of the main points of criticism the agrarians always raised when they tried to counter speculation was that futures trading was no more than a "monstrous gambling game between 'bulls' and 'bears.'" The "gigantic gambling device known as short-selling," they argued in one petition after another, "has been a potent cause in producing the ruinous agricultural depression from which the country has suffered."[43]

In 1892, the farmers' interest groups came extremely close to banning speculation in agricultural products by federal legislation. In preparation for the so-called Hatch Anti-Option Bill (intended to levy a prohibitive tax on futures dealings, and named after the chairman of the House Committee on Agriculture), hearings on the "Ficticious Dealing in Agricultural Products" were held. For the opponents of futures trading, they served as a welcome opportunity to put forward their accusations. Again and again, the farmers' witnesses stressed that speculation in futures was "gambling pure and simple, and the sense of all civilized communities is that gambling is wrong, and is justly the object of restraint by legislators."[44] By semantically blurring the distinction between gambling and speculation, the farmers' representatives intended fundamentally to discredit speculation as a regular economic activity. "Gambling in futures is wrong from every standpoint," a supporter of the bill stated; it "appeals to the cupidity and gambling propensity of the masses, ignores the law of nature in its effort to get a fortune without work [...] and under the guise of business assists and gives countenance to gambling which should be stopped."[45] In 1892, in the light of the looming elections and the additional importance the agrarian cause gained due to the initial success of the People's Party, a national ban on futures trading seemed, for the first and only time, to be within reach. The Hatch Bill passed both the House and the Senate with overwhelming majorities. It failed to become law only because the House minority was able to stall it until the end of the session. Repeated later attempts to prohibit futures dealing suffered a similar fate.[46]

The agrarian countermovement, however, was not the only challenge which endangered the still fragile status of financial speculation as a regular business activity in late nineteenth-century America. The second and equally important threat came from the growing importance of bucket shops. Bucket shops were establishments where small speculators who did not have access to the regular exchanges, or shunned them for other reasons, could wager money on the price movement of stocks or commodities.[47] In its outer appearance, a bucket shop completely resembled a broker's office. Its central element was the ticker which telegraphically received price quotations, which then were posted on huge blackboards. In honest bucket shops, the prices came "directly from the Stock Exchange ticker"; in less reputable outfits, the wire went nowhere and the quotations were a sham.[48] The major difference between a regular broker and a bucket shop was that the broker acted as the client's agent in buying or selling stocks or commodities on the floor of the exchanges, whereas the bucket shop proprietor took "one side of every deal that is made in his place, the patron taking the other, no article being bought or sold in any public market."[49] Consequently, bucket shop transactions had no effect on the market prices of stocks or agricultural products. The orders placed by brokers, on the contrary, formed the raw material for the process in which the prices were set by the interplay of supply and demand. All bucket shop transactions were margin deals for which the buyers had to deposit only a minor fraction of the prices posted for stocks or commodities. The margins, however, were much lower (usually in the range of 3 percent) than at the legitimate exchanges (normally 10 percent) and the required lot sizes were smaller. Thus, the bucket shops attracted an audience which wanted to speculate but did not have the opportunity to do it through brokers owing to insufficient financial means or because they were discriminated against for other reasons, e.g. they were women. When the bucket shops started to spread in the late 1870s, they were sometimes considered to be "a sort of democratized Board of Trade, where the common people could speculate without the intervention of brokers and where a large capital was not necessary for the making of a fortune."[50]

Within only a few years, however, the number of bucket shops increased tremendously; in 1889, it was estimated that five thousand of them existed all over the country. At the same time, they increasingly developed into an alternative market for speculation, where even speculators who formerly had been catered to by regular brokers placed their orders. This development posed a two-fold threat to the legitimate stock and produce exchanges. On the one hand, the bucket shops had become dangerous competitors which drew a considerable amount of business away from the exchanges. By 1889, the competition of the bucket shops "had pushed down the value of membership in the [New York] Stock Exchange from $34,000 to $18,000."[51] On the other hand, the business practices of the bucket shops, which clearly made them recognizable as places of wagering, and the multiple scandals which surrounded them, tainted the reputation of the established exchanges. This was even more the case since the public, politicians, and journalists often saw no difference between wagering on price movements in the bucket shops and options or futures trading on the floor of the exchanges. To them, there seemed to be "no legal or moral difference between ordinary Stock Exchange transactions and transactions in a bucket shop" and "the New York Stock Exchange [was] little more than a big bucket shop."[52]

Around 1880, the exchanges, led by the Chicago Board of Trade and the New York Stock exchange, started their campaign to stamp out the bucket shops, and this lasted until World War I. The exchanges fought the bucket shops on three different grounds. First, they lobbied state legislation in order to push through laws banning bucket shops on the basis that they violated the existing anti-gambling statutes. Moreover, they launched investigations into bucket shops themselves, the results of which they turned over to state prosecutors to help them with their cases. Second, the exchanges sought to stop the stream of telegraphically transmitted price quotations which was essential to the bucket shops' business model. After having tried, with limited success, to pressure the big telegraph companies to withhold the price quotations from the bucket shops, the organized exchanges began to sue their unincorporated competitors by claiming that the stock and commodity prices were their property, access to which they had the right to control.[53] Third, closely related to and in a certain sense underlying the other strategies, in a series of pamphlets and with the help of lawyers, journalists, and economists, the exchanges emphasized the fundamental difference between their own and the bucket shops' business models. Whereas the exchanges were sites of serious commerce, they contended, the bucket shop was "a gambling den, and nothing else."[54] Thus, they located themselves within the strong anti-gambling discourse of the period and made use of its arguments and images. At the same time, they took up the gambling accusations of the farmers' interest groups and redirected them against the bucket shops. By depicting the bucket shops as the *real* gambling hells, the official exchanges tried to purify themselves and to convince the public that they were nothing other than places of normal commercial activity.[55]

In their war against the bucket shops, which has attracted considerable attention in American economic history, the incorporated exchanges and their auxiliaries were successful in establishing an idea of the legitimate pursuit of self-interest, which included financial speculation and ostracized gambling as its negative foil. Predominantly, there were two lines of argument around which the concept of speculation as an honorable economic activity centered. First, the advocates of speculation employed the semantics of productionism which was dominant in nineteenth-century economic thinking. Originally, the farmers had accused the exchanges of producing nothing except "wind wheat" and thus contributing nothing to the national wealth.[56] The speculators now turned this idea on its head and claimed to be producers as well. But what did they produce? Organized speculation, to begin with, provided a "continuous market" for all those who wanted to buy or sell stocks or commodities. At the same time, the exchanges and most notably the trade in futures and options offered "the place where hedging in all its various forms may be best undertaken."[57] Thus, the speculative markets served as a "great system of insurance" against price variations.[58] The most important product of speculation, however, its supporters contended, was the market price itself. The organization of the official exchanges resulted in "the best price, the fairest price, and the most scientific price that human agencies [could] arrive at" because the quotations were "not a one-man affair, but the combined judgment of thousands of experts, bulls and bears, bankers and brokers, speculators and investors, all over the world, bidding and offering against each other by cable and telegraph." Moreover, the price quotations not only epitomized "the opinion of all these minds as to values to-day" but also their "critical look into the future" and therefore represented a piece of "'advance information'" which was "freely given" to all market participants.[59] According to this view, the speculators at the exchanges became knowledge producers who condensed all available economic information in the form of the market price, whereas the bucket shops were just "parasite[s]."[60] They did not contribute anything to the formation of prices but only acquired the quotations from the exchanges and abused them "as the basis of the bets made in their shops."[61]

Second, the defenders of speculation made claims about the individual character and personal qualities of speculators in order to separate them from the gamblers in the bucket shops. The "Committee on Speculation in Securities and Commodities," appointed by New York governor Charles Evans Hughes after the financial crisis of 1907, arrived at the conclusion that "a real distinction exists between speculation which is carried on by persons of means and experience, and based on an intelligent forecast, and that which is carried on by persons without these qualifications."[62] In the numerous interventions by the supporters of speculation, it was the *Homo Oeconomicus* who was at the core of the model of the honorable speculator and its definition of legitimate, self-interested behavior. The speculator was supposed to be the embodiment of competence, rationality, and self-discipline. The economist Henry Crosby Emery asserted:

> Only those men who have great experience, wide knowledge and the most improved means of obtaining information, combined with cool judgement, courage and the faculty of quick decision, are competent to forecast the course of future prices [...] And it is the great speculators who combine these qualities in the greatest degree.[63]

Hardly surprisingly, all these supreme qualities regularly went together with having command of abundant means for speculation. "The great evil of speculation," on the contrary, stockbroker W. C. van Antwerp argued, "consist[ed] in the buying of securities or real estate or anything else with borrowed money, by uninformed people who cannot afford to lose."[64] The exchanges did not conceal the fact that they themselves had had to fight overspeculation, price manipulation, and other "excesses."[65] But this had been in the past—"[t]he Exchange purified itself long ago of the old abuses" and met "new ones as they occurr[ed] [...] with severe disciplinary measures," the "most fruitful policy" comprising "measures which will lessen speculation by persons not qualified to engage in it."[66] The bucket shops, in contrast, did not have any intention to educate or discipline their clients, but simply thrived on attracting the "numberless small speculators, who are the social curse."[67] According to the advocates of speculation there could not be a bigger difference than that between the rational and well-informed speculator on the one hand, and the bucket shop gambler on the other, who only tried his luck and was after getting "something for nothing."[68]

In their battle against the bucket shops, the exchanges reached a landmark victory when the US Supreme Court in 1905 ruled in favor of the Chicago Board of Trade and against the Christie Grain & Stock Company, run by the so-called bucket shop king, C. C. Christie of Kansas City. The importance of the Supreme Court decision did not lie in immediately making the operation of the bucket shops illegal, but in the fact that it declared the price quotations to be the exchanges' property and thus gave them an instrument to deprive the bucket shops of their lifeblood over the following years. At the same time, the majority opinion of the court, which was delivered by Justice Oliver Wendell Holmes, clearly indicated that the idea of speculation as a legitimate economic activity strictly separated from gambling now had been widely accepted and gained the blessing of the highest US court. "Speculation of this kind by competent men is the self-adjustment of society to the probable," Justice Holmes reasoned. "Its value is well known as a means of avoiding or mitigating catastrophes, equalizing prices, and providing for periods of want." Far from being gamblers, the speculators at the exchanges were considered serious businessmen and producers. Their product, "the quotations of prices from the market," was "of the utmost importance to the business world." Consequently, the exchanges' price quotations were "entitled to the protection of the law" and were their exclusive property.[69]

Conclusion

With the rise of industrial capitalism in the nineteenth century, the idea that the pursuit of material self-interest was not only legitimate but perfectly compatible with public welfare became part and parcel of the dominant bourgeois ideology. What kind of self-interested behavior was acceptable, though, and when did it start to transgress the boundaries of the prevailing normative system and to endanger the very foundations of society?

In nineteenth-century America, the definition of legitimate material self-interest was neither stable nor uncontested. In the debate over the legitimacy of financial speculation and its relation to gambling, we can trace both the shifting boundaries and the constructivist character of what constituted a "normal" economic activity. The long-lasting struggle over the role of financial speculation can only be understood against the backdrop of the crusade against gambling which became a powerful trend in nineteenth-century American and global history alike. The anti-gambling movement was rooted in the evangelical revival, Enlightenment rationalism, the bourgeois work ethic and ideas of social reform, all emphasizing norms of discipline, temperance, and merit. Like most other countries, the United States reacted to the anti-gambling pressure by prohibiting or severely restricting lotteries, betting, and other games of chance.

Around 1800, for most contemporaries, speculation was hardly separable from gambling, both sharing the same bad moral reputation. Nevertheless, speculative practices increased massively in antebellum America owing to the rapid capitalist development of the country. The rise of speculation went hand-in-hand with its growing acceptance as a regular business activity. More and more people became convinced of its beneficial effects and saw it as distinct from ordinary gambling. This emancipation of speculation from gambling, however, was challenged again in the last decades of the nineteenth century. In the meantime, speculation in stocks and commodities, in options and futures had increased tremendously. Often, speculators made use of financial instruments, which had been developed originally in order to contain the new risks of rapidly changing market conditions. In the context of the surge of futures trading, the farmers' interest groups now accused the commodity exchanges of hosting reckless gamblers who were responsible for the downward trend of agricultural prices since the 1880s. At the same time, the spread of bucket shops not only entailed dangerous competition for the incorporated exchanges; it also invited the pointing out of the parallels between speculation at the exchanges and wagering in the bucket shops. In their defense on two fronts, the exchanges and their political and academic supporters were able to use bucket shops as a negative foil against which they could establish an idea of speculation which was based on a double demarcation from gambling. On the one hand, connecting to the ideology of productionism of the time, speculators were represented as producers of important economic knowledge in the form of prices. On the other hand, speculators—with their qualities of rationality, competence, self-discipline, and virility—were contrasted with irrational and emotional gamblers. Since the nineteenth century, the question of what is accepted as the legitimate pursuit of material self-interest has been decided by the discursive separation of the most innovative forms of financial speculation from gambling. The demarcation line between speculation and gambling, however, always has been precarious and will remain a matter of negotiation.

Notes

1 Albert O. Hirschman, *The Passions and the Interests: Political Arguments for Capitalism before Its Triumph* (Princeton: Princeton University Press, 1977).

2 Adam Smith, *An Inquiry into the Nature and Causes of the Wealth of Nations* (1776; repr. Petersfield: Harriman House, 2007), 293.

3 See David G. Schwartz, *Roll the Bones: A History of Gambling* (New York: Gotham Books, 2006), 143–52; John M. Findlay, *People of Chance: Gambling in American Society from Jamestown to Las Vegas* (London/New York: Oxford University Press, 1986), 31–34 and 40–42; John S. Ezell, *Fortune's Merry Wheel: The Lottery in America* (Cambridge, MA: Harvard University Press, 1960), 204–29.

4 Ann Fabian, *Card Sharps and Bucket Shops: Gambling in Nineteenth-Century America* (New York: Routledge, 1999), 31–53; Findlay, *People of Chance*, 95–100; Schwartz, *Roll the Bones*, 269–91.

5 See Gerda Reith, *The Age of Chance: Gambling in Western Culture* (London: Routledge, 1999), 156–81; Per Binde, "Gambling and Religion: Histories of Concord and Conflict," *Journal of Gambling Issues* 20 (2007): 145–65, here: 156.

6 See Jackson Lears, *Something for Nothing: Luck in America* (New York: Viking, 2003), 59–62; Elizabeth J. Clapp and Julie R. Jeffrey, eds., *Women, Dissent and Anti-slavery in Britain and America, 1790–1865* (Oxford: Oxford University Press, 2011); Nathan Hatch, *The Democratization of American Christianity, 1800–1860* (New Haven: Yale University Press, 1989).

7 Ian Hacking, *The Taming of Chance* (Cambridge: Cambridge University Press, 1990).

8 See Reith, *Age of Chance*, 24–33; Hacking, *Taming of Chance*, 1–15; Gerd Gigerenzer et al., *The Empire of Chance: How Probability Changed Science and Everyday Life* (Cambridge: Cambridge University Press, 1989), 1–36; Julia Jordan, *Chance and the Modern British Novel: From Henry Green to Iris Murdoch* (London: Continuum, 2010), 10–15; Thomas M. Kavanagh, *Enlightenment and the Shadows of Chance: The Novel and the Culture of Gambling in Eighteenth-century France* (Baltimore: Johns Hopkins University Press, 1993).

9 John A. Hobson, "The Ethics of Gambling," in: *Betting and Gambling. A National Evil*, ed. Benjamin Seebohm Rowntree (London: Macmillan, 1905), 1–20, here: 5–6.

10 Andreas Reckwitz, *Das hybride Subjekt. Eine Theorie der Subjektkulturen von der bürgerlichen Moderne zur Postmoderne*, 2nd ed. (Stuttgart: Velbrück Wissenschaft, 2012), 126.

11 A. M. Eli Hyde, *A Sermon; in which the Doctrine of the Lot is Stated, and Applied to Lotteries, Gambling, and Card-playing, for Amusement* (Oxford: John B. Johnson, 1812), 16.

12 Edmund Crapsey, *The Nether Side of New York or, the Vice, Crime and Poverty of the Great Metropolis* (New York: Sheldon & Company, 1872), 108.

13 Mason L. Weems, *Anecdotes of Gamblers, Extracted from a Work on Gamblers* (Philadelphia: Benjamin and Thoas Kite, 1816), 2.

14 Crapsey, *Nether Side*, 108.

15 Colonel Howard Vincent, quoted by John Hawke, "Our Principles and Programme," *The New Review* 10 (1894): 705–17, here: 711.

16 Anthony Comstock, *Traps for the Young*, 4th ed. (New York: Funk & Wagnalls Company, 1883), 126. Cf. Lears, *Something*, 170.

17 John P. Quinn, *Fools of Fortune* (Chicago: G. L. Howe, 1890), 190, 214.

18 See Cornelius Torp, "Glücksspiel und Zivilisierungsmission. Globalgeschichtliche Perspektiven auf das 19. Jahrhundert," *Geschichte und Gesellschaft* 43 (2017): 526–56.

19 Smith, *Wealth of Nations*, 74.
20 Alex Preda, *Framing Finance: The Boundaries of Markets and Modern Capitalism* (Chicago: University of Chicago Press, 2009), 33. Cf. Alex Preda, "The Investor as a Cultural Figure of Global Capitalism," in *The Sociology of Financial Markets*, ed. Karin Knorr-Cetina and Alex Preda (Oxford: Oxford University Press, 2005), 141–62.
21 David Miers and David Dixon, "National Bet: The Re-Emergence of Public Lottery," *Public Law* (1979): 372–403, here: 379.
22 See Stuart Banner, "The Origin of the New York Stock Exchange," *The Journal of Legal Studies* 27 (1998): 113–40, here: 114.
23 Henry W. Beecher, *Seven Lectures to Young Men, on Various Important Subjects* (Indianapolis: Thomas B. Cutler, 1844), 53. For an extensive analysis of the critique of speculation see Stuart Banner, Speculation. *A History of the Fine Line between Gambling and Investing* (Oxford: Oxford University Press, 2017), 14–27.
24 Michel Chevalier, "Society, Manners and Politics in the United States: Being a Series of Letters on North America [1839]," 305 (The Online Library of Liberty: https://oll.libertyfund.org/titles/chevalier-society-manners-and-politics-in-the-united-states).
25 See William J. Rohrbough, *The Land Office Business: The Settlement and Administration of American Public Lands, 1789–1837* (New York: Oxford University Press, 1968).
26 Logan Esarey, ed., *The Pioneers of Morgan County. Memoirs of Noah J. Major* (Indianapolis: Edward J. Hecker, 1915), 233.
27 T. Henry Dewey, *A Treatise on Contracts for Future Delivery and Commercial Wagers, including "Options", "Futures", and "Short Sales"* (New York: Bakers, Voorhis, 1886), 18.
28 Jonathan Levy, *Freaks of Fortune: The Emerging World of Capitalism and Risk in America* (Cambridge, MA: Harvard University Press, 2012).
29 Edwin T. Freedley, *A Practical Treatise on Business: Or How to Get, Save, Spend, Give, Lend and Bequeath: with an Inquiry into the Chances of Success and Causes of Failure in Business* (Chicago: D. B. Cooke, 1853), 109, 171, 167, 166. Cf. Levy, *Freaks*, 1–20.
30 Freedley, *Practical Treatise*, 167.
31 Thomas Corbet, *An Inquiry into the Causes and Modes of the Wealth of Individuals; or the Principles of Trade and Speculation Explained* (London: Smith, Elder, 1841), 159.
32 *The Eastern Argus*, December 5, 1815.
33 Chevalier, *Society*, 309. For the difference between France and the United States, cf. ibid., 166.
34 John R. McCulloch, *Principles of Political Economy*, 5th ed. (Edinburgh: Adam & Charles Black, 1864), 259.
35 Willard Phillips, *A Manual of Political Economy* (Boston: Hilliard, Gray, Little, & Wilkins, 1828), 50; Henry Vethake, *The Principles of Political Economy* (Philadelphia: Nicklin & Johnson, 1838), 233. Cf. Banner, *Speculation*, 35–40.
36 See Banner, *Speculation*, ibid., 40–55.
37 For this paragraph and the next one see William Cronon, *Nature's Metropolis: Chicago and the Great West* (New York: W. W. Norton, 1991), 97–147.
38 See Geoffrey Poitras, "The Early History of Option Contracts," in *Vinzenz Bronzin's Option Pricing Models: Exposition and Appraisal*, ed. Wolfgang Hafner and Heinz Zimmermann (Berlin: Springer, 2009), 487–528, here: 491.
39 See Jonathan I. Levy, "Contemplating Delivery: Futures Trading and the Problem of Commodity Exchange in the United States, 1875–1905," *American Historical Review* 111 (2006): 307–35, here: 311–12.

40 Morton Rothstein, "Frank Norris and Popular Perspectives of the Market," *Agricultural History* 56 (1982): 50–66, here: 58.
41 Cronon, *Nature's Metropolis*, 126; Levy, *Freaks*, 232–33; *Ficticious Dealing in Agricultural Products. Testimony Taken before the Committee on Agriculture during a Consideration of Bills Nos. 392, 2699, and 3870, Ristricting and Taxing Dealers in "Futures" and "Options" in Agricultural Products, and for other Purposes* (Washington: Government Printing Office, 1892), 10–12.
42 Statement of Mr. J. H. Brigham, Master of the National Grange, in: *Ficticious Dealing*, 261.
43 *Congressional Record: Containing the Proceedings and Debates of the 51st Congress, Second Session*, vol. 22 (Washington: Government Printing Office, 1891), 664–65.
44 Letter from David H. Gile, in: *Ficticious Dealing*, 322.
45 Letter from T. F. Brooks, in: *Ficticious Dealing*, 312.
46 Cedric B. Cowing, *Populists, Plungers, and Progressives. A Social History of Stock Commodity Speculation 1890–1936* (Princeton: Princeton University Press, 1965), 21–24; Banner, *Speculation*, 109–11.
47 The term "bucket shop" allegedly originated in early nineteenth-century England, where it referred to the places where poor boys came together to drink the beer which they previously had collected in buckets after it had been discarded by larger bars. Cf. John Hill, *Gold Bricks of Speculation: A Study of Speculation and Its Counterfeits, an Exposé of the Methods of Bucketshop and "Get-Rich-Quick" Swindles* (Chicago: Lincoln Book Concern, 1904), 39.
48 "The Bucket-Shop Curse," *New York Times*, June 7, 1892.
49 Hill, *Gold Bricks*, 38.
50 Charles H. Taylor, ed., *History of the Board of Trade of the City of Chicago*, vol. 1 (Chicago: Robert O. Law Company, 1917), 585.
51 "All Tickers Ordered Out. The Stock Exchange War on Bucket Shops," *New York Times*, June 1, 1891.
52 "As to the Bucket Shops," *New York Times*, November 1, 1887.
53 Cf. David Hochfelder, "'Where the Common People Could Speculate': The Ticker, Bucket Shops, and the Origins of Popular Participation in Financial Markets, 1880–1920," *Journal of American History* 93 (2006): 335–58, here: 354–55; Banner, *Speculation*, 98–104.
54 Hill, *Gold Bricks*, 20.
55 Fabian, *Card Sharps*, 188–202; Marieke de Goede, *Virtue, Fortune, and Faith: A Genealogy of Finance* (Minneapolis: University of Minnesota Press, 2005), 68–85.
56 Statement of Mr. J. H. Brigham, Master of the National Grange, in: *Ficticious Dealing*, 261.
57 Harrison H. Brace, *The Value of Organized Speculation* (Boston: The Riverside Press Cambridge, 1913), 178–79.
58 *House of Representatives, Hearings before the Committee on Agriculture during the Second Session of the Sixty-first Congress*, vol. I (Washington: Government Printing Office, 1910), 438.
59 W. C. van Antwerp, *The Stock Exchange from Within* (New York: Doubleday, Page, 1913), 10, 23.
60 W. T. Otis to Hon. Scott Ferris, March 30, 1908, *Congressional Record, Containing the Proceedings and Debates of the Sixty-first Congress, Second Session*, vol. 45 (Washington: Government Printing Office, 1910), 458.
61 Hill, *Gold Bricks*, 21. For this paragraph see Fabian, *Card Sharps*, 196–200; Urs Stäheli, *Spektakuläre Spekulation: Das Populäre der Ökonomie* (Frankfurt: Suhrkamp, 2007), 76–79.

62 *Report of Governor Hughes' Committee on Speculation in Securities and Commodities,* June 7, 1909, 4.
63 Henry C. Emery, "Legislation against Futures," *Political Science Quarterly* 10 (1895): 62–86, here: 79. Cf. also Henry C. Emery, *Speculation on the Stock and Produce Exchanges of the United States* (New York, 1896).
64 Van Antwerp, *Stock Exchange,* 50.
65 Regarding this paragraph and particularly the problem of "excess," see de Goede, *Virtue,* 75–81. Cf. also Fabian, *Card Sharps;* Stäheli, *Spektakuläre Spekulation.*
66 Van Antwerp, *Stock Exchange,* 65; *Report of Hughes' Committee,* 4.
67 Emery, "Legislation," 85.
68 Brace, *Value,* 198.
69 United States Supreme Court, 198 U.S. 236, Board of Trade of the City of Chicago v. Christie Grain Stock Company (1905). Cf. Levy, *Freaks,* 234–63; Banner, *Speculation,* 102–4.

11 Against self-interest

The codification of "disinterestedness" as an axiological operator in religion, aesthetics, and the ethics of intellectual professions[1]

Gisèle Sapiro

The concept of interest became widespread during the seventeenth century in the thoughts of moralists, who believed they had found a means to contain the passions, or at least to channel them.[2] In politics, the concept had been used in handbooks of advice to princes since Henri, duc de Rohan's *De l'intérêt des princes et états de la chrétienté*, published in 1634, which was well received in Britain.[3] It was extended from princes to, on the one hand, the court and the aristocracy's quest for prestige (by La Rochefoucauld, notably), and on the other to economic behavior (especially with Hume's reflection on promise, which in his view characterizes interested actions, and Adam Smith's paradigmatic formulation).[4]

However, just at the moment when the concept of self-interest was being adopted to explain human actions, a new moral category, that of disinterestedness, appeared. Pierre Force notes that in the first half of the seventeenth century, the word *désintéressé* is "used rather sparingly" and has "two related meanings": it is used to describe, first, someone who does not take sides in a dispute; and second, someone who is compensated or paid-off. He finds that the use of the term grew significantly in the second half of the century (there are 287 occurrences in the University of Chicago ARTFL, vs. 12 in the first half), starting with La Rochefoucauld's *Maxims*, where it means "to have motives other than self-interest." As Force puts it, "The notion of self-interest, brought forward by reason of State theory and its application to individual psychology, produces a new moral category, *désintéressé*, which is the opposite of *intéressé*."[5]

Force limits his in-depth analysis to religion and ethics. However, in the eighteenth century the concept of disinterestedness began to be claimed in other fields, moving from religion to art to literature to law. In these areas, self-interest was never recognized as a legitimate motivation of action. On the contrary, the rise of a market for symbolic goods, in Pierre Bourdieu's terms[6], and the growth of print capitalism were regarded as threats to the ethics of disinterestedness; and disinterestedness was considered essential to creative and intellectual activities. In a parallel way, modes of consumption of artistic works were hierarchized, placing what was defined as the aesthetic contemplative—or disinterested—attitude at the top. As Bourdieu argues, fields of cultural production asserted their autonomy from the market by producing an "interest in disinterestedness." [7]

This chapter will present initial hypotheses from a study on the sociogenesis, the circulation, and the social uses of the concept of disinterestedness.[8] I shall delineate a brief intellectual history of the concept of disinterestedness and of the system of oppositions in which this concept became meaningful in the eighteenth century, in order better to understand its uses as a category of ethics within the intellectual and artistic professions.[9] This concept of "disinterestedness," like that of "civilization," or later "freedom," functions as what I call an "axiological operator." Axiological operators give systems of cultural oppositions both their meaning and their position in a hierarchy of values, through spatial designators—in this case high and low—having moral connotations of worthy (*digne*) and unworthy or undignified (*indigne*).[10] The social efficacy of such operators comes from their ability symbolically to unify systems of classification or heterogeneous types of hierarchies in the order of values and institutions. Consequently, axiological operators play a major role in symbolic struggles, especially in periods of social transformation, but their own definitions and appropriation are also constantly struggled over. Interest played such a role, by designating rational action and the capacity for anticipation as opposite of passions, or the peaceful orchestration of actions against war. Other thinkers, however, counterposed to this idea motivations such as sympathy and altruism, and attitudes such as the contemplation of beauty.

The first section will examine how disinterestedness became a fundamental ethical concept identified with altruism, self-abandonment, and sacrifice as opposed to egoism, self-interest, and self-love. Introduced by La Rochefoucauld, this concept became central to the French theological "quarrel of pure love," which had echoes in Great Britain and the German-speaking areas. The second section will delineate the migration of the concept of disinterestedness from religion to aesthetics, a migration that can also be mapped from France to Great Britain to Germany. In the emerging area of aesthetics, disinterestedness was assimilated to a contemplative and distanced attitude opposed to drives (sensual pleasure), to need (utility), and to greed (the desire to possess), but also to calculation and knowledge. The values associated with the aesthetic attitude also had implications for artists' ethics in the conjuncture of the rising market for cultural goods, embodied for writers by copyright laws.[11] This matter of the ethics of the artist and the writer, which also concerned the legal profession, will be discussed in the third part. Established authors criticized the commodification of cultural products, seeing this as a threat to the disinterested motivations of authors and artists. Jean-Jacques Rousseau, however, adopted an original stance by criticizing them in turn for depending on the state and on patrons, and thus serving the latter's interests. He invented a new position, that of the independent writer, which would become a model in the nineteenth century.

By that time, the notion of disinterestedness had become primarily identified with indifference to wealth, as attested by the entry on "Désintéressement" in Denis Diderot and Jean le Rond d'Alembert's *Encyclopédie*: "*c'est cette disposition de l'âme qui nous rend insensibles aux richesses [...]*." And it is considered by the author, d'Alembert, as the first of virtues, "la première des vertus."[12] Following the restriction of the notion of interest to its rational and economic dimensions in the first half of the eighteenth century, as pointed out by Hirschman,[13] this definition of disinterestedness obscures a richer history of its usages.

(Self)-interest, self-love, and pure love

Echoes of this history can be found precisely in the *Encyclopédie* entry for "Intérêt." Interest is defined as: "this vice that makes us search for our advantages in contempt of justice and virtue, and it is a vile ambition; it's greed, the passion for money."[14] When referring to the interest of a person, a *corps*, or a nation, the word means whatever is convenient to its subject and not to others, in particular when the adjective *personnel* is added (*intérêt personnel*, or self-interest). The author of the entry, Jean-François de Saint-Lambert, criticizes the common confusion between interest and self-love, which he attributes to the French moralists of the previous century: Pierre Nicole, Blaise Pascal, and François de La Rochefoucauld.

The French moralists indeed analyzed the motivations of human actions based on the ideas of (self-)interest (*intérêt propre*) and self-love (*amour-propre*).[15] It is in this context that they introduced the concept of disinterestedness: "Interest speaks all sorts of tongues and plays all sorts of characters; even that of disinterestedness," wrote La Rochefoucauld, who also believed that: "The name of virtue is as useful to our interest as that of vice."[16] Close to the Jansenists, whom they echoed in the outside world, the moralists saw faith alone as a truly disinterested attitude. According to Antoine Arnauld, God wants to be loved in a disinterested manner; consequently, Arnauld criticized Nicolas Malebranche's interpretation of the Augustinian theory of pleasure in *De la Recherche de la vérité*: pleasure, according to him, is always the foundation of the quest for happiness.[17]

Although he formally combated the Jansenists, François Fénelon also regarded the love of God as the purest and most disinterested love. However, he believed that even religious faith's motivation may be interested: to believe in God out of fear of sanctions, hope for salvation, or expectation of happiness is not disinterested. In his *Explication des maximes des saints sur la vie intérieure* (1697), Fénelon, drawing on Paul, Augustine, and François de Sales, proposes a hierarchy of motives for loving God from the most interested to the most disinterested: 1) "servile" love in expectation for goods, which he attributes to "carnal Jews"; 2) expectation of happiness, which is self-love, or self-interest (*intérêt propre*); 3) hope, which is still interested despite beginning to be love of God for himself; 4) charity mingled with self-interest, but wherein disinterestedness is dominant; 5) pure charity, independent of any expectation of reward or fear of punishment, which is the highest form of love according to Augustine.[18]

In legitimizing the passive contemplative attitude as truly disinterested, all the while tracing limits to the mystical experience, Fénelon was trying to justify his friend Madame Guyon's quietist doctrine. Inspired by Italian quietists she had met in Turin and Vercelli, she had been arrested in 1695 and was accused of heresy by Jacques Bénigne Bossuet (*Instructions sur les états d'oraison*, 1696) because she held that one should never pray to God in order to gain anything for oneself, not even to be forgiven for one's sins. According to Fénelon, who learned it from her, only true love is disinterested, that is to say gratuitous, free from egoistic motivations, and it implies the sacrifice of one's own happiness and abandonment of oneself to God. He clearly identifies self-love with self-interest and opposes both to disinterestedness: the "disinterested soul" no longer desires God out of "self-love," because it is no longer stimulated by its *"propre intérêt"* (self-interest).[19]

This argument inspired the so-called *querelle du pur amour* (quarrel of pure love), led by Bossuet and Malebranche, who contested (among others) the idea that human will could be independent from the quest for happiness.[20] For Bossuet, who would have Fénelon's *Explication* condemned by the Pope in 1699, bringing about Fénelon's disgrace, the hope for eternal happiness (*beatitude*) and salvation could not be reduced to egoistic self-love. Fénelon reproached Bossuet for defining Madame Guyon's system as *"monstrueux"* (monstrous) and her aim as *"diabolique"* (diabolical), based on errors that could not be excused by the "ignorance" of her sex.[21] In practice, Bossuet blamed Fénelon for promoting the passive contemplative attitude instead of meditation, which includes acts such as prayer. He also rebuked him for writing in French rather than in Latin, thus addressing a wider audience, including women.

Malebranche, too, immediately reacted to Fénelon's *Explication* in his *Traité de l'amour de Dieu, en quel sens il doit être désintéressé* (1697). According to his Augustinian standpoint, love cannot, in order to be disinterested, exclude the very condition of love, that is to say an object of pleasure and a subject capable of feeling this pleasure. Love is disinterestedness because one adopts the interests of the beloved, and finds one's happiness in the beloved's pleasure. Malebranche also gave the example of sincere friendship as always disinterested.[22] Malebranche was attacked by François Lamy, who argued that love based on the quest for happiness is interested; he contended that true disinterested love of God should be disconnected from self-love, and depends on the will. In *Trois Lettres au R. P. Lamy* (1698) and in his *Réponse générale* (1700), Malebranche opposed François Lamy's idea of a *"désintéressement de l'Amour indépendant du motif d'être heureux"* (disinterestedness of love independent of the motive of being happy).[23] As Pierre Force emphasizes, Fénelon's extension to religious faith of the suspicion that La Rochefoucauld cast upon the motives of human action provided "theological and metaphysical foundations for the (now common-place) idea that the moral worth of an act is a function of the purity of its motives. Disinterestedness is now the foundation of morality."[24]

The quarrel, also named the "quietist affair," had immediate echoes in the German-speaking world as well as in England.[25] Gottfried Wilhelm Leibniz, who had written about "disinterested love," which he differentiated from "mercenary love" involving "material, pecuniary, or sensuous interest in its possession," as Emilienne Naert puts it,[26] was kept updated about the quarrel by Abbé Claude Nicaise.[27] Having asked Malebranche to send him his treatise, Leibniz recognized in his friend's position a stance close to his own concept of "disinterested love."[28] Baruch Spinoza considered that beatitude is not a reward of virtue but is virtue; the joy we experience does not result from the repression of penchants, but it is this joy that enables us to repress them.[29]

In England and Scotland, whereas Joseph Butler, in his *Fifteen Sermons* (1726), adopted Fénelon's view of disinterested love all the while criticizing the fanatics who supported the quietist doctrine, Anthony Ashley Cooper, Third Earl of Shaftesbury, Francis Hutcheson, and David Hume transposed the discussion to ethics. Shaftesbury introduced the concept of disinterestedness into his ethics in order to oppose Thomas Hobbes's political theory and, more broadly, the idea that ethics derive from egoistic motivations. As he argued in *Sensus communis* (1709), challenging Hobbes's view:

> You have heard it, my friend, as a common saying that "interest governs the world." But, I believe, whoever looks narrowly into the affairs of it will find that passion, humour, caprice, zeal, faction, and a thousand other springs, which are counter to self-interest, have as considerable a part in the movements of this machine. [...] The studiers of this mechanism must have a very partial eye to overlook all other motions besides those of the lowest and narrowest compass. It is hard that, in the plan or description of this clockwork, no wheel or balance should be allowed on the side of the better and more enlarged affections, that nothing should be understood to be done in kindness or generosity, nothing in pure good nature or friendship or through any social or natural affection of any kind, when, perhaps, the mainsprings of this machine will be found to be either these very natural affections themselves or a compound kind derived from them and retaining more than one half of their nature.[30]

And he blamed those philosophers who "explain all the social passions and natural affections as to denominate them of the selfish kind. Thus civility, hospitality, humanity towards strangers or people in distress is only a more deliberate selfishness."[31]

According to Stolnitz, while Shaftesbury used interest as an "axiological notion," to designate the "state of well-being or the genuine and long-range good," he also meant occasionally "self-interest" at the individual level, or "self-love."[32] However, in Malebranche's view, the quest for well-being was the expression of self-love.[33] Shaftesbury took a middle-ground position in the quarrel of pure love. Although he understood the arguments of the defenders of a rational approach to religion, he asked, in line with Fénelon: "For how shall one deny that to serve God by compulsion, or for interest merely, is servile and mercenary?" The quest for reward and fear of sanction is thus a servile and mercenary motivation for piety and religious acts. But, on the other hand, "the disinterested love of God," or "teaching the love of God or virtue for God or virtue's sake" had been "stretched too far, perhaps even to extravagance and enthusiasm." [34] "Enthusiasm," which referred in England to prophetic excesses, had become by that time a negative axiological operator for sectarianism, heresy, and intellectual fanaticism.[35] Shaftesbury's concept of love and self-love was closer to Malebranche's. Shaftesbury feared that the selfish quest for reward in the afterlife would overtake the disinterested pursuit of public good. For him, heroic virtues and private friendship were the best examples of disinterestedness.[36] Dealing like Shaftesbury with virtue, Hutcheson considered that truly virtuous action is disinterested, as it proceeds from love of esteem and love of benevolence, rather than from self-love or interest.[37]

Although the quarrel had ended with Fénelon's condemnation, the categories of the debate continued to be discussed in France. As we have seen, the author of the above-mentioned *Encyclopédie* entry on "Intérêt," Saint-Lambert, criticized the confusion between interest and self-love. In his view:

Self-love or continuous desire for well-being, attachment to our being, is a necessary effect of our constitution, of our instinct, of our sensations, of our reflections, a principle which, tending towards our preservation, and responding to nature's views, would be rather virtuous than vicious in the state of nature. But the man born in society draws from this society advantages that he must pay for with services: man has duties to fulfill, laws to follow, others' self-love (*amour-propre*) to respect.

His self-love is then just or injust, virtuous or vicious; and according to the different qualities it takes on different denominations: we saw that of interest, personal interest, and in what sense.[38]

He goes on to explain that self-love, when disordered, can turn into pride or vanity, but it can also "inspire passions" and look for "pleasures that are useful to order, to society." He gives examples of virtue motivated by self-love: a father's love for his children is a virtue, although he loves himself in them; serving the homeland is a virtue, even if "inspired by the desire to conserve our well-being" or by the love of glory; friendship is one as well, albeit based on the need for a kindred soul; and the passion for order, justice, is also anchored in self-love. After blaming the confusion introduced by the French moralists, he dedicates a paragraph to "Milord

Shafsburi," whose *Inquiry Concerning Virtue* had been adapted in French by Denis Diderot (*Essai sur le Mérite et la Vertu*, 1745), before his complete works appeared in French translation in Geneva in 1769. Saint-Lambert reproaches Shaftesbury for ignoring self-love because of his emphasis on the love of order, the love of moral beauty, and benevolence as our major motivations. In fact, Shaftesbury regarded this benevolence, and even self-sacrifice, as effects of self-love. However, according to Saint-Lambert, the "disinterestedness" (*désintéressement*) required by Shaftesbury "cannot be." Finally, the entry mentions the attacks against the author of *De l'Esprit*, that is to say Claude Adrien Helvétius, for confusing interest and self-love. (Diderot himself wrote some critiques in his *Réflexions sur le Livre de l'Esprit* of 1758.)

Thus, while "disinterestedness" had initially been opposed to both "self-interest" and "self-love", the antinomy between "disinterestedness" and "self-love" was challenged in the quarrel of pure love, leading to the dissociation of "self-interest" and "self-love." Jean-Jacques Rousseau would, in his *Discourse on Inequality* (1755), further distinguish *amour-propre* and *amour de soi*. Whereas *amour-propre* (translated as "self-esteem") refers to our quest for others' esteem, a negative sentiment which appears only in society (a critique which echoes both Hobbes and La Rochefoucauld), *amour de soi* (love of self) is, in his view, a natural and good sentiment, which when directed by reason and modified by pity leads human beings to virtue (a conception closer to Shaftesbury's ethics).[39]

From religion to aesthetics: Disinterestedness as a contemplative attitude

The religious sources of aesthetic theory are now clearly established.[40] It was, according to Cassirer, Shaftesbury, one of the most widely read thinkers of his time (his *Characteristics* also appeared in German translation in 1776–79), who first transposed the idea of disinterestedness to aesthetics, which he defined as disinterested pleasure.[41] It was his approach to morality and religion as loving their object for "its own sake," and his use of disinterestedness to designate not an action or a consequence but rather a "mode of attention and concern," as Stolnitz puts it,[42] that enabled the transfer of the concept to the aesthetic experience, as illustrated by the example of the pleasure one gets from listening to music, a pleasure for its own sake. Later, Shaftesbury would also oppose the disinterested contemplation of a beautiful object to the desire to possess it (he gives the example of the ocean). This opposition was picked up by Francis Hutcheson and Edmund Burke, who, while sharing the definition of the aesthetic state as the sensual perception of an object's beauty independently from its utility, used the concept of disinterestedness in slightly different ways: Hutcheson as an immediate perception prior to any calculation (and knowledge), Burke as an affective state of detached sympathy, opposed to greed.[43]

A similar idea could, however, already be found in Leibniz, who was, alongside Shaftesbury, another source for Kant's aesthetics.[44] In his attempt to define "disinterested love," Leibniz mentions the pleasure provided by the contemplation of beautiful things such as paintings by Raphael for themselves, and not for any utility.[45]

The idea of disinterestedness was adopted and systematized by Immanuel Kant, who, in his aesthetic philosophy, displaced it from sensualist psychology to transcendental judgment. In *Kritik der Urteilskraft* (*Critique of Judgment*) published in German in 1790, Kant made the distinction between judgments of taste and judgments of knowledge, characterizing the aesthetic taste as a judgment without a concept, which is subjective, just like any attraction to a source of pleasure. However, whereas the latter aims at satisfying inclinations and is thus interested, aesthetic pleasure is disinterested: "Everyone has to admit that if a judgment about beauty is mingled with the least interest then it is very partial and not a pure judgment of taste."[46] As Strube puts it, in Kant, the aesthetic pleasure does not stem from any need and does not produce one.[47] However, Kant does stress that this disinterested (*uninteressiert*) judgment can be interesting (*interessant*).[48] This also distinguishes it from moral judgment, which, when related to a concept, aims at satisfying a rational interest, or utility. Taste for the beautiful, on the contrary, is contemplative and an end in itself. When attached to a form of representation, this judgment is a "purposiveness without a purpose" (*"Zweckmässigkeit ohne Zweck"*), laying claim to universality despite its subjectivity.[49]

Adopting a social approach to the history of ideas, Martha Woodmansee has revealed other probable sources of Kant's theory besides Shaftesbury, situating it within the transformation of the conditions of artistic production. She particularly refers to Karl Philipp Moritz's "Versuch einer Vereinigung aller schönen Künste und Wissenschaften unter dem Begriff des in sich selbst Vollendeten" ("An Attempt to Unify all the Fine Arts and Sciences under the Concept of that which is Complete in Itself"), published in 1785.[50] This now-obscure text, which Kant had surely read, popularized the intense debates on art and beauty that had taken place in France after the publication of Charles Batteux's essay on *Les Beaux-Arts réduits à un même principe* (1746).

Batteux distinguished between the fine arts (*beaux-arts*), aimed at pleasure, and the mechanical arts (*arts mécaniques*), which responded to needs. He thus provided a theoretical foundation for the claim of visual arts (*arts plastiques*), which had been part of the mechanical arts, to be elevated to the liberal arts through an academic movement inspired by the literary.[51] In this treatise, the unity of the arts was advanced for the first time. Following Aristotle's theory, which had prevailed until then,[52] Batteux based this unity upon the imitation of nature, even if (like most theoreticians of his age) he saw this imitation not as an exact reproduction but as an idealization—the copy should not be a servile reproduction but instead present objects at their highest degree of perfection.[53] Batteux's theory was broadly disseminated by d'Alembert, who quoted it in his preliminary discourse to the *Encyclopédie* (1751), and it was widely received in the German-speaking world. His treatise (which Kant expressly refers to, alongside Lessing[54]) was translated in 1751, when Alexander Baumgarten had just founded his science of *anschauende Erkenntnis* (contemplative knowledge), also called aesthetics, the foremost objective of which was a general theory of the arts. Batteux's theory triggered a controversy that continued until 1770, consisting of defenses and refutations of his principle of unity.

One of the main protagonists of this controversy was Moses Mendelssohn, whose *Betrachtungen über die Quellen und die Verbindung der schönen Künste und Wissenschaften* (*Considerations on the Sources and the Connections of Fine Arts and Sciences*), published in 1757, decisively influenced Karl Philipp Moritz. In contrast to Batteux, Mendelssohn based the unity of the arts not on the imitation of nature but on their effects on the public, notably the capacity to move. According to Mendelssohn—a close reader of Shaftesbury, Hutcheson, and Burke, whose psychology of sensory perception he tried to bridge with the Pietist-influenced moral aesthetic[55]—what pleases is the sensual expression of perfection called beauty: the value of a work depends solely on the internal relations (harmony, symmetry, etc.) among its components. The artist is called upon to rise above common sense: re-creating beauty is his only object, and he has to feel free to concentrate it in his works in order to move us.

This theory was part of a larger current which, since Du Bos's 1719 *Réflexions critiques sur la poésie et la peinture* (*Critical Reflexions on Poetry and Painting*), located the artistic judgment in sentiment rather than in cognition, and thus displaced attention from the production to the reception of art. Mendelssohn's friend Gotthold Ephraim Lessing's insistence on the "*Liebhaber*," the amateur, in his *Laokoon* (1788) is inscribed in the same tradition, which supported the education of taste (aesthetics was introduced into academic curricula by the end of the century) and the development of artistic institutions.[56]

If Mendelssohn's disciple, Moritz, took up the idea of perfection underlying the theory of Ideal Beauty three decades later—and three years before Lessing published his *Laokoon*—it was in order to challenge his master's instrumentalist conception of the function of art as intended to provoke emotion. Moritz distinguished the Beautiful from the Useful. A useful object satisfies me insofar as I can use it, its aim resides outside of itself, whereas the beautiful object procures pleasure in itself, and is consequently "*in sich selbst vollendet*" (complete).

But when regarding the beautiful object, I roll the end out of myself and back into the object itself: I regard it as something that is not complete in me but is rather *complete in itself*, that thereby constitutes a totality in itself and affords me pleasure *for its own sake*; I do not so much give the object a relation to myself as give myself a relation to it.[57]

Moreover, Moritz hierarchized these two ways of perceiving objects. The pleasure provided by a beautiful object is superior to the satisfaction provided by a useful object. The latter is *"gröber"* (cruder), *"gemeiner"* (more "common"), whereas the former is *"feiner"* (finer) and *"seltner"* (rarer): "Pleasure in the merely useful is cruder and more common; pleasure in the beautiful is finer and rarer. We share the former, in a certain sense, with animals; the latter elevates us above them."[58]

Thus, according to Moritz, the difference between the artisan and the artist is that the artisan is subject to considerations of instrumentality, to the extent that objects from mechanical arts have no value outside their external purpose, whereas the artist is not subject to such constraints, since the fine arts have no purpose outside themselves and exist only for their own, internal perfection. Moritz concluded, therefore, that the artist has to seek out perfection in his work irrespective of its effect on the public.

This distinction between the artist and the artisan resonated with changes in the conception of art. In her study of the genesis of modern French aesthetics, Annie Becq suggests that during the eighteenth century the intellectualist (constructivist) rationalism that defined art as imitation yielded to a conception of creative reason that did not rule out sentiment, imagination, and talent, thus giving birth to the representation of the ingenious creative subject.[59] While the artisan's craft is predictable, the creator's work is not: art was unified under the notion of creation and originality, which distinguished it from both manual work and commercial products in the context of the rise of capitalism. This unification was even more specifically related to the rise of a market for cultural goods.

Professional ethics of intellectual professions: The artist, the writer, and the lawyer

Kant had certainly read Moritz's essay in the *Berlinische Monatsschrift*, where he himself had already published two pieces, one of which was *Was ist Aufklärung? (What is Enlightenment?)*.[60] Kant may also have found, as Moritz himself probably did, a similar idea in Shaftesbury's *Soliloquy, or Advices to an Author*, published in 1710, the very year when the first Copyright Act, the Statute of Anne, was adopted:

[A] real *Genius*, and thorow *Artist*, in whatever kind, can never, without the greatest unwillingness and shame, be induc'd to act below his Character, and for mere Interest be prevail'd with to prostitute his Art or Science, by performing contrary to its known Rules [...] Be they ever so idle, dissolute, or debauch'd; how regardless soever of other Rules; they abhor any Transgression in *their* Art, and wou'd chuse to lose Customers and starve, rather than by a base Compliance with the World, to act contrary to what they call the *Justness* and *Truth of Work*.[61]

This conception of the artistic ethos, a translation of "disinterestedness" in practice, took on its full meaning in the emerging market for cultural goods. The literary elite was concerned that it might make authors wish to flatter the public to the detriment of the quality of the work. For, according to Moritz, the public could be divided between the masses and a minority of persons of taste, who alone could appreciate beauty at its true value; the majority sought merely entertainment and pleasurable sensations. By making a work's perfection the artist's primary aim, Moritz defined the artwork as an end in itself and the ethos of the artist as this simple aim, which must not be subordinated to fame. Moreover, to distinguish aesthetic experience from sensory satisfaction, Moritz, who had been raised in the quietist tradition of German Pietism, transposed, as had Shaftesbury, the idea of disinterestedness from religious (love of God) to aesthetic experience by transferring contemplative practices from religion to aesthetics.[62] Beauty procures disinterested pleasure, an idea Kant (also from a Pietist background) would raise to philosophical fame five years later. By driving a rift between artistic creation and both artisanal and commercial activities, this theory created a hierarchy that placed the cultural practices of the "initiated" above those of the masses of laymen.

A purpose of the theory developed by Moritz, as Martha Woodmansee has emphasized, was practical: there are "interests in disinterestedness," she argues, using Bourdieu's expression.[63] For it corresponded to contemporary transformations in the book market, with the dissemination of new literary forms (such as novels, periodicals, and journals), and new channels of distribution (such as circulating libraries) among the emerging middle classes. After all, surveys on libraries have shown a "democratization" of reading from the 1760s onwards: the number of books lent doubled, borrowers were from more modest backgrounds, and the sentimental novel became more popular than "serious" genres.[64]

These transformations of the conditions of production led to the professionalization of writing. The phenomenon happened even more abruptly in Germany, where the patronage of authors had never been as widespread as in France, since provincial princes and aristocrats had shown little interest in art and absolutism had dragged down the emerging middle class. The movement was animated by about a hundred literati, philosophers, and poets, from Leibniz to Lessing, who used various means to disseminate literacy in the broadest sense: theatrical critiques, reading clubs, periodicals, etc.

In 1773, a discussion aiming at justifying literary property started in Prussia, in which Kant, like Friedrich Gottlieb Klopstock, Zacharias Becker, and Johann Gottlieb Fichte, was involved.[65] Kant contested the assimilation of the book to a commodity, emphasizing its immaterial dimension: authors should remain the owners of their thoughts, and only delegate their interests to the bookseller, as he would contend in his 1785 article "Unrechtmäßigkeit des Büchernachdrucks."[66] As argued by Woodmansee, the author's claims were based on the notions of originality and genius, which came to replace the neoclassical conceptions of craft and inspiration.[67]

France also experienced an unprecedented expansion of the book market in the second half of the eighteenth century. In order to reinforce their monopoly and protect themselves from counterfeiting, the powerful community of booksellers and printers claimed the exclusive privilege of printing. Denis Diderot's publisher asked him in 1763 to write a letter to justify their claim. It was in this *"Lettre sur le commerce de la librairie,"* the original version of which would be published only one century later, in 1861, that Diderot expressed the paradigmatic idea of the author's ownership of his writings:

> Indeed, what can a man possess, if a product of the mind, the unique fruit of his education, his study, his efforts, his time, his research, his observation; if the finest hours, the finest moments of his life; if his own thoughts, the feelings of his heart, the most precious part of himself, that part which does not perish, that which immortalises him, cannot be said to belong to him? [...] Who has more right than the author to use his goods by giving or selling them?[68]

In 1777, a royal decree on literary property granted for the first time—as a grace—to the author the right to earn royalties from his work, recognized as such. Legislation on literary property thus took note of the emerging group of authors who made a living, with greater or lesser efforts, from their writing. This right would be recognized during the French Revolution by two laws, adopted in 1791 and 1793, after a fierce debate in which the defenders of literary property confronted those who, like the Marquis de Condorcet, considered that ideas belong to everybody.[69] It is not by chance that the first legislation on publishing was adopted in Prussia the following year.

However, in France, literary authority had been recognized by the state long before, when Richelieu made the Académie française a *"corps de l'Etat"* in 1635, in exchange for services rendered to the state (the linguistic unification of the kingdom). By that time, the career of an author was less an end in itself than a means for social advancement. It was not until the Enlightenment that the profession of a man of letters became a "state" (*état*), as Duclos declared in his *Considérations sur les mœurs de ce siècle* (1750), without this "state" implying a professional status. On the contrary, those claiming to be part of the writing profession took care to distinguish themselves from the *"canaille écrivante"* stigmatized by Voltaire; that is, the literary *bohème* who, for want of anything better, aspired to living off their writing.[70] The "literary aristocracy" later condemned by the Revolution, with their privileges and grants through the system of patronage and sponsorship, charges, official functions and academic seats, had not imagined that literature could become a profession or, even worse, a trade. While printers and booksellers had started to experiment with capitalistic methods to make profit from books, this literary aristocracy applied the recommendations of Boileau, whose *Art poétique* warned against those who turned a "divine art" into a "mercenary trade":

Write for immortal Fame; nor ever chuse
Gold for the object of a gen'erous Muse.
I know a noble Wit may, without Crime,
Receive a lawful Tribute for his time:
Yet I abhor those Writers, who despise
Their Honor; and alone their Profit prize;
Who their *Apollo* basely will degrade,
And of a noble Science, make a Trade.[71]

The opposition between the literary establishment and literary bohemia was challenged by Jean-Jacques Rousseau, who criticized both positions as not guaranteeing the conditions for disinterestedness. In 1782, four years after his death, two books by him were released posthumously: *Les Confessions*, and *Rousseau juge de Jean-Jacques: Dialogues*. In the *Confessions*, Rousseau recounts his refusal of the king's offer of a life pension after the performance of his opera *Le Devin du village* (The village soothsayer) at the royal court at Fontainebleau in 1752. This refusal provoked an argument with his friend Diderot, who was angry with him for turning down the king's offer. In the *Confessions*, Rousseau claims that refusing the pension was a way to protect his "independence" and "disinterestedness."[72] As he made clear, a royal pension would have imposed upon him constraints which would have limited his commitment to truth, freedom, and courage, and condemned him either to flattery or to silence. In other words, getting a pension from the government implies serving its interests, or at least not being free to criticize it. Rousseau reasserted his position in the *Dialogues*, rejecting both the market and government pensions. He had always refused, he explained, to "prostitute" his talents; he could sell what his hands produced but not the "products of his soul": "it is their disinterestedness alone that can confer upon them force and elevation."[73] A couple of pages afterwards, he attacked the "illustrious Diderot" who, contemptuous of profit and "mercenary work," had criticized Rousseau for earning a living as a music copyist. But, argued Rousseau ironically, the work as a copyist had not enriched Jean-Jacques, and the philosopher Diderot's disinterestedness had not made him poorer. Indeed, Rousseau claimed that being a copyist was for him a way to earn a living without having to sell his own writings.[74]

Rousseau appears here as a "nomothete,"[75] inventing a new rule of the game: the independent, disinterested thinker should reject not only the law of the market but also the rule imposed by the government, as well as all forms of subordination through patronage, which characterize the figure of the courtier. The only possibility for a thinker to be independent and truly disinterested is to have a second occupation. Rousseau was to re-enact this rejection in England, where David Hume obtained for him a pension from the king; this refusal provoked the quarrel with Hume.

Rousseau's choice not to submit to the king in 1752 was premonitory. Voltaire himself would soon flee Frederick II's court after their dispute, and the *Encyclopédie* project would be suspended in France. His *Dictionnaire philosophique*, published anonymously in 1763, would be banned and burned in Geneva, Holland, Berne, and Paris. In this volume, Voltaire's article on "Lettres, gens de lettres" criticizes the figure of the courtier, whose sycophantic behavior he compares unfavorably with the courage of the writer who takes risks to tell the truth:

> Compose some odes in praise of my Lord Superbus Fadus, some madrigals for his mistress; dedicate a book on geography to his door-keeper, you will be well-received; enlighten mankind, you will be exterminated, Descartes was forced to leave his country, Gassendi was calumniated, Arnaud dragged out his days in exile; every philosopher is treated as the prophets were among the Jews.[76]

The ethos of disinterestedness was thus politicized through the attacks against the *philosophes* and the banning of their works, and would become a reference for the modern figure of the "intellectual."

The problem of disinterested professional ethics raised by Voltaire and Rousseau was not limited to writers and thinkers. In particular, the lawyers' professional organization, the Ordre des Avocats, claimed disinterestedness in order to assert the priority they attached to honor over fortune in carrying out their profession,[77] thus expressing superiority over commercial activities and manual labor. Rediscovered in the seventeenth century, the antique distinction that Roman law made between *operae liberales* and *operae illiberales* forbade that the former be submitted to a contract of service. It distinguished the *honorarium*, expressing the client's recognition for a service that could not be valued in purely financial terms, and the *merces*, reserved for manual work. As Karpik explains, "disinterestedness which, in its usual form, tightly associates a moral with a concrete experience, was early accompanied by a more general and extreme discourse which seemed to situate the profession out of the world and inscribe the lawyer in complete detachment from material interests."[78] This rhetoric, "which lodged economic relations in gift and counter-gift," appeared precisely in the eighteenth century. Karpik writes that "disinterestedness defined a strategy of rejecting the subordination to both the State and the market in order to connect to the public."[79]

How can a profession destined to provide the person who exerts it with the material means to earn a living be disinterested? Here, disinterestedness refers not so much to providing services free of charge as to the idea that professionals subordinate their own interests to those with which they are entrusted (that is, those of their clients, and more broadly the public).[80] This is comparable to the disinterestedness of civil servants, who have to subordinate their particular interests to the general interest.[81] The term "disinterestedness" would proliferate in nineteenth-century writings and discourse, notably in the duties with which the Conseil de l'Ordre (the council of representatives of the profession of lawyers) or the bar sought compliance, and in the inspiration the concept provided for many rules of professional ethics that laid down obligations toward clients.[82] This French model, asserting lawyers' autonomy in regard to both the state and the market, would be followed in other European countries in the nineteenth century.[83]

Conclusion

We have seen how the idea and concept of disinterestedness emerged by the end of the seventeenth century, in opposition to self-interest and self-love, in the French moralists' writings, and how its association with the contemplative attitude was transferred, via Leibniz, Shaftesbury, and Hutcheson, from religion to aesthetics in the process of the concept's migration to England and to the German-speaking areas, where Kant founded on it his definition of aesthetic judgment. "Disinterestedness" became an "axiological operator" opposed to interest(s), utility, greed, sensual pleasure, and vulgar emotions. The aesthetic (disinterested) attitude was distinguished from practical ends, the desire to possess (greed), and the quest for sensual pleasure (emotions), all motivated by self-interest. This distinction contributed to the hierarchization of different modes of consumption of artworks, placing aesthetic judgment at the top.

Having become widely used in discussions of morals, where it was opposed to self-interest, and especially to economic interest, with which the concept of interest was being more and more identified, the notion of disinterestedness also became central by the mid-eighteenth century in defining the ethics of intellectual professions, notably law, in order to assert the priority given by practitioners to honor over fortune. This aristocratic ethos was also adopted by the elite of authors, when confronted with the rise of the market for symbolic goods and the professionalization of writing. Market logic was considered to threaten the moral and intellectual quality of the works, and its rejection was connected, through the axiological operator of disinterestedness, to the idea that aesthetic judgment should prevail over other external criteria such as satisfying the demands of the audience. These two related uses of disinterestedness also favored the unification of literature and the fine arts around the notion of Beauty, and would ground their claims to autonomy throughout the nineteenth century. "Disinterestedness" thus became an axiological operator that served to indicate the professional ethos of cultural producers, to distinguish their products from other types of merchandise, and to create a hierarchy of forms of consumption in the context of the rise of capitalism.

Furthermore, as we saw, Rousseau played a major role in transposing the claim to disinterestedness and autonomy from the market to the state and to patrons. Politicized in the attacks against the *philosophes*, theorized by Voltaire, this rejection of the courtier ethos would become a reference for the figure of the writer as an independent intellectual whose responsibility is to tell his or her audience the truth, without being afraid to criticize the authorities, and more broadly for the modern figure of the "intellectual", as illustrated by Zola's paradigmatic position-taking in the Dreyfus Affair in the name of truth, with his *"J'accuse."*[84]

Notes

1   Parts of this paper were translated by Niall Bond, and parts directly written in English. I thank David Armitage, Thomas Becker, Karin Kukonnen, Juliane Vogel, and Christine Zabel for their valuable comments and suggestions.
2   Albert O. Hirschman, *The Passions and the Interests: Political Arguments for Capitalism before Its Triumph* (Princeton: Princeton University Press, 1977).
3   John A. W. Gunn, "'Interest Will Not Lie': A Seventeenth-Century Political Maxim," *Journal of the History of Ideas* 29, no. 4 (October–December 1968): 551–64.
4   Pierre Force, *Self-Interest before Adam Smith: A Genealogy of Economic Science* (Cambridge: Cambridge University Press, 2003), 175–79. Force rightly underscores that Smith's concept of interest is not purely economic: the pursuit of wealth is, in fact, motivated by vanity. On self-interested behavior at court, see Norbert Elias, *The Court Society* (New York: Pantheon Books, 1983).
5   Force, *Self-Interest before Adam Smith*, 183.
6   Pierre Bourdieu, "Le marché des biens symboliques," *L'Année sociologique* 22 (1971): 49–126; English trans. by Rupert Swyer, "The Market of symbolic goods," *Poetics* 14, no. 1-2 (1985): 13–44.
7   Pierre Bourdieu, "Un acte désintéressé est-il possible?" in *Raisons pratiques: Sur la théorie de l'action.* (Paris: Seuil, 1994), 147–74; English trans. "Is a Disinterested Act Possible?" in *Practical Reason: On the Theory of Action* (Cambridge: Polity, 1998), 75–91.
8   This research project was developed during the academic year 2018–19 at the Wissenschaftskolleg, which I thank for providing exceptional research conditions.
9   Gisèle Sapiro, "Une catégorie éthique de l'entendement lettré: Le concept de désintéressement," *Revue Silène* (2017): http://www.revue-silene.com/f/index.php?sp=comm&comm_id=201.
10   Gisèle Sapiro, "Défense et illustration de 'l'honnête homme': Les hommes de lettres contre la sociologie," *Actes de la recherche en sciences sociales* 153 (2004): 11–27.
11   Pierre Bourdieu, "Le marché des biens symboliques," *L'année sociologique* 22 (1971): 49–126; "The Market of Symbolic Goods," *Poetics, Journal of Empirical Research on Literature, the Media, and the Arts* 14 (1984): 13–44.
12   "Désintéressement (Morale)," in *Encyclopédie ou Dictionnaire raisonné des sciences, des arts et des métiers* (Paris, 1751–72) online: the ARTFL project, https://artflsrv03.uchicago.edu/philologic4/encyclopedie1117/navigate/4/4495/.
13   Hirschman, *The Passions*.
14   *"Ce vice qui nous fait chercher nos avantages au mépris de la justice et de la vertu, et c'est une vile ambition; c'est l'avarice, la passion de l'argent."* "Intérêt (Morale)," in *Encyclopédie*, online: https://artflsrv03.uchicago.edu/philologic4/encyclopedie1117/navigate/8/3384/.
15   Johan Heilbron, "French Moralists and the Anthropology of the Modern Era," in *The Rise of the Social Sciences and the Formation of Modernity*, ed. Johan Heilbron, Lars Magnusson, and Björn Wittroch (Dordrecht: Kluwer Academic, 1998), 77–106.

16 François Duc de La Rochefoucauld, *Reflections Or, Sentences and Moral Maxims*, nos. 39 and 187, English transl. online: Gutenberg project October 2005, last modified January 25, 2013, https://www.gutenberg.org/files/9105/9105-h/9105-h.htm#linkmaxims; original reference: *Maximes et Réflexions diverses* (Paris, Gallimard "Folio," 1976), 50 and 74.

17 *Réflexions philosophiques et théologiques sur le nouveau système de la nature et de grâce* (1685), cited in Force, *Self-Interest before Adam Smith*, 191.

18 François de Salignac de la Mothe Fénelon, *Explication des maximes des saints sur la vie intérieure* (Paris: B. Auboin, 1697), 1–12. On the notion of pure love before Fénelon and in his work, see Jacques Le Brun, *Le Pur Amour de Platon à Lacan* (Paris: Seuil, 2002).

19 Fénelon, *Explication*, 12.

20 On the political, social, and personal issues at stake in this quarrel, see Anne Ferrari, "Bossuet et Fénelon: la lettre qui tue," *Littératures classiques* 59, no.1 (2006): 299–316.

21 Jacques B. Bossuet, *Relation sur le quiétisme* (1698), in *Œuvres complètes de Bossuet, évêque de Meaux*, vol. 8 (Paris: Lefebvre), 320.

22 Malebranche, "Traité de l'amour de Dieu, en quel sens il doit être désintéressé (1697)," in Malebranche, *Œuvres complètes*, vol. 14 (Paris: Vrin/CNRS, 1963), 14 and 21.

23 Malebranche, *Trois lettres au Père Lamy* (1697), in Malebranche, *Œuvres complètes*, vol. 14 (Paris: Vrin/CNRS, 1963), 191 and 198.

24 Force, *Self-Interest before Adam Smith*, 192.

25 Christoph Schmitt-Maaß, "Quietistic Pietists? The Reception of Fénelon in Central Germany c. 1700," in *Fénelon in the Enlightenment: Traditions, Adaptations, and Variations*, ed. Christoph Schmitt-Maaß, Stefanie Stockhorst, and Doohwan Ahn (Rodopi: Brill, 2014), 147–70.

26 Emilienne Naert, *Leibniz et la querelle du pur amour* (Paris: Vrin, 1959), 61 (my translation). On Leibniz's early elaboration of this notion, see also Gregory Brown, "Disinterested Love: Understanding Leibniz's Reconciliation of Self- and Other-Regarding Motives," *British Journal for the History of Philosophy* 19, no. 2 (2011): 265–303.

27 See for instance (among others), Claude Nicaise to Leibniz, October 27, 1697 and February 27, 1698, in Gottfried W. Leibniz, *Sämtliche Schriften und Briefe*, ed. Berlin-Brandenburgischen Akademie der Wissenschaften und der Akademie der Wissenschaften zu Göttingen, Zweite Reihe, *Philosophischer Briefwechsel*, vol. 3 (Berlin: Akademie Verlag, 2013), no. 147 and nos. 156, 395 and 414, online: http://www.uni-muenster.de/Leibniz/DatenII3/II3_A.pdf.

28 Leibniz to Malebranche, March 13–23, 1699, in Leibniz, *Sämtliche Schriften*, nos. 204, 540.

29 Baruch Spinoza, *Ethics*, prop. XLII, trans. by Robert H. M. Elwes, 1883, Hypertext edition by Ron Bombardi, MTSU Philosophy WebWorks, 1997. Online: http://index-of.es/z0ro-Repository-3/Spinoza/Ethics%20Spinoza%20.pdf. See also Hirschmann, *The Passions*, 27.

30 Anthony A. Cooper, Earl of Shaftesbury, *Sensus Communis, an Essay on the Freedom of Wit and Humour* [1709], in Shaftesbury, *Characteristicks of Men, Manners, Opinions, Times* [1737], vol. 2, ed. Douglas D. Uyl (Indianapolis: Liberty Fund, 2001), 53–54; online: https://oll.libertyfund.org/titles/shaftesbury-characteristicks-of-men-manners-opinions-times-3-vols.

31 Ibid., 55.

32 Jerome Stolnitz, "On the Origins of 'Aesthetic Disinterestedness'," *The Journal of Aesthetics and Art Criticism* 20, no. 2 (1961): 131–43.

33 Malebranche, *Traité de l'amour de Dieu*, 14.

34 Shaftesbury, "The Moralists, a Philosophical Rhapsody [1709]," in Shaftesbury,*Characteristicks*, 267–68.

35 John G. A. Pocock, "Enthusiasm: The Anti-Self of Enlightenment," *Huntington Library Quarterly* 60 (1997): 7–28.

36 Shaftesbury, "The Moralists," 255; see also Force, *Self-Interest before Adam Smith*, 196–97.

37 Force, *Self-Interest before Adam Smith*, 198.

38 "*L'amour-propre ou le désir continu du bien-être, l'attachement à notre être, est un effet nécessaire de notre constitution, de notre instinct, de nos sensations, de nos réflexions, un principe qui, tendant à notre conservation, et répondant aux vues de la nature, serait plutôt vertueux que vicieux dans l'état de nature. Mais l'homme né en société tire de cette société des avantages qu'il doit payer par des services: l'homme a des devoirs à remplir, des lois à suivre, l'amour-propre des autres à ménager. Son amour-propre est alors juste ou injuste, vertueux ou vicieux; et selon les différentes qualités il prend différentes dénominations : on a vu celle d'intérêt, d'intérêt personnel, et dans quel sens.*" "Intérêt," in *Encyclopédie* (my translation).

39 Jean-Jacques Rousseau, "Discours sur les origines et fondements de l'inégalité parmi les hommes," in Rousseau, *Œuvres complètes*, vol. 3 (Paris: Gallimard "Bibliothèque de la Pléiade," 1964), 156 and 174.

40 The most recent work is Simon Grote, *The Emergence of Modern Aesthetic Theory: Religion and Morality in Enlightenment Germany and Scotland* (Cambridge, Cambridge University Press, 2017). However, Grote's very in-depth study omits to mention the reception of the French quarrel on pure love and of Fénelon's work in Germany, England, and Scotland, which appears to be a significant source of aesthetic theory.

41 Ernst Cassirer, *The Philosophy of the Enlightenment*, trans. Fritz C. A. Koelln and James P. Pettegrove (Boston: Beacon Press, 1955).

42 Stolnitz, *On the Origins of 'Aesthetic Disinterestedness'*, 133.

43 See Werner Strube, "Interesselosigkeit: Zur Geschichte eines Grundbegriffs der Ästhetik," *Archiv für Begriffsgeschichte* 23, no. 2 (1979): 148–74. On Burke, see also Paul Guyer, *A History of Modern Aesthetics*, vol. 1, *The Eighteenth Century* (Cambridge: Cambridge University Press, 2014), 153.

44 Clifford Brown, "Leibniz and aesthetics," *Philosophy and Phenomenological Research* 28, no. 1 (1967): 70–80.

45 Leibniz, preface to the translation of *Codex Juris Gentum Diplomaticus*, cited in Naert, *Leibniz*, 62.

46 Immanuel Kant, *Critique of Judgement*, §2, trans. Werner S. Pluhar (Indianapolis/Cambridge: Hackett, 1987), 46. Original text: "*Ein jeder muss eingestehen, dass desjenige Urteil über Schönheit, worin sich das mindeste Interesse mengt, sehr parteilich und kein reines Geschmacksurteil sei.*" *Kritik der Urteilskraft, Werkausgabe Band X*, ed. Wilhelm Weischedel (Frankfurt: Suhrkamp, "Taschenbuch Wissenschaft," 1977), 117.

47 Strube, *Interesselosigkeit*, 173.

48 Kant, *Kritik der Urteilskraft*, §2, 117 (note).

49 Kant, *Critique of Judgement*, §10, 65, §6.

50 Martha Woodmansee, *The Author, Art and the Market: Rereading the History of Aesthetics* (New York: Columbia University Press, 1994), 11–34.

51 Raymonde Moulin, "De l'artisan au professionnel: L'artiste," *Sociologie du travail* 4 (1985): 388–403; Martin Warnke, *Hofkünstler: Zur Vorgeschichte des modernen Künstlers*, 2nd ed. (Cologne: DuMont Buchverlag, 1996); Lary Shiner, *The Invention of Art: A Cultural History* (Chicago: University of Chicago Press, 2001).

52 Annie Becq, *Genèse de l'esthétique française moderne 1680–1914* (Paris: Albin Michel, 1994).

53   Charles Batteux, *Les Beaux-Arts réduits à un même principe* (Paris: Durand, 1746), 24.
54   Kant, *Kritik der Urteilskraft*, 214 (§33).
55   Leah Hochman, "The Ugly Made Beautiful," *Journal of Modern Jewish Studies* 5, no. 2 (2006): 137–61.
56   Élisabeth Décultot, "Le Laocoon de Gotthold Ephraim Lessing: De l'imagination comme fondement d'une nouvelle méthode critique," *Les Études philosophiques* 65, no. 2 (2003): 197–212.
57   Karl P. Moritz, "An Attempt to Unify All the Fine Arts and Sciences under the Concept of That Which Is Complete in Itself," trans. Elliot Schreiber, *Publications of the Modern Language Association of America* 127, no.1 (2012): 94–100 (citation 97). Original: "Versuch einer Vereinigung aller schönen Künste und Wissenschaften unter dem Begriff des in isch selbst Vollendeten (1785)," in Moritz, *Popularphilosophie, Reisen, Ästetische Theorie*, vol. 2, ed. Heide Hollmer and Albert Meier (Frankfurt a.M., Deutscher Klassiker Verlag, 1997), 943–49 (quotation 943).
58   Moritz, "An Attempt," 98 (Original: 944).
59   Becq, *Genèse de l'esthétique française moderne*. On the German debate, and more specifically on Lessing's reflections on genius and the question of rationality, see Frederick Beiser, *Diotima's Children: German Aesthetic Rationalism from Leibniz to Lessing* (Oxford: Oxford University Press, 2009), 254–59.
60   On the *Berlinischer Monatsschrift*, see Jonathan Hess, *Reconstituting the Body Politic. Enlightenment, Public Culture and the Invention of Aesthetic Autonomy* (Detroit: Wayne State University Press, 1999). Hess adds to Woodmansee a complementary understanding of the defence of aesthetic autonomy by Moritz and Kant in the context of the politics of this journal which, acknowledging the limits of its possibilities of political intervention, secures an alternative autonomous space besides the state. Schiller's later idea that artistic education can contribute to the enlightenment of people derives in part from this idea. Friedrich Schiller, *Über die aestetische Erziehung des Menschen in einer Riehe von Briefe, Sämtliche Werker* (1793), vol. 5 (Munich: Carl Hanser Verlag, 1980).
61   Shaftesbury, *Characteristicks*, vol. 3, 261. On the adoption of copyright in England, see Mark Rose, *Authors and Owners: The Invention of Copyright* (Cambridge, MA: Harvard University Press, 1993).
62   As shown by von Mücke in her survey of the impact of religious practices on redefining aesthetics during the Enlightenment. Dorothea von Mücke, *Practices of the Enlightenment: Aesthetics, Authorship and the Public* (New York: Columbia University Press, 2015).
63   Woodmansee, "The Interests in Disinterestedness," in *The Author, Art and the Market*, 11–33.
64   Rudolf Schenda, *Volk ohne Buch: Studien zur Sozialgeschichte der populären Lesestoffe, 1770–1910* (Frankfurt a.M.: Klostermann, 1970), 467.
65   Heinrich Bosse, *Autorschaft ist Werkherrschaft: Über die Entstehung des Urheberrechts aus dem Geist der Goethezeit* (Munich: Wilhelm Fink, 2014). See also Peter Baldwin, *The Copyright Wars: Three Centuries of Trans-Atlantic Battle* (Princeton: Princeton University Press, 2014).
66   *Berlinische Monat* 5. "On the Injustice of Reprinting Books" (1785), in *Primary Sources on Copyright (1450–1900)*, ed. Lionel Bently and Martin Kretschmer, accessed July 27, 2020: www.copyrighthistory.org. Kant develops this thesis more concisely under the title "What is a book?" in *Metaphysical Elements of Right* (*Metaphysische Anfangsgründe der Rechtslehre*, §31, 1797).
67   Woodmansee, *The Author, Art and the Market*, 35–55.

68   Denis Diderot, *Lettre sur le commerce de la librairie*, in Diderot, *Œuvres complètes*, vol. 8 (Paris: Hermann, 1976), 509–10. Translation of the quote in "Commentary on: Diderot's Letter on the book trade (1763)," *Primary sources on copyright*, accessed July 27, 2020: www.copyrighthistory.org.

69   Carla Hesse, "Enlightenment Epistemology and the Laws of Authorship in Revolutionary France, 1777–1793," special issue, *Representations* 30 (Spring 1990): 109–37; and *Publishing and Cultural Politics in Revolutionary Paris* (Berkeley/Los Angeles: University of California Press, 1991), chap. 3.

70   Robert Darnton, *The Literary Underground of the Old Regime* (Cambridge, MA: Harvard University Press, 1982), chap. 1; Roger Chartier, *Les Origines culturelles de la Révolution française* (Paris: Seuil, 1990), 76. The expression *"canaille écrivante"* appears in Voltaire's *Candide ou l'Optimisme* (chap. 21).

71   Nicolas Boileau, *The Art of Poetry*, trans. Sir William Soames and John Dryden (London: Bentley and Magnes, 1683), 61. Original text online: https://short-edition.com/fr/classique/nicolas-boileau/l-art-poetique-chant-iv.

72   Jean-Jacques Rousseau, "Les Confessions," in Rousseau, *Œuvres complètes*, vol. I (Paris, Gallimard Bibliothèque de la Pléiade, 1959), 380.

73   My translation: "c'est leur désintéressement qui peut seul leur donner de la force et de l'élévation." Jean-Jacques Rousseau, *Rousseau juge Jean-Jacques. Dialogue*, Rousseau, *Œuvres complètes*, vol. I 839–40.

74   Rousseau, *Rousseau juge Jean-Jacques*, 843.

75   I borrow this concept from Bourdieu, who used it to describe Flaubert and Baudelaire's invention of the autonomy of the literary field towards the market. Pierre Bourdieu, *The Rules of Art: Genesis and Structure of the Literary Field*, trans. Susan Emanuel (Cambridge: Polity Press, 1996). On Rousseau, see Christopher Kelly, *Rousseau as Author: Consecrating One's Life to the Truth* (Chicago: University of Chicago Press, 2003); Jérôme Meizoz, *Le Gueux philosophe (Jean-Jacques Rousseau)* (Lausanne: Antipodes, 2003); Benoît Mely, *Jean-Jacques Rousseau, un intellectuel en rupture* (Paris: Minerve, 1985).

76   Voltaire, *Voltaire's Philosophical Dictionary* (New York, Carlton House, 1950); online: Project Gutenberg, 2006, 91–92, http://www.gutenberg.org/ebooks/18569 (original: "Lettres, gens de lettres ou lettré," *Dictionnaire philosophique*, Paris, Imprimerie nationale, 1994, p. 324.)

77   Lucien Karpik, *Les Avocats: Entre l'Etat, le public et le marché. XIIIe–XXe siècle* (Paris: Gallimard, 1995), 89–91.

78   Ibid., 158 (Niall Bond's translation).

79   Ibid., 90–91.

80   Ibid., 38.

81   Pierre Bourdieu, "Un acte désintéressé est-il possible?," 167.

82   The deontological dispositions of the professions related to disinterestedness are distributed between those that prescribe the exercise of these professions with a non-mercantile goal, and those who affirm their incompatibiliy with other activities. See Joël Moret-Bailly, *Les Déontologies* (Aix: Presses Universitaires d'Aix-Marseille, 2001) 209 –215.

83   Hannes Siegrist, *Advokat, Bürger und Staat: Sozialgeschichte der Rechtsanwälte in Deutschland, Italien und der Schweiz (18.–20. Jh.)* (Frankfurt a.M.: Klostermann, 1996).

84   Didier Masseau, *L'Invention de l'intellectuel dans l'Europe du XVIIIe siècle* (Paris: PUF, 1994); Gisèle Sapiro, *La Responsabilité de l'écrivain: Littérature, droit et morale en France, XIXe–XXIe siècle* (Paris: Seuil, 2011).

Bibliography

Abolafia, Mitchel Y. "Markets as Cultures: An Ethnographic Approach." In *The Laws of the Market*, edited by Michel Callon, 69–85. Oxford: Blackwell, 1998.

Adelman, Jeremy, ed. *The Essential Hirschman*. 2nd ed. Princeton: Princeton University Press, 2015.

Adelman, Jeremy. *Worldly Philosopher: The Odyssey of Albert O. Hirschman*. Princeton: Princeton University Press, 2013.

Alff, David. *The Wreckage of Intentions: Projects in British Culture, 1660–1730*. Philadelphia, PA: University of Pennsylvania Press, 2017.

Allon, Fiona. "The Wealth Affect: Financial Speculation as Everyday Habitus." In *Bodies and Affects in Market Societies*, edited by Anne Schmidt and Christoph Conrad, 109–25. Tübingen: Mohr Siebeck, 2016.

Antwerp, W. C. van. *The Stock Exchange from Within*. New York: Doubleday, Page, 1913.

Appadurai, Arjun. "Introduction: Commodities and the Politics of Value." In *The Social Life of Things: Commodities in Cultural Perspective*, edited by Arjun Appadurai, 3–63. Cambridge: Cambridge University Press, 1986.

Ash, Eric. *The Draining of the Fence: Projectors, Popular Politics, and State Building in Early Modern England*. Baltimore, MD: John Hopkins University Press, 2017.

Attié, Katherine B. "Enclosure Polemics and the Garden in the 1650s." *Studies in English Literature, 1500–1900* 51, no. 1 (2011): 135–57.

Baker, Keith M., ed. *Inventing the French Revolution: Essays on French Political Culture in the Eighteenth Century*. Cambridge: Cambridge University Press, 1994.

Baldwin, Peter. *The Copyright Wars: Three Centuries of Trans-Atlantic Battle*. Princeton: Princeton University Press, 2014.

Banner, Stuart. "The Origin of the New York Stock Exchange." *The Journal of Legal Studies* 27 (1998): 113–40.

Banner, Stuart. *A History of the Fine Line between Gambling and Investing*. Oxford: Oxford University Press, 2017.

Banner, Stuart. *Speculation: A History of the Fine Line Between Gambling and Investing*. Oxford: Oxford University Press, 2017.

Bardhan, Pranab K. "Interlocking Factor Markets and Agrarian Development: A Review of Issues." *Oxford Economic Papers* 32, no. 1 (March 1980): 82–98.

Barlaeus, Caspar. *The Wise Merchant*. Edited by Anna-Luna Post. Translated by Corinna Vermeulen. Amsterdam: AUP, 2019.

Barnard, Toby. *Improving Ireland? Projectors, Prophets and Profiteers, 1641–1786*. Dublin: Four Courts Press, 2008.

Bassett, John S., ed. *Selections from the Federalist*. New York: Charles Scribner's Sons, 1921.

Baten, Joerg, and Jan L. van Zanden. "Book Production and the Onset of Modern Economic Growth." *Journal of Economic Growth*, no. 13 (2008): 217–35.

Batteux, Charles. *Les Beaux-Arts réduits à un même principe*. Paris: Durand, 1746.

Bayly, Christopher A. *Rulers, Townsmen and Bazaars: North Indian Society in the Age of British Expansion 1770–1870*. Cambridge: Cambridge University Press, 1983.

Becker, Gary S. *The Economic Approach to Human Behavior*. Chicago: The University of Chicago Press, 1976.

Becker, Gary S. "The Economic Approach to Human Behavior." In *Rational Choice: Readings in Social and Political Theory*, edited by Jon Elster, 108–22. Oxford: Blackwell, 1986.

Beckert, Jens. "The Great Transformation of Embeddedness: Karl Polanyi and the New Economic Sociology." In *Market and Society: The Great Transformation Today*, edited by Chris Hann and Keith Hart, 38–55. New York: Cambridge University Press, 2009.

Becq, Annie. *Genèse de l'esthétique française moderne 1680–1914*. Paris: Albin Michel, 1994.

Béguin, Katia. *Financer la guerre au XVIIᵉ siècle: La Dette publique et les rentiers de l'absolutisme*. Seyssel: Edition Champ Vallon, 2012.

Behar, Cem, and Yves Ducel. "L'Arithmétique politique d'Antoine Deparcieux." In *Arithmétique politique dans la France du XVIIIᵉ siècle*, edited by Thierry Martin, 147–61. Paris: INED, 2003.

Behrisch, Lars. *Die Berechnung der Glückseligkeit: Statistik und Politik im späten Ancien Régime*. Ostfildern: Jan Thorbecke Verlag, 2016.

Beiser, Frederick. *Diotima's Children: German Aesthetic Rationalism from Leibniz to Lessing*. Oxford: Oxford University Press, 2009.

Belmas, Elisabeth. *Jouer autrefois: Essai sur le jeu dans la France modern, XVIᵉ–XVIIIᵉ siècle*. Seyssel: Éditions Champ Vallon, 2006.

Berg, Maxine, and Elizabeth Eger. *Luxury in the Eighteenth Century: Debates, Desires and Delectable Goods*. Basingstoke: Palgrave, 2002.

Berg, Maxine. "In Pursuit of Luxury: Global History and British Consumer Goods in the Eighteenth Century." *Past and Present* 182 (February 2004): 85–142.

Berghoff, Hartmut, and Jakob Vogel, eds. *Wirtschaftsgeschichte als Kulturgeschichte, Dimensionen eines Perspektivenwechsels*. Frankfurt a.M.: Campus, 2004.

Binde, Per. "Gambling and Religion: Histories of Concord and Conflict." *Journal of Gambling Issues* 20 (2007): 145–65.

Blaufarb, Rafe. *The Great Demarcation: The French Revolution and the Invention of Modern Property*. Oxford: Oxford University Press, 2016.

Bloch, Camille. *Procès-verbaux du Comité des Finances de l'Assemblée Constituante*. Rennes: Impr. Oberthur, 1922.

Blom, Hans. *Morality and Causality in Politics: The Rise of Naturalism in Dutch Seventeenth-Century Political Thought*. Utrecht: H. W. Blom, 1995.

Blom, Hans. "Decay and the Political Gestalt of Decline in Bernard Mandeville and His Dutch Contemporaries." *History of European Ideas* 36 (2010): 153–66.

Bödeker, Hans E., and István Hont. "Naturrecht, Politische Ökonomie und Geschichte der Menschheit: der Diskurs über Politik und Gesellschaft in der Frühen Neuzeit." In *Naturrecht — Spätaufklärung — Revolution*, edited by Otto Dann and Diethelm Klippel, 80–89. Hamburg: Meiner, 1995.

Bondi, Yuri. "The Double Emergence of the Modified Internal Rate of Return: The Neglected Work of Duvillard (1755–1832) in a Comparative Perspective." *The European Journal of the History of Economic Thought* 13, no. 3 (2006): 311–35.

Bosse, Heinrich. *Autorschaft ist Werkherrschaft: Über die Entstehung des Urheberrechts aus dem Geist der Goethezeit.* Munich: Wilhelm Fink, 2014.

Bossenga, Gail. "Origins of the French Revolution." *History Compass* 5, no. 4 (2007): 1294–1337.

Bossenga, Gail. "Financial Origins." In *From Deficit to Deluge: The Origins of the French Revolution*, edited by Thomas Kaiser and Dale Van Kley, 37–66. Stanford: Stanford University Press, 2011.

Bourdieu, Pierre. "Le marché des biens symboliques." *L'année sociologique* 22 (1971): 49–126.

Bourdieu, Pierre. "The Market of Symbolic Goods." *Poetics: Journal of Empirical Research on Literature, the Media, and the Arts* 14, no. 1-2 (1985): 13–44.

Bourdieu, Pierre. "Un acte désintéressé est-il possible?" In *Raisons pratiques: Sur la théorie de l'action*, 147–74. Paris: Seuil, 1994.

Bourdieu, Pierre. *The Rules of Art: Genesis and Structure of the Literary Field.* Translated by Susan Emanuel. Cambridge: Polity Press, 1996.

Bourdieu, Pierre. "Die Biographische Illusion." In *Praktische Vernunft: Zur Theorie des Handelns.* 75–82. Frankfurt: Suhrkamp, 1998.

Bourdieu, Pierre. "Is a Disinterested Act Possible?" In *Practical Reason: On the Theory of Action*, 75–91. Cambridge: Polity, 1998.

Brace, Harrison H. *The Value of Organized Speculation.* Boston: The Riverside Press Cambridge, 1913.

Bracht, Johannes, and Ulrich Pfister. *Landpacht, Marktgesellschaft und agrarische Entwicklung. Fünf Adelsgüter zwischen Rhein und Weser, 16.–19. Jahrhundert.* Stuttgart: Steiner, 2020.

Braudel, Fernand. *Civilisation matérielle, économie et capitalisme, XVᵉ–XVIIIᵉ siècle.* 3 vols. Paris: Armand Colin, 1979.

Brown, Clifford. "Leibniz and Aesthetics." *Philosophy and Phenomenological Research* 28, no. 1 (1967): 70–80.

Brown, Gregory. "Disinterested Love: Understanding Leibniz's Reconciliation of Self- and Other-Regarding Motives." *British Journal for the History of Philosophy* 19, no. 2 (2011): 265–303.

Brugmans, Henri L. "Autour de Diderot en Hollande." *Diderot Studies* 3 (1961): 55–71.

Brun, Jacques Le. *Le pur amour de Platon à Lacan.* Paris: Seuil, 2002.

Bruner, Robert F., and Sean D. Carr. *The Panic of 1907: Lessons Learned from the Market's Perfect Storm.* Hoboken: John Wiley & Sons, 2009.

Buber, Martin. *Ich und Du.* Stuttgart: Reclam, 1995.

Bücher, Karl. *Die Entstehung der Volkswirtschaft.* Tübingen: Laupp, 1913.

Bunge, Wiep van. *From Stevin to Spinoza: An Essay on Philosophy in the Seventeenth-Century Dutch Republic.* Leiden: Brill, 2001.

Burguière, André. "L'État monarchique et la famille (XVIᵉ–XVIIIᵉ siècle)." *Annales. Histoire, Sciences Sociales*, no. 2 (March–April 2001): 313–335.

Capp, Bernard. *England's Culture Wars: Puritan Reformation and Its Enemies in the Interregnum, 1649–1660.* Oxford: Oxford University Press, 2012.

Cardoso, José L., and António de Vasconcelos Nogueira. "*Isaac de Pinto* (1717–1787): An Enlightened Economist and Financier." *History of Political Economy* 37 (2005): 264–92.

Cardoso, José Luís, and António de Vasconcelos Nogueira. "Isaac de Pinto (1717–1787) and the Jewish Problems: Apologetic Letters to Voltaire and Diderot." *History of European Ideas* 33, no. 4 (2007): 476–87.

Carrier, James G. "Maussian Occidentalism: Gift and Commodity Systems." In *Occidentalism: Images of the West*, edited by James G. Carrier, 85–108. Oxford: Clarendon Press, 1995.

Cassirer, Ernst. *The Philosophy of the Enlightenment.* Translated by Fritz C. A. Koelln and James P. Pettegrove. Boston: Beacon Press, 1955.

Chakrabarty, Dipesh. *Provincializing Europe: Postcolonial Thought and Historical Difference.* Princeton: Princeton University Press, 2000.

Chalk, Alfred F. "Mandeville's Fable of the Bees: A Reappraisal." *Southern Economic Journal* 33, no. 1 (July 1966): 1–16.

Chapman, Malcolm, and Peter J. Buckley. "Markets, Transaction Costs, Economists and Social Anthropologists." In *Meanings of the Market: The Free Market in Western Culture*, edited by James G. Carrier, 225–50. Oxford: Berg, 1997.

Charlier, Gustave. "Diderot et la Hollande." *Revue de littérature comparée* 82 (1947): 190–229.

Chartier, Roger. *Les Origines culturelles de la Révolution française.* Paris: Seuil, 1990.

Chenon, Emile. "De la transformation du domaine royal en domaine de la Couronne du XIVe au XVIe siècle." *Revue historique du droit francais et etranger* 4, no. 4 (1925): 528–30.

Clapp, Elizabeth J., and Julie R. Jeffrey, eds. *Women, Dissent and Anti-slavery in Britain and America, 1790–1865.* Oxford: Oxford University Press, 2011.

Cochrane, Richard. "The Tape Readers: Financial Trading as a Visual Practice." *Philosophy of Photography* 8 (2017): 109–17.

Cohen, Huguette. "Galiani, Diderot, and Nature's Loaded Dice." *Studies on Voltaire and the Eighteenth Century* 311 (1993): 35–59.

Condorelli, Stefano, and Daniel Menning, eds. *Boom, Bust, and Beyond: New Perspectives on the 1720 Stock Market Bubble.* Munich: De Gruyter, 2019.

Cook, Harold J. *Matters of Exchange: Commerce, Medicine and Science in the Dutch Golden Age.* New Haven, CT: Yale University Press, 2007.

Cormeré, Guillaume François Mahy de. *Mémoire général sur le crédit et sur les finances.* Paris: chez l'auteur, 1789.

Cowing, Cedric B. "Market Speculation in the Muckraker Era: The Popular Reaction." *Business History Review* 31 (1957): 403–13.

Cowing, Cedric B. *Populists, Plungers, and Progressives: A Social History of Stock and Commodity Speculation, 1890–1936.* Princeton: Princeton University Press, 1965.

Crafts, Nicholas F. R. "Explaining the First Industrial Revolution: Two Views." *European Review of Economic History* 15, no. 1 (April 2011): 153–68.

Crest, Aurélie du. *Modèle familial et pouvoir monarchique (XVIe–XVIIIe).* Vol. 1. Aix-en-Provence: Presses universitaires Aix-Marseille, 2002.

Cronon, William. *Nature's Metropolis: Chicago and the Great West.* New York: W. W. Norton, 1991.

Czarnecka, Agnieszka. "Taming Egoism: Adam Smith on Empathy, Imagination and Justice." *Cracow Studies of Constitutional and Legal History* 9, no. 2 (2016): 233–41.

Daal, Jan van, and Arnold Heertje, eds. *Economic Thought in the Netherlands, 1650–1950.* Aldershot: Avebury, 1992.

Dahrendorf, Ralf. *Homo Sociologicus. Ein Versuch zur Geschichte, Bedeutung und Kritik der sozialen Rolle.* 17th ed. Wiesbaden: VS Verlag für Sozialwissenschaften, 2010.

Darnton, Robert. *The Literary Underground of the Old Regime.* Cambridge, MA: Harvard University Press, 1982.

Davids, Karel. "From De la Court to Vreede: Regulation and Self-regulation in Dutch Economic Discourse from c. 1660 to the Napoleonic Era." *The Journal of European Economic History* 30, no. 2 (2001): 245–89.

Davids, Karel. "Economic Discourse in Europe between Scholasticism and Mandeville: Convergence, Divergence and the Case of the Dutch Republic." In *Departure for Modern Europe: A Handbook of Early Modern Philosophy (1400–1700)*, edited by Hubertus Busche and Stefan Heßbrüggen-Walter, 80–95. Hamburg: Felix Meiner Verlag, 2011.

De Angelis, Simone. "Lex naturalis, Leges naturae, 'Regeln der Moral': der Begriff des 'Naturgesetzes' und die Entstehung der modernen 'Wissenschaften vom Menschen' im naturrechtlichen Zeitalter." In *'Natur', Naturrecht und Geschichte: Aspekte eines fundamentalen Begründungsdiskurses der Neuzeit (1600–1900)*, edited by Simone De Angelis, Florian Gelzer, and Lucas M. Gisi, 47–70. Heidelberg: Winter, 2010.

De Angelis, Simone. *Anthropologien, Genese und Konfiguration einer "Wissenschaft vom Menschen" in der Frühen Neuzeit.* Berlin, New York: De Gruyter, 2010.

De Angelis, Simone. "Gedankenexperimente, Analogien und kühne Hypothesen: die Bedeutung der 'Wissenschaften vom Leben' für die Beziehung von Anthropologie und Geschichtsdenken in der Spätaufklärung — ein programmatischer Entwurf." In *Konzepte der Einbildungskraft in der Philosophie, den Wissenschaften und den Künsten des 18. Jahrhunderts*, edited by Rudolf Meer, Giuseppe Motta, and Gideon Stiening, 303–21. Berlin, Boston: De Gruyter, 2019.

Décultot, Élisabeth. "Le Laocoon de Gotthold Ephraim Lessing: de l'imagination comme fondement d'une nouvelle méthode critique." *Les Études philosophiques* 65, no. 2 (2003): 197–212.

Dejung, Christof. "Worldwide Ties: The Role of Family Businesses in Global Trade in the 19th and 20th Century." *Business History* 55 (2013): 1001–18.

Dejung, Christof, Monika Dommann, and Daniel Speich Chassé, eds. *Auf der Suche nach der Ökonomie: Historische Annäherungen.* Tübingen: Mohr Siebeck, 2014.

Dejung, Christof. *Commodity Trading, Globalization and the Colonial World: Spinning the Web of the Global Market.* New York: Routledge, 2018.

Derringer, Will. *Calculated Values: Finance, Politics, and the Quantitative Age, 1688–1766.* Cambridge, MA: Cambridge University Press, 2018.

Descimon, Robert. "Les Fonctions de la métaphore du marriage politique du roi et de la république, France, XVè–XVIIIè siècles." *Annales. Économies, Sociétés, Civilisations*, no. 6 (November–December 1992): 1127–1147.

Descimon, Robert. "L'Union au domaine royal et le principe d'inaliénabilité. La construction d'une loi fondamentale aux XVIè et XVIIè siècle." *Droits* 22, no. 1 (January 1995): 79–90.

Diatkine, Daniel. *Adam Smith. La Découverte du capitalisme et de ses limites.* Paris: Seuil, 2019.

Dilcher, Gerhard. "Alteuropäischer Adel: Ein verfassungsgeschichtlicher Typus?" *Geschichte und Gesellschaft, Sonderheft* 13 (1990): 57–86.

Dinges, Martin. "Wandel des Stellenwertes der Ökonomie in Selbstzeugnissen der Frühen Neuzeit." In *Menschen und Märkte: Studien zur historischen Wirtschaftsanthropologie*, edited by Wolfgang Reinhard and Justin Stagl, 269–90. Vienna: Böhlau, 2007.

Dixit, Avinash K., and Joseph E. Stiglitz. "Monopolistic Competition and Optimum Product Diversity." *American Economic Review* 67, no. 3 (June 1977): 297–308.

Douglas, Mary. *Natural Symbols: Explorations in Cosmology*. London: Cresset, 1970.

Doyle, Thomas. *Origins of the French Revolution*. Oxford: Oxford University Press, 1980.

Drayton, Richard. *Nature's Government: Science, Imperial Britain, and the 'Improvement' of the World*. New Haven, CT: Yale University Press, 2000.

Duflo, Colas. *Le jeu: De Pascal à Schiller*. Paris: PUF, 1997.

Dumont, Louis. *Homo hierarchicus. Le système des castes et ses implications*. Paris: Gallimard, 1979.

Dunkley, John. *Gambling: A Social and Moral Problem in France, 1685–1792*. Oxford: Voltaire Foundation, 1985, 188–217.

Dunn, Kevin. "Milton among the Monopolists: Areopagitica, Intellectual Property and the Hartlib Circle." In *Samuel Hartlib and the Universal Reformation: Studies in Intellectual Communication*, edited by Mark Greengrass, Michael Leslie, and Timothy Raylor, 177–92. Cambridge: Cambridge University Press, 1994.

Duranti, Alessandro. "Mediated Encounters with Pacific Cultures: Three Samoan Dinners." In *Visions of Empire: Voyages, Botany, and Representations of Nature*, edited by David P. Miller and Peter H. Reill, 326–334. Cambridge: Cambridge University Press, 1996.

Eamon, William R. "From the Secrets of Nature to Public Knowledge: The Origins of the Concept of Openness in Science." *Minerva* 23, no. 3 (September 1985): 321–47.

Edgeworth, Francis Y. *Mathematical Psychics. An Essay on the Application of Mathematics to the Moral Sciences*. London: C. Kegan Paul & Co, 1881.

Elias, Norbert. *The Court Society*. New York: Pantheon Books, 1983.

Ellenberger, Henry F. *Die Entdeckung des Unbewussten*. Stuttgart: Verlag Hans Huber, 1973.

Ellerbrock, Karl-Peter, and Clemens Wischermann, eds. *Die Wirtschaftsgeschichte vor der Herausforderung durch die New Institutional Economics*. Dortmund: Gesellschaft für Westfälische Wirtschaftsgeschichte, 2004.

Elster, Jon. *Sour Grapes: Studies in the Subversion of Rationality*. Cambridge, UK: Cambridge University Press, 1983.

Elster, Jon, ed. *Rational Choice: Readings in Social and Political Theory*. Oxford: Blackwell, 1986.

Elster, Jon. "Social Norms and Economic Theory." *Journal of Economic Perspectives* 3, no. 4 (1989): 99–117.

Elster, Jon. *Nuts and Bolts for the Social Sciences*. Cambridge, UK: Cambridge University Press, 1989.

Elwert, Georg. "Sanktionen, Ehre und Gabenökonomie: Kulturelle Mechanismen der Einbettung von Märkten." In *Wirtschaftsgeschichte als Kulturgeschichte, Dimensionen eines Perspektivenwechsels*, edited by Hartmut Berghoff and Jakob Vogel, 119–42. Frankfurt a.M: Campus, 2004.

Emery, Henry C. "Legislation against Futures." *Political Science Quarterly* 10 (1895): 62–86.

Emery, Henry C. *Speculation on the Stock and Produce Exchanges of the United States.* New York, 1896.

Esarey, Logan, ed. *The Pioneers of Morgan County. Memoirs of Noah J. Major.* Indianapolis: Edward J. Hecker, 1915.

Esmein, Adhemar. "L'Inalienabilite du domaine de la Couronne devant les Etats Generaux du XVIᵉ siècle." In *Festschrift Otto Gierke zum Siebzigsten Geburtstag,* 361–382. Weimar: Hermann Bohlaus Nachfolger, 1911.

Evans-Pritchard, Edward E. "Anthropology and History." In *Essays in Social Anthropology,* edited by Edward E. Evans-Pritchard, 172–263. London: Faber & Faber, 1962.

Evrigenis, Ioannis D., and Mark Somos, "Wrestling with Machiavelli." *History of European Ideas* 37, no. 2 (2011): 85–93.

Ezell, John S. *Fortune's Merry Wheel: The Lottery in America.* Cambridge, MA: Harvard University Press, 1960.

Fabian, Ann. *Card Sharps and Bucket Shops: Gambling in Nineteenth-Century America.* London/New York: Routledge, 1999.

Fabian, Johannes. *Time and the Other: How Anthropology Makes its Object.* New York: Columbia University Press, 1983.

Faccarello, Gilbert. "A Tale of Two Traditions: Pierre Force's Self-Interest before Adam Smith." *European Journal of the History of Economic Thought* 12, no. 4 (2005): 701–12.

Fairchilds, Cissie. "The Production and Marketing of Populuxe Goods in Eighteenth-century Paris." In *Consumption and the World of Goods,* edited by John Brewer and Roy Porter, 228–48. London: Routledge, 1993.

Feldmann, Reinhard. "Gräflich von Spee'sche Bibliothek Schloß Heltorf." In *Handbuch der historischen Buchbestände in Deutschland,* edited by Bernhard Fabian. Vol. 4. Hildesheim/Zürich/New York: Olms, 2003.

Ferrari, Anne. "Bossuet et Fénelon: la lettre qui tue." *Littératures classiques* 59, no.1 (2006): 299–316.

Fertig, Christine, and Ulrich Pfister. "Coffee, Mind and Body: Global Material Culture and the Eighteenth Century Hamburg Import Trade." In *The Global Lives of Things: The Material Culture of Connections in the Early Modern World,* edited by Anne Gerritsen and Giorgio Riello, 221–40. London: Routledge, 2016.

Findlay, John M. *People of Chance: Gambling in American Society from Jamestown to Las Vegas.* New York: Oxford University Press, 1986.

Finley, Moses. *The Ancient Economy.* Berkeley: University of California Press, 1999.

Firth, Raymond, ed. *Themes in Economic Anthropology.* London: Tavistock, 1967.

Fisher, Irving. *The Nature of Capital and Income.* New York: MacMillan, 1906.

Force, Pierre. *Self-Interest before Adam Smith: A Genealogy of Economic Science.* Cambridge: Cambridge University Press, 2003.

Forget, Evelyn L. "Evocations of Sympathy: Sympathetic Imagery in Eighteenth-Century Social Theory and Physiology." Annual supplement, *History of Political Economy* 35 (2003): 290–95.

Foster, Robert, and Timothy Tacket, eds. "The Origins of the French Revolution: A Debate." *French Historical Studies* 16 (1990): 741–65.

Foucault, Michel. *Security, Territory, Population.* Basingstoke: Palgrave Macmillan, 2007.

Fox, Justin. *The Myth of the Rational Market: A History of Risk, Reward, and Delusion on Wall Street.* New York: Harper Business, 2009.

Frank, Robert H. *Passions Within Reason: The Strategic Role of Emotions.* New York: W. W. Norton, 1988.

Fraser, Steven. *Wall Street: A Cultural History.* London: Faber & Faber, 2006.

Freer, Alan J. "Isaac de Pinto e la sua 'lettre à Mr. D[iderot] sur le jeu des cartes.'" *Annali della Scuola Normale Superiore di Pisa. Lettere, Storia e Filosofia, Serie II,* 33, no. 1/2 (1964): 93–117.

Freundlich, Francis. *Le monde du jeu à Paris 1715–1800.* Paris: Albin Michel, 1995.

Furet, François. *Penser la Révolution française.* Paris: Gallimard, 1978.

Perry, Gauci, ed. *Regulating the British Economy, 1660–1850.* Farnham: Ashgate, 2011.

Geerdink, Nina. *Dichters en verdiensten: De sociale verankering van het dichterschap van Jan Vos (1610–1667).* Hilversum: Verloren, 2012.

Gelderen, Martin van, and Quentin Skinner. *Republicanism: A Shared European Heritage.* 2 vols. Cambridge, NY: Cambridge University Press, 2002.

Giesey, Ralph E. "The Juristic Basis of Dynastic Right to the French Throne." *Transactions of the American Philosophical Society* 51, no. 5 (1961): 3–47.

Gigerenzer, Gerd, Zeno Swijtink, Theodore Porter, Lorraine Daston, John Beatty, and Lorenz Kruger. *The Empire of Chance: How Probability Changed Science and Everyday Life.* Cambridge: Cambridge University Press, 1989.

Gigerenzer, Gerd, and Peter M. Todd. *Simple Heuristics that Make Us Smart.* New York: Oxford, 1999.

Gillespie, Ryan. "Gilders and Gamblers: The Culture of Speculative Capitalism in the United States." *Communication, Culture & Critique* 5 (2012): 352–71.

Gintis, Herbert, Samuel Bowles, Robert Boyd, and Ernst Fehr. "Moral Sentiments and Material Interests: Origins, Evidence, and Consequences." In *Moral Sentiments and Material Interests: The Foundations of Cooperation in Economic Life,* edited by Herbert Gintis, Samuel Bowles, and Robert T. Boyd, 3–39. Cambridge, MA, London: MIT Press, 2005.

Glenn, Cheryl. *Rhetoric Retold: Regendering the Tradition from Antiquity through the Renaissance.* Carbondale and Edwardsville: Southern Illinois University Press, 1997.

Gobbers, Walter. *Jean-Jacques Rousseau in Holland: Een onderzoek naar de invloed van de mens en het werk (ca. 1760–1810).* Gent: secr. KVATL, 1963.

Godelier, Maurice. *Rationality and Irrationality in Economics.* New York: Monthly Review Press, 1972.

Goede, Marieke de. *Virtue, Fortune, and Faith: A Genealogy of Finance.* Minneapolis: University of Minnesota Press, 2005.

Goodfellow, David M. *Principles of Economic Sociology: The Economics of Primitive Life as Illustrated from the Bantu Peoples of South and East Africa.* London: Routledge, 1939.

Goody, Jack. *The East in the West.* Cambridge: Cambridge University Press, 1996.

Graaf, José Mulder van de, and Richard Rottenburg. "Feldforschung in Unternehmen. Ethnografische Explorationen in der eigenen Gesellschaft." In *Teilnehmende Beobachtung: Werkstattberichte und methodologische Reflexionen,* edited by Reiner Aster, Hans Merkens, and Michael Repp, 19–34. Frankfurt a.M: Campus, 1989.

Graber, Frédéric, and Martin Giraudeau, eds. *Les projets: Une histoire politique (XVIᵉ–XXIᵉ siècles)*. Paris: Presse des Mines, 2018.

Granovetter, Mark. "Economic Action and Social Structure: The Problem of Embeddedness." *The American Journal of Sociology* 91, no. 3 (November 1985): 481–510.

Greif, Avner. "Institutions and International Trade: Lessons from the Commercial Revolution." *The American Economic Review* 82 (1992): 128–33.

Gross, Thomas. "From Karl Bücher to the Formalist-Substantivist Debate." In *Karl Bücher: Theory – History – Anthropology – Non Market Economies*, edited by Jürgen G. Backhaus, 245–74. Marburg: Metropolis 2000.

Grote, Simon. *The Emergence of Modern Aesthetic Theory: Religion and Morality in Enlightenment Germany and Scotland*. Cambridge, Cambridge University Press, 2017.

Grotius, Hugues. *Le Droit de la guerre et de la paix*. Amsterdam: Pierre De Coup, 1724.

Gunn, John A. W. "'Interest Will Not Lie': A Seventeenth-Century Political Maxim." *Journal of the History of Ideas* 29, no. 4 (October–December 1968): 551–64.

Guyer, Paul. *A History of Modern Aesthetics*. Vol. 1. *The Eighteenth Century*. Cambridge: Cambridge University Press, 2014.

Hacking, Ian. *The Taming of Chance*. Cambridge: Cambridge University Press, 1990.

Hall, Peter A., and David Soskice. *Varieties of Capitalism: The Institutional Foundations of Comparative Advantage*. Oxford: Oxford University Press, 2001.

Hann, Chris. *Social Anthropology*. London: Hodder & Stoughton, 2000.

Hann, Chris. "Tradition, sozialer Wandel, Evolution. Defizite in der sozialanthropologischen Tradition." In *Rationalität im Prozess kultureller Evolution: Rationalitätsunterstellungen als eine Bedingung der Möglichkeit substantieller Rationalität des Handelns*, edited by Hansjörg Siegenthaler, 283–301. Tübingen: Mohr Siebeck, 2005.

Hann, Chris, and Keith Hart, eds. *Market and Society: The Great Transformation Today*. Cambridge: Cambridge University Press, 2009.

Hansen, Kristian B. "Contrarian Investment Philosophy in the American Stock Market: On Investment Advice and the Crowd Conundrum." *Economy and Society* 44 (2015): 616–38.

Hasenberg-Butter, Irene. *Academic Economics in Holland, 1800–1870*. Den Haag: Nijhoff, 1969.

Hatch, Nathan. *The Democratization of American Christianity, 1800–1860*. New Haven: Yale University Press, 1989.

Hayek, Friedrich August von. *Individualism and Economic Order*. Chicago: Chicago University Press, 1996.

Heilbron, Johan. "French Moralists and the Anthropology of the Modern Era." In *The Rise of the Social Sciences and the Formation of Modernity*, edited by Johan Heilbron, Lars Magnusson, and Björn Wittroch, 77–106. Dordrecht: Kluwer Academic, 1998.

Henderson, David. *Misguided Virtue: False Notions of Corporate Social Responsibility*. London: The Institute of Economic Affairs, 2001.

Henning, Friedrich-Wilhelm. "Dienste und Abgaben der Bauern im 18. Jahrhundert." In *Quellen und Forschungen zur Agrargeschichte*, edited by Wilhelm Abel and Günther Franz. Stuttgart: Fischer, 1969.

Henry, Aaron J. "William Petty, the Down Survey, Population and Territory in the Seventeenth Century." *Territory, Politics, Governance* 2, no. 2 (2014): 1–20.

Hersh, Jonathan, and Hans-Joachim Voth. "Sweet Diversity: Colonial Goods and the Rise of European Living Standards after 1492." *CEPR Discussion Paper* 7386, no. DP7386 (2009)

Herskovits, Melville. "Economics and Anthropology: A Rejoinder." *Journal of Political Economy* 49 (1941): 269–78.

Herskovits, Melville. *Economic Anthropology: A Study in Comparative Economics.* New York: A. Knopf, 1952.

Hess, Jonathan. *Reconstituting the Body Politic. Enlightenment, Public Culture and the Invention of Aesthetic Autonomy.* Detroit: Wayne State University Press, 1999.

Hesse, Carla. "Enlightenment Epistemology and the Laws of Authorship in Revolutionary France, 1777–1793." Special issue, *Representations* 30 (Spring 1990): 109–37.

Hesse, Carla. *Publishing and Cultural Politics in Revolutionary Paris.* Berkeley/Los Angeles: University of California Press, 1991.

Hill, John. *Gold Bricks of Speculation: A Study of Speculation and Its Counterfeits, an Exposé of the Methods of Bucketshop and "Get-Rich-Quick" Swindles.* Chicago: Lincoln Book Concern, 1904.

Hirschman, Albert O. *The Passions and the Interests: Political Arguments for Capitalism before Its Triumph.* Princeton: Princeton University Press, 1977.

Hirschman, Albert O. *The Passions and the Interests. Political Arguments for Capitalism Before Its Triumph*, 3rd ed. Princeton: Princeton University Press, 2013.

Hirschman, Albert O. "Political Economics and Possibilism." In *The Essential Hirschman*, edited by Jeremy Adelman, 1–34. 2nd ed. Princeton: Princeton University Press, 2015.

Hobson, John A. "The Ethics of Gambling." In *Betting and Gambling. A National Evil*, edited by Benjamin Seebohm Rowntree, 1–20. London: Macmillan, 1905.

Hochfelder, David. "'Where the Common People Could Speculate': The Ticker, Bucket Shops, and the Origins of Popular Participation in Financial Markets, 1880–1920." *Journal of American History* 93 (2006): 335–58.

Hochfelder, David. *The Telegraph in America, 1832–1920.* Baltimore: Johns Hopkins University Press, 2012.

Hochman, Leah. "The Ugly Made Beautiful." *Journal of Modern Jewish Studies* 5, no. 2 (2006): 137–61.

Hogan, Sarah. *Other Englands: Utopia, Capital, and Empire in an Age of Transition.* Stanford: Stanford University Press, 2018.

Holzhey, Tanja, Kornee van der Haven, and Rudolf Rasch, ed. *Nil Volebtibus Arduum. Tieranny van eigenbaat (1679). Toneel als wapen tegen Oranje.* Zoeterwoude: Astraea, 2008.

Hont, István, ed. *Jealousy of Trade: International Competition and the Nation-State in Historical Perspective.* Cambridge, MA/London: Harvard University Press, 2005.

Hont, István. *Jealousy of Trade: International Competition and the Nation-State in Historical Perspective.* Cambridge, MA: Harvard University Press, 2005.

Hont, István. "Luxury and Commerce." In *The Cambridge History of Eighteenth-Century Political Thought*, edited by Mark Goldie and Robert Wokler, 379–418. Cambridge: Cambridge University Press, 2006.

Hont, István. "The Early Enlightenment Debate on Commerce and Luxury." In *The Cambridge History of Eighteenth-Century Political Thought*, edited by Mark Goldie and Robert Wokler, 379–428. Cambridge, NY: Cambridge University Press, 2006.

Hont, István. *Politics in Commercial Society: Jean-Jacques Rousseau and Adam Smith*. Cambridge, MA: Harvard University Press, 2015.

Hoppit, Julian. "The Contexts and Contours of British Economic Literature, 1660–1760." *Historical Journal* 49, no. 1 (March 2006): 79–110.

Hoppit, Julian. *Britain's Political Economies: Parliament and Economic Life, 1660–1800*. Cambridge: Cambridge University Press, 2017.

Horne, Thomas A. *The Social Thought of Bernard Mandeville: Virtue and Commerce in Early Eighteenth-Century England*. London: Macmillan, 1978.

Howe-Adams, Jedediah. "Concerning the Physician's Finances." *Medical Times* 32 (1908): 161–68.

Richard, Hoyle, ed. *Custom, Improvement and the Landscape in Early Modern Britain*. Farnham: Ashgate, 2011. http://www.historicum-estudies.net/epublished/netzbiographie/preussische-zeit/mineralbrunnen/.

Hume, David. *Enquiries Concerning the Human Understanding and Concerning the Principles of Morals*. Oxford: Clarendon, 1902.

Humphries, Jane, and Jacob Weisdorf. "Unreal Wages? Real Income and Economic Growth in England: 1260–1850." *Economic Journal* 129, no. 623 (October 2019): 2867–87.

Hundert, Edward J. *The Enlightenment's Fable: Bernard Mandeville and the Discovery of Society*. Cambridge: Cambridge University Press, 1994.

Hunt, Lynn. *Politics, Culture and Class in the French Revolution*. Berkeley: University of California Press, 1984.

Ingram, John K. *A History of Political Economy*. New York: The Macmillan Company, 1902.

Isambert, Decrussy, and Taillandier, eds. *Recueil general des anciennes lois francaises depuis l'an 420 jusqu'à la Révolution de 1789*. Vol. 14. Paris, 1829.

Isambert, Decrusy, and Taillandier, eds. *Recueil general des anciennes lois francaises depuis l'an 420 jusqu'à la Révolution de 1789*. Vol. 15. Paris, 1829.

Isenmann, Moritz. "Die langsame Entstehung eines ökonomischen Systems: Konkurrenz und freier Markt im Werk von Adam Smith." *Historische Zeitschrift* 307 (2018): 665–69.

Israel, Jonathan. *The Dutch Republic: Its Rise, Greatness and Fall, 1477–1806*. Oxford: Clarendon Press, 1998.

Israel, Jonathan. *Radical Enlightenment: Philosophy and the Making of Modernity, 1650–1750*. Oxford: Oxford University Press, 2001.

Jacob, Margaret C., and Catherine Secretan, eds. *The Self-Perception of Early Modern Capitalists*. New York, NY: Macmillan, 2008.

Jacob, Margaret C. *The First Knowledge Economy: Human Capital and the European Economy, 1750–1850*. Cambridge: Cambridge University Press, 2014.

James, Harold. *Krupp: A History of the Legendary German Firm*. Princeton: Princeton University Press, 2012.

James, Susan. *Passion and Action: The Emotions in Seventeenth-Century Philosophy*. Oxford: Clarendon Press, 1997.

Johannes, Gert-Jan, and Inger Leemans. *Worm en Donder. Geschiedenis van de Nederlandse Letterkunde 1700–1800*. Amsterdam: Prometheus, 2013.

Johannes, Gert-Jan, and Inger Leemans. "O Thou Great God of Trade, O Subject of my Song!": Dutch Poems on Trade, 1770–1830. *Eighteenth-Century Studies* 51, no. 3 (Spring 2014): 337–356.

Johannes, Gert-Jan, and Inger Leemans. "'Van den handel zou hij zingen'. Nederlandse koophandelsgedichten 1770–1830." *De Negentiende Eeuw* 40, no. 1 (2016): 1–33.

Johannes, Gert-Jan, and Inger Leemans, "'O Thou Great God of Trade, O Subject of my Song!' Dutch Poems on Trade 1770–1830." *Eighteenth-Century Studies* 51, no. 3 (2018): 337–56.

Jones, Edward D. *Economic Crises*. New York: Macmillan, 1900.

Jordan, Julia. *Chance and the Modern British Novel: From Henry Green to Iris Murdoch*. London: Continuum, 2010.

Journeaux, Isabelle. "Le jeu à travers les romanciers français et anglais du XVIIIᵉ siècle." *Revue d'histoire moderne et contemporaine* 40, no. 1 (1993): 49–85.

Kahneman, Daniel, and Amos Tversky. "Prospect Theory: An Analysis of Decisions Under Risk." *Econometria* 47, no. 2 (March 1979): 264–91.

Kahneman, Daniel, and Amos Tversky. *Choices, Values, and Frames*. Cambridge, UK: Cambridge University Press, 2000.

Kahneman, Daniel. "Maps of Bounded Rationality: Psychology for Behavioral Economics." *The American Economic Review* 93, no. 5 (Dec 2003): 1449–495.

Thomas, Kaiser, and Dale Van Kley, eds. *From Deficit to Deluge: The Origins of the French Revolution*. Stanford: Stanford University Press, 2011.

Kamarck, Andrew M. *Economics as a Social Science: An Approach to Nonautistic Theory*. Ann Arbor: University of Michigan Press, 2002.

Kantorowicz, Ernst H. *The King's Two Bodies: A Study in Medieval Political Theology*. Princeton: Princeton University Press, 1957.

Kaplan, Steven L. *Bread, Politics and Political Economy in the Reign of Louis XV*. 2nd ed. London: Anthem Press, 2015.

Kapossy, Béla, Isaac Nakhimovsky, and Richard Whatmore, eds. *Commerce and Peace in the Enlightenment*. Cambridge: Cambridge University Press, 2017.

Kargol-Wasiluk, Aneta, Anna Wildowicz-Giegiel, and Marian Zalesko. "The Evolution of the Economic Man: From Homo Oeconomicus to Homo Moralis." *Gospodarka Narodowa* 29, no. 1 (February/March 2018): 33–57.

Karpik, Lucien. *Les Avocats: Entre l'etat, le public et le marché. XIIIᵉ–XXᵉ siècle*. Paris: Gallimard, 1995.

Kavanagh, Thomas M. *Enlightenment and the Shadows of Chance: The Novel and the Culture of Gambling in Eighteenth-century France*. Baltimore: Johns Hopkins University Press, 1993.

Kavanagh, Thomas M. "The Libertine's Bluff: Cards and Culture in Eighteenth-Century France." *Eighteenth-Century Studies* 33, no. 4 (2000): 505–21.

Kavanagh, Thomas M. *Dice, Cards, Wheels: A Different History of French Culture*. Philadelphia: University of Pennsylvania Press, 2013.

Kaye, Frederick B., ed. *The Fable of the Bees: Or, Private Vices, Public Benefits: by Bernhard Mandeville*. Oxford: Clarendon Press, 1924.

Keinemann, Friedrich. *Vom Krummstab zur Republik: Westfälischer Adel unter preußischer Herrschaft 1802–1945*. Bochum: Brockmeyer, 1997.

Keller, Vera. "Mining Tacitus: Secrets of Empire, Nature and Art in the Reason of State." *British Journal for the History of Science* 45, no. 2 (2012): 189–212.

Keller, Vera. *Knowledge and the Public Interest, 1575–1725*. Cambridge: Cambridge University Press, 2015.

Keller, Vera, and Ted McCormick. "Towards a History of Projects." *Early Science and Medicine* 21, no. 5 (2016): 423–44.

Kelly, Christopher. *Rousseau as Author: Consecrating One's Life to the Truth.* Chicago: University of Chicago Press, 2003.

Kirkpatrick, Kate. *Becoming Beauvoir: A Life.* London/New York: Bloomsbury Academic, 2019.

Kloek, Joost J., and Wijnand W. Mijnhardt. *1800: Blueprints for a National Community.* Assen: Van Gorcum, 2004.

Knight, Frank. "Anthropology and Economics." *Journal of Political Economy* 49 (1941): 247–68.

Knight, Frank. *Reading the Market: Genres of Financial Capitalism in Gilded Age America.* Baltimore: Johns Hopkins University Press, 2016.

Kocka, Jürgen, and Marcel van der Linden, eds. *Capitalism: The Reemergence of a Historical Concept.* London: Bloomsbury, 2016.

Koppers, Wilhelm. "Die ethnologische Wirtschaftsforschung: Eine historisch-kritische Studie." *Anthropos. Internationale Zeitschrift für Völker- und Sprachkunde* 10 (1915): 611–651.

Koppers, Wilhelm. "Die ethnologische Wirtschaftsforschung: Eine historisch-kritische Studie." *Anthropos. Internationale Zeitschrift für Völker- und Sprachkunde* 11 (1916): 971–1070.

Kriedte, Peter, Hans Medick, and Jürgen Schlumbohm. *Industrialization before Industrialization: Rural Industry and the Genesis of Capitalism.* Cambridge/Paris: Cambridge University Press/Maison des Sciences de l'Homme, 1981.

Lamb, Robert B. "Adam Smith's System: Sympathy Not Self-Interest." *Journal of the History of Ideas* 35, no. 4 (1974): 671–82.

Langsæther, Peter E., and Geoffrey Evans. "More than Self-Interest: Why Different Classes Have Different Attitudes to Income Inequality." *The British Journal of Sociology* (February 2020). DOI:10.1111/1468-4446.12747.

Latour, Bruno. *We Have Never Been Modern.* Cambridge, MA: Harvard University Press, 1993.

Laurence, Fontaine. *L'Économie morale: Pauvreté, credit et confiance dans l'Europe préindustrielle.* Paris: Gallimard, 2008.

Lawson, Thomas. *Frenzied Finance: The Crime of Amalgamated.* New York: Ridgway, 1905.

Lears, Jackson. *Something for Nothing: Luck in America.* New York: Viking, 2003.

Leemans, Inger, and Wouter de Vries. "Why Wind? How the Concept of Wind Trade Came to Embody Speculation in the Dutch Republic." *Journal of Modern History.* Forthcoming.

Lefèvre, Edwin. *Sampson Rock of Wall Street.* New York: Harper & Brothers, 1907.

Legêne, Susan. "The European Character of the Intellectual History of Dutch Empire." *BMGN—Low Countries Historical Review* 132, no. 2 (2017): 110–20.

Lemay, Edna H. *Dictionnaire des Constituants 1789–1791.* 2 vols. Paris: Universitas, 1991.

Lemire, Beverly. *Fashion's Favourite: The Cotton Trade and the Consumer in Britain: 1660–1800.* Oxford: Oxford University Press, 1991.

Leng, Thomas. *Benjamin Worsley (1618–1677): Trade, Interest and the Spirit in Revolutionary England.* Woodbridge: Royal Historical Society/Boydell Press, 2008.

Lesger, Clé. "Merchants in Charge: The Self-Perception of Amsterdam Merchants, ca. 1550–1700." In *The Self-Perception of Early Modern Capitalists*, edited by Margaret C. Jacob and Catherine Secretan, 75–97. New York: Palgrave Macmillan, 2008.

Lévi-Strauss, Claude. *Anthropologie structural*. Paris: Plon, 1958.

Lévi-Strauss, Claude. *La Pensée sauvage*. Paris: Plon, 1962.

Levy, Jonathan. "Contemplating Delivery: Futures Trading and the Problem of Commodity Exchange in the United States, 1875–1905." *American Historical Review* 111 (2006): 307–35.

Levy, Jonathan. *Freaks of Fortune: The Emerging World of Capitalism and Risk in America*. Cambridge, MA: Harvard University Press, 2012.

Levy, Jonathan. "Accounting for Profit and the History of Capital." *Critical History Studies* 1, no. 2 (Fall 2014): 171–214.

Lips, Julius E. *The Savage Hits Back*. New Haven: Yale University Press, 1937.

Lorenz, Chris, and Stefan Berger. *The Contested Nation: Ethnicity, Class, Religion and Gender in National Histories*. Basingstoke, New York: Palgrave Macmillan, 2008.

Lubinski, Christina. *Familienunternehmen in Westdeutschland: Corporate Governance und Gesellschafterkultur seit den 1960er Jahren*. Munich: Beck, 2010.

Luhmann, Niklas. *Die Wirtschaft der Gesellschaft*. Frankfurt a.M.: Suhrkamp, 1988.

Lütge, Friedrich. *Deutsche Sozial- und Wirtschaftsgeschichte: Ein Überblick*. 3rd ed. Berlin/Heidelberg/New York: Springer, 1979.

Macinnes, Allan I. "Covenanting Ideology in Seventeenth-Century Scotland." In *Political Thought in Seventeenth-Century Ireland: Kingdom or Colony*, edited by Jane H. Ohlmeyer, 191–200. Cambridge: Cambridge University Press, 2000.

Magnot-Ogilvy, Florence, ed. *Gagnons sans savoir comment: Représentations du Système de Law du XVIIIᵉ à nos jours*. Rennes: Presses Universitaire de Rennes, 2017.

Maissen, Thomas. "Der Staatsbegriff in Machiavellis Theorie des Wandels." In *Niccolò Machiavelli, Die Geburt des Staates*, edited by Manuel Knoll and Stefano Saracino, 55–70. Stuttgart: Steiner, 2010.

Maitland, Frederick W. "The Crown as Corporation." In *Maitland: Selected Essays*, edited by Harold D. Hazeltine, Gaillard Lapsley, and Percy H. Winfield, 108. Cambridge: Cambridge University Press, 1936.

Malinowski, Bronisław. "The Primitive Economics of the Trobriand Islanders." *Economic Journal* 31 (1921): 1–16.

Malinowski, Bronisław. *Argonauts of the Western Pacific: An Account of Native Enterprise and Adventure in the Archipelagoes of Melanesian New Guinea*. London: Routledge, 1922.

Marchal, Guy P. "Das 'Schweizeralpenland'. Eine imagologische Bastelei." In *Erfundene Schweiz: Konstruktionen nationaler Identität*, edited by Guy P. Marchal and Aram Mattioli, 37–49. Zurich: Chronos, 1992.

Masseau, Didier. *L'Invention de l'intellectuel dans l'Europe du XVIIIᵉ siècle*. Paris: PUF, 1994.

Mauss, Marcel. *The Gift: The Form and Reason for Exchange in Archaic Societies*. New York: Norton, 1990.

Mauzi, Robert. "*Écrivains et moralistes* du XVIIIᵉ siècle devant les jeux de hazard." *Revue des sciences humaines* 90 (1958): 219–56.

Mayer, Jean. "La philosophie de Diderot: une philosophie de joueur." *Le Jeu au XVIIIe siècle.* Aix-en-Provence: Edisud, 1976.

McCloskey, Deirdre. *Bourgeois Dignity: Why Economics Can't Explain the Modern World.* Chicago, IL: University of Chicago Press, 2010.

McCormick, Ted. *William Petty and the Ambitions of Political Arithmetic.* Oxford: Oxford University Press, 2009.

McLeod, Christine. *Heroes of Invention: Technology, Liberalism and British Industry, 1740–1914.* Cambridge: Cambridge University Press, 2007.

McRae, Andrew. *God Speed the Plough: The Representation of Agrarian England, 1500–1660.* Cambridge: Cambridge University Press, 1996.

Medema, Steven G. *The Hesitant Hand. Taming Self-Interest in the History of Economic Ideas.* Princeton: Princeton University Press, 2009.

Medick, Hans. *Leben und Überleben in Laichingen 1650–1900: Lokalgeschichte als Allgemeine Geschichte.* Göttingen: Vandenhoeck & Ruprecht, 1996.

Meizoz, Jérôme. *Le Gueux philosophe (Jean-Jacques Rousseau).* Lausanne: Antipodes, 2003.

Mely, Benoît. *Jean-Jacques Rousseau, un intellectuel en rupture.* Paris: Minerve, 1985.

Menning, Daniel. *Politik, Ökonomie, Aktienspekulation: 'South Sea Bubble und Co.' 1720.* Berlin/Boston: DeGruyter, 2020.

Messina, Luisa. "Les jeux de cartes dans le roman libertin du dix-huitième siècle." *Les chantiers de la création* 11 (2019). https://doi.org/10.4000/lcc.1562.

Middleton, Simon, and James E. Shaw, eds. *Market Ethics and Practices, 1300–1850.* Oxford/New York, NY: Routledge, 2017.

Miers, David, and David Dixon. "National Bet: The Re-Emergence of Public Lottery." *Public Law* (1979): 372–403.

Miert, Dirk van. *Humanism in an Age of Science: The Amsterdam Athenaeum in the Golden Age.* Leiden: Brill, 2009.

Mokyr, Joel. *Industrialization in the Low Countries, 1795–1850.* New Haven, CT: Yale University Press, 1976.

Mokyr, Joel. *The Gifts of Athena: Historical Origins of the Knowledge Economy.* Princeton: Princeton University Press, 2002.

Mokyr, Joel. *The Enlightened Economy: An Economic History of Britain 1700–1850.* New Haven: Yale University Press, 2009.

Mokyr, Joel. *A Culture of Growth: The Origins of the Modern Economy.* Princeton: Princeton University Press, 2017.

Moore, Robbie. "Ticker Tape and the Superhuman Reader." In *Writing, Medium, Machine: Modern Technographies,* edited by Sean Pryor and David Trotter, 137–52. London: Open Humanities Press, 2016.

Moret-Bailly, Joël. *Les Déontologies.* Aix: Presses Universitaires d'Aix-Marseille, 2001.

Moszkowski, Max. *Vom Wirtschaftsleben der primitiven Völker (Unter besonderer Berücksichtigung der Papua von Neuguinea und der Sakai von Sumatra).* Jena: Gustav Fischer, 1911.

Moulin, Mathilde. "Les rentes sur l'Hôtel de Ville." *Histoire, économie et société* (April 1998): 623–48.

Moulin, Raymonde. "De l'artisan au professionnel: L'artiste." *Sociologie du travail* 4 (1985): 388–403.

Mücke, Dorothea von. *Practices of the Enlightenment: Aesthetics, Authorship and the Public.* New York: Columbia University Press, 2015.

Mukerji, Chandra. *Impossible Engineering: Technology and Territoriality on the Canal du Midi*. Princeton: Princeton University Press, 2015.

Murphy, Anne. *The Origins of English Financial Markets: Investment and Speculation before the South Sea Bubble*. Cambridge: Cambridge University Press, 2009.

Murphy, Anne. "'We Have Been Ruined by Whores': Perceptions of Female Involvement in the South Sea Scheme." In *Boom, Bust, and Beyond: New Perspectives on the 1720 Stock Market Bubble*, edited by Stefano Condorelli and Daniel Menning, 261–84. Munich: De Gruyter, 2019.

Murphy, Antoine. "John Law and the Assignats." In *La Pensée économique pendant la Révolution française*, edited by Philippe Steiner and Gilbert Faccarello, 431–48. Grenoble: University of Grenoble Press, 1990.

Naert, Emilienne. *Leibniz et la querelle du pur amour*. Paris: Vrin, 1959.

Nagy, Piroska. "History of Emotions." In *Debating New Approaches to History*, edited by Marek Tamm and Peter Burke, 189–202. London: Bloomsbury Academic, 2019.

Nakhimovsky, Isaac. "The Enlightened Prince and the Future of Europe: Voltaire and Frederick the Great's Anti-Machiavel of 1740." In *Commerce and Peace in the Enlightenment*, edited by Béla Kapossy, Isaac Nakhimovsky, and Richard Whatmore, 44–77. Cambridge: Cambridge University Press, 2017.

Neal, Larry. *The Rise of Financial Capitalism: International Capital Markets in the Age of Reason*. Cambridge: Cambridge University Press, 1990.

Nijenhuis, Ida. *Een Joodse Philosophe: Isaac de Pinto (1717–1787)*. Amsterdam: NEHA, 1992.

North, Douglass C. *Institutions, Institutional Change and Economic Performance*. Cambridge: Cambridge University Press, 1994.

Novak, Maximillian E., ed. *The Age of Projects*. Toronto: University of Toronto Press, 2008.

Oexle, Otto G. "Aspekte der Geschichte des Adels im Mittelalter und in der Frühen Neuzeit." *Geschichte und Gesellschaft, Sonderheft* 13, (1990): 19–56.

Ogilvie, Sheilagh C. "Consumption, Social Capital, and the Industrious Revolution in Early Modern Germany." *Journal of Economic History* 70, no. 2 (June 2010): 287–325.

Olivier-Martin, François. "La Reunion de la Basse-Navarre à la couronne de France." *Anuario de historia de derecho español* 9 (1932): 249–89.

Orain, Arnaud. *La politique du merveilleux: Une autre histoire du Système de Law (1695–1795)*. Paris: Fayard, 2018.

Overmeer, Paul C. H. *De economische denkbeelden van Gijsbert Karel van Hogendorp (1762–1834)*. PhD diss., Tilburg University, 1982.

Ozouf, Mona. *"L'homme régénéré: Essais sur la Révolution française*. Paris: Gallimard, 1989.

Pantaelleoni, Maffeo. *Principii di Economia Pura*. 2nd ed. Firenze: G. Barbèra, 1894.

Patrick, George T. W. "The Psychology of Crazes." *Popular Science Monthly* 18 (1900): 285–94.

Paul, Helen. "Rousseau in de Republiek: Nederlandse reacties op de burgerlijke godsdienst van Jean-Jacques Rousseau." *Groniek* 3 (1999): 103–13.

Paul, Laurie A. *Transformative Experience*. Oxford: Oxford University Press, 2014.

Pearson, Harry W. "The Secular Debate on Economic Primitivism." In *Trade and Market in Early Empires: Economies in History and Theory*, edited by Karl Polanyi, Conrad Arensberg, and Harry Pearson, 3–11. Glencoe, IL: The Free Press, 1957.

Pelckmans, Paul. "Le 'Voyage en Hollande' de Diderot." *Neuphilologische Mitteilungen* 86, no. 3 (1985): 294–306.

Persky, John J. "The Ethology of Homo Oeoconomicus." *Journal of Economic Perspectives* 9, no. 2 (1995): 221–31.

Pfister, Ulrich. "The Proto-industrial Household Economy: Toward a Formal Analysis." *Journal of Family History* 17, no. 2 (April 1992): 201–32.

Pfister, Ulrich. *Die Zürcher Fabriques: Protoindustrielles Wachstum vom 16. zum 18. Jahrhundert.* Zürich: Chronos, 1992.

Pincus, Steven. "Neither Machiavellian Moment nor Possessive Individualism: Commercial Society and the Defenders of the English Commonwealth." *The American Historical Review* 103 (1998): 705–36.

Plattner, Stuart, ed. *Economic Anthropology*, Stanford: Stanford University Press, 1989.

Plumpe, Werner. "Die Geburt des 'Homo oeconomicus': Historische Überlegungen zur Entstehung und Bedeutung des Handlungsmodells der modernen Wirtschaft." In *Menschen und Märkte: Studien zur historischen Wirtschaftsanthropologie*, edited by Wolfgang Reinhard and Justin Stagl, 319–52. Vienna: Böhlau, 2007.

Pocock, John G. A. *The Machiavellian Moment: Florentine Political Thought and the Atlantic Republican Tradition.* Princeton: Princeton University Press, 1975.

Pocock, John G. A. "Enthusiasm: The Anti-Self of Enlightenment." *Huntington Library Quarterly* 60 (1997): 7–28.

Poitras, Geoffrey. "The Early History of Option Contracts" In *Vinzenz Bronzin's Option Pricing Models: Exposition and Appraisal*, edited by Wolfgang Hafner and Heinz Zimmermann, 487–528. Berlin: Springer, 2009.

Polanyi, Karl. *The Great Transformation.* New York: Farrar & Rinehart, 1944.

Polanyi, Karl, Conrad Arensberg, and Harry Pearson, eds. *Trade and Market in Early Empires: Economies in History and Theory.* Glencoe, IL: The Free Press, 1957.

Polanyi, Karl. "The Economy as an Instituted Process." In *Trade and Market in Early Empires: Economies in History and Theory*, edited by Karl Polanyi, Conrad Arensberg, and Harry Pearson, 243–70. Glencoe, IL: The Free Press, 1957.

Polanyi, Karl. *The Great Transformation: The Political and Economic Origins of Our Time.* 1944. Reprint, Boston: Beacon, 2001.

Pollock, Sir Frederick and Frederic W. Maitland. *The History of English Law before the Time of Edward I.* 2nd ed. Cambridge: Cambridge University Press, 1968.

Popkin, Richard H. "Hume and Isaac de Pinto." *Texas Studies in Literature and Language. A Journal of the Humanities* 12 (1970): 417–30.

Popkin, Richard H. "Hume and Isaac de Pinto, II. Five New Letters." In *Hume and the Enlightenment: Essays Presented to Ernest Campbell Mossner*, edited by William B. Todd, 99–127. Edinburgh: Edinburgh University Press, 1974.

Prak, Maarten. *The Dutch Republic in the Seventeenth Century: The Golden Age.* Cambridge: Cambridge University Press, 2005.

Prass, Reiner. *Grundzüge der Agrargeschichte. Vol. 2. Vom Dreißigjährigen Krieg bis zum Beginn der Moderne (1650–1880).* Cologne: Böhlau, 2016.

Preda, Alex. "In the Enchanted Grove: Financial Conversations and the Marketplace in England and France in the 18th Century." *Journal of Historical Sociology* 14, no. 3 (2001): 276–307.

Preda, Alex. "The Investor as a Cultural Figure of Global Capitalism." In *The Sociology of Financial Markets*, edited by Karin Knorr-Cetina and Alex Preda, 141–62. Oxford: Oxford University Press, 2005.

Preda, Alex. *Framing Finance: The Boundaries of Markets and Modern Capitalism.* Chicago: University of Chicago Press, 2009.

Pross, Wolfgang. "Die Begründung der Geschichte aus der Natur: Herders Konzept von 'Gesetzen' in der Geschichte." In *Wissenschaft als kulturelle Praxis 1750–1900,* edited by Hans E. Bödeker, Peter H. Reill, and Jürgen Schlumbohm, 187–225. Göttingen: Vandenhoeck & Ruprecht, 1999.

Pross, Wolfgang. "Geschichte als Provokation der Geschichtsphilosophie, Iselin and Herder." In *Isaak Iselin und die Geschichtsphilosophie der Europäischen Aufklärung,* edited by Lucas M. Gisi and Wolfgang Rother, 201–265. Basel: Schwabe, 2011.

Quinn, John P. *Fools of Fortune.* Chicago: G. L. Howe, 1890.

Ratcliffe, Marc J. *The Quest for the Invisible: Microscopy in the Enlightenment.* Farnham: Ashgate, 2009.

Ray, Rajat K. "Asian Capital in the Age of European Domination: The Rise of the Bazaar, 1800–1914." *Modern Asian Studies* 29 (1995): 449–554.

Reckwitz, Andreas. *Das hybride Subjekt. Eine Theorie der Subjektkulturen von der bürgerlichen Moderne zur Postmoderne.* 2nd ed. Stuttgart: Velbrück Wissenschaft, 2012.

Reddy, William. *The Rise of Market Culture: The Textile Trade and French Society: 1750–1900.* Cambridge/Paris: Cambridge University Press/Editions de la Maison des Sciences de l'Homme, 1984.

Reif, Heinz. *Westfälischer Adel 1770–1860: Vom Herrschaftsstand zur regionalen Elite.* Kritische Studien zur Geschichtswissenschaft 35. Göttingen: Vandenhoeck & Ruprecht, 1979.

Reif, Heinz, ed. *Adel und Bürgertum in Deutschland: Entwicklungslinien und Wendepunkte im 19. Jahrhundert.* Berlin: Akademie, 2001.

Reif, Heinz. "Adel, Aristokratie, Elite: Sozialgeschichte von Oben: Elitenwandel in der Moderne." *Historische Zeitschrift* 13, no. 2 (2016): 323–330.

Reill, Peter H. "Das Problem des Allgemeinen und des Besonderen im geschichtlichen denken und in den historiographischen Darstellungen des späten 18. Jahrhunderts." In *Teil und Ganzes: Zum Verhältnis von Einzel- und Gesamtanalyse in Geschichts- und Sozialwissenschaften, Beiträge zur Historik,* edited by Karl Acham and Winfried Schulze, 141–68. Munich: DTV, 1990.

Reill, Peter H. "Eighteenth-century Uses of Vitalism in Constructing the Human Sciences." In *Biology and Ideology: From Descartes to Dawkins,* edited by Denis R. Alexander and Ronald L. Numbers, 61–87. Chicago, London: University of Chicago Press, 2010.

Reinhard, Wolfgang, and Justin Stagl, eds. *Menschen und Märkte: Studien zur historischen Wirtschaftsanthropologie.* Vienna: Böhlau, 2007.

Reith, Gerda. *The Age of Chance: Gambling in Western Culture.* London: Routledge, 1999.

Riello, Giorgio, and Tirthankar Roy, eds. *How India Clothed the World: The World of South Asian Textiles 1500–1850.* Leiden: Brill, 2010.

Riley, James C. "French Finances 1727–1768." *The Journal of Modern History* 2, no. 92 (June, 1987): 209–43.

Robb, George. "Ladies of the Ticker: Women, Investment, and Fraud in England and America, 1850–1930." In *Victorian Investments: New Perspectives on Finance and Culture,* edited by Nancy Henry and Cannon Schmitt, 120–40. Bloomington: Indiana University Press, 2009.

Robotham, Don. "Afterword: Learning from Polanyi." In *Market and Society: The Great Transformation Today*, edited by Chris Hann and Keith Hart, 272–83. Cambridge: Cambridge University Press, 2009.

Roche, Daniel. *The Culture of Clothing: Dress and Fashion in the "Ancien Régime."* Cambridge: Cambridge University Press, 1994.

Rogall, Holger. *Neue Umweltökonomie – Ökologische Ökonomie: Ökonomische und ethische Grundlagen der Nachhaltigkeit, Instrumente zur Durchsetzung.* Opladen: Leske + Budrich 2002.

Rogall, Holger, and Katharina Gapp. "Homo heterogenus – das neue Menschenbild in den Wirtschaftswissenschaften." In *Wirtschaftsanthropologie*, edited by Claus Dierksmeier, Ulrich Hemel, and Jürgen Manemann, 99–115. Baden-Baden: Nomos, 2015.

Rohrbough, William J. *The Land Office Business: The Settlement and Administration of American Public Lands, 1789–1837.* New York: Oxford University Press, 1968.

Rose, Mark. *Authors and Owners: The Invention of Copyright.* Cambridge, MA: Harvard University Press, 1993.

Rothschild, Emma. *Economic Sentiments: Adam Smith, Condorcet, and the Enlightenment.* Cambridge, MA: Harvard University Press, 2002.

Rothstein, Morton. "Frank Norris and Popular Perspectives of the Market." *Agricultural History* 56 (1982): 50–66.

Rottenburg, Richard. "Von der Bewahrung des Rätsels im Fremden." In *Neue Perspektiven der Wissenssoziologie*, edited by Dirk Tänzler, Hubert Knoblauch, and Hans-Georg Soeffner, 119–36. Konstanz: UVK, 2006.

Rouselet, Anne. *La Règle de l'inaliénabilité du domaine de la couronne: Étude doctrinale de 1566 à la fin de l'ancien régime.* Paris: LGDJ, 1997.

Rühle, Susanne. *Guanxi Capitalism in China: The Role of Private Enterprises and Networks for Economic Development.* Marburg: Metropolis, 2012.

Samuelson, Paul A. "A Note on the Pure Theory of Consumer's Behavior." *Economia* 5, no. 17 (1938): 61–71.

Sapiro, Gisèle. "Défense et illustration de 'l'honnête homme': Les hommes de lettres contre la sociologie." *Actes de la recherche en sciences sociales* 153 (2004): 11–27.

Sapiro, Gisèle. *La Responsabilité de l'écrivain: Littérature, droit et morale en France, XIXᵉ–XXIᵉ siècle.* Paris: Seuil, 2011.

Sapiro, Gisèle. "Une catégorie éthique de l'entendement lettré: Le concept de désintéressement." *Revue Silène* (2017): http://www.revue-silene.com/f/index. php?sp=comm&comm_id=201.

Sarasin, Philipp. "Replik." *Internationales Archiv für Sozialgeschichte der deutschen Literatur* 36 (2011): 183–85.

Schaffer, Simon. "The Earth's Fertility as a Social Fact in Early Modern Britain." In *Nature and Society in Historical Context*, edited by Mikulás Teich, Roy Porter, and Bo Gustafsson, 124–47. Cambridge: Cambridge University Press, 1997.

Schama, Simon. *The Embarrassment of Riches: An Interpretation of Dutch Culture in the Golden Age.* London: Collins, 1987.

Schama, Steven. *The Embarrassment of Riches: An Interpretation of Dutch Culture in the Golden Age.* Berkeley/Los Angeles, CA: University of California Press, 1988.

Schenda, Rudolf. *Volk ohne Buch: Studien zur Sozialgeschichte der populären Lesestoffe, 1770–1910.* Frankfurt a.M.: Klostermann, 1970.

Schier, Donald. "Diderot's Translation of 'The Gamester.'" *Diderot Studies* 16 (1973): 229–40.

Schiller, Friedrich. *Über die aestetische Erziehung des Menschen in einer Riehe von Briefe, Sämtliche Werker (1793)*. Vol. 5. Munich: Carl Hanser Verlag, 1980.

Schmitt-Maaß, Christoph. "Quietistic Pietists? The Reception of Fénelon in central Germany c. 1700." In *Fénelon in the Enlightenment: Traditions, Adaptations, and Variations*, edited by Christoph Schmitt-Maaß, Stefanie Stockhorst, and Doohwan Ahn, 147–70. Rodopi: Brill, 2014.

Scholten-Buschhoff, Friederike. *Die Bewirtschaftung adliger Güter in Rheinland und Westfalen: 1650–1850*, Manuscript PhD diss. Münster: University of Münster, 2020.

Schönfuß, Florian. "Bewirtschaftung des Roisdorfer Mineralbrunnens." In Netzbiographie – Joseph zu Salm-Reifferscheidt-Dyck (1773–1861), edited by Martin O. Braun, Elisabeth Schläwe, und Florian Schönfuß. Last modified January 24, 2017. Accessed April 16, 2018.

Schüttpelz, Erhard. *Die Moderne im Spiegel des Primitiven: Weltliteratur und Ethnologie (1870–1960)*. Munich: Wilhelm Fink, 2005.

Schwartz, David G. *Roll the Bones: A History of Gambling*. New York: Gotham Books, 2006.

Schwartz, Leon. *Diderot and the Jews*. Vancouver: Fairleigh Dickinson University Press, 1981.

Secretan, Catherine, ed. *Le "Marchand philosophe" de Caspar Barlaeus. Un éloge du commerce dans la Hollande du siècle d'or. Étude, texte et traduction du Mercator Sapiens*. Paris: H. Champion, 2002.

Secretan, Catherine, and Willem Frijhoff, *Dictionnaire des Pays-Bas au siècle d'or*. Paris: CNRS, 2018.

Seiser, Gertraud. "Neuer Wein in alten Schläuchen? Aktuelle Trends in der ökonomischen Anthropologie." *Historische Anthropologie* 17 (2009): 157–77.

Sen, Amartya K. "Rational Fool: A Critique of the Behavioral Foundations of Economic Theory." *Philosophy and Public Affairs* 6 (1977): 317–44.

Sen, Amartya K. "Behavior and the Concept of Preferences." In *Rational Choice: Readings in Social and Political Theory*, edited by Jon Elster, 60–81. Oxford: Blackwell, 1986.

Shepard, Alexandra. *Accounting for Oneself: Worth, Status, and the Social Order in Early Modern England*. Oxford: Oxford University Press, 2015.

Shiner, Lary. *The Invention of Art: A Cultural History*. Chicago: University of Chicago Press, 2001.

Sidis, Boris. "A Study of the Mob." *The Atlantic Monthly* 75 (1895): 188–97.

Sidis, Boris. *The Psychology of Suggestion: A Research into the Subconscious Nature of Man and Society*. New York: D. Appleton, 1903.

Siebenhüner, Bernd. *Homo Sustinens. Auf dem Weg zu einem Menschenbild der Nachhaltigkeit*. Marburg: Metropolis, 2001.

Siegenthaler, Hansjörg. "Geschichte und Ökonomie nach der kulturalistischen Wende." *Geschichte und Gesellschaft* 25 (1999): 276–301.

Siegrist, Hannes. *Advokat, Bürger und Staat: Sozialgeschichte der Rechtsanwälte in Deutschland, Italien und der Schweiz (18.–20. Jh.)*. Frankfurt a.M.: Klostermann, 1996.

Sikora, Michael. *Der Adel in der Frühen Neuzeit: Geschichte Kompakt*. Darmstadt: WBG, 2009.

Simmel, Georg. *The Philosophy of Money*. 1900. Reprint, London: Routledge, 2011.

Simon, Herbert. "Bounded Rationality and Organizational Learning." *Organization Science* 2, no. 1 (1991): 125–134. https://doi.org/10.1287/orsc.2.1.125.

Skidelsky, Robert. *Money and Government: The Past and Future of Economics.* New Haven: Yale University Press, 2018.

Sklansky, Jeffrey. *The Soul's Economy: Market Society and Selfhood in American Thought, 1820–1920.* Chapel Hill: University of North Carolina Press, 2002.

Slack, Paul. *The Invention of Improvement: Information and Material Progress in Seventeenth-Century England.* Oxford: Oxford University Press, 2015.

Smyth, William J. *Map-Making, Landscapes and Memory: A Geography of colonial and Early Modern Ireland c. 1530–1750.* Cork: Cork University Press, 2006.

Sombart, Werner. *Der moderne Kapitalismus: Historisch-systematische Darstellung des gesamteuropäischen Wirtschaftslebens von seinen Anfängen bis zur Gegenwart.* Munich: Duncker & Humblot, 1928.

Somló, Felix. *Der Güterverkehr in der Urgesellschaft.* Brussels: Misch & Thron, 1909.

Spang, Rebecca. "The Ghost of Law: Speculation on Money, Memory and Mississippi in the French Constituent Assembly." *Historical Reflections/Réfléxions Historique* 31, no. 1 (Spring, 2005): 3–25.

Spang, Rebecca. *Stuff and Money in the Time of the French Revolution.* Cambridge, MA: Harvard University Press, 2015.

Spies, Marijke. "De koopman van Rhodos: Over de schakelpunten van economie en cultuur." *De zeventiende eeuw* 61 (1990): 166–73.

Stäheli, Urs. *Spektakuläre Spekulation: Das Populäre der Ökonomie.* Frankfurt: Suhrkamp, 2007.

Stapelbroek, Koen. *Love, Self-Deceit and Money: Commerce and Morality in the Early Neapolitan Enlightenment.* Toronto: University of Toronto Press, 2008.

Stapelbroek, Koen. "The Haarlem 1771 Prize Essay on the Restoration of Dutch Trade and the Economic Branch of the Holland Society of Sciences." In *The Rise of Economic Societies in the Eighteenth Century,* edited by Koen Stapelbroek and Jani Marjanen, 257–84. Basingstoke: Palgrave Macmillan, 2012.

Stapelbroek, Koen. "Dal sistema di Utrecht (1713) al sistema di Vattel (1758); attraverso l'Observateur Hollandois e 'quelques arpents de neige' in America." *Rivista Storica Italiana* 129, no. 2 (2017): 495–535.

Stapelbroek, Koen. "From Jealousy of Trade to the Neutrality of Finance: Isaac de Pinto's 'System' of Luxury and Perpetual Peace." In *Commerce and Peace in the Enlightenment,* edited by Béla Kapossy, Isaac Nakhimovsky, and Richard Whatmore, 78–109. Cambridge: Cambridge University Press, 2017.

Stapelbroek, Koen, "The History of Trade and the Legitimacy of the Dutch Republic." In Histories of Trade as Histories of Civilization, edited by Antonella Alimento and Aris Della Fontana, Basingstoke: Palgrave MacMillan, 2021/forthcoming.

Stapelbroek, Koen. "Carthage Must Be Preserved: The Neutrality of Trade and the End of the Dutch Republic." Forthcoming.

Stewart, Larry. *The Rise of Public Science: Rhetoric, Technology, and Natural Philosophy in Newtonian Britain, 1660–1750.* Cambridge: Cambridge University Press, 1992.

Stolnitz, Jerome. "On the Origins of 'Aesthetic Disinterestedness.'" *The Journal of Aesthetics and Art Criticism* 20, no. 2 (1961): 131–43.

Strathern, Marilyn. *The Gender of the Gift: Problems with Women and Problems with Society in Melanesia.* Berkeley: University of California Press, 1988.

Strien-Chardonneau, Madeleine van. *Le Voyage de Hollande: Récits de voyageurs français dans les Provinces-Unies, 1748–1795.* Oxford: Voltaire Foundation, 1992.

Strube, Werner. "Interesselosigkeit: Zur Geschichte eines Grundbegriffs der Ästhetik." *Archiv für Begriffsgeschichte* 23, no. 2 (1979): 148–74.

Sturkenboom, Dorothee. *De ballen van de koopman: Mannelijkheid en Nederlandse identiteit in de tijd van de Republiek.* Gorredijk: Sterck & De Vreese, 2019.

Sutcliffe, Adam. "Can a Jew Be a Philosophe? Isaac de Pinto, Voltaire, and Jewish Participation in the European Enlightenment." *Jewish Social Studies* 6, no. 3 (2000): 31–51.

Sutton, Elizabeth A. *Capitalism and Cartography in the Dutch Golden Age.* Chicago, IL: University of Chicago Press, 2015.

Tackett, Timothy. *Becoming a Revolutionary: The Deputies of the French National Assembly and the Emergence of French Revolutionary Culture (1789–1790).* Philadelphia: The Pennsylvania State University Press, 2006.

Tanner, Jakob. "Die ökonomische Handlungstheorie vor der 'kulturalistischen Wende'? Perspektiven und Probleme einer interdisziplinären Diskussion." In *Wirtschaftsgeschichte als Kulturgeschichte. Dimensionen eines Perspektivenwechsels*, edited by Hartmut Berghoff and Jakob Vogel, 69–98. Frankfurt a.M.: Campus, 2004.

Tarlow, Sarah. *The Archeology of Improvement in Britain, 1750–1850.* Cambridge: Cambridge University Press, 2007.

Taveneaux, René. *Jansénisme et prêt à intérêt: Introduction, choix de textes et commentaires.* Paris: Vrin, 1977.

Taylor, Charles H., ed. *History of the Board of Trade of the City of Chicago.* Vol. 1. Chicago: Robert O. Law Company, 1917.

Taylor, James. *Creating Capitalism: Joint-Stock Enterprise in British Politics and Culture, 1800–1870.* Woodbridge: Boydell, 2006.

Terjanian, Anoush F. *Commerce and its Discontents in Eighteenth-Century French Political Thought.* Cambridge: Cambridge University Press, 2013.

Thaler, Richard H., and Cass R. Sunstein. *Nudge: Improving Decisions About Health, Wealth and Happiness.* New Haven, CT: Yale University Press, 2008.

Thaler, Richard H. *Misbehaving: The Making of Behavioral Economics.* London/ New York: W. W. Norton & Company, 2015.

Thirsk, Joan. *Agricultural Change: Policy and Practice, 1500–1750.* In *Chapters from the Agrarian History of England and Wales, 1500–1750*, edited by John Chartres, 54–109. Vol. 4. Cambridge: Cambridge University Press, 1990.

Thomas, Keith. "History and Anthropology." *Past and Present* 24 (1963): 3–24.

Thompson, Edward P. "Time, Work Discipline and Industrial Capitalism." *Past and Present*, no. 38 (December 1967): 56–97.

Thompson, Edward P. "The Moral Economy of the English Crowd in the Eighteenth Century." *Past and Present* 50 (February 1971): 76–136.

Thuillier, Guy, ed. *Le premier actuaire de France: Duvillard (1755–1832).* Paris: Sans Coll, 1997.

Thurnwald, Richard. *Die menschliche Gesellschaft in ihren ethno-soziologischen Grundlagen.* Vol. 3. *Werden, Wandel und Gestaltung der Wirtschaft.* Berlin: De Gruyter, 1932.

Thurnwald, Richard. *Economics in Primitive Communities.* London: Oxford University Press, 1932.

Torp, Cornelius. "Glücksspiel und Zivilisierungsmission. Globalgeschichtliche Perspektiven auf das 19. Jahrhundert." *Geschichte und Gesellschaft* 43 (2017): 526–56.

Trivellato, Francesca. *The Promise and Peril of Credit: What a Forgotten Legend about Jews and Finance Tells Us about the Making of European Commercial Society.* Princeton: Princeton University Press, 2019.

Turner, Victor. *From Ritual to Theatre: The Human Seriousness of Play.* New York: Performing Arts, 1982.

Usher, Dan. *The Economics of Voting: Studies of Self-Interest.* Oxford/New York: Routledge, 2015.

Velde, François, and David Weir, "The Financial Market and Government Debt Policy in France, 1746–1793." *The Journal of Economic History* 52, no. 1 (March 1992): 1–39.

Velema, Wyger, and Arthur Weststeijn, eds. *Ancient Models in the Early Modern Republican Imagination.* Leiden: Brill 2017.

Verburg, Rudi. "The Dutch Background of Bernard Mandeville's Thought: Escaping the Procrustean Bed of Neo-Augustinianism." *Erasmus Journal for Philosophy and Economics* 9, no. 1 (2016): 32–61.

Verheyen, Nina. "Gemeinschaft durch Konkurrenz. Georg Simmel und Ellenbogenmenschen des Kaiserreichs." *Merkur* 10/11 (2013): 918–27.

Vliet, Pieter van der. *Onno Zwier van Haren (1713–1779): Staatsman en dichter.* Translated by Han van der Vegt. Hilversum: Uitgeverij Verloren, 1996.

Vovelle, Michel. "L'Historiographie de la Révolution française à la veille du bicentenaire." *American Historical Review* 272 (1988): 113–26.

Vries, Jan de, and Ad van der Woude. *The First Modern Economy: Success, Failure, and Perseverance of the Dutch Economy, 1500–1815.* Cambridge: Cambridge University Press, 1997.

Vries, Jan de. *The Industrious Revolution: Consumer Behaviour and the Household Economy: 1650 to the Present.* Cambridge: Cambridge University Press, 2008.

Vries, Marleen de. *Beschaven!: Letterkundige genootschappen in Nederland, 1750–1800.* Nijmegen: Vantilt, 2001.

Wagner-Hasel, Beate. "Hundert Jahre Gelehrtenstreit über den Charakter der antiken Wirtschaft. Zur Aktualität von Karl Büchers Wirtschaftsanthropologie." *Historische Anthropologie* 17 (2009): 178–201.

Wallace, Mike. *Greater Gotham: A History of New York City from 1898 to 1919.* Oxford: Oxford University Press, 2017.

Warde, Paull. "The Idea of Improvement, c. 1520–1700." In *Custom, Improvement, and the Landscape in Early Modern Britain,* edited by Richard W. Hoyle, 127–48. New York: Routledge, 2011.

Warnke, Martin. *Hofkünstler: Zur Vorgeschichte des modernen Künstlers.* 2nd ed. Cologne: DuMont Buchverlag, 1996.

Weatherill, Lorna M. *Consumer Behaviour and Material Culture in Britain: 1660–1760.* London: Routledge, 1996.

Weber, Max. *The Protestant Ethic and the Spirit of Capitalism,* trans. Talcott Parsons. London: Allen & Unwin, 1930.

Weber, Max. *Die protestantische Ethik und der Geist des Kapitalismus.* Tübingen: Mohr, 1934.

Weber, Max. *Economy and Society: An Outline of Interpretive Sociology.* Vol. 1. Berkeley: University of California Press, 2013.

Weber, Peter K. "Adeliges Unternehmertum im Rheinland: Aktivitäten und Mentalitäten." In *Europäischer Adel als Unternehmer im Industriezeitalter*, edited by Manfred Rasch and Peter K. Weber, 57–72. Essen: Klartext, 2017.

Webster, Charles. *The Great Instauration: Science, Medicine and Reform, 1626–1660*. London: Duckworth, 1975.

Weir, David. "Tontines, Public Finance, and Revolution in France and England, 1688–1789." *The Journal of Economic History* 49, no. 1 (March 1989): 95–124.

Wellman, Kathleen. *Making Science Social: The Conferences of Théophraste Renaudot, 1633–1642*. Norman: University of Oklahoma Press, 2003.

Weststeijn, Arthur. "From the Passion of Self-love to the Virtue of Self-Interest: The Republican Morals of the Brothers De la Court." *European Review of History: Revue européenne d'histoire* 17, no. 1 (2010): 75–92. DOI: 10.1080/13507480903511934.

Weststeijn, Arthur. *Commercial Republicanism in the Dutch Golden Age: The Political Thought of Johan & Pieter de la Court*. Leiden: Brill, 2012.

Wilk, Richard. *Economies and Cultures: Foundations of Economic Anthropology*. Boulder: Westview Press, 1996.

Withington, Phil. *The Politics of Commonwealth: Citizens and Freemen in Early Modern England*. Cambridge: Cambridge University Press, 2005.

Wolfe, Charles T. "Smithian Vitalism?" *Journal of Scottish Philosophy* 16, no. 3 (2018): 264–271.

Woodmansee, Martha. *The Author, Art and the Market: Rereading the History of Aesthetics*. New York: Columbia University Press, 1994.

Yale, Elizabeth. *Sociable Knowledge: Natural History and the Nation in Early Modern Britain*. Philadelphia: University of Pennsylvania Press, 2015.

Yale, Elizabeth. "With Slips and Scraps: How Early Modern Naturalists Invented the Archive." *Book History* 12 (2009): 1–36.

Yamamoto, Koji. "Reformation and the Distrust of the Projector in the Hartlib Circle." *The Historical Journal* 55, no. 2 (2012): 375–97.

Yamamoto, Koji. *Taming Capitalism Before its Triumph. Public Service, Distrust & 'Projecting' in Early Modern England*. Oxford: Oxford University Press, 2018.

Yanagisako, Sylvia J. *Producing Culture and Capital: Family Firms in Italy*. Princeton: Princeton University Press, 2002.

Zabel, Christine. "Challenges of Food Security: Free Trade, Distribution and Political (In)Stability in Mid 18th Century France." *European Journal for Security Research* 3 (2018): 35–50.

Zabel, Christine. "From Bubble to Speculation: 18th Century Readings of the 1720s." In *Boom, Bust and Beyond: New Perspectives on the 1720 Stock Market Bubble*, edited by Stefano Condorelli and Daniel Menning, 303–32. Berlin/Boston: De Gruyter, 2019.

Zimmerman, David A. *Panic! Markets, Crises, & Crowds in American Fiction*. Chapel Hill: University of North Carolina Press, 2006.

Zuñiga y Postigo, Gloria. "Adam Smith on Sympathy: From Self-Interest to Empathy." In *Propriety and Prosperity, New Studies on the Philosophy of Adam Smith*, edited by David F. Hardwick and Leslie Marsh, 136–46. London: Palgrave Macmillan, 2014.

Index

Printed in the United States
By Bookmasters